London's Criminal Underworlds, c. 1

London's Criminal Underworlds, c. 1720–c. 1930

A Social and Cultural History

Heather Shore
Reader in History, Leeds Beckett University, UK

palgrave
macmillan

First published 2015 by
PALGRAVE MACMILLAN

Palgrave Macmillan in the UK is an imprint of Macmillan Publishers Limited, registered in England, company number 785998, of Houndmills, Basingstoke, Hampshire RG21 6XS.

Palgrave Macmillan in the US is a division of St Martin's Press LLC, 175 Fifth Avenue, New York, NY 10010.

Palgrave Macmillan is the global academic imprint of the above companies and has companies and representatives throughout the world.

Palgrave® and Macmillan® are registered trademarks in the United States, the United Kingdom, Europe and other countries.

ISBN 978-1-349-33845-0   ISBN 978-1-137-31391-1 (eBook)

DOI 10.1057/9781137313911

This book is printed on paper suitable for recycling and made from fully managed and sustained forest sources. Logging, pulping and manufacturing processes are expected to conform to the environmental regulations of the country of origin.

A catalogue record for this book is available from the British Library.

Library of Congress Cataloging-in-Publication Data
Shore, Heather, 1964–
London's criminal underworlds, c. 1720–c. 1930 : a social and cultural history / Heather Shore.
pages cm
Includes bibliographical references.
ISBN 978-0-230-30404-8
1. Crime—England—London—History. 2. Criminals—England—London—History. I. Title.
HV6950.L7S56 2015
364.109421—dc23   2014038810

Typeset by MPS Limited, Chennai, India.

*In memory of my parents
Ellen and Allan Shore*

Contents

List of Illustrations and Maps

Cover illustration: Gustave Doré, 'Wentworth Street, Whitechapel, 1872', from G. Doré and B. Jerrold, *London A Pilgrimage: With Illustrations by Gustave Doré* (London).

Illustrations

Maps

Acknowledgements

This book has been a long time coming and I owe a debt of gratitude to many friends and colleagues who encouraged and supported my efforts over the years. This includes archivists and librarians at the Bodleian Library, British Library, British Library Newspapers Colindale, Cambridge University Library, Corporation of London Record Office, Finsbury Library, Guildhall Library, Institute of Historical Research, London Metropolitan Archives, Museum of London Picture Library, National Archives and Tower Hamlets Library.

I consider myself lucky to have a great group of colleagues in Cultural Studies at Leeds Beckett University, including my fellow historians, Matthew Caygill, Helen Dampier, Kelly Hignett, Simon Morgan and Rachael Rich. Particular thanks go to Shane Ewen, Grainne Goodwin, Stephen Mosley, Alison Oram and Ruth Robbins all of whom have either read parts of the book or provided a sounding board about the book at various stages. The Leeds Beckett University Centre for Culture and the Arts paid for the cover image, illustration and maps. I'd also like to thank my former colleagues and continuing friends at the Universities of Portsmouth and Northampton – Brad Beaven, Ken Lunn, Cathy Smith, Matthew Taylor and the late Bob Kiehl.

The research for and writing of a book benefits from the discussions we have as historians. I've been very lucky to count amongst my friends and advisors the following, who have kindly read various parts of the book during its long gestation: Andrew Davies, Barry Godfrey, Drew Gray, Louise Jackson, Tim Hitchcock, Dick Hobbs, Bob Shoemaker, Stefan Slater and John Carter Wood. I owe special thanks to two of those friends. Tim Hitchcock, who has been generous with his time and support since he first taught me as an undergraduate at the Polytechnic of North London, and Louise Jackson, who has gently but firmly encouraged me to finally finish this book.

I have also benefitted from discussions with friends and colleagues who have advised and provided intellectual support over the years, notably John Beattie, Alyson Brown, Carl Chinn, Mary Clayton, Penelope Corfield, Pam Cox, Clive Emsley, Nathasha Glaisyer, Gordon Johnston, Helen Johnston, Peter King, John Langbein, Emma Robertston, Helen Rogers, Lisa Taylor, Suzie Thomas, Janice Turner and Chris Williams. I would also like to thank my editors at Palgrave Macmillan, Jen McCall and Holly Tyler, for their patience and 'chivvying'. My thanks are also extended to the anonymous reader at Palgrave. Finally, I would like to thank my family, Tim Shore, Ian Shore and their respective partners, Gary and Laura, and also Heather, Colin and Isla for 'putting me up'.

The cover image from G. Doré, 'Wentworth Street, Whitechapel, 1872', from G. Doré and B. Jerrold, *London A Pilgrimage: With Illustrations by Gustave Doré* (London) is from the Museum of London. The illustration on p. 58 is by William Hogarth, *A Harlot's Progress*, Plate 3, 1732, with the permission of The Trustees of the British Museum. The maps on pp. 51, 95 and 177 are from the London Metropolitan Archives, City of London. I would particularly like to thank Jeremy Smith for his help in selecting them. An earlier version of Chapter 3 was published in article form in the journal *Social History*, which has kindly given permission for it to be republished in a revised form here. (H. Shore (2009), '"The Reckoning": Disorderly Women, Informing Constables and the Westminster Justices, 1727–1733', *Social History*, 34, pp. 409–27.) Some parts of Chapter 8 were first used in article form in H. Shore (2011), 'Criminality and Englishness in the Aftermath: The Racecourse Wars of the 1920s', *Twentieth Century British History*, 22, 4, pp. 474–97.

All citations from the Old Bailey Proceedings (including the Trials, Sessions, Ordinary's Accounts and Statistics) are taken from the online version, Tim Hitchcock, Robert Shoemaker, Clive Emsley, Sharon Howard and Jamie McLaughlin, et al., *The Old Bailey Proceedings Online, 1674–1913* (www.oldbaileyonline.org, version 7.0). All references to documents digitised by the London Lives project are from Hitchcock, Robert Shoemaker, Sharon Howard and Jamie McLaughlin, et al., *London Lives, 1690–1800* (www.londonlives.org, version 1.1).

Abbreviations

CLRO Corporation of London Record Office
LL   London Lives
LMA   London Metropolitan Archives
OBP   Old Bailey Proceedings
ONA   Ordinary of Newgate's Account
TNA   The National Archives

1
Introduction

COURT. Soams is your Name? How long have you gone by that Name?

ISABELLA EATON. About a 12 Month.

COURT. I think I have try'd you here by another Name.

EATON. Very like you might try me, my Lord, and by another Name too; but what if you did, I was Innocent, and my Jury acquitted me. I never came here for my Crimes, but my Passions.[1]

WILLIAM SHEEN: 'I have known what it is to stand at that bar myself, and have been as lenient to the prisoner as if she had been my own child – I have no doubt you are aware of what I was here for – they think they have a right to rob me – I was never a thief in my life – I feel for the prisoner, but she has robbed my sister four sessions ago'.[2]

We are not an 'organised' gang and never have been. So far from encouraging feuds and outbursts I have endeavoured in every possible way to keep the warring factions wide apart so that there should be no violent conflicts of any description.[3]

These vignettes remind us that criminals have more than one identity. As the accused, as witnesses, as victims and as members of communities, they contribute to the narratives of crime that were woven around them by magistrates and lawyers, policemen, journalists and other commentators. Isabella Eaton gives evidence at the Old Bailey trial of Jane Murphey alias Macloughlane in December 1732, and in doing

1

so defends her own right to a voice. In February 1847, William Sheen stands his ground in the courtroom, when he accuses his servant Mary Ryley of taking various items from his lodging house in Whitechapel. In September 1922, Charles 'Darby' Sabini defends his reputation and that of his associates in an interview with the Sunday paper, the *Empire News*. Whilst we can never be sure of the extent to which published words are an accurate reflection of reality, these statements capture fleeting moments of negotiation with respectable society. They demonstrate that the underworld and the upperworld overlapped. As Richard Evans noted in his study of German criminals, 'the boundaries of the underworld were always more fluid than commentators maintained'.[4]

The underworld and the ways in which it has been constructed in different historical periods inform this book. Theoretically, cultural, social and political ideology about criminal subcultures accelerated during the twentieth century.[5] However, in terms of the ties that bind criminals to their communities and to kin, and in the spatial footsteps from where they originate, connections with traditional 'underworlds' remained. Thus, this book is an attempt to think about the changing nature of the language used by police and law enforcers, by journalists and writers, by victims and witnesses and by criminals themselves. It looks at some of the interactions that have shaped the historical construction of the underworld. Regulatory frameworks, criminal law and practice, styles of journalism and popular crime writing have all influenced the way in which the public has come to understand organised crime. This book considers some of these processes over a broad chronological period. That the examples come from the early eighteenth century until the interwar period of the twentieth century is not accidental. It was in the eighteenth century that the idea of a criminal underworld became more coherent and more embedded in popular culture. In a period in which the criminal justice system was being vigorously remade, cultural production, the texts, literatures and narratives through which the underworld was and is narrated, was expanding and becoming more accessible to a wider range of society.

The book ends in the interwar period of the twentieth century.[6] Both criminals and representations of criminals were influenced by external factors in this period, marking it as a significant watershed. Thus concepts of organised crime were much more distinctly influenced by North American representations of gangsters by the early 1930s.[7] Arguably it is in the 1920s and 1930s, and amongst the networks and alliances concerned in converging illegal economies, that the roots of modern organised crime can be found. Whilst considerations of change over time are inevitable, the intention of this book is not to provide a sequential history or complete survey of the underworld. Rather, key examples and case studies are used to explore a set of themes that have been identified from the press, criminal and police records, and the historically constructed narrative of the underworld.

An important focus of the book is what might be broadly described as crime networks. As Paul Griffiths has noted of early modern London:

> The evident distortions of a constructed 'underworld' or calculated political boundaries do not mean that we should limit criminal communities to a minor role in early modern London. Instead of a parallel criminal universe, we should hunt for the jigsaw pieces that, when put together, show associations or networks of criminals.[8]

Some of those jigsaw pieces are examined in three chapters (3, 5 and 8) which provide detailed studies of individuals and groups of closely connected criminals who became known to the public for parts of their life. For these mainly plebeian Londoners, interactions with the courts could be significantly shaped by the socially constructed representations of the gangs and confederacies to which they were believed to belong. However, the book argues that kinship, ethnic and community networks also structured these connecting criminal lives. Whilst these individuals and groups were not always welcome residents, they were neighbours and did flow in and out of local communities. Moreover, the way in which the press and other crime literatures contributed to the visibility of certain 'noted' individuals is also crucial. This visibility can also be seen in other chapters in this book (2, 4, 6 and 7), which focus on the relationship between criminality and press and courtroom constructions of criminal typologies. Gang crime, informers, hustlers, the swell mob, swindlers, the long firm and fighting gangs are some of the labels used by the press and other authorities to describe forms of criminal activity. These chapters cover longer chronologies, combined with close examination of a smaller group of trials from the Old Bailey. The rest of this introduction outlines the key themes and chapter structure of the book. To start, a brief exploration follows of the use of the word 'underworld' in both contemporary writings and in the more recent work by academics and authors of popular crime histories.

Underworld Terminology

Writers continue to evoke the liminality, marginality and otherness of the underworld to cloak descriptions of criminality in the eighteenth, nineteenth and twentieth centuries.[9] The terminology of the 'criminal underworld' has become deeply embedded in our cultural psyche: the 'underworld' is presented as a solid entity, a set of behaviours, activities and spaces that exist alongside the upperworld. Indeed, the term has had a profound power in the modernity of the twentieth and twenty-first centuries. As a collective way of describing bad behaviour it is compelling; and its imprecision ensures that it remains a key trope in press reportage. The process of how the underworld became embedded in our cultural, social and political language is partly the focus of this book. Despite its prevalence as a noun used to describe collective criminal activity, 'the underworld' was not used consistently until the later nineteenth century. One of the earliest books to refer to the underworld in its title was the work of the pseudonymic George Ellington, who in 1869 published *The Women of New York; or, The Under-world of the Great City ....* This was followed in 1899 by the work of Helen Campbell, also writing about prostitution, in *Darkness and Daylight; or, Lights and Shadows of New York Life.*[10] By the early decades of the twentieth century the use of the term had become fairly common in descriptions and accounts of urban criminal milieux in America and Britain.[11]

An early newspaper reference to the underworld is found in *The Times* in 1864, in an editorial that attempts to explain the 'belief in an underworld of crime and horrors'.[12] According to the writer, this was a 'fanciful idea of metropolitan wickedness'; and that 'the dark chambers of Ainsworth's novels, in which thieves and thief-catchers played their desperate game against each other, no longer exist'.[13] The author saw communities of thieves as something belonging to the past: 'the superior efficiency of our modern police saves us from depredations on a grander scale'. The police were no longer interested in the encouragement of crime and the 'detestable trade of Jonathan Wild is suppressed'. The thieves remained but 'are no longer so gregarious in their habits, that they do not congregate, as they once did, in certain quarters, or meet so regularly at certain "flash houses," but are more dispersed through the whole population, and often carry on honest trade in their spare hours'. This editorial can be read as a moment of mythologisation. The references to Ainsworth's novels and to G. M. W. Reynolds's *Mysteries of London* are significant.[14] Thus, at this mid-Victorian point of time the narrative trope of the underworld was one that was powerfully shaped by the relationship between the press, law enforcement and broader print culture.[15] Yet, these narrative connections originated in the previous century, as the reference to Jonathan Wild suggests. Eighteenth-century print culture celebrated the criminal, and underwent a significant trans-formation.[16] Even before this, the concept of alternative deviant worlds can be found in the detailed iconography of pre-modern underworlds. Literary and semi-literary accounts, such as John Awdeley's *Fraternity of Vagabonds* in 1561, and other rogue literature of the Elizabethan and early Stuart period, described an alternative world with a specific language, codes of behaviour and a distinct geography.

The prevalence of published crime literature – the criminal biography written by hack Grub Street writers in the eighteenth century, the social investigations of the nineteenth and the true crime of the twentieth – has led to some reticence on the part of historians in dealing with the underworld paradigm.[17] Exceptions to this include the work of Paul Griffiths and John McMullan on early modern London and Alyson Brown and Stefan Slater's work on the early twentieth century.[18] Richard Evans' work on narratives of the underworld in nineteenth-century Germany provides a useful discursive framework.[19] Other work has focused on cultural production and its role in shaping the representa-tion of criminality. For example, Andrea McKenzie has written on crime print culture in the eighteenth century and authors such as Rosalind Crone and Judith Flanders have written in a similar vein about the nineteenth century.[20] Esther Snell and Richard Ward have explored dis-courses around criminality in the eighteenth-century press. John Carter Wood and Matt Houlbrook have written about the relationship between crime stories, press representation and mass culture in the interwar period of the twentieth century.[21] Outside these serious studies there exists a parallel popular history of crime. Thus, in a number of popular texts the underworld is described as a real historical and social space.[22] This is most apparent in genre studies of the underworld by true-crime writers such as James Morton and Brian McDonald.[23] The way in which such writers employ evidence and narrate stories about historical organ-ised crime is inherently problematic. Arguably there are processes of mythologising in this history that have been shaped over time by the public demand for crime stories. As Roland Barthes suggested, 'Myth lends itself to history in two ways: by its form, which is only relatively motivated; by its concept, the nature of which is historical'.[24] The late modern mythologising of crime stories mirrors the earlier proliferation of print culture; the particular success of the 'black and red' true-crime genre since the 1980s, specialising in villains' memoirs, resonates with the biographies of highway robbers, footpads and fraudsters.[25] Moreover, the narrative of organised crime has also undergone a process of 'genealogising' by writers who see criminal groups and individuals such as the Sabinis (Chapter 8) on a continuum; the connections and inheritances (of criminal business, of territory) echoing the predominance of the 'family firm' in later-twentieth-century narratives. Thus the 'racecourse wars' of the interwar period, and the activities of the Sabini family in particular, have been mythologised and genealogised through a number of literary media, including press, police biography, memoirs and novels, as well as true crime writing.

However, the underworld has not only been constructed through contemporary print culture and true crime mythologies. Organised crime networks have been the subject of systematic study by sociologists and criminologists.[26] British organised crime has tended to be seen as a more recent phenomenon.[27] Dick Hobbs notes that in Britain the concept of organised crime has only relatively recently been deployed by political institutions (politicians and senior police officers): 'this shift in perception is a direct consequence of a particular reading of globalization and its attendant attributes, in particular the expansion of illegal economic activity and its cosmopolitan associations'.[28] This approach, Hobbs argues, defines organised crime as a distinctly modern phenomenon that largely ignores the persistent elements of criminal organisation that can be identified in past societies. Historians also have generally seen forms of criminal organisation as culturally and politically constructed. There is no underworld, only elite interpretations of the lives of the poor and working class; a collection of ideas about crime mediated through cultural and legal apparatus. This view is supported by cultural historical approaches which privilege the place of language and discourse. The disentanglement of 'the underworld' from its literary and cultural contexts renders it meaningless; the understanding of criminal organisation that relates it to bureaucracy, structure and hierarchy is essentially unhelpful.

Close reading of historical sources suggests a more flexible and fluid (and arguably disorganised) set of relationships. In the 1980s, criminologist Peter Reuter coined the term 'disorganised' crime, arguing that in reality criminal networks were more diverse and fragmented than the traditional picture had supposed.[29] This is a more useful means of categorising the criminal activity in which some individuals and groups were involved, and is suggested by the fundamentally loose nature of many of the alliances described in this book. Individuals shifted allegiances and groups joined forces in response to a variety of external or internal factors. Whilst alliances could be shaped by the overlapping networks to which people belonged, other forces also engendered commonalities and confederacy. As Chapter 7 will demonstrate, groups of youths in late-Victorian and Edwardian London formed and re-formed alliances which were often transient and short-lived. What were perceived as gang formations gained a public profile as a result of shifting territorial conflicts. Similar patterns of disorganisation have been identified by Andrew Davies in his study of gangs in interwar Glasgow.[30] Moreover, roles such as fence or informer or thief were flexible rather than occupying a rigid and hierarchical bureaucracy.[31] Indeed gang terminology is inherently tricky. Whilst criminal confederacies and gangs certainly existed historically we need to be aware of the nuances of the language used by contemporaries.[32] For example, the criminologist Simon Hallsworth has written about the problematic way in which definitions of the 'gang' are used in modern assessments of 'gangland Britain'. He notes, 'far from the streets being overrun by "gangs", the most pervasive street collectives appeared to comprise volatile peer groups randomly and erroneously labelled as "gangs" by control agencies'.[33] As the research for this book demonstrated, control agencies, including law enforcers (police, constables, thief-takers and magistrates), the courts, as well as the press, frequently used the term 'gang' to describe a range of collective activities. For example, at different times groups of youths who came together for fighting, hustling or 'holding the street' were often described as belonging to gangs by the police, who tended to see such activity as systematic and collectively organised. When witnesses and police described their knowledge of the gang, it acted as a means of conferring authority on their evidence. But the police identification of gangs (of coiners, of burglars, of thieves) often described loose associations and confederacies between individuals. As we will see in Chapter 6, gangs of coiners were often constituted of members of households, husbands and wives, lodgers and children.

Themes

The reconstruction of criminal lives has been a piecemeal process, reliant on case studies and on the tantalising glimpses of criminal activity that can be identified in the records of the criminal justice system. Whilst these were lives that were frequently lived on the margins and on the periphery, more recent explorations in social and cultural history have sought to understand the ways in which individuals and groups negotiated the criminal justice system and, in some cases, the impact this had on practices on the ground.[34] Key issues include concerns about gangs; practices of informing; relationships between police and criminals; the role of the historical media; the ordering of the parish and of the street; the control

of vice, prostitution and gambling; and the place of criminal and plebeian agency. Whilst many of these matters inform the chapters that
follow, four themes have been identified which will be introduced in
more depth here: print culture, public crime, criminal networks and
territory. Each chapter illustrates, to a greater or lesser degree, aspects of
these themes. Overall they present a portrait of a period during which
pressures on growing urban communities, policing and legal practice,
and an expanding print culture, mutually reinforced the crime stories
that have been told as part of the 'invention' of the underworld from
the early eighteenth century.

Print Culture and Public Crime

From the eighteenth century the crossover between literary representation and media coverage increased, marking it as a period in which the
underworld was substantially remade.[35] Moreover, as Bob Shoemaker
has argued, the explosion of printed literature fundamentally shaped
attitudes towards crime.[36] For Shoemaker, despite the expansion of
crime coverage in the press during the later eighteenth century, the
period between the 1690s and 1770s was 'a golden age of writing
about crime, in which crime was a key theme in print culture ... and
the voices of criminals and their victims could clearly be heard'.[37] The
burgeoning print culture found a receptive audience as well as a willing
cast. Individual criminals struck bargains with the hack journalists who
exploited their desire for immortality, for justice and/or revenge on former confederates, or simply for financial remuneration (for condemned
felons, this could be money for their burial and for their families).[38] As
the next chapter will demonstrate, the 1720s and 30s were significant
decades for the transmission of criminal print cultures. The intensifica-
tion of crime reporting in this period may have had a very real impact
on criminal justice practices. As Richard Ward has suggested, by the
1740s, 'the increasingly prominent and powerful forces of print culture and public opinion were intimately linked to, and could have a
potentially significant impact upon, the administration of law'.[39] The
responses of the press and broader print culture to crime 'events', and
the way in which they sought to identify and publicise criminal confederacy, drew on practices honed in previous decades. Thus, from the
1690s there had been a growth of 'crime stories' about particular types
of offender, most notably the highway robber. However, these representations owed more to traditional forms of rogue literature that depicted
a mobile, sturdy and threatening world of criminals and vagabonds.[40]

Beattie argues in contrast that from the 1720s the Sessions Papers, Ordinaries' Accounts and newspapers, 'introduced more authentic reports of offenders and trials'.[41]

Nevertheless, whilst the eighteenth-century press was suffused with crime news, there was not yet the culture of the crime leader or the moral editorial. In papers like the *Daily Post*, the domestic or London news was often on the front page, but these papers generally only consisted of two sheets and the second sheet often consisted of advertisements and lists of trade prices. However, it did mean that reports about criminals, about the sessions of the Old Bailey or the Guildhall, about executions, were accessible and visible. Moreover, from the 1720s, arguably, the relationship between the magistracy and the press was increasingly intimate. London magistrates at times actively courted the press and, indeed, the press keenly reported on their activities.[42] Other contemporary sources also reflect the importance of the interconnections between the public, the press and the police. William Hogarth's *A Harlot's Progress*, based on events reported in the press in the summer of 1730, was a clever hybrid of print culture, crime story and the public taste for celebrity criminals such as James Dalton and the rapist and seducer, Colonel Charteris.[43] It was the coincidence of broader structural changes linking the press, law enforcement, criminal justice and the public sphere that make the decades from the 1720s so meaningful.

In the eighteenth century, at least up until the 1770s, the proliferation of print culture meant that the most visible and notorious offenders had some sort of public profile. At that point, according to Robert Shoemaker, 'the character of printed literature about crime changed significantly, due to both new financial and official constraints on publication and the shifting cultural preoccupations of readers, as respectable society lost interest in the life experiences of members of the deviant lower classes'.[44] During the early nineteenth century, individual criminals were accorded the infamy of being identified in criminal broadsheets and the popular press, such as *Bell's Life in London, and Sporting Chronicle* (c.1822), and its rival, *Life in London* (1821).[45] The crime broadsheet or broadside industry was most notably associated with Jeremiah Catnach, who ran a very productive business from Monmouth Street in the heart of Seven Dials.[46] The most lucrative subject for the broadsides would shift from highway robbery to bloody murder. Whilst murder had always sold, the shockwave that was sent through the country by the Ratcliff Highway murders in 1811 arguably established a taste for 'bloody' broadsides.[47] The extent to which murder had seeped into nineteenth-century culture is deftly illustrated by Rosalind Crone, who points to the 'material culture of murder', and manufacture of ephemera celebrating violent crime.[48] Tales of robbers and highwaymen did survive in the form of the 'Newgate novel', which included the work of William Harrison Ainsworth and Edward Bulwer-Lytton, as well as Charles Dickens's *Oliver Twist*.[49] Moreover, Dickens's preoccupation with the workhouse and the environments in which crime thrived were reflected in the emerging genre of social investigation by the mid-nineteenth century, most strongly associated with the *Morning Chronicle* and the 'investigative journalism' pioneered by Henry Mayhew.[50]

Social investigation was driven by a range of interests. On the one hand, authors were motivated by political, reformist and religious sensibilities. For example, James Greenwood wrote a number of investigative accounts that explored the poorest districts of London, with an eye to commentary on social inequality.[51] Reviewing *The Seven Curses of London*, in 1869 the *Era* commented that it, 'lays bare some of the most appalling wounds that are not yet closed up on the body of English society'.[52] On the other hand, Andrew Mearns, a Congregational minister, and author of the reform tract, *The Bitter Cry of Outcast London* (1883), was more typical of a strand of religious writing which contributed to the genre of social investigation during the nineteenth century.[53] Many of these accounts were highly sensational and melodramatic and, indeed, reform (whether politically or spiritually driven) and sensation were not mutually exclusive. The majority of these texts presented general and often very stereotypical accounts of the problem of crime and poverty. The celebration of crime that was often implicit in earlier biographical accounts, and the low-life literature of the early nineteenth century, was largely absent. Nevertheless, the sheer abundance of investigation into crime, the conceptualisation of a 'criminal class', the introduction of more systematic recording and classification of criminals, and the detailed trial reportage to be found in the press, mean that 'career' criminals can be occasionally identified. This can be seen from the reconstruction of William Sheen's life (Chapter 5), and accounts of 'professional' criminals like James Townsend Saward (Chapter 6).

By the later nineteenth and early twentieth centuries, newspapers would increasingly become the more natural home for social journalism, drawing together the elements of older prescriptive literatures, pamphlets and journals into headlines, editorials and columns regularly reporting the crime problem.[54] One new form of print culture that proliferated by the interwar period was the police biography. The earliest biographies appeared in the late nineteenth century and were closely influenced by the vogue for detective fiction. In particular, the publication of Arthur

Conan Doyle's Sherlock Holmes stories from the 1880s, helped to grow the market for real-life detective stories.[55] From its earliest incarnations, police biography would be influenced by broader print culture. As Haia Shpayer-Makov has argued, a key function of the memoir was 'to reinforce support for the legal system in the country'. Hence, good 'police' and bad 'villains' were often drawn in very broad brushstrokes. Former police detectives such as Tom Divall (1929), Fred Wensley (1931) and Frederick 'Nutty' Sharpe (1938) draped their accounts of the events with both machismo and close 'knowledge'. Divall, for example, was keen to stress his intimacy with the gangs, 'I had friends among both lots …'.[56] Typically, accounts were subject to institutional or self-aggrandisement. As Sharpe wrote in 1938, 'I don't think that I make any unfair boast when I say that these yellow livered, rotten little bullies and cowards are dead scared of the Flying Squad'.[57]

By the interwar period, the influences on press portrayals of crime, and indeed on police biography, would be shaped by other external cultural influences, what one contemporary newspaper called 'the Chicagoan Complex'.[58] As early as 1922 the *Empire News* was describing the racecourse gang conflicts, discussed here in Chapter 8, as 'resembling the methods of the mafia gangs of Italy and America'.[59] Other contemporary authors wrote the racecourse wars into their narrated lives. The most notorious of the racecourse gangs, the Sabinis, appeared in the posthumously published biography of the nightclub owner Kate Meyrick. She closely echoed contemporary press rhetoric when describing the 'gangsters', noting, 'The West End of London was at this period a regular hotbed of lawlessness; then and for another four years or so Soho suffered a reign of terror'.[60] The evoking of terror and terrorism was common in press constructions of the racecourse wars, and of gang crime more generally.[61] Fiction writers, such as Graham Greene and Peter Cheney, would also help to retrospectively construct the mythology of the racecourse wars.[62] Moreover, such narratives have been recycled into the linear genealogies presented by writers such as McDonald and Morton, as well as the pulp fiction account of Darby Sabini's life, published by former crime correspondent Edward T. Hart.[63] In the merging of literary representation, print culture and criminal lives, the Sabini family were a natural fit. But even in the early 1920s, stereotypes of what Andrew Davies has called 'the Romantic Outlaw' were used to describe Darby Sabini in the press.[64] In the *Empire News*, Sabini was described as, 'A dapper, sturdy-looking little man with the quick, flashing eyes of his race'.[65] Here Darby was cast as 'leading man', in an era in which celebrity was becoming a powerful force.

Public Enemies?

The emergence of the gangster trope in the interwar years of the twentieth century, however, was not unprecedented. The overlapping forces that combined to produce interactions between law enforcement and print culture also contributed to the emergence of a cultural form which focused on the life of the individual criminal (or groups of criminals). With its roots in the highwayman literature of the late seventeenth century, it flourished from the early eighteenth century with the emergence of the 'Grub-Street' milieu and particularly (by the 1720s) with the influence of individuals like Daniel Defoe and the printer, John Applebee, in publicising crime stories.[66] Wild's 'career' can be seen as a significant turning-point for the publicity of crime, not least because Wild himself manipulated his public profile as a way of furthering his influence. The notoriety of Wild, and the short, brutal lives of many of those who were connected to him, would be valuable fodder for the writers of criminal biography. Thus print culture not only reflected public and policing rhetoric on the state of crime in the metropolis, but also identified specific groups or individuals as troublemakers, feeding into a process that enabled the stigmatisation of particular individuals and/ or communities. Individuals were visibly and publicly recorded in the proliferation of texts that charted crime and disorder in the metropolis: the *Proceedings of the Old Bailey*, the *Ordinary of Newgate's Account*, the *Select Trials*, the *Newgate Calendar*. These joined with the daily reporting of criminal news to provide both plebeian and elite communities with knowledge of who the 'villainous' were. The press focused attention on those that they identified as being key actors in the criminal milieu. At key points, the interrelationship between the incidence of crime, the enforcement of order and the reporting of crime resulted in heightened knowledge and visibility of criminality. Clearly, decisions were made about which crimes were to be reported, and whilst serious violent crime and robbery would always be worthy of column inches, the activities of notorious criminals like Jonathan Wild, Jack Sheppard and Dick Turpin could be followed in minute detail.[67] The case studies provided in this book illustrate the powerful ability of the press to focus the attention of the public upon specific individuals and to reinforce criminal typologies and stereotypes – rather than reflecting the shared experience that may have characterised the lives of Mary Harvey and Isabella Eaton, the Sheen family, the Sabinis and the other women and men of their communities.

Cases like these help us to say something about the relationship between cultural production and legal process, and the way in which it contributes to the historical construction of criminality. Descriptions of criminal behaviour and criminal types were not just plucked out of thin air; rather they were based on real people who had real experiences in the criminal justice system. Moreover, care needs to be taken with the crime stories told in print culture. Whilst some individuals and groups of offenders were the subject of intense interest; many offenders escaped notice. Indeed, the representations that were generated could be based on a narrow interpretation of real-life events, on a limited number of actual criminals and often on recycled evidence. For example, William Augustus Miles's interviews with juvenile offenders on the *Euryalus* hulk in the 1830s, were recycled in the Select Committee on Gaols and Houses of Correction in 1835, the Constabulary Commission of 1836–39 (for which he was a researcher), and his own book, *Poverty, Mendicity and Crime*, published in 1839. Miles presented the boys' stories as evidence of widespread criminal organisation.[68] Miles's ubiquity at this point, and his status of expert might suggest that evidence from a small number of juvenile boys about a small number of offenders was likely to have been passed around a large number of contemporary commentators and practitioners.[69]

From the early nineteenth century, criminal histories of individuals other than those found guilty of murder were less popular. Without the culminating terror of the noose, narratives of pickpockets, thieves and receivers of stolen goods did not have the same currency as violent criminals whose story arc more often ended up on the gallows. Moreover, even in its early-nineteenth-century incarnations, the *Newgate Calendar* tended to focus mostly on the classic narratives of highwaymen and robbers from the previous century.[70] There were some notorious, non-homicidal criminals who caught the eye of the print media. Probably one of the most visible criminals in early nineteenth century print culture was the London Jewish fence and thief, Isaac 'Ikey' Solomon, a 'career' criminal who was active in London from c. 1810.[71] By the mid-1820s, he was well known to the police, both for his activities as a receiver of stolen goods and as a dealer in stolen bank notes. However, Solomon's fame came largely as a result of a notorious escape from custody in 1827. Joining his separately convicted wife in Van Diemen's Land, Solomon was the subject of a legal battle, culminating in his being shipped back to England to stand trial in 1830. The involvement of the Colonial and Home Office in the case put the seal on his notoriety. Solomon was tried on a number of indictments at the Old Bailey in 1830, after which he was sentenced to transportation for 14 years and returned to Van Diemen's Land in November 1831.[72] Solomon was no ordinary offender. Like the most notorious criminals of the previous century, he had crossed the line that brought him into public repute. As John Tobias points out, 'Despite the predominance of this period in our criminal history, none of the ordinary criminals of the day, it seems to me, are known by name to the general public'. He cites Solomon as an example of a man 'engaged in ordinary crime'.[73] Yet, it is the exceptional elements of Solomon's public story that allow the historian to trace his progress through both official records and print culture.[74]

In the twentieth century, a similar tendency of the press and other print culture to identify and select particular individuals as 'public' criminals can also be found. Thus Dick Hobbs points out that few might have heard of Billy Hill and Jack 'Spot' Comer (the 'bosses' of the London underworld in the later 1930s and 40s) had they not caught the attention of biographers like Duncan Webb and the pulp fiction writer, Hank Janson.[75] Similarly, there was little or no mention of the McDonald family from South London, until Brian McDonald, the nephew of 'gangleader' Charles 'Wag' McDonald, published his history and part-memoir, *Elephant Boys: Tales of London and Los Angeles Underworlds*, in 2000.[76] The book drew on 'Uncle Wag's' diaries, which he had conveniently kept. Since then, true crime authors have written the McDonald family firmly into the family tree of gangsterdom. Of course it may be that the McDonalds were actually very good at being criminals, avoided arrest and resisted the temptation to make their mark as visible hard men. Certainly figures like Spot and Hill, and their successors, Ronald and Reginald Kray, could not resist the lure of being 'public' criminals.[77] In 1955 Hill published his immodestly titled, *Boss of Britain's Underworld*. It had been ghost-written by the crime correspondent of the *People*, Duncan Webb. The Kray twins 'invited' John Pearson to write their biography in 1967. Indeed, the powerful pull of criminal celebrity and criminal association should not be underestimated. Thus, when Raphael Samuel interviewed the former criminal Arthur Harding about his life in East London, Harding placed himself firmly in the criminal networks of the early twenties, with references to the Sabinis and to the Jewish bookmaker Edward Emmanuel. Whilst Harding did have a criminal and penal record and most notably gave evidence to a Royal Commission on policing in 1908, his reflections on proximity to the Sabinis may have been aspirational or a reflection of the local mythologies (and press coverage?) that he would have access to as an East End resident.[78]

Criminal Networks: Families, Communities, Workplace

In exploring the individuals and groups who have become the substance of this book, I have found that relationships, networks and communities fundamentally underpin the crime stories that make up the underworld.[79] Thus, criminal organisation is characterised by the same relationships of exchange and reciprocity that structure everyday society. Moreover, these criminal communities are rarely fixed in their identities. Rather, networks overlap and communities might come together in a fragile and often short-lived way that then defines them as 'criminal' or 'deviant'. Indeed, Matt Neale has cautioned against the use of the term 'criminal networks', describing the circulation of stolen goods in eighteenth-century Bristol as 'myriad social and economic connections that were constantly in flux'.[80] Gangs could represent multiple identities, not just criminal identities. For Peter Linebaugh, the gang represented the meeting of class identities, the apparent rules and conduct of the gang echoed forms of labour organisation.[81] However, this book demonstrates the importance of family and kinship bonds to the connections that made up criminal networks. As Paul Griffiths notes in his account of early modern London between 1550 and 1660, '"Criminals" crossed spatial, residential and work borders all the time'.[82] The exchanges, interactions and 'boundary-hoppings' described by Griffiths for the late sixteenth and seventeenth centuries, equally work to describe overlapping networks and criminal communities from the early eighteenth century.[83] Accounts of criminals are shaped by alliance and connection. Some alliances are deep-seated, based on family and on deep connections to communities. Thus, Moll Harvey worked mainly with her sister, Isabella Eaton; Sheen's main confederates were his elderly, roguish parents; the Sabinis were brothers; other members of the 'gang' were close neighbours. In all three cases, our protagonists operated in well-defined areas – networks of streets, pubs and lodging houses. Moreover, siblings, husbands and wives, children, parents, neighbours and lovers frequently populated the gangs identified by such gang-busting magistrates as De Veil and the Fieldings in the eighteenth century. For example, the Black Boy Alley Gang, the name used to identify a cluster of individual and associated offenders in the Chick Lane and Field Lane area during the 1740s, were bound as much by territorial and familial alliances as criminal organisation.[84] Criminal activity then needs to be understood in the context of community, and particularly the makeshift economies of the poor that transformed familial, class or ethnic identity into criminal identity. Neighbours and community were also party to the processes that shaped criminal identity. Even in more short-lived and less deep-rooted liaisons and networks, such connections were present.

One of the ways in which individuals and groups interconnected for illegal purposes was through contacts made at work. In the nineteenth century, when the experience of work and the workplace developed for the working and lower middle-class, confederacies formed through work become more visible in the criminal justice system. Arguably, white-collar crime has long been seen as a form of organised crime. However, it sits problematically in relation to the overlapping criminal communities that are examined in this book. These communities have not only been formed by the illegalities, strategies and economies of those involved in them, but also through the series of interactions with criminal justice, with law enforcement and with print culture. White-collar criminals, for the most part, have historically managed to evade these agents. The term itself is associated with the work of Edwin Sutherland in 1939, used to describe 'a crime committed by a person of respectability and high social status in the course of his occupation', and the limited historical investigations into white-collar crime have concentrated for the most part on company and corporate fraud.[85] Yet, at the Old Bailey, as we see in the account of frauds and long-firm crimes described in Chapter 6, the relationship and networks that framed the crimes were those of financial transaction, the workplace and economic or business partnership. In these often complicated cases, involving multiple defendants, the circles that overlapped were those of clerks, travelling salesmen, shopkeepers, commission agents and managers. It may be that the increasing visibility of these cases in the Old Bailey from the mid-nineteenth century does mark a shift away from the crimes of the overlapping communities of families and neighbours to be found in the earlier period. On the other hand, as John Langbein has shown, similar relationships structured the 'gang' of the corrupt solicitor William Wreathock in the 1730s, whose network was composed of attorneys, clerks and their enforcers.[86] Finally, work, at least in part, contributed to the formation of identity amongst the youth gangs of late-Victorian and Edwardian London, as will be shown in Chapter 7. Thus, the boys and young men involved in street and fighting gangs may have strongly identified with the neighbourhood territory, but they also had shared common ground as manual and semi-skilled workers.

Territory and Crime: Margins, Boundaries and Contested Spaces

Whilst information about criminal lives is inevitably fragmentary, in the case studies presented here we find patterns relating to territory and urban space. Territory has shaped the history of ideas about the underworld and about criminal organisation. In contrast to late modern society, where organised crime and the underworld are defined through globalised black economies and technologies, criminal communities in the past were strongly tied to urban terrains.[87] Whilst crime networks could operate in provincial towns and rural areas, urban streets and ghettos dominate narratives of the underworld.[88] The clusters of streets that were identified as trouble spots by the authorities and by other 'experts' were predictably economically deprived areas. Moreover, as Clive Emsley has pointed out:

> It is clear that the police stigmatised certain lodging house districts as criminal and, while these were generally the cheapest and poorest, the labelling may have become to some extent self-fulfilling with those who could avoid lodgings in a stigmatised area making every effort to do so.[89]

However, there were other notable features of the streets and street-clusters in the metropolis that became associated with crime. The crime stories told in the chapters that follow frequently take place in contested spaces. The conflicts between Mary Harvey and her neighbours, described in Chapter 3, took place in the vicinity of Hedge Lane, a road in the Haymarket area notoriously associated with prostitution.[90] Areas associated with vice are inherently contested spaces, as Simon Gunn has noted, 'The sexual regulation of public space is indeed one of the most pervasive and least remarked, features of urban modernity'.[91] In Hedge Lane, tensions between 'disorderly' residents and their more respectable neighbours would escalate to the point at which the latter would collude with the constables and the reforming magistracy in order to reclaim their streets. Characteristically, law enforcers and police are at the root of such conflicts over space and territory. Indeed, as Steve Herbert has argued, police officers (and their early modern counterparts) regularly exercise territoriality, seeking to influence social action through the control of space, 'Police efforts to claim sovereignty over the street, however, are always subject to contestation'.[92]

Historically, these battles for street terrain have frequently involved young men. Two chapters in this book deal with the relationship between youth and territory. Whilst most discussions of historical youth gangs date from around the 1870s, as Chapter 3 demonstrates, concerns about gangs of youths surfaced much earlier. Hence, an increasing number of prosecutions involving (mainly) young men described as 'hustling' and 'surrounding' their victims, often in a large crowd assembled to watch a procession or ceremony, appeared at the Old Bailey in the 1810s and 1820s. Whilst these gangs of young men may have been drawn to the fairs, parades and processions because of the opportunities provided by the assembling of crowds, they were also engaged in a contest about how to use that territory. For the election crowd gathered at the hustings, or the Carolinian crowd coming out in support of the queen, the street was a political space as well as one of disorder or larceny. As cabinet-maker, Henry Cotton described, as he watched the queen passing near Waterloo Place in September 1820, 'My hands were pinioned down by a gang, who hustled me against the carriage, and I felt my watch go from my fob'.[93] According to Old Bailey accounts, when metropolitan streets were claimed for the rituals of procession and public spectacle, 'hustling gangs' took advantage of the opportunity to rob bystanders and spectators. In many of these cases the descriptions of hustling gangs are vague, with often a hazy estimate of the number of people apparently involved. It is impossible to even tell who or how many were involved in the actual commission of crime. Thus descriptions of large groups, claiming street space, characterise these accounts.

Such descriptions of hustling gangs demonstrate the continuing constellation of concerns about groups of young men on public streets. Their aggressive group behaviour, their fight for territory on the street, ripple down to the accounts of 'fighting gangs', ruffianism and hooliganism that can be found later in the century. Whilst the gangs of young men described in late-Victorian and Edwardian London may have shared features with the hustling youths of the Regency, there are distinctions. From its earliest appearance in the press, hustling had been strongly associated with the City. As one writer remarked in the *World*, in October 1788, 'To the reproach of the City Police, a most daring set of villains infest the very center of it, especially Fleet-street. Parties of them skulk in Courts; and, on a signal given, they assemble, and proceed to what they call "hustling"'.[94] The City was essentially a contested terrain. As Paul Griffiths notes of early modern London, 'London was a city of overlapping circles and this disarray was a root cause of its tensions. The city map was complicated by crisscrossing jurisdictions. Wards and parishes overlapped, trespasses made explicit in boundary contests'.[95] For the gangs of youths who fought on late-Victorian and Edwardian streets, their terrain had shifted to the margins of the City and the areas that fringed the centre of London. Main thoroughfares that formed boundaries were frequently the site of conflict between young people and other street users. Thus, the group of youths described in Chapter 4, who paraded along Pentonville Road in November 1820, 'hustling, tripping up, and knocking down every person they met', were contesting the terrain of Pentonville Road in a way very similar to the later groups of roughs, ruffians and hooligans described in Chapter 7.[96] It is perhaps no coincidence that Pentonville Road was a site of conflict. Indeed, the sections of the modern London Inner Ring Road, Marylebone Road, Euston Road, Pentonville Road and City Road, were all part of a terrain used by groups of youths.

The youths charged with the murder of Joseph Rumbold in Regent's Park in May 1888, had been walking and fighting on the Marylebone Road the day before the attack on Rumbold.[97] The fight was apparently the climax of a series of confrontations between the Fitzroy Place Lads and the Lisson Grove Lads. Fitzroy Place was just off Euston Road, near the junction with the Marylebone Road. Lisson Grove was also off Marylebone Road, to the west. These roads, along with Pentonville and City Road to the East, formed part of a major boundary – the New Road, a turnpike road which was opened in 1756. Indeed, for much of the eighteenth century, the New Road was virtually London's northern boundary. By the later nineteenth century, whilst London had spilt over and beyond this boundary it still retained its importance as a key highway.[98] Karen Spierling and Michael Halvorson, commenting on early modern communities, see boundaries as places where those communities intersect: 'it is at the margins or boundaries of these circles, where insider meets outsider, where group identities are tested, shaped, and ultimately accommodated or rejected'.[99] This resonates with the late-Victorian and Edwardian accounts of youth gangs, for whom the street was a place where they meet other youths, workmates, family members and youths from adjacent territories. They also met the police, as Spierling and Halvorson note, 'Conflict at the boundaries of these communities might arise between members of rival groups, but it could also be set off by the tensions inflicted on an individual or group of people caught in the competing demands of different community networks or emerging bureaucratic institutions'.[100]

Boundaries between parishes can be seen as liminal spaces, disputed territories. Arguably, where the boundary was not only between parishes, but between the county and the City, the status and reputation of such areas was even more problematic. Thus, the reputation of the Clerkenwell rookery may have been linked to its specific position on the margins of the City.[101] Confederacies of thieves, robbers, footpads and thief-takers had been historically associated with a tightly delineated set of streets and lanes on the boundaries of the City of London. Black

Boy Alley and Chick Lane, later West Street, Field Lane and Saffron Hill, had long been at the centre of the spatial map of metropolitan crime.[102] Areas such as this were problematic for the authorities. As John Carter Wood notes, 'Some neighbourhoods may have received little protection from the authorities, allowing alternative powers to assert themselves, and there may even be "no-go" areas in which the police are normally absent'.[103] Certainly, the Clerkenwell rookery was not a safe place for law enforcers. In the 1740s it took the increase of rewards by the authorities to encourage thief-takers and constables into the area.[104] By the early nineteenth century, law enforcers still faced considerable danger when they had to venture into the area. John Barnley, a beadle of St Andrew's parish described a visit to Field Lane in evidence given to the 1817 Select Committee on Police, 'I lately went to fetch a thief who had committed a highway robbery: he came out very gently with me, and after I was out of the house, and had gone about an hundred yards, I was surrounded by twenty or thirty people, who had come out of that very house to rescue him...'.[105] The area would finally be wiped out with the development of the Fleet valley and the building of the Farringdon Road in the mid-nineteenth century. Elaine Reynolds has suggested that in parishes that were adjacent to the City traditional informal law enforcement strategies might have been more effective. However, she argues, during the nineteenth century, 'as overcrowding and immigration into the East End increased over the course of the century, this sense of social harmony altered'.[106]

By the 1880s tensions in Whitechapel escalated dramatically and arguments about jurisdiction and territory would become an issue in the police response to the Whitechapel murders.[107] But the reputation of Whitechapel and Spitalfields as urban frontier-towns was apparent long before the 1880s. The Sheen family (Chapter 5) had moved from one marginal space (off Rosemary Lane, close to the Mint and to St Katherine's) to another, when they colonised lodging houses on Wentworth Street. Thus, the street's reputation may have reflected its status both as the boundary between Whitechapel and Spitalfields, and at its west end, with the City. The proximity of such areas to the City was also a reflection of the historical development of the suburban parishes. Areas like Clerkenwell, Whitechapel and Spitalfields had developed as satellites to the City and, with suburban development during the eighteenth and nineteenth centuries, they would predominately house the poor and manufacturing industry.[108] Moreover, these areas would attract new communities seeking to gain a foothold in the economic and social life of the metropolis. For instance, successive waves of Italian migrants had come to London throughout the nineteenth century.[109] The earliest settlers were skilled craftsmen who had settled in Holborn; later migrants settled in nearby Clerkenwell. As we will see in Chapters 7 and 8, the contest over urban space shaped the development of territorial conflict in the later nineteenth and early twentieth centuries. In Clerkenwell, confrontations between youth street gangs and young men from the Italian community reflected the intricate negotiations of newly shared street space. By the interwar period, the territorial activities of the Sabini family and their associates may have been a legacy. As Wood notes, 'Concepts of spatial belonging are affected by issues including class, sex, age, status, ethnicity and profession, and violence can play a role in all aspects of territoriality: identifying who has the right to be within a particular space, establishing the boundaries of that space and excluding those who do not belong'.[110]

Approaching the Underworld

By using a case study approach and providing snap-shots of deviant cultures and behaviours, this book aims to explore the overlapping communities which were identified by local, cultural and political authorities as constituting the 'underworld'. This process could be described as one of ethnographic 'thick description', in particular in those chapters (3, 5 and 8) concerned with small groups of individuals. Malcolm Gaskill has argued that 'we need to concentrate on smaller contexts of lived experience at the heart of ... society: the market-place, work-shop, parish church, courtroom, ale-bench, winter fireside, birthing-chamber and so on'.[111] Similarly, in this book, the minutiae of ordinary life come together with more extraordinary narratives of criminal justice. Peter Burke has noted the problems with such detailed studies of individuals or groups of individuals, 'One might begin with the charge that the micro-historians trivialize history by studying the biographies of unimportant people or the difficulties of small communities'.[112] Yet, as he goes on to argue, the micro-historian should aim to demonstrate the links between small communities and macro-historical trends. Like Richard Evans' collection of micro-histories from nineteenth-century Germany, the narratives constructed from the snapshot records of the lives of Harvey and Eaton, the Sheens and the Sabinis attempt to address bigger questions about social relations, community, policing prosecution practices and print culture.[113] But other methodological problems and issues remain. The first is the issue of recorded plebeian and/or working-class speech. Here, the words of street robbers and hustlers, fraudsters and hooligans are overwhelmingly mediated through the press, courtroom testimony and the records of law enforcers. Plebeian language is often diluted and restructured and may be far from verbatim. Nevertheless, I would argue that these words are all we have to reconstruct these lives. Moreover, one of the advantages of digital searching has been the ability to probe the record below the more obvious and accessible. Tweaking searches and wildcards often provide minute fragments that add nuance to our histories of individuals. For example, such deep searching found the words attributed to the elderly Sarah Roberts, a neighbour of the Sheens and hugely indignant at the 'mob in the street', who had assembled upon the release of William Sheen. Roberts had gone to see the Lambeth magistrate, Mr Curtis, in order to make a complaint about threats of violence she had received from the Sheens.[114] She told the magistrate, 'he [Sheen] was marching about in his shirt sleeves like any lord ...', later in the interview she concluded, 'Ah, ah! He's a bad boy, Sir ...', suggesting that her life was in danger if some action was not taken. These words do not come from the Old Bailey, do not even come from a magistrate trial, and the incident was not widely reported. Just because something is not often recorded or repeated does not, of course, make it more authentic. Ultimately all we can do as historians who are interested in plebeian lives is try to piece together the fragments of evidence to create some impression of those lives.

Another arguably problematic feature of this study is the focus on the metropolis (and particularly on the Old Bailey courtroom). I make no apologies for concentrating here on that most dominant of urban spaces, London, which has historically been seen as the home of the underworld.[115] A number of characteristics explain its central importance. As well as its heavily urbanised nature, it also had a busy port, and a highly transient population. During the course of the nineteenth century increasing concerns about immigration, disease and public health would contribute to the process of a marginalisation and segregation of poor communities, producing an 'underworld' which was ever more territorially designated. The social and economic are married to the cultural in the construction of London as a criminogenic environment. Whilst 'underworlds' can exist anywhere, the metropolis, as studies of New York, Paris and Berlin suggest, is the centre of gravity in the paradigmic history of the underworld.[116] Only more recently, with the impact of globalisation and the Internet, has the underworld loosed its moorings from the metropolitan city. Nevertheless, a focus on London, and particularly on the Old Bailey, does have its limitations. Recent work by Matt Neale has concluded that 'studies which are based on London may have only a limited relevance to helping us understand crime in other English cities'.[117] On the other hand, my intention in this book has not been to provide a model to explain criminal confederacy, but rather to explore the myriad ways in which real lives and real relationships may have both shaped, and been shaped by, contemporary and historical understandings of the underworld.

A social and cultural history – evaluating cultural production alongside archival findings – provides us with a solid empirical basis from which to explore criminal lives. A partial reconstruction of poor lives can be mediated through elite sources. Historians can recapture the words of the criminal and the poor in the rich sources which we have at our disposal: these include the Old Bailey Sessions Papers; the records of the Home Office and Metropolitan Police; records of the Quarter Sessions, the police court and the parish; the investigations carried out on behalf of and the evidence submitted to Select Committees and Royal Commissions; newspaper reports and the writings of Grub Street hacks; the commentaries, memoirs and reports of social investigators, philanthropists, reformers and representatives of the criminal justice system. These writers and authors mediated their 'knowledge' of criminal lives in a variety of print forms in increasing numbers during the period covered by this book. Our ability to dissect criminal lives in forensic detail is in large part due to significant developments in the availability of primary source materials. Most important for this book has been the digitisation of the Old Bailey Proceedings. The work of the project team, and particularly its directors, Tim Hitchcock, Robert Shoemaker and Clive Emsley, has been significant in shaping the way in which historians and other researchers interpret and analyse evidence from the trials.[118] The work on individual criminals that I started on the microfilm copies and completed on the digitised version has substantially expanded. This has enabled me to place individuals, their confederates and other associates within a broader set of interconnecting networks and to produce a much deeper and arguably more meaningful snapshot of their lives.

The chapter that follows explores the relationship between law enforcement and the narratives and networks of criminals in the early eighteenth century. In particular it will look at the decades of the 1720s and 1730s, a period in which the underworld more significantly and substantially became part of the public discourse about crime and deviance. This chapter and the next pinpoint some ways in which the outlined themes took form during this important period. Chapter 3 focuses on a specific group of criminals and their activities in a short period between the late 1720s and early 1730s. By following Mary Harvey, her sister Isabella Eaton and her confederate Mary Sullivan through their series of interactions with the criminal justice system, themes relating to print culture and to Harvey's reputation as a 'public criminal', to overlapping communities and territorial contests, are explored. Chapter 4 examines the changing language of robbery in the later eighteenth and early nineteenth century, narrowing its focus to the surge in hustling cases to be found from the 1810s as a way of considering how concerns about young men, violence and territorial infringements may have underpinned the surfacing of anxiety about 'new' forms of crime and robbery. Chapter 5 unpicks the life of William Sheen and his family over two decades in the early to mid-nineteenth century. Sheen's public reputation and contemporary notoriety, the connecting narratives of his family and the local community, and the territorial importance of the Wentworth street area are key themes. Chapter 6 considers the evolution of 'modern' ideas about crime, and the contemporary understanding that new forms of criminality were becoming more common, by exploring the patterns of activity and prosecution in crimes broadly described as fraud and swindling. This includes coining, forgery and long-firm frauds, crimes which would be prosecuted in increasing numbers in the Old Bailey from the middle of the nineteenth century. Nevertheless, within these cases, the identified themes can still be found: overlapping communities of family, neighbours and colleagues characterise many of these interactions. Moreover, print culture played a significant role in suggesting new forms of organisation to patterns of criminal activity that had long been troubling the authorities. Chapter 7 returns to the consideration of youth, violence and territory in the later nineteenth and early twentieth centuries, by exploring the reporting of street fighting gangs in the Victorian and Edwardian press. It looks in detail at the young men and women who were involved as protagonists, victims and witnesses, the communities to which they belonged and the territories with which they associated. Finally, Chapter 8 will consider the racecourse wars of the interwar period, and particularly focus on the involvement of the Sabini family, returning the book to an exploration of the themes of community, territory and the publicity of crime in a period which is often seen as crucial in the evolution of 'modern' organised crime activity.

2
'Now we have the Informing Dogs!': Crime Networks and Informing Cultures in the 1720s and 1730s[1]

Introduction

The criminal career of Jonathan Wild, executed at Tyburn on 24 May 1725, has for many commentators become a fixed point in the history of the underworld.[2] Wild was a criminal, an informer, a thief-taker and a thief-maker; a man who artfully navigated the entrepreneurial justice system of the early eighteenth century. Our knowledge of Wild's activities is shaped by the long repetition of his story in the print culture that he was said to have courted.[3] His most thorough biographer, Gerald Howson noted, 'Certainly he resembled the gangster of the twentieth century more closely than he did his famous contemporaries in Europe ... He was the first criminal to become a "celebrity" ...'.[4] Indeed, Wild's story is frequently re-imagined through the lens of later twentieth-century gang culture (in itself a constructed narrative), which reframes Wild as an eighteenth-century criminal mastermind.[5] In this chapter I am less concerned with the reiteration of his story and more with the significance of the era as one in which Wild and his associates were able to thrive, and in which the 'underworld' narrative would find a more stable niche.

Whilst rudimentary forms of criminal organisation had long been part of the metropolitan economy, Wild can be seen as a moderniser in his grasp of the networks of enterprise and control.[6] Hence, Wild prospered in the early-eighteenth-century metropolis because of his skilful manipulation of the climate of informing that had proliferated with the system of rewards established from the 1690s, encouraging criminals to turn on their companions and associates. Practices of informing were also encouraged through the campaigns for moral reform from the late seventeenth century, and the support of the magistracy and the investment of authority in their actions would enable enterprising men to become informing 'professionals' working closely with law enforcers. In the 1720s and 1730s informing, rewards and reforming would help create a visible culture of criminal confederacy, which was enabled by the development of the press and in the printed literature of crime that privileged 'crime stories' about notorious individuals and gangs.

This chapter and the one that follows focus on the interaction between print culture, law enforcement and criminal activity in the 1720s and 1730s, decades in which new models of criminal confederacy were being constructed and shaped. The first part of the chapter explores the evolution of the gang in print culture in the early eighteenth century, arguing that gang terminology was inherently problematic. The next part of the chapter briefly contextualises law-enforcement strategies in this period and the influence of the moral reformation campaign before focusing in more detail on the practices of informing that flourished in these decades. It explores a group of men whose lives were intertwined by informing in order to illustrate the blurred boundaries between the worlds of law enforcement and criminality in this period: the informing constables, Thomas, Michael and Robert Willis, the street robber, James Dalton, and the 'professional' informer, John Waller. The chapter that follows illustrates some of the broader themes raised here, by providing a detailed study of Mary 'Moll' Harvey's gang, looking more closely at the overlapping networks of crime, community and kinship through a series of interactions with law enforcement and print culture.[7]

There had been heightened concerns about crime from the 1690s when a series of acts had established rewards for the conviction of highwaymen, coiners and burglars.[8] However, after the end of the War of the Spanish Succession in 1713, arguably there was something of a 'social panic' about crime. John Beattie has convincingly demonstrated that by the 1720s there was an increase in prosecutions of violent crime, particularly robbery and burglary, in the metropolis. Beattie links this to heightened concerns about gangs that were increasingly widely reported by the press.[9] From the early eighteenth century, the street-robber had emerged as a distinct type of criminal both in the Old Bailey Sessions and in the wider print culture. Moreover, this representation was distinguished from former depictions of the footpad as being essentially an urban problem.[10] Whilst not all criminals were robbers, the most visible criminals in the early decades of the eighteenth century had often been convicted of some form of street robbery. There are a number of explanations for this. Firstly, the likelihood of being sentenced to death if found guilty of forms of robbery was comparatively high, contributing to the visibility of criminals whose story would be made 'public'. Most offenders who were prosecuted and found guilty of highway robbery at the Old Bailey were sentenced to death (84.7 per cent).[11] The proportion actually executed is less clear. Richard Clark's estimates show that highway robbers as a proportion of those who were executed at Tyburn increased from the early eighteenth century; in the decade between 1725 and 1734, highway robbers constituted 48.11 per cent of those hanged.[12] However, whilst robbers may have been the most common occupants of the Tyburn Tree, the application of the death penalty was not the only explanation for their dominance in accounts of criminal confederacy. For example, in Surrey between 1749 and 1775, a period by which the robber was a declining figure in print culture, the robber still accounted for over half of those who were hanged.[13] Secondly, the rewards system that encouraged informing was skewed towards anxieties about urban disorder. Hence, robbery out in the open (in public, on the street, in the community) was a significant concern. Finally, the theme of criminal confederacy was strikingly apparent in the print culture that proliferated in this period, with the urban robber as a dominant character. From the early eighteenth century this combination of factors meant that robbery was the dominant trope in crime narratives and commentaries.

However, crime commentaries and criminal justice policy focused on what in reality was likely to have been a small cohort of offenders. This means that the contemporary criminal networks that we can identify frequently overlapped. After the death of Wild it may be that the vacuum that was left produced an environment in which criminal activism around informing was more intense. Moreover, it is likely that the authorities were keen to mop up the networks which Wild had identified and/or was associated with. Certainly, it is a period that allows us to trace some of the key themes of this book: the interactions between print culture and criminal and informing networks; the role of kinship and community networks; and the visibility of the metropolitan underworld. There are limitations to how far criminal networks can be traced. However, we are able to trace networks and connections, albeit in a limited way, because individuals or groups have become visible through the mechanisms of criminal justice and print culture. Groups of criminals identified as 'gangs' would inform episodic escalation of popular fear throughout much of the century, often focused on the metropolis. The most well known, the Gregory or Essex gang, associated with Richard Turpin, garnered considerable publicity in the 1730s, and a number of historians have noted the role of the print media in reinforcing the notoriety of Turpin and his gang.[14] As Erin Mackie has noted, 'He is repeatedly referred to as the "Famous Turpin" in a press that had itself contributed to that fame'.[15] Later, in the mid-1740s, the activities of the Black Boy Alley Gang were highlighted through a combination of press activity, public attention and print culture.[16] Whilst the arrests and reporting of the Black Boy Alley Gang can be understood in terms of 'moral panic', these events were also part of a broader landscape of criminal, informer and thief-taking networks which have been described in painstaking detail by Ruth Paley.[17] Not only does Paley trace connections between the infamous McDaniel gang of thief-takers who were prosecuted in 1754, with 'criminal gangs' such as the Black Boy Alley Gang and the Royal Family, she also demonstrates the complicated relationships between such networks and key magistrates such as Sir Thomas De Veil and Henry and John Fielding from 1748.[18] Moreover, criminal networks and criminal gangs did not disappear after the mid-century. By 1785 Martin Madan complained, 'Our gangs of thieves are grown too numerous, and the individuals too desperate and dangerous, to be controuled [sic] by the comparatively feeble powers of a private magistrate, or of the common parochial constable'.[19] Yet, the 1720s and 1730s remain pivotal in the evolution of the underworld narrative. To a large extent this can be explained by the changing nature of print culture.

Print Culture

Print culture concerned with crime expanded rapidly in the early eighteenth century and its proliferation has been seen as crucial to the development of discussions of crime in the public sphere.[20] During the 1720s the printed accounts of the trials at the Old Bailey became an increasingly popular publication. From December 1729 various changes were made to the format, including cross-referencing between trials, advertisements and the greater use of verbatim accounts. Hence, by the 1730s the accounts had expanded from around six to eight pages to often more than 20 pages.[21] In parallel with this, the Ordinary's *Account*, which chronicled the lives of the condemned, became a more substantial publication, and pamphlet accounts of crime proliferated. Whilst cradle-to-grave accounts of criminals and their heinous acts had been published in increasing numbers since the mid-seventeenth century, the vast majority of these were more often concerned with murder and the occasional highwayman.[22] During the 1720s there was a qualitative shift in the nature of these publications, with the robber, the burglar and the gang joining the typologies already being extolled.[23]

For instance, the year 1722 saw the publication of *A Compleat and True Account of All the Robberies Committed by James Carrick, John Malhoni, and Their Accomplices ...*, *A Full, True and Impartial Account of All the Robberies Committed in City, Town, and Country, for Several Years Past by William Hawkins ....*, as well as accounts of William's brother John Hawkins and of Benjamin Child, '*Lately Executed for Robbing the Bristol Mail'*.[24] Over the following decade the publicity of crime grew alongside the perceived crime wave, creating an atmosphere of intense speculation and moral rhetoric about crime. The theatricality of Wild's story, with its various dramatic elements, was capitalised upon by both hack Grub Street authors and social satirists.[25] Hence, Mandeville's discourse on public execution, Defoe's biographies of Wild and Sheppard, various pamphlets on street robbery and Gay's *Beggar's Opera* (1728) amounted to an unprecedented level of crime stories in cultural form.[26]

Undoubtedly the events leading up to the conviction and execution of Jonathan Wild can be seen as something of a spur to this flowering of crime literature. Criminal gangs were frequently identified by the authorities and named as such in the press. Nevertheless, as Shoemaker has noted, robberies were disproportionately reported given that they accounted for only a very small number of crimes tried at the Old Bailey.[27] Even in the 1720s, the decade in which Wild's influence may have affected the number of prosecutions for robbery, thefts involving violence accounted for only 6.55 per cent of crimes prosecuted at the court.[28] In addition, the rhetoric employed across the printed media to describe crime events can be questioned. Drilling down into newspaper references to gangs reveals a more nuanced picture. For example, a search of the Burney Collection of newspapers for the year 1723 reveals 210 references to 'gang' and 'gangs'.[29] These ranged from the gang of 'banditti or Robbers' reported in Venice in the *Evening Post* of 24 January, several references to the gang of the celebrated French robber Cartouche and numerous references to gangs of 'Blacks', such as the activities of the Berkshire Blacks reported in the *Daily Post* of 14 May.[30] In this year at least, events on the continent and in the English countryside had as much impact on the rhetoric employed by the press as any urban crime wave. Moreover, in the Old Bailey Sessions of that year there were no references to gangs. There were 20 references to prosecutions for highway robbery, which described 14 cases. There were only six references to violent robbery and only three of these were different 'events' to those categorised under highway robbery.[31]

As suggested earlier, much of the print culture that was generated about crime in this period was based on a narrow range of evidence and offenders. Thus, the most notable criminal biographies of the 1720s focused on the activities of a number of gangs involved in robberies. However, the majority of the accounts from these years revolved around the activities of a relatively small number of criminals. These included Edward Burnworth, Benjamin Child, James Carrick, William Hawkins, Ralph Wilson, Jack Sheppard, Martin Bellamy, James Dalton and Thomas Neaves (also spelt Neeves).[32] The relationships of these men were intricately bound. Both of the Hawkins, Child, Carrick, Burnworth and Wilson were linked together through Jonathan Wild. According to Gerald Howson, Wild had taken it upon himself to break the London gangs between 1721 and 1723; these included the Hawkins gang, Carrick's gang, Burnworth's gang and James Shaw's gang.[33] Moreover, he suggests that Wild was implicated in the capture of Child, who had been tried at the Aylesbury Assizes.[34] He was hanged close to the site of the robbery near Slough and his body gibbeted on Hounslow Heath.[35] Howson tells us that Jack ('John') Hawkins 'swore ... that he'd be revenged on somebody for poor Child's sake'.[36] John Hawkins was executed at Tyburn in May 1722 after being impeached upon by Ralph Wilson; his body would join Child's on the gibbet.[37] William Hawkins, the brother of John, in turn impeached on his confederates and was transported to South Carolina.[38] Martin Bellamy had stolen from Wild, and had also, according to Philip Rawlings, impeached on James Dalton.[39] James Dalton and Jack Sheppard were two of the biggest prizes on the list distributed by Wild, 'The Prisoner, in the Morning before his Tryal came on, dispersed about the Court a considerable Numbers of printed Lists of the Felons that he had apprehended ...'.[40] These networks should be seen as less a manifestation of organised crime in the modern sense and more as a collection of relationships or loose confederacies. Hence, there was a high level of public consciousness about such groups and networks in the period of Wild's operation and for some time after his death; we know that the printed media engaged vociferously with Wild's 'career' and subsequently those who were in any way associated with him. Thus, the Wild era resulted in the higher visibility of criminal 'organisation' at this time. Wild knowingly used the media in order to publicise his legal activities. In turn this may have produced both more opportunities for criminal enterprise and contributed to an environment which favoured illegitimate economies.

Other factors would help bolster Wild's legacy and sustain public interest in the 'underworld'. Arguably, the reward system expanded and made statutory by government from the 1690s had created the climate in which criminal entrepreneurs like Wild were able to flourish. Whilst rewards had been used as a strategy to target highwaymen and burglars from the 1690s, in January 1720 a Royal Proclamation was published offering a £100 reward (above the statutory £40), for 'whoever shall discover and apprehend any Person or Persons who have at any time within three Months last past committed; or who hereafter shall commit any Robbery, either in the publick Streets or Highway or Road, in or near our Cities of London and Westminster ...'.[41] It also contained the provision of pardoning for accomplices. This was clearly designed to persuade members of gangs to impeach their confederates, in other words, an attempt to break criminal networks.[42] Moreover, the reward was also an attempt to encourage private thief-takers such as Wild to use the prosecution system, rather than acting as a go-between. Arguably, over the following decades the proclamation, which was to stay in force almost continuously until 1745, had a substantial impact on both the prosecution of offenders and the interactions between criminals, courts and law enforcers.

Moral Reformation

Law enforcement was intricately bound up with the moral reformation project in this period, as we will see from the activities of men like the Willis brothers and John Waller, who traded their skills as informers and enforcers in the reform environment. The Society for the Reformation of Manners had first emerged during the critical decade of the 1690s. These societies were proactive and campaigning organisations, and as Faramerz Dabhoiwala points out, 'These groups ... set out to prosecute immorality using the secular law'.[43] They drew upon a range of prosecutorial tools: the recognizance, the indictment and the blank warrant. The latter was printed by the society to be filled in by their constables and informers; it would then be presented to a magistrate who would sign it, thereby setting the process in train for the arrest of the accused.[44] The range of behaviour and disorder policed by the societies was broad, but their most energetic efforts do seem to have been directed toward what can be essentially seen as street-cleansing operations.[45] The grassroots impact of moral reformation was to result in the campaigns to control and punish the most visible and public forms of vice. However, despite the involvement of some middling and elite men as clients, the vices that were aimed at were class specific. Generally the societies aimed to curb the immorality of plebeian London, not the *demi-monde*. Moreover, the campaigns often focused their efforts on sexual immorality, and in particular, prostitution.[46] And so their main targets were women and the men with whom they shared their lives; bullies and pimps, but also husbands and family members. Indeed these were not mutually exclusive categories. Moreover, such women were seen as ciphers for broader cultures of immorality and, as Shoemaker has demonstrated, they were suspected not only of prostitution but also of theft, vagrancy and other disorderly behaviour.[47] This point was clearly made in the Tower Hamlets Society in the 1690s when it linked the impudence of harlots to a whole range of debauchery, crime, vice and disorder.[48] Their success in pursing such campaigns was achieved with the acquiescence of local law enforcers and found support from a significant portion of the magistracy as well as householders, merchants and shopkeepers who were seemingly plagued by the 'contagion' of vice.[49] To some extent, it was the local activity of the reformers that shaped the policing of criminal networks in these decades. Thus, as we will see in the chapter that follows, campaigns against specific localities were frequently initiated by the societies in response to local petitioning and salaried agents were employed to undertake the job of detecting and prosecuting bawdy houses. These agents would be accompanied by one or two helpers, and by sympathetic constables and magistrates. As we will see, the Willis brothers were occupied in this activity, although contemporary references to them as 'constables' are often ambiguous and it is unclear how official their tenure was. It is important to recognise the pragmatic approaches of the grass-roots campaign. It seems clear that the activities associated with the campaign provided a spur to those reform-minded magistrates and local residents who sought to combat disorder in their locality. Moreover, as Dabhoiwala argues, these connections were facilitated by significant financial rewards. This points to the importance of the reformation of manners in invigorating the policing of vice and crime, 'to increase the efficiency of existing methods of policing'.[50]

In the 1720s and 1730s local magistrates and constables would play an active role in the suppression of immorality, often specifically on behalf of the Society for the Reformation of Manners. This suppression could be targeted at particular individuals and specific localities, which in turn drew on the local knowledge provided by the magistracy and their constables. The metropolitan magistrate played a central role in the identification and policing of criminal networks in the eighteenth century, taking advantage of the system of rewards and the culture of informing. Hence, the use of various financial strategies to encourage the formal turning over of information from the 1690s seems to have galvanised thief taking and other less legitimate forms of 'witnessing'.[51] If the state had provided the thief-taker and other entrepreneurial individuals with the tools to make crime their business, the magistrate was a crucial figure in the law enforcement nexus that developed in this period. The added evangelicalism of the tide for moral reform seems to have helped produce a particularly vigorous magistracy. The unpopularity of magistrates like Sir John Gonson (d. 1765) and Sir Thomas De Veil (1684–1746) was satirised by Hogarth in the 1730s. In his portrayal of Justice Gonson, harrying the harlot Moll Hackabout, his constables armed with staves (Figure 3.1), Hogarth implies the relentlessness of the magistrate's campaigns against disorderly houses in 1730.[52] His satire of De Veil as a drunken Freemason (Hogarth and De Veil were apparently both members of the Freemasons) in plate 4 of his 'Time of Day' series, was a pointed commentary on De Veil's aggressive enforcement of the 1736 Gin Act.[53] Sir John Gonson was one of the key magistrates pursuing the reformation of manners agenda in the 1720s and 1730s.[54] Others included the Middlesex justices Nathanial Blackerby, Thomas Railton and Thomas Boteler.[55] In 1729, Blackerby and Railton were attacked publicly by William Rowland, a clergyman, who published 'a false and scandalous libel, signed Sodomastix', which effectively accused the two magistrates of taking bribes in sodomy cases.[56] A generous view might be that the justices were practising a little mercy in such cases, given the potential severity of penalty against mollies at this time.[57] Rowland was found guilty and sentenced to the pillory, where he continued castigating the justices much to the public's concern according to the *London Journal*.[58]

As we will see in the next chapter, John Gonson was the key protagonist in a series of raids on disorderly houses that took place in 1730 and had publicly instructed the Grand Jury a number of times in 1728 and 1729, pushing a proactive moral reformation.[59] The extent of Gonson's direct intervention might be disputed, but certainly for cultural commentators he seems to have become the magistrate most vividly associated with 'moral reformation'. Hogarth was not alone in satirising Gonson's hunger for reform and in the mid-1730s Pope wrote of 'the storm of Gonson's lungs', presumably a reference to his fervour, in *The Fourth Satire of Doctor John Donne*.[60] Moreover, he seems to have been unpopular with plebeian London. On a night in November 1730, according to the *Daily Journal*, Gonson was insulted and threatened by a soldier and another man, a pickpocket named Luke Powel. He was apparently rescued by a crowd of people who had gathered to watch a bonfire. Powel had in fact encountered Gonson a few months earlier, when the magistrate had committed him to the Tothill Fields Bridewell after being caught with a number of handkerchiefs on his person.[61]

The metropolitan magistrate then, was a public figure who was perhaps not so distant from those he was policing. Whilst we are familiar with the role of discretionary justice in this period, in the early eighteenth century Justices of the Peace were also more proactive in the pre-trial stages of law enforcement.[62] In the context of moral reforms such as those pursued by the reformation campaign, or in relation to gin prosecutions, individual justices often took a vigorous role in the processes of 'policing'. Those magistrates who were seen to step over the mark in actively pursuing prosecution were open to accusations of corruption at this time, and there was clearly a fine line between those who encouraged business and those who abused their position of authority.[63] Moreover, as Norma Landau has noted, 'to the eighteenth century, the trading justice was not merely criminal; he actually caused crime'.[64] Busy urban magistrates were particularly open to these sorts of accusations, given that they were likely to be issuing large numbers of recognizances to appear at the sessions. However, it is probable that in urban settings, and particularly the metropolis, justices played a much more influential and proactive role, not seeing it only as a way of making money.[65]

Law Enforcement and Informing

The move towards greater financial reward for information should be considered as part of a broader pattern in which law enforcement was no longer a civic duty, but rather a paid office. In the early eighteenth century the combination of financial inducement, moral reformation and vigorous individual urban magistrates encouraged an environment in which entrepreneurial approaches to law enforcement flourished. Whilst the societies and local magistrates might have had certain offenders or groups of offenders in their sights, the broad currency of information meant that the former's desire to clean up vice and the latter's desire to control crime became close bedfellows. Thus, law enforcement in the early-eighteenth-century metropolis would be characterised by the involvement of a group of men who occupied the liminal spaces of the underworld. Constables, informing constables, professional informers and criminal informers were actively involved in attempts to control the overlapping criminal networks of the metropolis. Both individuals and collectives of informers could be a powerful tool in providing evidence to bring prosecutions. Whilst informers were motivated by financial rewards, there is also evidence to suggest that previous connections and confrontations fuelled the informing culture. Hence, the relationships between informers and the networks that they policed were far from clear-cut. In fact, informers and informing constables themselves were liable to end up in court on charges such as assault and barratry (the instigation or encouragement of prosecution on false grounds). The relationship between the office of constable, informing and thief-taking had been commented on since the late seventeenth century when the emergence of the rewards culture engendered, in the 1690s, a febrile culture of information. The boundaries between those men holding the parochial office of constable and those operating as thief-takers could often be blurred. As Beattie notes, in 1690s coining and clipping cases, some constables were hard to distinguish from thief-takers.[66] However, from the early eighteenth century references to 'informing constables' started to appear. It is likely that the informing constable emerged in the specific context of the campaign for reformation – a hybrid of the constable, the thief-taker and the informer, who operated within the vice remit of the societies. Certainly, this relationship can be confirmed later in the century through the activities of the informing constable William Payne, sworn in as an extra constable in 1764, and closely involved with the recently re-established Society for the Reformation of Manners.[67]

The informing constable was a problematic figure from his earliest appearances. An early-eighteenth-century reference can be found in verses printed in the *London Spy* (first published in book form in 1703), titled 'Informing Constables, and other Informers', illustrating the contempt in which such men were held, 'with a Painted Staff, and Awful Threat Of bawling them before some Magistrate'.[68] In 1723, they were described in the *Authentick Memoirs of the Life Intrigues and Adventures of the Celebrated Sally Salisbury* as 'those *Religious Officers*, the *Informing Constables* ...'.[69] By 1733, the Grand Jury were pronouncing on 'vexatious' prosecutions, and drawing attention to the problem of 'Clerks and Sollicitors in Confederacy with a Set of People calling themselves informing Constables'.[70] Such men were mistrusted by plebeian Londoners who were frequently on the receiving end of the constables often aggressive attentions. In January 1722, Edward Vaughan and Philip Cholmley were charged with the murder of Henry Bowes.[71] In their defence a warrant was produced, 'for searching Gaming and other disorderly Houses, sign'd by Ten Justices of the Peace ... According they went to several lewd Houses, from whence they took divers into Custody ...'. At the final house they entered the inhabitants were waiting brandishing brickbats and drinking pots as weapons and shouting, 'Now we have the informing Dogs! Murder them, Murder them!'. It is unclear how formal a role was taken by Cholmley and Vaughan, who were, unsurprisingly, acquitted.[72] However, they were accompanied by George Cartwright and Thomas Burt, who were witnesses in a related trial in February in which Charles MacCave, Edward Dun and Edward Galloway were found guilty of breaking the peace, 'Riotously assaulting several Constables, in the execution of their Office'.[73] Attacks on informing (or reforming) constables did happen periodically, and a well-known early case was the murder of John Dent by a group of soldiers in 1709, after the apprehension of a disorderly woman.[74]

Despite the informing constables' unpopularity with the public, the magistracy generally supported those who strayed over the line. It seems that a certain level of legitimate violence was to be expected in the commission of moral reform; in 1721, when constable Edward Arnold was charged with assaulting William Saunders at the Five Bells in St Clements Dane, and taking from him a silver headed cane and three shillings, 6d in money, the apparent robbery was judged a 'lawful action' by the court.[75] A more complex case was reported in the press in November 1729. A constable for St George's Hanover Square had been taken into custody 'on his being charged with searching Several Houses for disorderly persons, without any Legal Authority'.[76] According to the press, this constable was one of a number who had acted on the information of a ten-year-old boy, William Abourne, who had impeached various individuals for robbery and murder. This case has the taint of false witness, as there seemed to be little evidence to support the allegations. Nevertheless, several constables followed up the information leading to a charge of entering the house of a Mr Taylor at the Gold Lion in King's Street, St James, 'in a violent and riotous Manner, without Legal Authority ... and putting the said Mr Taylor in fear of his life, by presenting a loaded pistol to his Breast'.[77] As *Fog's Weekly Journal* derisively noted, 'This may be a Memorandum to such Constables who are too busy in their Office'.[78] What is interesting in this case is the term 'legal authority'; the implication is that the magistrates were willing to turn a blind eye to violence in the commission of the constable's role, but not the transgression of authority.[79] In other words, so long as the constable was armed with the weapon of the warrant, a certain level of violence was legitimate, as seen in the case of Edward Arnold.

Informers can be loosely identified as belonging to social networks.[80] Such informing networks could include a range of individuals who used information for a variety of ends. Thus the informing constable can be understood as a node or actor in a network in which the other nodes to which they are connected might be other informing constables, other individuals who sought to make money out the informing culture ('professional informers') or criminal informers. Moreover, informers could be bound by other relationships and/or allegiances. Research by Warner, Ivis and Demers on social networks of informers against the Gin Act of 1736 suggests that the flurry of informing that accompanied the Act was largely opportunistic and that links between the informers were generally weak.[81] Whilst they did identify 'career informers' (those who informed more than once) their careers seem to have been generally short-lived, with the longest career lasting three years. Moreover, over half the gin informers identified by Warner and colleagues were women. In contrast, the informers for the reformation of manners campaign were male and some were active for a number of years.

Informing Constables: The Willis Brothers

The nature of the men who operated in the shadowy nexus between formal law enforcement and the networks of informers can perhaps be best illustrated by the activities of a group of men who were definitely working as informing constables in the 1720s and early 1730s and may have been active as early as the 1710s. There were at least three Willises – Thomas, Michael and Robert – and whilst they are referred to as siblings it is possible that there may be more than one generation of Willises. They were certainly active in the business of the societies and were apparently involved in the arrest of Jonathan Wild.[82] The earliest possible reference to a Willis is found in the Bridewell records from 1717, where a Thomas Willis appears in the minutes of the Court of Governors involved in the arrest of suspected disorderly persons; Robert Willis appears from 1722 and Michael Willis in 1725.[83] Moreover, a number of recognizances from 1725 relating to prosecutions for being idle and disorderly were initiated by Thomas and Robert Willis, confirming their active participation in the prosecutorial process.[84] It is difficult to verify the relationships between the Willises with complete certainty. Their names are not systematically recorded, and often they do not appear on the recognizances or indictments for the trials with which they are most strongly associated in the print literature. A further barrier to identifying such informers is in the diversity of the language used to describe them. In the case of the Willis brothers they were referred to variously as 'informers', 'informing constables', 'constables' and 'thief-takers'. According to Howson, Robert Willis arrested William Field in April 1725 and had also been present (along with another Willis) at the arrest of Wild, although I have found no clear evidence of this.[85] Nevertheless, given the ambiguity of their role and their closeness to law enforcement networks it would not be surprising if one or more of the brothers had been present. They certainly arrested the six street-robbers who were impeached by James Dalton in 1728 and the highwayman John Everett in 1730, who was armed with a pistol when the Willises took him in Fore Street.[86] According to evidence given by Mr Thomas Willis at the trial of three of the men, Christopher Rawlins, Isaac Ashley and John Rowden, they had come across Dalton whilst they were searching disorderly houses, 'who made an Ingenious Confession, and said, if he could be admitted as an Evidence, he could be of great Service to the Publick'. Apparently Dalton then directed Thomas and his brother Robert Willis to a house in Chick Lane, Smithfield, where they found the defendants.[87]

Whilst the Willises were formally described as constables in these accounts, they were also referred to as informers or 'informing constables' in the context of searching disorderly houses and bawdy houses and serving warrants for offences connected with disorderly activities. The notoriety of the Willises is captured in a reference to the informers in *Villany Exploded: or, the Mistery of Iniquity laid open*, an account of the activities of a so-called gang of street-robbers in Newgate written in 1728 at least in part by Daniel Defoe. The main protagonist, a street-robber named Peter Levee, was arrested by a Mr Willis after being betrayed by his wife.[88] In a struggle with Willis, Levee pulled a pistol on him, which misfired, with the result that Levee was ordered for execution. Later in the same document the author included a 'Copy of Articles ... which were sign'd by a Gang of Street-Robbers and House-Breakers, who are now all, or most of them detected and executed'. Article number 2 states:

> That he who shall be so idle, and extravagant, as to sell, or pawn his Sword, or Pistol, with which he shall be provided, when he enters into this Society, shall have but one half of the Booty, which comes to his Share, for a whole Month after; the other half shall go towards the Expence of Feeing Coachmen, informing Constables and Watchmen; and he who shall neglect knocking down any Watchman, who shall refuse a Fee, may he be pox'd by the first Whore he lies with, and his Pistol miss fire, when he is pursu'd by Willises.[89]

The Willises were undoubtedly boundary-spanners, falling somewhere between thief-takers and informers, as well as treading the line of illegality themselves. Thomas Willis was one of the ring-leaders of a number of informing constables who were tried for assault in 1731.[90] The trial took place at the Court of King's Bench on Saturday 11 December. The men had assaulted Charles Geery after he was found with Elizabeth Noon and Anne Lewis, who by implication were prostitutes, in Noon's room. According to the evidence, 'Willis came to the Window, which had neither Shutter nor Curtain, and in an effeminate Voice call'd out, Nanny, Nanny, open the Door'. A frightened Noon blew out the candles, and pleaded with Geery to keep quiet; in response an indignant Geery, stating he had nothing to fear, opened the door, where he was grabbed by the defendants. Geery immediately demanded what authority they had seized him upon, in response to which another of the constables, Adams, said 'Damn you, I'll shew you my Authority'. Geery was then struck on the head with the constable's staff, receiving several blows, 'His Cloaths were torn off, and he was naked to the Wall, if a Man can be said to be naked who was covered with Blood and Dirt'. Geery begged to be taken before the Constable of the Night, in response to which one of the defendants said, 'You Dog, we are Constable enough for you; damn you, we have managed many such a killing Captain as you'.[91]

As this incident and confrontations such as those explored in the next chapter demonstrate, the Willises were particularly active in their dealings with men and women accused or suspected of sexual delinquencies. As well as their extensive involvement in the searches and raids of disorderly houses, at least one Willis was involved in the attacks on the molly houses that occurred sporadically throughout the period, with a flash point around 1726. However, there is some ambiguity in these trials since the Willises are referred to plurally or as Mr Willis, and no first name is given. In July 1726, William Brown was found guilty of assaulting Thomas Newton with intent to commit sodomy. Thomas Newton was the decoy set by Willis and another constable to trap Brown. As Newton recalls, 'I went with them to an ale house in Moorfields where we agreed that I should go out, and pick one up, and they'd wait at a proper Distance'. Once the bait was caught, literally as Brown had his hand down Newton' breeches, 'I held him fast, and call'd out to my Companions, who coming up we carry'd him to the Watchhouse'.[92] According to Rictor Norton, Newton was a known hustler who had encountered Willis when he had gone to give bail for Mother Clap, a notorious molly-house madam. Willis persuaded him to give information and used him in what was clearly a case of entrapment.[93] Here the Willis involved is specifically designated as a constable, armed with warrants to apprehend sodomites.

There was clearly something to be gained from the interrelationship between moral authority and financial inducement that came from the association with the reformation campaign. Thus, as informing constables for the society the Willis brothers gained respectability and credibility. Moreover, the association with the Westminster justices, as well as with the various wealthy tradesmen and residents who were involved with the societies and petitioned the justices to clean up the streets, was advantageous to the brothers.[94] Although according to Ned Ward the reforming constables also benefitted financially from the disorderly houses, 'They are only encouragers of what they pretend to suppress, protecting those people for bribes which they should punish, well knowing each bawdy-house they break is a weekly stipend out of their own pockets'.[95] Indeed, in November 1729 it was reported in the *Daily Journal* that one of the constables for the Parish of St George's Hanover Square had been charged with 'searching Several Houses for disorderly persons, without any legal Authority, and for extorting money from the keepers of several notorious brothels as a gratuity for his pretended civility in not taking away their creatures'.[96] Clearly informing was a pervasive and often insidious practice. It could also be extremely lucrative.[97] For men like the Willises, who can be characterised as boundary-spanners navigating the networks that linked more formal law enforcement with less credible culture of informing, rewards were probably their livelihood. However, criminals may have informed from a much more basic instinct: to save their lives.

Informers and Evidences

Accomplice testimony was used increasingly in the criminal justice system from the early eighteenth century. John Langbein demonstrates how the witness and reward systems were closely related. Some of the reward statutes promised pardons. However, more often accomplice testimony simply led to non-prosecution of the informer.[98] Nevertheless, money could be made. For example, in 1744, William Harper, known as 'Old Daddy', (a 26-year-old so named 'on account of his being more grave in company than the others'), impeached six members of the so-called Black Boy Alley Gang for which he received 102*l* 10s.[99] Ann Wells, the wife of another member, received £17 for impeaching her husband and other members of the gang.[100] In 1731, it was reported in the *Gentleman's Magazine* that of the ten malefactors executed at Tyburn on 20 December, the reward for apprehending seven of them amounted to nearly one thousand pounds.[101] Langbein points out that for much of the eighteenth century 'the crown witness system was practically the only resort of the London-area authorities in dealing with gang crime', and certainly impeachment of criminal confederates seems to have been a common practice amongst such criminals.[102] Indeed, one of the explanations for the increasing numbers of criminal biographies from this period may in part be the need for those criminals who had impeached to provide justification and rationale for their actions. For example, Ralph Wilson, William Hawkins, James Dalton and Thomas Neaves all turned evidence, and 'authored' biographies. As we saw earlier, Wilson gave evidence against John Hawkins and George Simpson in May 1722, who were being tried for the robbery of the Bristol Mail in April of that year. At the trial both Hawkins and Simpson protested against Wilson's evidence, 'The prisoners in their Defence, objected against Wilson's Character, as being guilty by his own Confession'. Moreover, Wilson's motivation for turning evidence, according to the defendants, was that he himself had been impeached by Hawkins' brother, William.[103] William Hawkins, also involved in highway robbery, had given information to Jonathan Wild against Butler Fox and James Wright.[104] James Dalton and Thomas Neaves were awarded a pardon in 1728, after giving evidence at various trials.[105] Dalton gave evidence at the May trials of William Russell, William Holden and Robert Crouch for highway robbery and Christopher Rawlins, Isaac Ashley and John Rowden for robbery and highway robbery.[106] In his defence Dalton said:

> but going on in my old Way, I was presently after taken up, and for the Preservation of my own Life, was obliged to turn evidence. There were six of my Companions hang'd upon my Information; and I protest that they were every one guilty of their Crimes they suffered for.[107]

He directed much of his anger towards Thomas Neaves, whom he accused of giving evidence against an innocent man, Richard Nicholls.[108] He was particularly aggrieved that he had received only £40 for his evidence, rather than the £140 that he felt was his due.[109]

Dalton was no stranger to the culture of informing and he was a pivotal actor in the networks of the 1720s. He was closely associated with William Field, who was notorious for his impeachment of Wild, Jack Sheppard and other well-known criminals; he also had dealings with the Willis brothers, and he would ultimately become the victim of the professional informer, John Waller.[110] According to the various narratives that describe him, James Dalton's birth and upbringing made his ultimate fate inevitable: 'from his infancy he was a thief and deserved the gallows almost as soon as he wore breeches'.[111] A popular story recounted how his own father had been executed for street-robbery; the young Dalton had been anchored between his father's legs as he travelled in the cart to Tyburn.[112] Despite his long career (by eighteenth century standards) and centrality to criminal networks, his closeness to the world of informing left him a marked man. In 1727, he was held in safe custody in Wood Street Compter, which seems to have been used for criminals giving evidence, presumably in order to protect them from the inmates of Newgate where the accused men lay.[113] When Dalton was brought before the court to take trial in January 1730 for attempting to rob the renowned physician Dr Mead, the *Daily Journal* reported that a woman in the crowd had thrown a bottle at his head and he had been badly cut.[114] The *Daily Courant* noted that 'One Mary Harvey, having some words, with James Dalton the noted Street Robber, she cut his Head in a terrible manner with a Quart Bottle'.[115] Moreover, the following Wednesday it reported that he was to be 'tried at the next sessions for dangerously wounding a man yesterday in the hold by cutting him in a desperate manner with a knife'.[116] Dalton was himself to suffer from the tide of impeachment, when the notorious 'affidavit-man' John Waller gave evidence against him in April 1730.[117] His execution was at Tyburn on the 12 May, the *Country Journal, or Craftsman* reported that he 'drank Part of two Pots of Beer at the Place of Execution and utterly denied the Fact for which he died'.[118]

There seems to have been a veritable rush to impeach in the 1720s, and Wild's fingerprints can be seen on so many of these trials that it is hard not to conclude that there was a deliberate policy aimed at breaking up gangs at this time. However, informing was also an attractive business opportunity to those on the periphery of criminal networks, with many informers being accused of playing false witness. For example, when Edward Joire was found guilty of highway robbery in April 1724, he denied any knowledge of the witness: 'The Prisoner deny'd the Fact, or his having any Knowledge of John Godfrey the Evidence, and call'd Evidences to his Reputation, and also that should prove that he was elsewhere, at the Time when the Fact was committed' (perhaps unsurprisingly Wild was also present at the trial).[119] Moreover, informing could also be used as a way of settling grievances. In 1744, Mary Kemp had lived in the house of Hannah Eastwood, who accused her of taking several items of clothing. According to Eastwood, she had asked the accused to return the stolen goods, but then had later found her near Bond Street with a cloak, apron and shift, 'When I asked her for the things, she run out into the street and said, D-n you, you b-h, if you offer to touch me, I'll swear a street robbery against you, and buy twenty times as much with the reward'. Kemp was found guilty and sentenced to be whipped, despite two witnesses who gave damning evidence against Eastwood to the effect that she 'makes it her business to indict people to extort money from them'.[120] Not surprisingly, criminals who turned evidence to save their own skins also spotted the opportunities afforded by informing. Thomas Neaves had turned evidence in a number of trials, indeed in his *Life*, which was published in 1729, it suggests that Neaves had become a professional informer, 'he resolv'd on a new Employment, which was to apprehend Felons, or those that were noted for that course of Life, from whom he us'd to extort Money, and then set them at Liberty; he had an idea that Jonathan Wild had got considerably by that Business'.[121] When Thomas Neaves was tried for the theft of a coat at the Old Bailey in January 1729 he claimed in his defence that he had actually been pursuing the thief who had stolen the coat, 'it having been his practice for some time to catch thieves, but he having been formerly an evidence, and hang'd a great many men, people had an ill opinion of him'.[122] Despite his protestations Neaves was hung at Tyburn on the 7 February. His autobiography, *The Life of Thomas Neaves*, was advertised in the *Daily Post* the following Monday.[123]

Some of the worst abuses of the rewards system were related to the activities of what can be described as 'professional' informers. These were individuals who essentially adopted informing as a trade; although they could also have links to more established law enforcers and thief-takers. According to Langbein, by the 1730s it was scandals about the misuse of the system that would lead to judges admitting defence counsel in this period.[124] A well-known 'career' informer was John Waller, who informed (apparently falsely) against James Dalton in the trial that would lead to his execution in May 1730.[125] As the title page of the narrative of his *Life* announced, it would contain 'the Villanies, Tricks, and Devices, which he practised in defrauding and cheating People, and in swearing robberies against innocent Persons, to take away their Lives, for the sake of the Rewards granted by Act of Parliament'.[126] Waller's career may well have been lucrative, however, he frequently ran into trouble. His *Life*, written very much in the style of the standard criminal biography, records that he was the son of the executioner of Halifax, who left Yorkshire 'addicted to roving', and embarked on a life which was to take advantage of the flexible law enforcement system. At different times he became a bailiff's follower, a solicitor, a blackmailer and an informer.[127] He seems to have started his informing career around the mid-1720s. Thus, in February 1728, Edward Gear and Constantine Canaway were committed to Newgate in February 1728 for robbing

'Mr John Waller, Cook to one of his Majesty's Ships of War', as he was coming over the fields from Islington in December 1727.[128] In Waller's *Life* Gear is not mentioned, however, an assault by a Constantine Connoway is.[129] They were apparently acquitted which may explain their absence from the Old Bailey Proceedings. According to the *Life*, he was then prosecuted at the Guildhall. This seems to have been for some sort of impersonation and possibly robbery. After this he again spent some time as a cook upon a man-of-war.[130]

Between 1729 and 1730 he seems to have returned to his former activities, with the notorious James Dalton very much in mind. Thus, in early 1730, in Newgate after being found guilty of the attempted robbery on Dr Mead, Dalton was charged with robbing John Waller the previous November.[131] At the trial in April, Waller said that he had met Dalton at the Adam and Eve public house at Pancras; on the walk back to London they had shared a Link (a light), and in a field between Tottenham Court Road and Bloomsbury Dalton had pulled out a Pistol and robbed him. Dalton was absolutely indignant, accusing Waller of being 'a Man of vile character ... a common Affadavit Man'.[132] The *Life* records that Dalton directly accused Waller in his last dying speech:

> He acknowledged that he had been a most profligate sinner, guilty of many street-robberies, addicted to whoring, drinking, and swearing; but declared, that as he hoped for mercy in the other world, he was entirely innocent of that particular fact for which he was to die, and that the said John Waller had sworn his life away merely for the sake of the reward given by Act of Parliament.[133]

In May 1730, John Wells and Charles Ditcher were tried for assaulting John Waller on the highway and taking a cloth coat from him.[134] According to Waller, Wells said to him 'you are the honest Man that are going to hang Dalton'. It seems that Waller was suggesting that the attack was motivated from his involvement with the Dalton trial. This attack had taken place in March, at which time Dalton was in Newgate awaiting trial for his supposed attack on Waller – indeed, in the 25 April edition of the *London Evening Post*, reporting on the committal of Charles Ditcher, it was noted, 'There are now four Persons in Newgate to be try'd next Sessions, being charged with robbing the said Waller; two for the Highway, and two for picking his Pocket'.[135] The men were acquitted when at least two witnesses who had been threatened by Waller gave evidence against him.[136]

The early parts of Waller's career are much less clearly delineated in the *Life*; however there is evidence that he was operating before 1727.

The *Life* suggests that Waller specialised in impersonation. One of the people he impersonated was Robert Willis. In January 1726, *Parker's Penny Post* reported that Waller had been tried at the Guildhall Sessions accused of assaulting Richard Preston and Elizabeth Wilkinson.[137] He had apparently assumed the name of one Mr Willis, 'a person who has been long engaged with the Society for the Reformation of Manners, and always behaved with the utmost integrity', intending, so it was surmised, to extract money from his victims whom were suspected of being lewd persons.[138] Preston and Wilkinson reacted indignantly, calling a proper officer who 'thought fit to provide a Lodging that Night for his pretended Brother Constable in the Compter'.[139] A set of recognizances from the Guildhall Sessions in August 1725 provide further insight into Waller's activities. Whilst not all of these references can be connected to our John Waller with absolute certainty, they do suggest a man well used to the conflict inherent in the trade of informing. These include a recognizance for Richard Preston requesting his appearance at the Guildhall Sessions in order to prosecute and give evidence against John Waller for assaulting and beating him and presumably leading to the trial in January. Another recognizance summoned John Clark to prosecute and give evidence against John Waller for assault. Another called John Waller to give evidence against one William Fuller for assaulting him in the streets and robbing him of a periwig.[140] If these traces refer to the same John Waller, it would suggest that he was taking advantage of the ubiquity of the Willises who were particularly active that August and are also referred to in the Sessions file.[141]

With the execution of James Dalton in May 1730, Waller would gain further notoriety.[142] A story is told in Waller's *Life* of him talking with one of the Newgate servants who had asked him how much he had received for a particular conviction (James Dalton), Waller answered £80, and upon being asked what he was going to do with it replied that he planned to become a Holland Trader, a trade in which he had previously been engaged. The servant suggested that this was probably a good idea since, 'probably some of the persons, or their friends, against whom he had sworn, might watch an opportunity of knocking his brains out in the night'. Waller 'offered to swear that the servant threatened to knock out his brains, or if he did not do it himself, he would procure one that should'. When Waller later accused two women, Ann Hill alias Wild and Moll MacCartney, of robbing him, that same Newgate servant told the magistrate, Sir Richard Brocas, of Waller's reputation. With Waller's character blackened, the women were discharged.[143] Whilst Waller certainly continued in these activities after his impeachment of Dalton, in this conviction he made a severe miscalculation.[144] Within two years of Dalton's death Waller himself was to become a victim. In May 1732, at the Old Bailey, he was convicted of falsely charging two men with involvement in a robbery.[145] He was sentenced to be placed in the pillory with his head uncovered for two hours on three days.[146] On the first day, 13 June 1732, at 11 o'clock in the morning, he was almost immediately pulled from the pillory and beaten to death with hardened cauliflower stalks. Three men were later charged with his murder, William Belt (alias Worrel, a prisoner who had been charged with overseeing Waller's punishment), Richard Griffiths (alias Serjeant) and Edward Dalton, the younger brother of James.[147] The men were executed October 1732. According to the *Ordinary's Account*, Dalton denied that he'd threatened to revenge his brother's death, until he reached the place of execution, 'where he acknowledged his inhumanely treating of Waller upon the pillory'.[148]

Conclusion

This chapter has explored the interrelated changes that established the 1720s and 30s as key decades in the development of an underworld narrative. Moreover, the belief of contemporaries that they were experiencing high levels of crime marks the era as one in which the combination of cultural production, state activity and criminal activism produced an unprecedented focus on the problem of criminal confederacy. As E. P. Thompson wrote, 'if that unsatisfactory term "crime wave" could ever be used with conviction, it might possibly be applied to the early 1720s'.[149] Whilst Thompson may have been referring to the context of rural crime and the origins of the Black Act of 1723, there is little doubt that metropolitan observers felt that they were under siege from gangs of highway robbers and criminal gangs. Moreover, the exposure and execution of Jonathan Wild in 1725 profoundly shaped the ways in which contemporaries understood the 'crime problem' over the following decade or more. The pivotal influence of Jonathan Wild's career, arrest and execution is hard to deny. Arguably Wild was at the nexus of a criminalised culture which, at least in part, accounts for the vivid and characterful narratives that remain from this period. Indeed, one of the central ways in which historians have been able to explore this early-eighteenth-century crime culture has been through the expansion of print. The growing press, the evolution of the Old Bailey Sessions Papers and the rising publication of other crime literatures in this period confirm the importance of these decades to the study of the relationship between print culture and crime activism. As Andrew Pepper has noted, 'the 1720s, in England, and more particularly in London, constitute a significant moment in the early development of writing about crime'.[150] Not only was it a period during which the transmission, distribution and diversity of print culture would grow exponentially, but it was also one in which a number of strands of legislation, practice and culture of law enforcement meshed in a way which led to an apparently more visible underworld of criminals, gangs and informers.

When the Society for the Reformation of Manners emerged in the febrile decade of the 1690s, it was war, unemployment, harvest failure and trade disruptions that contributed to rising prosecutions for property crime. Beattie argues that these factors and the consequent economic distress helped 'stimulate a campaign of social and religious discipline'.[151] By the 1720s and 1730s the society was increasingly the target of criticism. Nevertheless the adherents of 'moral reformation' continued to exploit their connections with metropolitan magistrates in order to target what they perceived as disorderly communities. They were able to do this not only because of a supportive and proactive magistracy, but also because of the informing culture which proliferated in this period. As this chapter has argued, networks of informers, criminals and law enforcers were far from mutually exclusive. Whilst such interweaving had been a feature of the metropolitan criminal landscape since the late seventeenth century, in the 1720s and 1730s the visibility of crime was boosted by the cultural and legal responses to informing: the activities of the authorities, or at least their representatives, in concert with the societies; the role of constables who exploited their knowledge of crime and criminal connections for money; the activism of criminals who bartered their confederates lives for the chance of survival or to provide financial recompense to their families, or for a fleeting moment of fame; and finally, the enterprising individuals who took advantage of the law to make a living.[152]

In this chapter it has also been suggested that the rhetoric that developed to describe criminal gangs was problematic. Once again, print culture was often responsible. As David Lemmings has noted in his study of one metropolitan newspaper, 'in the 1720s aggregated reports in the *London Journal* would have conveyed the impression that parts of the east end of London were virtually seminaries for gangs of thieves and housebreakers'.[153] Whilst confederacies of criminals certainly existed, to retrospectively cloak them with the language of the 'underworld' and 'organised' criminality, leads to a limited understanding of the reality of the role played by crime in plebeian communities. Moreover, the agency of individual plebeian Londoners who brushed up against the criminal justice system needs to play a larger part in the exploration of crime cultures in this period. So-called gangs and confederacies were shaped as much by relationships of community and kin as the commission of crime. Thus fraternal and other familial relationships remain essential to the networks and communities explored here: brothers such as James and Edward Dalton, John and William Hawkins, Robert, Michael and Thomas Willis, and sisters such as Mary Harvey and Isabella Eaton to whom we turn in the next chapter.

3

'A Noted Virago': Moll Harvey and her 'Dangerous Crew', 1727–1738[1]

Gallows confessions and criminal biography provided eighteenth-century readers with unparalleled access to a version of criminal enterprise and confederacy. This unprecedented circulation of crime print culture enables historians to catch sight of the criminal through a series of interactions with justice, albeit a somewhat selective version of events.[2] Through these interactions we can capture fragmentary evidence of plebeian Londoners negotiating the criminal justice system, dealing with law enforcers and experiencing sanctions such as the pillory, the House of Correction, transportation and the gallows. As Tim Hitchcock and Robert Shoemaker have argued, 'the tactics of the poor and the criminal are in direct, imaginative and constructive dialogue with the institutions and individuals which administer criminal justice and poor relief'.[3] Often, the most detailed criminal lives and most sustained connections with criminal justice come from those 'notorious' offenders whose lives end at Tyburn. However, other criminals, who were not amongst the condemned, gained a public and visible reputation through their encounters with the criminal justice system.[4] Mary 'Moll' Harvey was such an individual. Between 1727 and 1732, she was as much an object of public curiosity as her fellow 'criminals', such as James Dalton, Mother Needham and the aristocratic rake Colonel Charteris. Variously referred to as 'famous', 'notorious' and 'noted', Mary's antagonistic relationship with justice, particularly during 1730 to 1731, was well known to early eighteenth-century Londoners.[5] It may in part have been Mary's gender that made her a particular target of the press. Her willingness to confront and to negotiate with justice arguably set her apart, and the connections between her gender, her notoriety and her 'public' life were frequently alluded to in the press, for which she was 'a noted Virago, who has been so frequently mentioned in the News Papers for the Exercise she has given to the Justices of the Peace in Westminster'.[6]

This chapter will reconstruct the offending lives of Harvey, her sister Isabella Eaton and confederate Mary Sullivan for the relatively short period in which they are visible to history. Overlapping networks and communities are at the heart of this story, which reveals the interactions between the local justice system and a particular plebeian community in the neighbouring parishes of St Martin in the Fields and St James.

In the 1720s and early 1730s, the disorderly house campaigns involved justices, constables and the local community, both respectable and disorderly. Whilst these campaigns were to be one of the last purges of the early-eighteenth-century incarnation of the Society for the Reformation of Manners, this chapter will demonstrate that they were also a vehicle which local magistrates and informing constables would utilise to target specific troublesome individuals. As Dabhoiwala and Gowing have demonstrated, local communities were familiar enough with the mechanics of justice to turn to the local magistracy and paid constables and informers to deal with nuisance neighbours.[7] Whilst Harvey and Eaton, both keepers of 'disorderly' taverns in the St James's district, were likely anyway to have been swept up by the disorderly house raids, it is clear that their more respectable neighbours, individual constables and the magistracy deliberately sought to break down the community from which the women came, and of which Mary Harvey was a significant member. Over a number of years we see the women avoiding conviction, instigating counter-convictions and negotiating the justice system in order to protect themselves and their livelihoods. Whilst we can only read the lives of Mary and Isabella through the lens of criminal administration, it is possible to tell a story about plebeian agency and the social significance of the law. Thus, despite the concerted efforts of some powerful justices of the peace, Harvey and Eaton both played the system and fought it.

The women were arguably connecting points on a number of overlapping networks – as criminals, as inn-keepers, as neighbours (however unwelcome) – and the events fundamentally reveal the escalation of tensions between the communities who shared proximity. Indeed, locality and community are hugely important in how we think about these interactions. Community is undoubtedly a problematic term, suggesting a cohesion that is not necessarily evidenced in the socially mixed neighbourhood that Mary inhabited.[8] However, it does provide a way of referring to the interconnectedness of different local networks and the local relationships that can be traced in these events. Historical communities have tended to be painted as stable, involved and tightly-knit, but, as Withington and Shepard have argued, 'Community, as a state of interpersonal relations, did not preclude conflict. On the contrary, conflict was intrinsic to such relations, and the precepts and practices of community were invariably crystallised through attempts to resolve or contain it'.[9] When overlapping communities are contesting the same spaces, we can define them essentially as territorial conflicts. Thus, 'ordinary citizens' sought to protect their homes and businesses from criminality, disorder and vice in these central metropolitan parishes. As we saw in Chapter 1, streets and areas associated with vice are inherently contested; however, the streets of St James were also home to Mary Harvey and her community. The taverns run by Harvey and Eaton (in Hedge Lane and Sherwood Street, see Map 3.1) were defined

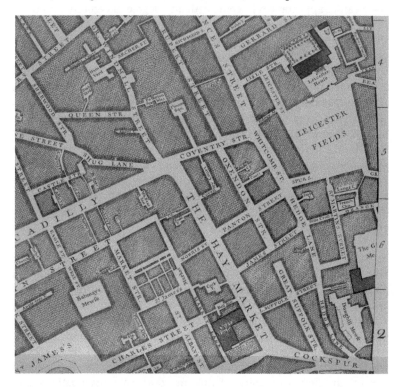

Map 3.1 'The taverns run by Harvey and Eaton (in Hedge Lane and Sherwood Street...) were defined as disorderly by their respectable neighbours and by the Westminster justices.' Detail from John Rocque, *A Plan of the Cities of London, Westminster and Southwark*, 1746 (26 inches to the mile). (Courtesy London Metropolitan Archives.)

as disorderly by their respectable neighbours and by the Westminster justices; nevertheless, these businesses did not exist in isolation, but were spaces where the local plebeian community could drink, talk, fight, sing and copulate.

Protagonists and Trials

Mary Harvey is visible as a public offender from December 1727 when she starts to make regular incursions onto the criminal justice stage. Her criminal 'career' before that date is ambiguous. It seems unlikely that Harvey and her confederates had not encountered the law before 1727. However, the women used a variety of aliases, making it impossible to trace earlier appearances in court with any degree of certainty. All three of the women took the names of various 'pretend' husbands and seem to have been known interchangeably by these names throughout the period. A 'Mary Harvy als Coates' was tried at the Old Bailey in 1721 for stealing from Daniel Cassel, found guilty of felony, pickpocketing, and transported to Annapolis, arriving in July 1722.[10] If this is Mary Harvey, she negotiated a return from transportation.[11] Gerald Howson connects this early appearance with the Mary Harvey who 'was later referred to as a "Queen of the Underworld" by Defoe in his last pamphlet (*Street Robberies*)...'.[12] Howson also connects Mary Harvey to the wave of arrests leading up to the trial of Jonathan Wild.[13] Of course if she had been on the fringes of Wild's networks, this might provide an explanation for why she became such a target of the Westminster justices by the later 1720s and for the Willis brothers, with whom, if this was the case, she would have had a history.

So whilst we cannot trace the women with any certainty before the winter of 1727–28, from this period Harvey and her confederates, her sister Isabella Eaton, John Eaton (the 'pretend' husband of Isabella Eaton) and Mary Stanly [sic] (an alias of Mary Sullivan), featured as witnesses and defendants at a number of trials, including the murder trial of Richard Savage, the poet and friend of Samuel Johnson.[14] On 28 February Mary Harvey and John Eaton were tried on two indictments. The first was for the theft of various goods belonging to Jane Fielding.[15] Their victim had previously been 'acquainted with the prisoners in Bristol' and perhaps because of this the court was unsympathetic and resolved that both the prosecutor and prisoners were a 'contentious and malicious People'. Harvey and her co-defendants were acquitted.[16] The second trial was that of Mary Harvey and John Eaton for an assault on Henry Wilcox.[17] Wilcox had been tried for Highway Robbery in December 1727 when John Eaton and Mary Stanley (alias Sullivan) had been prosecution witnesses.[18] In early 1728 Wilcox had received a pardon in order to qualify him to counter-prosecute Mary Harvey, John Eaton and Mary (Isabella) Eaton for highway robbery.[19] The jury decided that Wilcox's charge was unjust and acquitted the prisoners.[20] These early trials introduce important elements that would recur in the trials of Mary Harvey, Isabella Eaton and their various husbands and confederates over the following years. For example, the suggestion of prostitution is often implicit in cases involving the women, as is the frequenting of and location of disorderly spaces (inns, taverns and coffee-houses). Wilcox had been drinking with Mary Stanley in John Eaton's coffeehouse, near Leicester Fields, when the alleged robbery took place. Clearly the women were engaged in a series of events that involved alcohol, seduction and (alleged) theft. Moreover, their places of residence and the local networks to which they had recourse were in close proximity to areas such as Haymarket, long established as a centre for prostitution.

Anthony Henderson has argued that recourse to prostitution might be seen as one of a range of available sources of income available to plebeian women, and thus the extent to which we characterise Harvey as being formally involved in vice (i.e. as a madam or procuress) is debatable.[21] More likely, the opportunities for sex were part of the economy of taverns in the area inhabited by Harvey and Eaton, with an understanding that men who indulged would pay a 'reckoning' to the house. The expectation of payment of the reckoning, however, would often lead to conflict. Drunken men would refuse to pay or would make accusations of robbery. The authorities were sometimes unwilling to bring in guilty verdicts given the complicity of the male prosecutor/ victim in going willingly with the girls, or at the very least the ambiguous position of prosecutors who had often been drinking. Moreover, in pub and tavern life, paying the reckoning could refer to other forms of transaction (drink, food, labour) as well as sexual intercourse.[22] As one contemporary, a Mr Thomas Brown, wrote in 1730, 'Here I live at Ease and in Plenty, swagger and carouse, quarrel with the *Master*, fight the *Drawer*, and never trouble my self about paying the *Reckoning*, for one Fool or other pays it for me.'[23]

The Policing of Disorder

Until the 1752 Disorderly Houses Act, successful prosecutions of bawdy houses were often difficult to obtain.[24] Before this, as we saw in the previous chapter, the authorities preferred to use summary proceedings and periodic purges as a means of keeping the disorderly houses under control. In some years there were more focused campaigns, with the magistrates using warrants to purge particular areas; campaigns against disorderly houses were initiated in 1728, and later, in 1730–31, targeting areas in Covent Garden, St Martin in the Fields and St James.[25] Arguably the societies had become a handy vehicle for local people and active local justices who wanted to move out undesirable neighbours and consequently the rhetoric of moral reformation was a very useful tool for putting known, troublesome, individuals out of action.[26] As Shoemaker concluded of the judicial system in this context, 'the discretion it accorded to plaintiffs and justices allowed the law also to be used aggressively to see the punishment of adversaries ... whose activities were not necessarily criminal'.[27] In the case of Mary Harvey, increasingly this strategy would fail to stymie her activities and the authorities would turn to the indictment, and other means, to control her. For example, in December 1729, *Fog's Weekly Journal* reported that Mary had been admitted to bail, 'and has opened her tavern near Golden Square'.[28] Thus if the justices were using moral reformation as a blunt tool to close down disorderly taverns and houses, keepers were likely to respond by re-opening in a different location. Moreover, they would use the law themselves to initiate prosecutions of overzealous constables. Indeed, in 1728 the Westminster justices had petitioned the Secretary of State to provide financial support to protect constables who were the subject of essentially malicious prosecutions.[29] This insurance would prove to be particularly pertinent in dealings with Harvey and her confederates.[30]

The following year the house of Mary Harvey was raided. By this time she was based in Shug Lane, close to her sister Isabella who kept the Crown Tavern in Sherrard (Sherwood) Street (see Map 3.1).[31] In August 1729 it was reported in the *British Journal or Censor*, that some constables who had been to search Harvey's house, had been 'lock'd in by her, who charged 'em with the Watch, thereby hindering 'em in their Duty'.[32] On 9 October, Justice Cook committed Isabella Eaton to the Gatehouse prison upon the oath of three constables (James Body and the Willis brothers), whom she had threatened to shoot in the head at the Crown Tavern. She was also charged with keeping an ill-governed disorderly house. The same day, Mary was bound over by Justice John Ellis to await trial at the Westminster Sessions for keeping a disorderly house and for 'grossly abusing Justice Cook in his Office'.[33] On Thursday 30 October, Bourke committed her to Newgate, 'for assaulting and wounding a Constable and his Assistants, in executing a Warrant for a Felony committed at the Crown Tavern in Sherrard Street, St James'. Isabella Eaton was committed to New Prison to await further examination, on suspicion of robbing a gentleman in the tavern.[34] These attacks on the constables need to be read with a caveat. The events may have originated in resisting arrest although, through the lens of indictment and press report, they appeared as assaults, wounding and attacks. As Jennirie Hurl-Eamon points out, in a number of cases of violence directed against constables there is evidence of venality on the part of the constables. Thus, constables 'manufactured' assaults, and later dropped the charges in exchange for payment.[35] According to Hurl-Eamon, female participation in attacks on constables between 1680 and 1720 was low. Nevertheless, plebeian Londoners were vigilant against the constables overstepping their authority, suggesting that much of the violence was a result of resisting arrest, either by the accused or by the local community.[36]

By early November 1729, both Mary and Isabella were committed to Newgate upon charges of felony.[37] On Friday 21 November the *Daily Journal's* London news was taken up with the account of the arrest of Mary Sullavan [*sic*], 'a notorious Pick-pocket', in Southwark by a warrant drawn up by Justice Bourke. She was committed to the Gatehouse charged with being involved with Mary Harvey and privately stealing, 'from a Gentleman at the Standard Tavern in Leicester Fields, a Diamond Ring and a Silver gilt Snuff-Box of a considerable value'. She was also charged (with Isabella Eaton) for the Crown Tavern robbery.[38] At the Old Bailey Sessions in January 1730, Mary Sullivan and Isabella Eaton were tried on two indictments: first for the theft of the diamond ring and snuff box from William Burroughs in the Standard Tavern in Leicester Fields on 16 October 1729; second for the theft of two Guineas from Henry Crew on 25 October 1729.[39] The evidence in this case is convoluted, and even during the proceedings there is confusion over dates. Prosecution evidence was provided by John Davis and Mary West (alias Elizabeth Ryley), with Davis giving evidence to the effect that Sullivan and Eaton were involved in the theft.[40] Mary Harvey gave evidence that Davis had accused her of stealing the ring, for which she had been committed to prison. In the second felony, Henry Crew was clearer in his evidence, although he admitted to having been drinking. In this case he was picked up by a woman (Anne Cragg, described by the prosecution as a 'Whore and a Thief') near Leicester Fields, and then went for a drink with her at the Crown Tavern. The woman was thrown out of the tavern by Mary Sullivan ('hussy, what do you do here? Get you gone') who then stayed to drink with Crew. After some more wine, Sullivan 'fell to playing at my Cod-piece', and Crew realized he was being robbed. At this point Mary demanded the Reckoning ('G-d D-n you, pay your Reckoning, and get you out of the House'), which Crew could not pay since she had stolen his money. The next day he took out a warrant against Eaton (as the mistress of the house) and Sullivan. Mary West, a servant at the Crown Tavern, gave evidence for the prosecutor again, stating that Ann Cragg, Mary Sullivan and Isabella Eaton had shared the two guineas between them.[41] Harvey gave evidence for the defence, stating that West was a thief, 'and made a long harangue about two Plates, and of her having Money for being an Evidence against the Prisoners'. Both women were acquitted.[42] The third of the indictments that had originally been drawn against Eaton and Sullivan in early December 1729 was not tried until early April 1730. This was for the theft of a gold watch and 28 guineas from a person unknown, an event that had apparently taken place at the Crown Tavern in late October 1729. The women were acquitted.[43]

In 1730 there began a sequence of events that were to effectively keep Mary Harvey in some sort of custody for much of the next two years. In early July it was reported that the Westminster justices had granted a warrant against several people who 'frequented the house of Moll Harvey'.[44] According to the reports, the constables who went to serve the warrants were beaten by Harvey and her husband; fresh warrants were granted and a number of Moll's 'gang' (as they were now generally referred to), though not Mary herself, were sent to the Gatehouse. As the *Daily Journal* pointed out, 'This is the same Gang that swore against Wilcocks of Bristol, and there are now in the Gaols of this Town at least 10 of this dangerous Crew'.[45] If we consider these events alongside the previous confrontations with the constables, we can see that Mary Harvey and her associates did not take the arrival of the constables and the threat of the warrant lightly. The escalation into violent conflict could be read as a householder protecting her home rather than simply as a prostitute or disorderly housekeeper, or indeed criminal offender, resisting arrest. Whilst the magistrates were keen to protect their constables from 'vexatious' and malicious prosecution, some of these prosecutions may have been justified.[46] What is clear is that the authorities had identified a community that they wanted to purge. Harvey and Eaton, and their various family members, associates, friends and confederates, were at the centre of this community. Nevertheless, the community was also composed of plebeian Londoners. Perhaps significantly, this was an Irish community. It is already clear from the prosecution involving the theft of Jane Fairfax's goods in February 1728, that Harvey and the Eatons had networks beyond the environs of Westminster.[47] How important was Harvey's identity, and that of her associated community, as Irish?

The Irishness of the community was increasingly commented upon from 1730 onwards, and several of the men associated with Harvey and Eaton were identified as Irish. These were men like William Macheig, James Devins, Alexander Bourk and Edward Hearn, who gave evidence for the prosecution in the trial of the Willis brothers.[48] When Edward Hearn, described as Eaton's 'bully' (or pimp), was arrested in September 1730 and committed to hard-labour at the Bridewell the *British Journal* commented that sending an Irishman to work was as 'contrary to the Grain of an Irishman as Swines Flesh to a Jew'.[49] The extent to which the attack on Harvey's community was related to ethnic identity, rather than or in addition to its criminal identity, is difficult to gauge. We have no clear estimate of the extent of the Irish community in London at this time. In 1736, economic protests against Irish labour took place, spreading from Shoreditch, into Spitalfields and Whitechapel.[50] Linebaugh estimated that around 14 per cent of those hanged at Tyburn in the eighteenth century had been born in Ireland, though the dispersal of that community over time, let alone the size of the second-generation Irish community, is again seemingly impossible to measure.[51] Certainly, by the 1730s there was an Irish community in the Rosemary Lane area of East London; an area known as 'Little Dublin' was more centrally located in St Giles.[52] The distinctiveness of Harvey's community in the 1720s and 1730s may have been at least in part a product of its Irish complexion; on the other hand, it may have been more personal, face-to-face interactions which shaped the fortunes of the women, and of their community, from 1730.

The 1730 Disorderly House Campaign

In the spring and summer of 1730, the confrontational relationship between Harvey, Eaton and the brother constables, Thomas and Michael Willis, was central to events. Arguably it is at this point when local agendas and moral reformation politics more sharply coalesced. Clearly, the Westminster justices in the shape of Cook and Bourke had failed, despite their numerous attempts, to control or indeed, remove, Harvey and Eaton. With the entrance of Sir John Gonson (the Chairman of the Westminster Sessions), and the stepping up of the campaign, Mary Harvey's fortunes were set to take a turn for the worse.

The raids of 1730 were to be immortalised in *A Harlot's Progress* (see Figure 3.1). In plate 3 the prostitute, Moll Hackabout, is portrayed in the grip of steady decline in a Drury Lane garret. As Jenny Uglow describes it in her biography of Hogarth, 'This is the point of her second fall, from whoring to crime, as she swings the stolen watch from her fingers. And this too, is the moment of her legal fall – it is not a bold young lover but ... Justice Gonson who steps thoughtfully through the door, finger to lips, followed by the watchmen with their wooden staves'.[53] The series was executed by Hogarth over the summer of 1730.[54] Clearly a keen observer of the daily news, the series contains allusions to several notorious criminals and bawds of the day.[55] Hogarth's record reflects the point at which Harvey became a 'public' criminal.

Criminal celebrity during this period is discussed tangentially by Ruth Penfold-Mounce in her study of modern crime. Explaining how such celebration of crime occurs, she notes, 'Interest crime refers to criminals whose actions engage with a controversial or contentious issue within society which excites public resonance and results in celebrity

Figure 3.1   William Hogarth, *A Harlot's Progress*, Plate 3, 1732. (Courtesy The Trustees of the British Museum.)

status, whether or not the criminal is seeking such prominence'.[56] The delinquencies of Harvey and her community, performed as they were against the background of moral reformation, became of intense interest to a print culture that was keenly reporting the activities of reforming magistrates and their constables, as well as providing titbits of gossip about noted criminals. Reporting upon an altercation between Harvey and Michael Willis at Newgate, the *Grub Street Journal* remarked, 'I think Willis ought to resign his Post to this Virago: the ensign of whose authority should be a Pewter Chamber-pot'; Moll had apparently hit Willis with a chamber-pot.[57]

Dahboiwala suggests that the impact of these particular disorderly house raids was limited, 'it was not accompanied by any major effort against street-walking'.[58] Arguably this is because the raids were less about prostitution per se and more about trying to tackle local social problems. Certainly, these social problems spread further afield than St James's parish. In fact, the initial meetings were responding to petitions by local tradesmen and respectable residents of St Martin's in the Field, who were becoming increasingly intolerant of the behaviour of the inhabitants of the less salubrious parts of the neighbourhood of Drury Lane.[59] By July, petitions had also been received from the residents of St Paul's, Covent Garden, complaining of the 'frequent outcrys in the night, fighting, robberies, and all sorts of debauchery committed by them all night long to the great inquietude of his majesties good subjects'.[60] In response to this a committee of justices was set up in order to inquire into the problem. By mid-July, petitions from neighbouring parishes had extended the raids to St Margaret's, St Anne's, St John the Evangelist, St George's in Hanover Square and St James.[61] The petitions, and the meetings they prompted, were also widely reported in the daily press.[62] Arguably these petitions from residents enabled a more formal and organised campaign, spearheaded by Gonson. Certainly this series of raids were to continue throughout the rest of 1730, until the early months of 1731.[63] According to a report into the raids, the committee appointed to look into the complaints by local residents met at the vestry 42 times.[64] In this time they bound over 48 persons for keeping and maintaining disorderly houses; admitted to prison 16 persons for keeping disorderly houses and ill-governed houses; and indicted 24 persons for keeping disorderly houses at the Sessions for the City and Liberty of Westminster. Using the much discredited general warrants resulted in the committal of 127 men and women to Tothill Fields house of correction, apprehended in disorderly houses or on the streets (the legality of the warrant had been confirmed and approved by the Court of King's

Bench).[65] Most of these were later discharged. The report singled out Mary Harvey and Isabella Eaton:

> That amongst the disorderly houses so suppressed one formerly kept by one Mary Harvey als Mackeige being the Blackmores head & Sadlers arms in or near hedge lane & also the house of Isabella Eaton als Gwyn being the Crown tavern in Sherrard Street St James were two of the most notorious for harbouring and entertaining Gangs of Thieves, pickpockets & desperately wicked felons.[66]

The Westminster justices had ensured that their constables were protected by writing to the Secretary of State. A response from Lord Harrington (Secretary of the State of the Northern Department) congratulated Gonson upon the good work being done to suppress the disorderly houses and confirmed the government's financial support for the activities of the Westminster justices and their constables:

> the Sollicitor of the Treasury is ordered to defend, at his Majestys Expence, the Constables and other Peace Officers, in any Actions or Suits that may be brought against any of them for what they shall do in the faithful Discharge of their Duty of their Offices, in putting in Execution the Warrants issued to them by the Justices of the Peace.[67]

At the Sessions of the Peace for the City and Liberty of Westminster, which started on Monday 17 August 1730, John Gonson took the opportunity to explain the 'Nature, Design and most extensive Power' of the constables, all of whom had been ordered to attend the court.[68] At the same adjournment, and it would be nice to think at the point that Gonson was pontificating, Mary Harvey vocally made herself known. She was taken into custody for 'breeding a Disturbance in the Court, and abusing the Justices on the Bench'. Upon the attempts to take her into custody, Mary physically resisted: 'she beat them with such Violence, and so resolutely defended herself, that they could not get her out of Court for some time'.[69] On Thursday 20 August, the Westminster justices met in the vestry room of St Paul's, Covent Garden.[70] Isabella Eaton attended the meeting in order to present a petition to the justices, who had charged Harvey with contempt of court. The petition acknowledged her insolent behaviour and asked that she should be admitted to bail. In response the justices charged Mary Harvey with receiving stolen goods – a pair of diamond earrings.[71] She was charged with receiving the earrings from Mary Sullivan, 'knowing them to be stolen, and for insisting on 15 Guineas for restoring the same which is Death by a Statute of the 5th of Queen Anne, upon which the late Jonathan Wilde was convicted'.[72]

These interactions with the criminal justice system provide a lens into the ways in which plebeian Londoners negotiated with the justices and other officials of the court. Whilst clearly the women were at a disadvantage, it is important not to underestimate the sorts of knowledge that women like Harvey and Eaton had gained through their experiences. This might suggest that repeat offenders like Harvey and Eaton had more 'tools' at their disposal, demonstrating agency, albeit in a limited way. Indeed, Hitchcock and Shoemaker see such actions by the poor and criminals as a way of achieving a particular outcome, rather than conscious proto-political agency.[73] Nevertheless, as Andy Wood has argued in relation to plebeian agency, deference and defiance are essentially intertwined, and whilst the actions of Harvey and Eaton may be read as defiant, their attempts to negotiate were limited by elite authority.[74] Thus, Eaton adopted the strategy of deference when she appealed to the court on behalf of her sister.

Within a week of Isabella's appearance at the vestry room in August 1730, Mary Harvey was brought from the Gatehouse to the Old Bailey in order to give evidence against the Willises.[75] In court Harvey was described as being 'more modest than usual', although the press were at pains to point out that this was only because she had been threatened with confinement. The trial apparently lasted several hours and the Willises were 'honourably' acquitted.[76] Whilst the press reported it as the trial of Michael and John Willis, it was in fact the trial of Michael and Thomas Willis (who was already under indictment for his part in the attack on Charles Geery).[77] The trial referred to the events of October 1729, when the Willises and the parish constable James Body had taken up Isabella Eaton at her home as a result of complaints by various neighbours.[78] A full-scale fight had ensued, initiated (according to the Willises) largely by Mary Harvey, who, 'attended by several people with Clubs', attempted to rescue her sister and in the process 'beat and abused' Michael Willis in a violent manner. In her evidence Harvey said that the Willises had assaulted her, kicked and punched her, snatched gold rings off her fingers, and generally caused an affray. The trial brought forth a number of witnesses on behalf of Harvey, including William Macheig (Harvey's common-law husband) and Isabel Gwyn (Eaton). This evidence suggests that the accused were well known as informers, but also described quite lurid levels of violence and a very public fight between Harvey and the two defendants. In their defence, the Willises protested that they had only been doing their duty as informers. Moreover, according to Michael Willis, this was personal, 'she has frequently threatened to be reveng'd on us; and that she had declar'd since the Indictment was found, that Robbery or no Robbery, she would hang me'.[79] James Body, the parish constable, deposed, 'That having taken up Mrs Eaton by a Warrant, Mrs Philips (Harvey) came with several Men with Mop-Staves and Broomsticks to rescue her Sister, and had in her Hand a Meat-Fork to stick the Persons who had her Sister'. The Willises were acquitted after calling a number of the Westminster magistrates to defend their reputations, including Justices Gonson, Railton and De Veil (here spelt Du Val). The magistrates testified that the Willises had been 'very serviceable in suppressing the disorderly houses; and gave the Prosecutor the Character of a very turbulent and disorderly Woman, and one of the vilest of her sex'.[80] Mary Harvey was returned to the Gatehouse.

September was to be a particularly active month for Sir John Gonson, the Westminster justices and their constables. A number of arrests were made in Drury Lane, and a number of women committed to the Tothill Fields Bridewell, including several women out of a 'house in Hedge-lane where Mary Harvey lately lived' on the night of 24 September.[81] Isabella Eaton was also charged and committed to Newgate for involvement in the robbery of the diamond rings received by Harvey. Mary Sullivan had been committed by Justice Bourke some time during the previous month.[82] Finally, on 14 October 1730 the three women came to trial at the Old Bailey for the robbery, and in the case of Harvey, receiving stolen goods.[83] This trial sounds suspiciously contrived, the evidence was imprecise to the point that the witnesses were not even able to specify the date of the robbery, stating it to have happened sometime in the last two to four months. Considering that Mary Harvey, at least, was in prison for much of the previous two to four months, it is perhaps unsurprising that all the prisoners were acquitted. However, this did not amount to a release from custody, as by the end of that week Harvey and Eaton were attempting to be admitted to bail on another indictment, for 'wilful and corrupt Perjury', against the Willises.[84]

On the morning of October 31, Mary Harvey was brought to the King's Bench Bar through means of a habeas corpus directed to the keeper of the Gatehouse.[85] It was not unusual for disorderly house keepers to have cases removed to higher courts in order to delay prosecution, which may explain the shift from the Middlesex Sessions to King's Bench in these events. Her counsel argued that given that she had been confined in the Gatehouse for so long (since 17 August that year), she should be bailed, with the proviso that she would undertake to appear at the next Westminster Quarter Sessions, and also to ask pardon 'of the Worshipful Bench for her rude and indecent Behaviour'.[86] However, the justices refused to show Harvey any mercy, and instead responded by confronting her with another three charges, indicting her twice for keeping a disorderly house and once for beating a constable. According to the justices, since she had failed to appear and plead to the indictments her bail was forfeited. Clearly they were determined not to let Harvey escape their grasp this time and she was committed to the King's Bench prison until she found bail.[87] After that she was to be remanded back to the Gatehouse until, 'she shall make such a Submission as the Chairman and the rest of the Justices of Westminster shall think proper to accept of, and until they shall think fit to discharge her'.[88]

Despite her predicament, the fact that she had recourse to legal counsel does tell us something about Mary's importance. She was not simply a 'disorderly' woman, but an innkeeper, and arguably a woman of some standing within her plebeian community. As Tony Henderson suggests, bawdy house keepers could maintain a degree of respectability.[89] Moreover, there are similar cases of 'disorderly' women using the writ of habeas corpus at this time. For example, Mary Freman [*sic*], alias Talby (also Moll Freeman, alias Talboy), who challenged her commitment in November of 1730, was described as having five counsel, 'This creature is supported by several noted gamesters and sharpers about Covent-Garden'.[90]

Moll Harvey at Large

The friction between Mary's community and the Westminster justices was deepening by the autumn of 1730, with continued meetings of what was now referred to as the Disorderly House Committee and a series of warrants and commitments to Bridewell throughout November and December. On 11 November Mary Sullivan was committed to the Gatehouse for two felonies (picking pockets) and David Hamilton, described as one of Harvey's gang, was charged on warrant of detainer for involvement in one of the felonies.[91] The Westminster justices were making sure they mopped up as many of Moll Harvey's 'gang' as possible.[92] In late November (25) Mary was given notice at the King's Bench prison of her trial for perjury at the next Sessions of the Old Bailey.[93] However, she was not moved to Newgate to await her trial since she was still awaiting trial at King's Bench. Harvey was found guilty of keeping a disorderly house at the sitting of Nisi Prius of the King's Bench on

3 December 1730, but not sentenced at this point.[94] Meanwhile, on 9 December Mary Sullivan came to trial for the theft of two guineas from John Richards.[95] Isabella Eaton was also tried for the same felony. The evidence recorded at the Old Bailey amounts to little more than a drunken tit-for-tat over the reckoning at the Crown Tavern. The women were acquitted, but Isabella was to be removed to the Gatehouse, 'she being charg'd with diverse crimes by Justices of the Peace for the City and Liberty of Westminster'.[96] At this point, with both Harvey and Eaton in custody awaiting their trial for perjury, Moll Harvey tired of trying to negotiate the justice system.[97] On the morning of Wednesday 13 January 1731 Mary broke out of the King's Bench prison in Southwark, apparently taking several other prisoners with her.[98] She was retaken on 3 February in Holborn and returned to King's Bench prison.[99]

The following week she finally went to King's Bench to receive her sentence, which was to 'stand in the Pillory at Charing Cross between the Hours of Twelve and Two, to pay one Mark Fine, to be imprison'd three Months, and to give Security for her good Behaviour for five Years'. She was also charged on a perjury indictment to which she pleaded not guilty. On the journey from King's Bench (held in Westminster Hall) to King's Bench prison (in Southwark) Mary escaped again, near the door of the Fountain Alehouse (close to the court, in King's Street).[100] That evening, Justice De Veil committed four Irishmen to Newgate for helping Mary escape.[101] According to the *Grub Street Journal*, she was retaken again on King's Street. The following Tuesday (16) the *Daily Journal* reported that she had been arraigned at the King's Bench on Friday (12) and that Isabella Eaton and the husband of Mary Harvey would be tried for the same offence.[102]

There is clearly some confusion in the newspapers around this time as to whether Mary Harvey was at large or not. It seems at some point after the 12 February 1731 she escaped yet again since she disappeared from the press record until 20 May, from which point several newspapers reported that she had been retaken on Monday night (17 May) at Wapping, 'in Bed with one Maccage, her pretended Husband'.[103] The conflicting stories of what happened to Harvey during her absence suggest that the press were anxious to sustain a narrative around Harvey and her confederates. As Richard Ward has noted, 'mid-eighteenth-century editors were forced to rely on a varied range of sources for crime news, including other forms of print, readers' correspondence, so-called "newsgatherers", rumour, criminal justice officers, and the usual informants'.[104] This is important in thinking about how 'crime stories' developed in the eighteenth-century press, and how the repetition of an account could give it an authority which may be misleading. Thus Ward points to the large number of identical reports in the mid-eighteenth-century press, suggesting that editors were relying on a select number of news-gatherers. Hence, at the end of May, the *Daily Post* published a long report describing how Harvey had apparently sailed to Rotterdam with the intention of opening a tavern. However, the Dutch government had been 'informed of her Exploits in England', and ordered Mary and her sister (as Isabella seems to have escaped as well) to be put on the 'Black List'. The *Daily Post* reported that the consequence of this being a pos-sible commitment to the Rasp House, 'to work for seven or fifteen Years, or perhaps for Life', they decided to come back to England.[105] The extent to which this was a reliable account is debatable. Whilst the story of Mary and Isabella's exploits 'on the run' in the Netherlands undoubtedly has piquancy, the narrative structure, so suggestive of the travel tales of many contemporary criminal biographies, is arguably suspect. The foreign journey, usually linked to colonial transportation, was a com-mon feature of eighteenth-century criminal biography, suggesting the gossip, rumour and editorial creativity, drawing on the informal sources described by Ward, may have filled in the gap of Harvey's absence in a way that would be familiar to readers.[106]

Harvey's reappearance and arrest in Wapping was widely reported. According to the *Daily Post*, on her return from the Netherlands she 'lurked' around Wapping for some weeks, until she quarrelled with one of her gang, who 'out of Revenge discover'd her to the Constables'. She put up a fight upon arrest, 'so that they were forced to tie her Hands together, and with much Difficulty get her to Prison'. The *Universal Spectator and Weekly Journal* noted that Harvey's 'pretended husband' had been charged on Thursday (20) by warrant of detainer, and Isabella Eaton had been committed to New Prison the same day.[107] On Monday 24 May, Eaton and Mackeig were brought to King's Bench bar by writ of habeas corpus and committed to King's Bench prison.[108] According to the *London Evening Post* (25 May) and the *Daily Journal* (27 May) Mary Harvey was also supposed to have been brought to King's Bench on an habeas corpus.[109] However, on either Sunday (23) or Monday (24) she managed to escape again by dressing in men's clothes, but was retaken on Monday or Tuesday afternoon, 'at a publick House in St George's Fields'.[110] In mid-June it was reported that Harvey and her 'accomplices' (including Isabella Eaton and William Mackeig) had broken out of New Prison.[111] They were tried in their absence upon the perjury charge at Guildhall Sittings of the King's Bench and found guilty.[112] On Friday night, 25 June, Mary and Isabella were found making a disturbance in St Giles's and returned to the New Gaol in Surrey where they were to stay until they received their judgment in the perjury case at King's Bench.[113] The case was argued in King's Bench from Friday 19 November and would not be resolved until the end of the month. The substance of the legal arguments about the case was concerned with the specific nature of the indictment. Thus, the three prisoners (Harvey, Eaton and William MacKeig) were found guilty on one indictment, but each one of them should have been indicted separately 'that the crimes were distinct and separate'.[114] Eventually, on 27 November 1731 the judgment was reversed, and Isabella Eaton and William Mackeig were discharged. Mary Harvey was to return to court on Monday 29, as there were other charges against her. However, despite learned argument by counsel, 'there not being sufficient Proof of them, the Court discharged her'.[115] Given the range of indictments and informations that had been found against Mary Harvey during the previous year or more, it is very tempting to conclude that these charges were spurious. As far as can be told, she was only found guilty of one of the charges, for keeping a disorderly house, for which she had been found guilty at King's Bench in December 1730.[116] On every other charge she was either acquitted, or in the case of the perjury case, the verdict was reversed. This points to the absolute determination of the Westminster justices to close down Mary Harvey's operation, and their willingness to use methods of dubious legality whilst at the same time working within the strictures of the formal justice system. Moreover, it is likely that the cases in which the women were involved were particularly difficult to try given that the prosecutors had been drinking, and the accusations of theft were made in the context of sexual congress, or in the process of the 'reckoning'.

After her discharge in November 1731, Mary Harvey went to ground, or at least the press had (for now) tired of her. Whilst the influence of the reformation of manners campaign was declining, the Westminster justices had achieved what they had set out to do by purging the most notorious disorderly houses. In the short term this was a successful strategy. Disorderly women and men were fined, or sent to the House of Correction and, if not reformed, hopefully stymied. In the longer term, given the inability to permanently remove prostitution from areas like Drury Lane and Haymarket, these campaigns arguably had a limited impact.[117] Nevertheless, contemporaries regarded the campaigns as a success. In 1731, an anonymous publication attributed to Daniel Defoe dealt with the campaign against vice, singling out the work of the magistrates of Westminster.[118] The vigorous conduct of the Westminster justices in 'attacking the Crowd of disorderly people' should set an example, 'for certainly the City and Liberties of Westminster (tho' bad enough) are not the only Places which want to be reformed; there are other Sinks of Wickedness which want cleaning, besides those in the Dominion of MOLL HARVEY'.[119] In 1732, a satirical poem published in the *Craftsman*, apparently as a response to news about trained bands in Middlesex and Westminster, included the following verse: 'Nor does Sir *John* require your Aid, But wishes you would mind your Trade, Whist He alone can serve you; For by his own unwearied Pains, *Sharpers* and *Whores* He leads in Chains, And triumphs O'er *Moll Harvey*'.[120] The involvement of Thomas Willis in the assault on Charles Geery seems to have spelt the end for the careers of the Willises as constables (at least in Middlesex and London).[121] Arguably, despite the brothers being found innocent of the highway robbery charge in 1730, the guilty verdict against Thomas and the publicity attracted by the perjury case had tarnished their reputation. Or it may be that since the Westminster justices had achieved their main aims by 1732, and since the society was on the wane, their services were no longer required. Indeed, whilst one publication contained a laudatory account of the Westminster justices campaign against the disorderly houses, it also described how the reforming societies had gone seriously awry, with accusations of scandal and bribes. At the root of this corruption were the constables:

> Among these are to be reckon'd Mercenary Watchmen, Hired Constables, and especially those they call the Reforming Constables; an officious pretending People, who, under the Appearance of Zeal for Reformation of Manners, have by Connivance, and more especially by notorious Bribery and Corruption...propagated that fatal Degeneracy of Manners.[122]

Conclusion

In conclusion, it would be misleading to suggest that Mary 'Moll' Harvey was an 'ordinary criminal'. However, her notoriety does allow us a different way of thinking about the mechanisms of justice in the early eighteenth century. Whilst most accounts have necessarily focused on the administrative machinery and essentially the law enforcers perspective, the cases presented in this chapter, particularly as they deal with the same people over a substantial period of time, have enabled a number of insights into the grass-roots impact of the policing of the poor. Firstly, the events described in this chapter point to the importance of face-to-face relationships in criminal justice systems, and particularly in the early eighteenth century, when the parish still predominated in local policing arrangements. The direct involvement of the magistracy, their interaction with the constables, the confrontations between the magistrates, the accused and the broader community, underline the important role of this figure in pre-modern law enforcement. Indeed, from these cases we see that justice had a wide range of tools to draw upon in the maintenance of local order. Thus the tools of criminal justice – the warrant, the indictment, the court-room, the lock-up, the prison, as well as the force and organisation of civic bodies – were drawn upon in these attempts to curtail Mary Harvey's activities in their locality. The strong connection between vice and disorderly spaces which characterised much of the propaganda of the Society for the Reformation of Manners was a gift to local justices and local 'respectable' residents, who were able to enforce control of disorder in their own backyards, cloaked in the rhetoric of national, moral reformation. The 1730 campaign effectively sought to kill two birds with one stone, to stymie Harvey and her confederates and at the same time round up the usual disorderly suspects.

This chapter has also shown that, in this case, justice bit off rather more than it could chew. Thus the second strand of my argument has been to show how Mary Harvey was equally to take advantage of the flexibility and discretion inherent in the early-eighteenth-century system. Whilst this half of the story is much less visible (Harvey's counsel is rarely heard), it is significant that in the nine Old Bailey trials that the women collected between them, there was only one clear guilty verdict, for Mary Sullivan in 1732. Moreover, in the King's Bench perjury trial, the verdict was reversed. Whilst we have to be careful in how we use notions of agency (as can be seen by the women's fate below) this case provides an extensive example of plebeian Londoners interacting with, resisting and in some ways shaping justice. I would argue that it is necessary to look beyond the actions of Mary Harvey and her immediate circle and consider the wider community and networks involved in this story. Thus, reading between the lines of Harvey's tumultuous life, we can glimpse disorderly, plebeian communities attempting to assert their place in the local community. As much as their disorderly pubs and taverns and nightly disturbances might have upset their respectable neighbours, the community resisted the constables and 'bred disturbances' until local residents were forced to resort to the criminal justice system to purge their nuisance neighbours.

Moreover, despite the involvement of the Westminster justices, in the form of Gonson and, latterly, Colonel Thomas De Veil, the women continued to maintain a presence (albeit a more subdued one) in the courts and in the press as witnesses and occasionally as the accused, for a while after these events. Mary Sullivan was to end her 'career' in July 1732, when she was found guilty of picking the pocket of George Anderson who had been drinking with Sullivan and Eaton in a pub in Drury Lane.[123] She was transported to Virginia in October that year.[124] Mary Harvey, after a short hiatus, reappeared at the Old Bailey, but was acquitted. By July 1732 she was up to her old tricks, accused of abusing a constable and keeping a disorderly house. The *Grub Street Journal*, in its version of the events published on 6 July, could not resist commenting, '*Either he was not a man, or she more than a woman*'.[125] She had disappeared from the record by January 1733, except for a tantalising reference in the *Daily Courant*, later that year: '*Dublin, Dec. 15*. On Saturday last, the notorious Moll Harvey, so often mentioned in the English News Papers, was tried at the Thosel, and found guilty of picking the Pocket of one Mr Morgan of seven Moiés, and was ordered for Transportation'.[126] Isabella Eaton was to trouble the justices for a little longer. She had appeared alongside Mary Sullivan in July 1732 and also as a witness in the trial of Jane Murphey in December that year.[127] Isabella was rarely in evidence over the following few years, until the summer of 1735 when she was committed to Newgate for insulting and abusing Sir William Billers, the justice, in the execution of his office.[128] This 'office' seems to have been in relation to the Willis case, for which Eaton and a woman described as her chambermaid, Elizabeth Walker, were accused of conspiracy.[129] Isabella was tried in January 1736 at the General Quarter Sessions of the Peace at Guildhall, for the City of London, found guilty and sentenced to pay a £5 fine, spend a year in Newgate and find securities for her good behaviour.[130] By 1737, Isabella was still in prison, petitioning for a release that was at least eight months overdue.[131] Her last known brush with the law was in June 1738, when she was committed to Newgate by Justice De Veil, for picking a gentleman's pocket. During her long examination by De Veil she abused him 'prodigiously', threatened him and attempted to beat him.[132] The following year, the *Daily Post* contained the following brief report on the front page of its edition for Friday 27 October 1738: 'On Monday last died in a Cellar in St Giles's, the famous Isabella Eaton, who many times was committed to Newgate, and to most of the Gaols about Town. She died in a poor miserable Condition; a just Example to all such notorious Cheats'.[133]

4
'The pickpockets and hustlers had yesterday what is called a *Grand Day*': Changing Street Theft, c. 1800–1850[1]

In the late eighteenth and early nineteenth centuries established models of robbery and new definitions of pickpocketing combined in a form of street theft that fashioned novel ways of referring to the dangers of public streets. The writing of journalists and social investigators, the evidence of police, victims, witnesses and the accused, contributed to a shifting rhetoric of robbery. It was no longer solely the dark alleys and quiet dead ends in which danger lurked. Rather, the crowded thoroughfares of the developing metropolis presented the potential for daylight robbery. As one provincial journalist noted in 1820, 'the state of the metropolis is become dangerous and disgraceful. There can be no concourse of people without the most atrocious robberies'.[2] Street robbery has been the subject of a number of studies by historians who are interested in the relationship between violent street theft and the ways in which print culture has shaped the terminology and representations of such crimes. Whilst forms of street robbery have been a perennial feature of the urban criminal milieu, the visibility of the footpad, the highwayman and the garrotter reflect the periodic fusing of the forces of print culture, public anxiety and criminal justice policy: identifying them as 'public enemies'.[3] Through these various incarnations the robber has remained a significant and persistent actor in the underworld narrative. Yet, at the Old Bailey robbery would only ever generate a small cohort of offenders, and for much of its history the incidence of violent robbery has been distorted. As Bob Shoemaker has noted (about the eighteenth century), 'Robberies were disproportionately reported, accounting for 44.2 per cent of all crime reports, despite the fact that they accounted for only 6.8 per cent of the crimes tried at the Old Bailey'.[4] From the later eighteenth century perceptions of and attitudes to street robbery underwent significant change. This can partly be explained by structural factors such as the growth of new financial instruments that took away the need to carry cash and valuables, improvements to the roads around London and the developments in policing, particularly after 1790.[5] Prosecutions which referred to robbery on or near the highway were less common by the late 1820s, when the broader terminology of robbery, robbery with violence or felonious assault would more often be used.[6] The decades of the late eighteenth and early nineteenth centuries saw a profound shift in prosecution practices. As John Beattie has noted, in this period the decline in prosecution of robbery was clearly related to changes in the law relating to picking pockets. As a result of these changes, prosecutions of the latter increased between the 1810s and 1820s.[7]

This chapter will consider the changing landscape of interpersonal danger in the metropolis by exploring a form of robbery that appeared in print culture, courtroom and police records from the late eighteenth century. Victims and witnesses described the experience of robbery as being 'hustled' and 'surrounded' by gangs of youths or men. However, despite the perception of hustling as a form of violent street theft, many of these prosecutions were not for robbery or highway robbery, but rather for larceny from the person, more colloquially described as picking pockets. Whilst young men and youths committing street robberies and/or picking pockets had long been a feature of metropolitan street life, the hybrid figure of the hustler blended concerns about gangs of young males, pickpockets and street robbers that in the early decades of the century developed in diverse ways. Whilst the vocabulary of hustling was common in the press from the late 1780s, by looking in detail at a small group of cases from the 1810s and 1820s, it becomes clear that a specific set of events coloured the perception of threat on London's streets, provided increased opportunity for crime and led to increased policing of prospective street robbers. The experiences of the London crowds who joined processions and demonstrations, and the authorities' concerns about both potential and actual unrest, would shape representations of street robbery in this period.[8] The second part of the chapter will consider the ways in which police and law enforcers handled these cases, suggesting that hustling trials provide a window onto the changing strategies of prosecution and punishment in the years leading up to the Metropolitan Police Act of 1829. The final part of the chapter considers a further manifestation of the robber vocabulary, which once again reframed street robbery and theft from the 1830s and 1840s. The 'swell mobsman' was depicted as a skilful hustler, and hustling as part of an arsenal of cunning techniques of thievery. By 1844, even the prime minister's brother, the Reverend Mr Peel, was being 'hustled by the swell mob in the playing fields, at Eton College...'.[9]

This chapter draws on a series of trials at the Old Bailey in which offences of robbery and larceny from the person are recast as incidents of hustling.[10] Between 1815 and 1825 there were 106 trials in which 'hustling', 'hustle' or 'hustled' was referred to. All but six of these trials refer to hustling as an experience of interpersonal street crime: 55 of these were prosecutions for picking pockets, 41 were for highway robbery, three for robbery and one for grand larceny. The 100 trials involved 145 individual defendants.[11] Whilst hustling was just one way of describing robbery and a relatively small number of trials at the Old Bailey specifically refer to being hustled, these cases enable us to examine the way in which victims described their experience of being robbed in public spaces. John Beattie has noted the growing number of robberies at the Old Bailey which involved victims being attacked by a group of offenders, 'Almost half the cases tried at the Old Bailey between 1810 and 1830 were robberies in which victims were surrounded by offenders and hustled while their pockets were rifled or their watches snatched'.[12] Close examination of such cases can provide insights into the policing and prosecution strategies that were adopted to deal with the perennial issue of street theft. In order to examine the problem of 'hustling' more closely, the main focus here is upon highway robbery, robbery and pickpocketing trials where incidents of hustling are described in the ten-year period from the end of the French Wars in 1815. Whilst the terms 'hustling', 'hustled' and 'hustler' are found sporadically in the eighteenth-century trials, their use would peak in 1819 and 1820. These cases predominantly described robbery in public, in the daytime and frequently against the backdrop of civic events and places where the public gathered, signalling a shift from the types of robbery that took place under the cloak of darkness or with the force of a pistol or knife. More broadly, this small set of cases represent prevailing concerns about the picking of pockets, a form of crime which was far from novel but which by the early decades of the nineteenth century became commonplace at the Old Bailey courtroom.

The major distinction between violent theft and other forms of theft was in the level of violence employed by the accused, demonstrated in the use of wording such as 'against his will' and 'putting in fear' in the indictment. In theory, distinctions between highway robbery and pickpocketing cases were clear-cut. Highway robbers used violence as a blunt tool, putting their victim 'in fear', and were more likely to commit crime in the dark, near or on the King's highway. Pickpockets worked in the daytime, in crowds, at the very least near or in public venues, and their crimes were subtle and undetected by their victim. The importance of the time of day has been demonstrated by Deirdre Palk who found, in her study of pickpockets between 1780 and 1808, that male pickpockets were more likely to commit offences in the daylight and in public spaces: 'as a rule, men and boys did their private stealing amongst crowds watching processions, at public hangings, at fights, in crowds watching "the quality" pass by, at horse fairs and in theatre foyers, and were pulling handkerchiefs from pockets in the streets in broad daylight'.[13] Palk comments that the original pickpocketing statute had stipulated that the theft was one effected without the knowledge of the victim. The law was further refined in the late eighteenth century:

> The statute was 'intended to suppress a certain species of dexterity, against the success of which the common vigilance of mankind was found not to be an adequate safeguard and protection, and therefore if the larceny is in the slightest degree detected at the time it is committing, the offender is not within the penalty of the act'.[14]

Such issues of interpretation arguably impacted on prosecution practices, and there was a growing lack of clarity in the transforming legislative landscape of the early nineteenth century.[15] Samuel Romilly's 1808 Act dealing with larceny from the person changed the nature of the offence so that robbers who did not use weapons or effect serious violence could essentially be prosecuted as pickpockets.[16] The statute had the effect of increasing prosecutions for pickpocketing but also blurred the boundaries between what constituted robbery and what larceny from the person.

Moreover, in this period the concerns of criminal justice practitioners and commentators were shifting. Whilst young men had long predominated at the quarter sessions and assizes, from the early nineteenth century they became a significant focus for reformers.[17] It was in such an environment, when legislative change and reform imperatives were combining, that robberies involving encounters with large gangs of mostly young men in public streets, often in broad daylight, were being reported with increasing frequency. During such episodes victims of robberies would describe being 'hustled', 'surrounded', 'pushed', 'pulled' and 'jostled' by large 'groups', 'gangs', crowds', 'packs' or 'mobs' of youths and young men. Hustling 'gangs' were described as using their physical mass against their intended targets to effect robberies on the crowded metropolitan streets. For example, in August 1820 John Middleton was robbed on the King's highway by a crowd of people whom he met near Southampton Street, off the Strand.[18] He told the court, 'I was surrounded by them, they jostled me with their shoulders and elbows – I then thought they were about to rob me, and endeavoured, with all my force, to get into a shop – the door being open, I got within about a yard of the door, when some of the gang got between me and door, and prevented me'. When asked how many there were, he continued, 'I was much alarmed, and unable to count them, but suppose there were twenty or more'. Middleton clearly had no idea who had robbed him. George Taylor, a Clerkenwell officer who had witnessed the incident and retrieved Middleton's pocketbook, recounted the dramatic circumstances of the attack and chase: 'I was making my way out from them, and they sung out, "Chiv him!" which means to use their knives. I got a cut over my knuckle, my hand was all over blood(y)'. Such was the melee described by Taylor and his companion, a broker named William Colton, that it was almost impossible to be clear about identifying the main offenders. Colton described a group of 25 or 26 men, 'many of them genteelly dressed'. William Sidney Smith, a 19-year-old shoemaker who was eventually found guilty of the robbery and sentenced to death, described how he had been apparently innocently walking from Oxford Street in order to see the Queen: 'I met the procession in Piccadilly'.

Hustlers, Pickpockets and Robbers

Specific references to the practice of being hustled in the course of a robbery can be found during the eighteenth century. In 1751, Smollet had his character Trunnion being 'hussled' in *The Adventures of Peregrine Pickle*.[19] In 1762, a watchmaker named James Planch was watching the passing of Prince Henry's coach at the entrance to St James's when he was pushed and the watch he was delivering was taken.[20] The evidence was confused and the accused, Francis Jones, was acquitted. From the 1780s, the experience of being robbed in the daytime whilst attending a public event seemed to be an increasing risk of town life. At the Old Bailey are found victims such as John Ferdinand Dalziel Smith, who was hustled 'in the crowd on St David's day, between twelve and two' in April 1784; William Wickham who was witnessed being hustled in a crowd that had assembled to see the King and Queen leave the Drury Lane theatre in February 1785; and, in April that year, William Tubb, who was hustled near Tottenham Court Road, where a crowd had gathered to the see 'the balloon going off with Count Zambeconi'.[21] A report of the event in the *General Evening Post* noted, 'Many of the light fingered gentry made a good days business yesterday around the spot from which the balloon ascended'.[22] From the 1810s, forms of street robbery were frequently undifferentiated in the writings of contemporary observers. As a letter from 'A Citizen' to the *Morning Post* explained in 1813, 'the streets of the *City* are most shamefully infested day and night by organised gangs of *pickpockets, hustlers,* and *street robbers,* and that the losses sustained by the public in consequence have been very considerable'.[23]

Whilst not all street robbery was described as hustling, contemporary commentators clearly had it in mind when they voiced their concerns about metropolitan street crime. In 1816 the Select Committee on Police had bemoaned the increasing problem of open and forceful street robbery, singling out the problem of 'taking property by force from the person or by hustling'.[24] And the 1817 Committee made further comments about 'those fellows who hustle passengers in the street'.[25] In 1816 and 1817 the problems of post-war demobilisation may well have boosted concerns about street robbery. Certainly, by the late 1810s guidance on how to deal with street robbers could be gleaned from the *The London Guide and Stranger's Safeguard Against the Cheats, Swindlers, and Pickpockets that Abound Within the Bills of Mortality,* published in 1818. In a chapter entitled, 'System of Walking – Caution', the author pointed out the danger to strangers and those from outside town, who tended to awkwardly pass the streets by walking on the kerb stone, which apparently made them conspicuous to robbers and pickpockets. The author advised, 'A pickpocket will hustle such a one against his accomplice in the day time ... *Money* in the *breeches* pockets, can only be come at in a crowd, or by *flooring* the victim; the former of which is most usually ... performed in the day time'.[26] The following year the notorious thief James Hardy Vaux published his memoirs, in which he described the 'STALL UP', a term used by pickpockets:

> To *stall* a person up ... is to surround him in a crowd, or violent pres-
> sure, and even sometimes in the open street, while walking along,
> and by violence force his arms up, and keep them in that position
> while others of the gang rifle his pockets at pleasure, *the cove* being
> unable to help or defend himself; this is what the newspapers
> denominate hustling, and is universally practiced at the doors of
> public theatres, at boxing matches, at ship-launches and other places
> where the general anxiety of all ranks, either to push forward, or to
> obtain a view of the scene before them, forms a pretext for jostling,

and every other advantage which the strength and numbers of one party gives them over a weaker one, or a single person.[27]

For the press hustling had become an epithet for street robbery, reflecting a new sort of public danger. The lonely highway, the heaths and the commons had long been spaces vulnerable to the threat of the highway robber and footpad; now the dense and crowded urban streets and spaces of the metropolis were providing cover for another sort of predator. Old fears were repackaged using the new language of hustling. Thus it was believed that the intermingling of bodies in the public streets, at processions, at fairs, at pleasure gardens, outside theatres and at the races provided opportunities for gangs to 'surround' and to 'hustle' the unwary victim. Victims included The Right Honourable Thomas Lord Foley, who was hustled at the hustings in Covent Garden in February 1819. Lord Foley described how a party rushed on both sides of him, held one arm up, the other down, and took his watch and pocketbook. Similarly, Mr John Prior was, 'hustled by a gang of fellows' at two o'clock in the afternoon in October 1819, whilst he stood with a crowd watching the launch of an air balloon near the Belvidere Tavern in Pentonville.[28] Whilst such venues had traditionally been hunting grounds for male pickpockets, private stealing involving stealth and subtlety was, at least in 1819 and 1820, replaced with open and public shows of force.

Characteristically hustling gangs were male and young. Very few cases involved women. Between 1815 and 1825, of the 145 defendants prosecuted in hustling cases, 142 were prosecuted for picking pockets (78), highway robbery (61) and robbery (3).[29] Another three men were found guilty of grand larceny in a case from 1815, though in all other aspects this was a typical hustling case, involving a group of men hustling their victim's silk handkerchief whilst he watched the Lord Mayor's Procession.[30] Only 16 of the 145 defendants were women, and they were prosecuted for picking pockets or for highway robbery.[31] In customary fashion, groups of women, or women with men, often robbed their victim inside or upon leaving or entering a house or pub.[32] For example, in June 1820, when William Burgess claimed to have been hustled in a passage in Wentworth Street by Eliza Brown, Lucy Saunders and Edward Crispin, it turned out he had spent much of the night drinking with the women; as the watchman Samuel Starkey testified, 'he was very drunk, the women could hardly keep him from falling'.[33] If street hustlers were overwhelmingly male, they were also overwhelmingly young men. Yet, despite the preponderance of prosecutions for juvenile pickpockets in this period, very young boys were not generally involved in hustling gangs.[34] Whilst the occasional 15 or 16 year old would be prosecuted with a group of older youths, specific gangs of juvenile robbers were not singled out. There were exceptions. For example, in December 1818 Charles Russell, the 14-year-old servant to a tobacconist, had been hustled by a group of boys, 'making a noise like a parcel of dogs'.[35] Nevertheless, violent street robbery and hustling was a young man's game. Between 1815 and 1825, 82 of the 145 defendants surveyed were aged 25 or under. Given that in the case of 45 of the defendants no age was given (usually indicating a verdict of not guilty), 80.29 per cent of the convicted hustlers were aged 25 and under, and 9.92 per cent were aged under 17; hence just seven convicted hustlers were aged over 25.[36] It is perhaps worth noting that whilst youths and young men predominated, older men were occasionally identified amongst the hustling gangs. For example, in July 1836 30-year-old John Nelson and 35-year-old John Wilson were identified as part of a gang who had hustled Hugh Poole in the City, near St Dunstan's. Both men were found guilty and sentenced to death.[37] Whilst hustling and gang robberies took place in both the day and the evening or night, the press clearly reserved their most scandalised commentary for those robberies that had taken place in daylight. Whilst being violently accosted by a robber in the dark was nothing new, being hustled by a large gang in broad daylight apparently was. As *The Times* noted in December 1820, 'crime increases to such a pitch that, in passing through Fleet-street and the Strand in the middle of the day, people are hustled and robbed with impunity'.[38] However, in the summer of 1819, when a number of hustling robberies were widely reported in the press, it was the sheer level of violence displayed and the apparent numbers of youths involved which seems to have particularly outraged contemporary commentators.

The West End Fair Gang and Violent Robbery

Despite the concerns about daytime robbery, it was a series of violent robberies that took place on three summer evenings in July 1819 which seem to have caused the initial wave of concern about hustling and street robbery. The events of the West End Fair in Hampstead on 28, 29 and 30 July attracted substantial press coverage and would result in 12 trials for highway robbery and pickpocketing at the Old Bailey between September 1819 and February 1820.[39] Whilst descriptions of 'The West End Fair Gang', and references to the 'Captain of the Gang' John Henley, recall models of criminal confederacy evoked in earlier accounts of highway robbery and footpaddery, these events, wrapped as they were in the language of hustling, also reflect some of the newer concerns about public space in this period.[40] After an initial outbreak of violence on Monday, special constables were drafted in to deal with what were described as 'armed gangs of robbers'.[41] Indeed, the police presence at the fair seems to have been considerable, with several parish watchmen who had been attending the fair for pleasure also becoming embroiled in the violence. One victim of hustling was the watchman of St Martin-in-the-Fields, Timothy Ryan, who was at the fair with his wife and child. He described being attacked and hustled by a group of five men who forced him down on his knees and surrounded him. Philip Cameron, a 31-year-old, was identified as being the man who pushed Ryan to his knees, whilst 19-year-old William Carter had struck him. Whilst attempting to arrest the two men with the aid of John Furzeman, a constable of St Giles who was also at the fair with his family, they were apparently attacked by a crowd of about 50 or 60 who marched on them with bludgeons and short sticks.[42] The description of the violence, the openness of the robberies, the numbers described, the suggestion of organisation and the adoption of the language of hustling would set the tone for reporting of gang robbery from this point. According to *The Times*, 'The ruffians were divided into gangs ... estimated at more than 150'; the alleged 'leader' of the gang, John Henley, was described as repeatedly shouting, 'Let's hustle the b...r'.[43] Another witness who attempted to beat off the robbers, reported cries of 'Stall him, cut his b...y throat!'.[44] Three youths, 21-year-old Edward Cassidy, 20-year-old John Henley and a 15-year-old Romany named Henry Lovell, would eventually be executed on 26 November 1819 in front of an 'immense multitude'.[45]

Later that year the Hampstead vestry would appoint a committee specifically to look into the events, and the following July a force of 150 men, including 50 special constables, were assembled by local magistrates with the backing of the Home Office, the local vestry and local householders, to ensure that the fair was not held.[46] Whilst this suppression was not strictly legal, by 1822 they would have been able to resort to the Metropolitan Police Act, which allowed for uncharted fairs to be declared illegal.[47] The reporting of the West End Fair marked a heightened concern about hustling incidents between 1819 and 1821, when 49.02 per cent of the defendants would be tried (all but one for picking pockets, highway robbery or robbery).[48] The sheer coverage that these events were given arguably contributed to the visibility of hustling gangs after this point. Increasingly, the reporting of large gangs of robbers in public spaces would be boosted by the courtroom language of witnesses and of victims who were voluble in their descriptions of being violently hustled. Moreover, growing anxiety about 'the crowd', and particularly the political crowd, would be accompanied by the adoption of hustling rhetoric.

Hustlers, Radicals and the Crowd

The resurrection of radical mass politics in this period led to a dramatic increase in riots and public order disturbances. This return to the radicalism that had been driven underground during the wars was partly due to the economic distress that was affecting London at this time. Unemployment from the loss of war contracts and poor harvests, combined with the return of men from the army and navy, provided a fertile ground for post-war radicalism.[49] In London this resulted in a litany of public order disturbances, as well as demonstrations and processions, through the late 1810s and early 1820s. The problems of controlling large crowds had already been sharply illustrated by the events at Spa Fields in December 1816 and sporadic episodes of crowd violence had continued to burden the authorities. However, from the autumn of 1819 the tumult and intensity of the London crowd was providing ample opportunities for street robbery.[50] Reports of hustling would gather intensity over the course of the following year, peaking to something of a crisis by December 1820. Coverage of radical crowds in this period frequently commented on the prevalence of hustling gangs amongst the mob. For example, in September 1819 a number of arrests were made during Henry Hunt's 'Triumphal Entry' into London after the events at Peterloo and before his arrest in 1820.[51] James Whitehair was hustled as he waited for Mr Hunt's procession to pass through Bishopgate, 'I found myself surrounded by a crowd, who were hustling me, and attempted to take my pocket-book'. Daniel Huffman, a 16-year-old, was accused of the robbery and sentenced to transportation for life.[52] The Chairing of Francis Burdett in April 1820 was another political event that drew crowds and provided opportunities for robbery. Whilst attending the Chairing with two ladies, Robert Mayne had his watch and seals stolen. He attempted to seize the thief and was immediately 'surrounded by a gang of them. They took him from me after a great resistance. The prisoner bit my thumb; he is not the person who took my watch, but he was one of the party – there were about twelve of them ...'.[53] The anti-Burdett *Morning Post* satirically commented on the 'plentiful harvest to the rogues and pick-pockets' afforded by the baronet's vanity.[54] Thus, by

1820, the proliferation of processions, marches and demonstrations of the London radicals would be characterised as creating not only problems of public order, but also undermining the safety of the public who it seems could hardly walk in the open streets without the risk of being hustled.[55]

These were significant years for processions. Over half the references to processions in the Old Bailey Sessions Papers fall in the first half of the nineteenth century, with just over a third of these falling in the years between 1819 and 1821.[56] The only other year with a significant number of references to processions was 1848, when they mostly relate to Chartist activity. Prothero notes that the organisation of support for Queen Caroline intensified from her return to England in June 1820, and her trial for adultery which ran from 19 August to 8 September, and then through most of October.[57] Accordingly, between June and December 1820 there were 35 trials involving victims having their pockets picked whilst in some proximity to a procession; at least 23 of these took place when the Queen was passing or during processions taking place to support her.[58] For example, in the October Sessions at the Old Bailey, we find 21-year-old Thomas Dorset who took advantage of the assembled crowds to hustle James Pickles, a clerk watching the procession. A witness saw Dorset in 'the centre of a gang of sixty or seventy'.[59] In the same session, 25-year-old Lewis Lazarus and 'a gang of well-known pickpockets' made use of the crowds gathered to see the Sawyers' Procession returning from Brandenburgh House (the Queen's residence), to surround a passer-by, James Filor, and snatch his watch. Also in October, 21-year-old William Penny was found guilty of picking the pocket of Richard Cornelius, who was surrounded by a gang whilst 'a procession was going to the Queen'.[60] Indeed, through the second half of 1820, commentary on the prevalence of 'barefaced' and 'audacious' robbery in daylight amongst crowds who gathered to watch processions or took part in demonstrations often accompanied press reports as a matter of course. In some of the reporting there was a suggestion that the hustling gangs and the political mob were of a shared persuasion. Thus in November, on the evening after the Coopers' Procession had returned from Brandenburgh House, a gentleman was robbed on Long Acre by 'a numerous gang of villains, who were calling out "the Queen! The Queen! For ever"'.[61]

Elsewhere the press took the opportunity to draw attention to the apparent inadequacies of the police in dealing both with the Carolinian crowds and with the hustling gangs. As the *Morning Post* noted on the occasion of the radical leader's address to the Queen in October 1820, 'The public peace, then, is again to be interrupted, the industrious men are to be drawn aside from their employ and their families, and the unsuspecting are to be exposed to gangs of street robbers. We trust the Police will be on the alert'.[62] There are indications that the policing presence had been increased. In the City a list of special constables had been drawn up at the request of the Lord Mayor John Atkins in the previous year.[63] Evidence of a more proactive approach was reported upon in October 1820, when there was a confrontation between a hustling gang and several constables who had 'collected in a body, for the purpose of apprehending some of the leaders of the gang'. About 30 men had 'hustled, tripped up, and knocked down, several persons, whom they robbed of pocket-books, money, and watches', between Brandenburgh House and Knightsbridge. The confrontation occurred outside Knightsbridge Barracks, and, despite the constables being armed with pistols and cutlasses, no arrests were made.[64] The radical-leaning *Morning Chronicle* weighed in with criticism, commenting in November on the occasion of the Queen's visit to St Paul's, that pickpockets had become so numerous due to the 'shameful negligence of the police'.[65] In December the *Morning Post* was suggesting that some of the special constables sworn in to preserve order had 'been amongst the most expert pickpockets of the metropolis' who, according to the *Post*, had turned a blind eye to the activities of their accomplices who had 'hustled and robbed every person they could'.[66] Clearly these accounts are problematic and reflect contemporary political tensions. The City had come out in support of Caroline and it was in the interests of the Mayor and Aldermen to maintain orderly demonstrations and processions. On the other hand, the Tory press was quick to criticise the police, and dismiss the Queen's supporters at best as a 'mob' and at worst as pickpockets, thieves and robbers. Moreover, the chaotic and open nature of these street robberies and the political contexts in which they were being reported, were also being played out in an era during which existing law enforcement arrangements were coming under increasing pressure. By December 1820, the Lord Mayor of the City himself was casting aspersions on the ability of the police to deal with 'those persons who associated together with the view of hustling and robbing passengers'.[67]

Demonstrations and crowd disturbances would continue into 1821, and indeed intensify after the death of the Queen in August. However, the reporting and prosecuting of incidents involving hustling gangs would decrease by that spring. Indeed the Queen's funeral, which took place on 14 August 1821 and was the cause of such tumult and riot amongst the London populace, did not result in a rash of arrests; certainly none were tried at the Old Bailey. The Mansion House police office went as far as issuing a statement, reprinted in the *Morning Chronicle* on 16 August:

> In justice to the proper feeling and peaceable conduct of the immense multitude of persons, of both sexes, that were drawn together from all quarters into the City on Tuesday, when the Queen's Funeral Procession passed through, we feel it our duty to notice that not the slightest accident of any kind occurred, within the knowledge of any of the officers, on the whole line from Temple-bar to Whitechapel; not the smallest violence or even insult were offered to the soldiery, but, on the contrary, they were almost constantly cheered by the populace with the cries of 'the Blues' 'the Blues for ever,' the whole of the way; and yesterday morning not a single prisoner was in custody, either at this office or at the Guildhall Justice-room, for picking pockets, or any act of riot, tumult, or disorder, committed during the time of, or in any manner attributable to, the passing of the procession through the City.[68]

It is hardly surprising that the police would be keen to stress the order of the proceedings, given the concerted efforts of demonstrators to reroute the procession through the City. Arguably, the concerns about hustling in 1820 had played a part in the calls for an increase in police strength. According to Elaine Reynolds, it was the perceived increase in street robbery that had led to changes to the horse and foot patrol in 1821.[69] The expansion of the foot patrol in the centre and the creation of the 'dismounted horse patrol' to police those areas immediately outside the centre (within five miles of Bow Street) was masterminded by Lord Sidmouth, who had called for change as a result of 'the alarming increase of street robberies within the metropolis'.[70] The foot patrol increased its numbers and four police districts outside of the centre were created, patrolled by 22 men, two sub-inspectors and an inspector.[71] Moreover, the authority of the magistracy would be further enforced by police legislation in 1821 and 1822.[72] At a local level, such proactive policing seems to have made a difference. Thus, by May 1821, the Chairman of the Watch Committee wrote to Sidmouth that, 'Street Robberies in our Parish are less frequent since we have had our additional Patrol…'. [73]

Law Enforcement, Discretion and Cases of Mistaken Identity

In the case of hustling and gang robberies, prosecutors were faced with a number of problems in dealing with such large groups. Indeed, victims' and constables' estimates of the numbers of robbers who had 'surrounded' and 'hustled' them seemed to rise with the increased prosecution of such cases. Reports ranged from descriptions of 'several' men to a 'great number' to counts of 'five men', 'two dozen', '50', '60 or 70', and '100'. The chaos and confusion of such robberies and the problems of identification meant that for witnesses it was important to impress upon the court the sheer mass and the significant physical presence such large numbers represented. However, not only were there issues in determining who had committed the robbery, but the level of violence and the extent to which that violence had been used in the commission of the crime were also far from clear-cut. Arguably, in 1819 and 1820, this led to a highly discretionary approach to dealing with these cases in order to achieve a successful prosecution. Clive Emsley has pointed out that, 'the two offences [robbery and larceny from the person] overlap and the eventual way in which a crime was recorded could depend on how the victim and/or police wished to conceive of "violence"'.[74] This certainly seems to be the case in the early nineteenth century, when not only were the distinctions between highway robbery and pickpocketing increasingly blurred, but the need to prosecute street robbers may have conflicted with the desire to pay attention to the letter of the law. The 1808 Larceny Act had loosened the definition of pickpocketing so that victims no longer needed to prove that the theft had been committed without their knowledge. However, whilst a wider range of thefts from the person could now be prosecuted under this statute, the (legal) distinctions between larceny from the person and violent robbery remained.[75] In 1815, these distinctions between forms of robbery and stealing from the person preoccupied the Old Bailey courtroom. Thus in the case of a robbery by John Lane in October 1815, despite the considerable violence he resorted to in resisting arrest, the court was keen to stipulate that the actual theft had been achieved without the use of 'force and violence', hence the crime did not amount to a highway robbery.[76] The sometimes subtle distinctions between capital and non-capital crimes were also illustrated in another case from 1815. At the trial of Isaac Davis and Moss Jacobs, for feloniously assaulting Margaret Quinland on the highway and taking from her two shawls and money, the court deliberated over the specific use of force used to get the shawl. If the shawl was simply snatched, then this was not enough to result in a capital sentence; but if the victim had resisted the robbery, and held on to the shawl, and if the defendant had 'succeeded in getting it, that would be force and violence enough to constitute a highway robbery'.[77]

However, in hustling cases the series of events was frequently so chaotic and confused that it was simply not always possible to make these distinctions. More often than not such cases were prosecuted as larcenies from the person, despite considerable evidence of violence, precisely because of the problems of identification and confusion over the issue of 'force and violence'. For example, when Charles Smith and George Mason were accused of robbing Robert Chapman in August 1820, witnesses gave conflicting accounts. One witness described seeing Smith striking Chapman; another witness did not see the robbery, but saw the watch in Smith's hand; Robert Chapman himself described being 'surrounded by the gang' and seeing his son knocked down, but did know either of the prisoners, and another witness stated 'I rather think Smith struck him in the mouth'. The defendants were prosecuted for picking pockets and, in this case, found not guilty.[78] However, such series of events – the uncertainty of identification and the lack of clear connection between the defendant and a violent robbery – were common in hustling cases. For example, in July 1820 John Teasdale, who was watching the Glassblowers' Procession from Devonshire Street, was violently accosted at midday by a gang of youths. He described scuffling with the youths whilst they attempted to take his watch and seals, being hit in the neck by one youth, who he failed to identify, and having stones thrown at him by the rest of the gang. He described being 'very much beaten'. Nevertheless, he did not connect any of the three boys, who were eventually prosecuted with larceny from the person, with specific acts of violence.[79] They were part of a crowd that had hustled him violently.

It may be that from this period larceny from the person was a much more effective tool in waging war against street robbers. Thus crimes that would previously have been prosecuted as robbery on the highway were now prosecuted as larceny from the person. The larceny statute of 1808 not only repealed the death sentence and changed the wording so that the theft no longer had to be effected 'privily'. It also stipulated that those who were 'present, aiding and abetting' were to be punished in the same way as the principal offenders.[80] This was effectively a mandate for joint enterprise or common purpose.[81] Moreover, whilst Romilly had originally wanted to punish pickpocketing with a maximum sentence of transportation for seven years, a rather more draconian majority in the House of Commons made sure that the maximum sentence of transportation for life was imposed for all but the least serious of larcenies from the person. According to Radzinowicz, for the architects of the 1808 Act, 'the elimination of offenders from society was held to be the best safeguard against crime'.[82] Thus, in hustling cases, where identification was frequently shaky and where evidence of violent robbery was far from clear-cut, a charge of larceny from the person could offer a better chance for a successful prosecution and permanent removal of the offender from the metropolitan streets.

However, the decision-making process that connected the accused to a violent act was far from straightforward in highway robbery cases. For example, Michael Harley was one of a large gang who hustled a tailor named Hugh Mackay at a procession on the Strand in December 1820. Whilst Mackay identified 23-year-old Harley as having pulled his watch chain, there was no clear accusation of violence against him. Mackay claimed to have been beaten so badly by this gang that, 'My head was so swelled with the blows I could not put my hat on for several days'.[83] However, there seems to have been significant confusion about the identification made by Mackay. Originally Mackay had accused another man, James McFarlane, and sworn to a positive identification. McFarlane had apparently denied involvement, exclaiming, 'I wish those who had actually robbed you had beaten out your b…y brains, then you would not have been able to swear so falsely against me'.[84] It is unclear what happened to McFarlane, as he disappears from the record. However, in January 1821 Michael Harley was identified instead as the man who robbed Hugh Mackay. Harley had been identified in a police line up; Mackay told the courtroom 'If he was tarred and feathered all over except his face I could swear to him'.[85] However, in a further twist to the case, after being sentenced to death and ordered for execution on 13 February 1821 Harley was saved from the gallows when it transpired that he had in fact been in police custody at time that he was supposed to have been committing the robbery.[86] *The Times* commented that another man of loose countenance, who was so like the prisoner 'that they are scarcely to be known apart … must have been the person so pointed out to the prosecutor on the Saturday he mentioned'.[87]

The credibility of identifications in hustling cases was problematic for prosecutors, victims and police. In the chaos of being hustled by a large gang, was it really possible to say with any certainty who had robbed you? William Sidney Smith, who was prosecuted for highway robbery and sentenced to hang in September 1820, would subsequently have his sentence respited when it turned out he had been the victim of a mistaken identity.[88] It transpired that the robbery had been witnessed by Sheriff Parkin who, attending the procession in his official capacity, had identified a robber who bore a strong resemblance to Smith. This robber, a butcher named James Edrop, was eventually sentenced to life transportation in February 1822.[89]

Other law-enforcement practices contributed to the increasing prosecution of street crime and to the confusion as to identification in some of these cases. In the case of William Sidney Smith, a key witness was a broker named William Colton, who clearly worked alongside the police in some capacity. In the 1820s and 1830s, he appeared as a witness in a large number of larceny trials. At the trial of James Edrop, he appeared again as a witness, this time describing himself as a 'constable of Pancras'.[90] Colton was particularly interested in pickpockets. Thus the *Morning Post* reported on the arrest of one Martin Bulmer in August 1823, by William Colton, 'a constable, with attempting to pick several gentleman's pockets the proceeding evening at White Conduit House, on their coming out of the Garden from seeing the balloon'.[91] The extent to which Colton may have manufactured evidence in such cases is unknowable. However, his intervention in the criminal justice process is a reminder that practices of informing survived in this period, and that outcomes could be influenced by such interactions in the prosecution process.

Finally, the value of the goods stolen could have a bearing. For example, Joseph Ellinger, a 21-year-old who was executed on 5 December 1820, was part of a gang who hustled and surrounded John Aird at the opening of the Regent's Canal.[92] Several bank notes, amounting to £43, were found in Ellinger's pocket. Reporting on his execution, *The Times* noted that the robbery 'had been marked with those aggravations of cruelty and personal violence which of late have so attended the atrocious street-robberies that disgrace the metropolis and its vicinity'.[93] More generally though, a comparison of the stolen goods in hustling cases found little difference between highway robbers and pickpockets. Most stole watches, seals, chains and pocketbooks.

It may be that prosecutions of highway robbery were more likely to be used in those hustling cases where a death sentence was desired in order to make an example. Consequently, five sentences of death resulted from the events of the West End Fair, suggesting that in that particular outbreak of hustling and gang robbery an exemplary punishment was needed. This led to the triple execution of Henley, Cassidy and Lovell in November 1819. However, it is difficult to draw any firm conclusions from the death sentences passed at the Old Bailey. Whilst highway robbers were the most likely offenders to be sentenced to death, significant numbers had their charge reduced to larceny from the person.[94] This disinclination to use the full force of the law may have been an indication of the relative youth of the accused. Peter King has suggested that by the early 1820s offenders in their late teens were rarely hung and that by 1827 no offender aged under 20 went to the gallows.[95] Nevertheless, a small number of executions did include those of teenagers. Most poignant was the case of 18-year-old William Knight. One of the earliest hustling cases, in September 1818 Knight and another youth, Edward Evans, were accused of robbing Robert Lowe and his young son who were walking through Whitechapel when they met with the funeral party of a member of the Odd Fellows Society. Lowe was hustled by a gang of about 20 people. His watch was pulled from the fob by Knight and handed over to Evans. He managed to hold onto Knight whilst being kicked and beaten by the gang. Local constables who happened to be attending the funeral were also 'assailed with sticks and stones'. Whilst at no point were Knight and Evans specifically accused of violence, both youths were found guilty of highway robbery and sentenced to death.[96] Knight was executed in January 1819. According to the *Morning Chronicle*, at the scaffold he declared that whilst he was present at the time that the transaction took place, he was innocent of the crime of which he was accused, 'After the rope was adjusted and his face covered, he called out several times in a loud tone, "I am innocent, I am innocent; I am dying not guilty"'.[97]

The Swell Mob

In 1831, a man named Joseph Payne felt moved to privately publish a poem called, 'Lord Mayor's Day'. It connected hustling specifically to the ceremonial crowd. It also connected hustling to a form of criminal confederacy that was fast emerging in accounts of metropolitan criminality: the swell mob. He wrote:

> Policemen are staving
> On heads misbehaving:
> Ward beadles bustling,
> Pickpockets hustling;
> People tip-toeing it;
> Swell mob are going it,
> Making sly snatches
> At brooches and watches.[98]

From the late 1820s and early 1830s, in newspaper accounts and contemporary writing and journalism, hustling was frequently undertaken by the 'swell mob'. The rough and tumble hustling crowd, with its multiple potential suspects, was superseded by a specialised class of thief. Echoing the incipient concept of the 'criminal class', the swell mob was organised, cunning and sophisticated.[99] As Superintendent Lincoln, of D Division (Marylebone Lane) reported in c. 1835, 'There are two classes – The higher and lower sort – they never associate – the lower class sat about – play skittles – dominoes – pitch at the mott – and shove halfpenny – The higher sort he calls Swell mob – Race Men – Thimblemen – and cracksmen'.[100] George Laval Chesterton, the governor of Coldbath Fields, offered a more detailed account of the swell mob and their methods to the Constabulary Committee in 1839, apparently based on narratives from the inmates of Coldbath Fields:

> There are different terms made use of expressive of their various methods of stealing from the person. In hustling, the victim of plunder is surrounded in a push, and, as will be presently shown, he is robbed of every valuable article in his possession ... another is particularised by violence; the mob meets a man, hustles him; if he will not quietly drop, but becomes obstreperous, he is knocked down and robbed ... They soon mark a victim; they follow him till a push occurs, either accidently by meeting a group of people, or intentionally made by themselves. Two go before the man, the others close up behind; their victim is hemmed in, a push takes place, he is jostled and hustled about, the thieves cry out to those behind not to press so, the press is increased; the victim being surrounded, his pockets are generally turned inside out.[101]

Later in his evidence, to clarify the position of the swell mob in the classification of crime, Chesterton identified the less-educated swell mobsman, who was 'able to assist in hustling a man for the purpose of robbing him' but was not elevated enough to 'mix in the higher circles of society, gaining a livelihood by practicing on the credulity of mankind'.[102]

Popular publications also referenced the methods of the swell mob. For example, *Helps and Hints How to Protect Life and Property. With Instructions in Rifle and Pistol Shooting, & c.* was published by Charles Random, self-styled Baron De Bérenger, a firearms expert and manager of the Cremorne Gardens, in 1835.[103] De Bérenger recommended the following course of action upon being careless enough to have fallen victim to the swell mob:

> Should members of the SWELL MOB or other fellows have taken advantage of your carelessness so as to have succeeded in closely

SURROUNDING or HUSTLING you, either with a view to confine
your arms or to deduct from the force of your stick, by your being
prevented from striking with your point ... immediately seize your
stick in the middle, as it will enable you to hit or to parry with either
end ....[104]

Similarly, in 1847, in the *Chambers's Edinburgh Journal*, it was noted that
the swell mob 'subsists chiefly by "hustling" or robbing in crowds'.[105]
The swell mobsman was in many ways an odd figure; he retained characteristics of the pickpocket and the street robber, but also elements of
the picaresque. This was the world that in 1821 had been conjured in
Pierce Egan's, *Life in London*, in which the friends Corinthian Tom and
Jerry Hawthorn experienced the 'Day and Night Scenes' of London,
the 'vulgar' amusements of popular theatres, sports, particularly those
of pugilism and the turf.[106] Thus the swell mob roved the fairgrounds,
racecourses and highways of Victorian England, just as the highwayman
and footpad had troubled an earlier generation. Yet, by the 1830s and
1840s the swell mob generally referred to a specific sort of group or gang
of thieves who had skills and experience and, as a result of this, a social
mobility. The 'top' swell mobsmen could move around polite society
through the shared spaces of the racecourse, prize fights and theatre.
This ability to dissemble and impersonate is characteristic in descriptions of the swell mob. As Partridge notes, the swell mob were 'Such
pickpockets as, to escape detection, dress and behave like respectable
people'.[107]

Whilst they rarely became editorial or headline fodder, the swell mob
featured regularly both in serious reporting of trials and the police
courts, as well as in contemporary journalism. The earliest reference
is in the *Standard* (July 1827), which described, 'members of what are
termed the "swell mob" or in plainer English, gentlemen professors of
the art of picking pockets'.[108] In 1829, *The Times* reported when several
pickpockets were charged before Sir Richard Birnie 'with attempting
to lighten the pockets of various individuals in front of St Martin's
Church yesterday, on the occasion of the Welch charity children being
paraded there for the purpose of attending divine service'. Pickpockets
George Kimmis and one Smith, 'better known by the cognomen' of
"the Marquis"', were apparently known to the police as being members
of the swell mob.[109] Only a few references to the swell mob occur at
the Old Bailey. The first of these is in September 1830, and provides
many of the elements that would be typical in accounts of such thieves.
Twenty-three-year-old John Hemmings was found guilty of picking the

pocket of Robert Chisholme, a visitor from the United States, outside the Haymarket Theatre. One witness, John Groom, remarked that 'there were a great many of what they call the swell mob' at the scene of the crime.[110] The connection between the swell mob and picking pockets is confirmed in the Old Bailey. In the 22 references to be found to the swell mob, 14 refer to pickpocketing.[111] Most are in the 1830s, but the last reference, to a prisoner who had apparently given information against the swell mob, was in December 1856.[112] However, the relative scarcity of the term in the Old Bailey does not reflect the broad reference to the swell mob in the contemporary press.[113]

By the 1840s, the swell mobsman had become a universal figure. Henry Mayhew, both in his own journalism and in his capacity as the editor of *Punch*, has much to answer for in this characterisation and proliferation of the well-attired swell mobsman:

> He usually dresses in the same elaborate style of fashion as a Jew on a Saturday (in which case he is more particularly described by the prefix 'swell'), and 'mixes' generally in the 'best of company', frequenting – for the purposes of his business – all the places of public entertainment.[114]

This representation of the swell mob as aspirational and fashionable was not original. As early as the mid-1830s, boys on the *Euryalus* prison hulk, moored at Chatham, described the dress of the swell mobsman, 'curled hair, blue frock coat to the knees, blue trowsers tight to the knees ... velvet collar waistcoat, low fancy worked shoes ... hat, generally on one side ... go about with a cigar in their mouth'.[115] A superintendent of the Mayfair and Soho division around the same time referred to a well-known young thief named William Nelson, who 'is about twenty-three years old, of excellent address and manners, he has been transported and many times in prison ... the officers at Marlborough street say that he makes more than any other of the swell mob'.[116] Moreover, the swell mob was increasingly seen as representing not simply an element of the 'criminal class', but rather a generation of thieves with ideas above their station. For example, an anonymous publication satirised the links between the 'swell mob' and the upwardly mobile 'millocrats' of the 1840s, in a 'Petition to the "Swell Mob" from the Tribe of "blacklegs, Prigs, & Pickpockets," Requesting to Enjoy the Same Privileges as Their "brethren" the "millocrats"'.[117] Charles Dickens referred to the journalistic swell mob in *Household Words*.[118] By the 1850s attempts were made to elevate the swell mobsman to the stage in a domestic drama of two acts, 'The swell mob's man, or, The housebreaker of White Chapel'. A license was requested for the Pavilion Theatre in Whitechapel Road in October 1852, but was turned down by the Lord Chamberlain's Office.[119] By the mid-nineteenth century, the swell mob was firmly entrenched in popular culture. However, by the 1860s the press had a new set of villains in its sights, and whilst the swell mobsman was an increasingly scarce visitor to the news sheets, a new folk devil appeared in the guise of 'the rough'.

Conclusion

In a seminal article of 1980, Jennifer Davis argued that the 'garotting panic' of 1862 was orchestrated by the press and by government actions in order 'to promote new measures for its control'.[120] According to Davis the result was a clear path to reform of the criminal law. Similarly, in the early nineteenth century it could be argued that anxieties about hustling foreshadowed the police reform of 1829, as demonstrated by Lord Sidmouth's expansion of the foot patrol and dismounted horse patrol in 1821. In the same year, an Act was passed 'for the more effectual Administration of the Office of the Justice of the Peace'. In the City the number of extra constables hired by wards had tripled by 1820 and continued to rise after this point.[121] Certainly, by the time of the 1822 Select Committee on Police, witnesses were remarking that the expansion of the Bow Street foot patrol had had a significant impact on the activities of pickpockets and street robbers. Moreover it recommended further expansion 'because robbery from the person is probably more frequent by day than at any other time'.[122] At the very least, these events shed light on the transformation of metropolitan policing in the years leading up to 1829 and provide a window into concerns about urban unrest, plebeian crowds and street crime. M. J. D. Roberts has examined the control of metropolitan public space in the late 1810s and early 1820s, noting the 'increased visibility of behaviour'. The coincidence of these events with the debate about vagrancy, leading up to the passage of the 1822 Vagrancy Act, clearly signals the increasing intolerance of street disorder in this period.[123] Arguably, violent street robbers, vagrants and plebeian demonstrators were all part of the same problem. The 1822 Act would harden the stop and search powers that would be used to sweep beggars from the streets. However, in 1819 and 1820 prosecutors, concerned about the apparent threat of street robbery, were increasingly flexible in their use of larceny from the person as a way of permanently hoovering up disorderly, criminal and perhaps potentially radical groups of youths.

This chapter has explored changing forms of criminal vocabulary by focusing closely on the hustler and the swell mob. As Shoemaker has demonstrated, print culture in the later eighteenth century reproduced the shifting cultural attitudes that indicated a growing intolerance for violence and radically changed perceptions of street robbery.[124] In the 1810s and 1820s this perception shifted again. The flood of pickpockets that came through the courts from the 1810s fundamentally shaped attitudes to robbery and danger on the streets. Consequently, the figure of the 'hustler' combined older fears and understandings of street robbery with a new form of public danger: being 'hustled and robbed with impunity' in the daytime or early evening, in the crowd, in the open, in public.[125] By the 1830s and 1840s, accounts of being hustled in a large crowd were less common and hustling had become a technique of the swell mob. However, concerns about robbery and interpersonal danger in the metropolis also echoed newer concerns about large groups of urban youth and the threatening presence of gangs of young men. Hence, a press report from November 1820 described a Saturday evening in town:

> a most impudent gang of thieves, between 30 and 40 in number paraded along Pentonville towards the Bell-gate, hustling, tripping up, and knocking down every person they met with, treating the women with rudeness, and tearing their pockets off their sides, robbing them of their shawls, scarfs ... and robbing the men of their watches, money, hats ....[126]

A similar account from *The Times* in March 1831 reported an attempted street robbery that took place during a City procession, 'The gang, who belonged to what is called the "Swell Mob," finding themselves thus foiled ... set up a general cry of "Serve him out;" "Knock his hat off?"'.[127] Underpinning these early-nineteenth-century constructions of the experience of robbery is the undeniable manifestation of territorial contest. Thus, in a period when concerns about young male offenders were rapidly growing, we see youths and young men committing crimes, parading and 'owning the street' and marking their territory in a way which would again be associated with troublesome and troubling youth by the later nineteenth century.[128]

5
'There goes Bill Sheen, the Murderer': Crime, Kinship and Community in East London, 1827–1852

In the early nineteenth century, despite the popularity of low-life narratives such as Pierce Egan's *Life in London* or the memoirs of the pickpocket and swindler James Hardy Vaux, the taste for more traditional forms of criminal biography had waned.[1] Nevertheless, late Regency and early Victorian readers' enthusiasm for deviance was far from dead; rather it had shifted from the life-narratives of robbers and thieves to bloody spectacle. As Rosalind Crone has demonstrated, the Victorians would absorb gruesome, graphic re-enactments of violence into their mainstream print culture.[2] However, whilst criminal biography may have been a moribund form, the lives of individual criminals continued to be documented in detail in early-nineteenth-century print culture as well as in the writings of reformers and other investigations into crime and poverty. Parliamentary Select Committees and inquiries into crime and policing proliferated in the early decades of the nineteenth century, with reformers, practitioners and politicians seeking to find common ground between local and state strategies to deal with what were perceived as the increasing social costs of urbanisation and migration.[3] As a result, a number of documents survive that specifically refer to individuals, public houses, police officers and crime events that can be corroborated in conjunction with court records from the Old Bailey and contemporary press reports.

One such individual was William Sheen, a repeat offender whose 'career' straddles the end of the Regency and the first decades of the Victorian era. This chapter will reconstruct Sheen's (adult) life history in order to demonstrate the circuitous relationship between criminal networks, policing strategies and print culture. A detailed reconstruction of Sheen's offending life illustrates a number of the key themes of this book. Firstly, print culture continues to be paramount, rendering criminal activity and criminal individuals more visible. Whilst 'criminal lives' lacked the currency they had in the previous century, the column inches allocated to individual criminals and the motivations and decision-making which shaped print culture remain a significant factor. Secondly, community and family networks are central to our understanding of the ways in which illegal and makeshift economies shifted and rubbed together in Sheen's life. Thirdly, the interactions between and within individual lives, overlapping networks and street-level law enforcement will again be traced here. But this chapter introduces other elements that in the nineteenth century would drive the 'underworld' narrative. Descriptions of the physical and spatial dimensions of the underworld would become increasingly vivid in early Victorian accounts of criminality. Prescriptions for control and management of crime focus on the relationship between slum and slum dweller in the creation of the underworld.

While the streets that made up 'Jack Ketch's warren', the boundary area between the City and Middlesex, continued to attract the outcast and the incomer, from the early nineteenth century another liminal space on the eastern border of the City would come to dominate developing narratives of crime.[4] Rosemary Lane, and the warren of streets around the Mint, had been linked to the criminal fraternity in the eighteenth century. During the nineteenth century, the areas adjacent to the City borders would become increasingly associated with cultures of poverty, crime, low lodging houses and prostitution.[5] The spatial map of Sheen's life traces a cluster of streets in which he and his family lived their lives: Rosemary Lane, Wentworth Street, Keate Street, Christopher's Court, White's Yard. The Lambeth Street Police Office sat at the centre of these streets (within a short walk of all of them) signifying its important relationship to the immediate community.[6] In particular, Wentworth Street (see Map 5.1), on the border of Spitalfields and Whitechapel, would gain a notorious reputation as a district for low lodging houses. Henry Mayhew would note by the 1850s, 'The worst places, both as regards filth and immorality, are in St. Giles and Wentworth Street, Whitechapel.'[7] Moreover, the Wentworth street lodging houses were identified by contemporaries as 'resorts of juvenile thieves and prostitutes', reflecting the increasing preoccupation with the problem of juvenile crime from the early nineteenth century.[8]

Despite being a serial and notorious offender, William Sheen would eventually slip into obscurity in the annals of crime. Nevertheless, he is an identifiable figure whose presence can be traced through a wide range of documents. However, Sheen's identification by contemporaries in such texts was due to the event for which he gained his initial infamy. In late May 1827, William Sheen ('The Younger') was tried at the

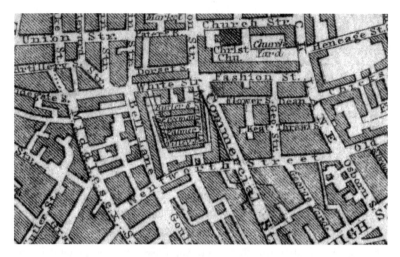

Map 5.1 'The areas adjacent to the City borders would become increasingly associated with cultures of poverty, crime, low lodging houses and prostitution... In particular, Wentworth Street, on the border of Spitalfields and Whitechapel, would gain a notorious reputation.' By Charles Knight for the Society for the Diffusion of Useful Knowledge c. 1852 (3.5 inches to the mile, detail). (Courtesy London Metropolitan Archives.)

Old Bailey for the murder of Charles William Beadle, his four-month-old child. Sheen's first trial at the Old Bailey established many of the characteristics that would later inform the reporting of his life: violence, kinship and community. The murder had apparently taken place on Thursday 10 May at his home in Christopher's Court, off Lambeth Street in Whitechapel. This incident can be initially read as a singular event. It becomes the start point in Sheen's story and would subsequently define him in the following decades. What is unclear is the extent to which the murder proved to be the spark which would propel Sheen and his extended family into crime or whether the family were already involved in criminal activity. Moreover, by defining Sheen and his family through their involvement in illegal activities or in associations with other offenders and/or police, we have to consider how unusual or unorthodox this family's experiences were. How far can the experiences of the Sheen family be understood as aspects of the myriad ways in which plebeian Londoners lived their lives and constructed their local and familial networks? Certainly, they lived in an area well known for disorder. Sheen and his wife Lydia lived close to the Irish community of Rosemary Lane. His father, also William, lived nearby in White's Yard. As the Lambeth Street police officer, Ebenezer Dalton testified, 'there are a great many Irish in

Whitechapel ... there are frequent disturbances amongst them'.[9] By the time of the murder Sheen was already 26.[10] If he had been involved in petty crime or illegalities these were likely to have been tried at petty sessions, which were not systematically reported at this period.[11] The crimes for which Sheen and his family were tried after the murder are not easily defined as survival or economic crimes. Charges of theft, burglary, fencing and brothel-keeping were accompanied by episodes of violence, often alcohol fuelled, which brought the family into contact with the police and the magistracy. Before we move on to considering the Sheen family network, the extraordinary events of 1827 require closer inspection.

The Murder

The 'Dreadful Murder in Whitechapel' and the trials that followed were widely reported both in the metropolis and beyond during the summer of 1827. Jeremiah Catnach quickly capitalised on the general horror expressed and published a broadside, 'A Horrible Murder, A Father Cutting his Child's Head off!', outlining the sordid details of the crime and including 'A Copy of Verses':

> The murderers name is William Sheen
> O horrible to write,
> The wicked wretch did often swear
> He'd take his infants life.
> On Thursday night he bade his wife
> To go to buy some tea,
> That he, the monster might complete
> The horrid tragedy.[12]

Charles William Beadle was the illegitimate son of William Sheen and his wife Lydia Beadle, whom he had married after the boy's birth.[13] The baby had been born to Lydia in Mr Willis's Poorhouse in Lombard Street and baptised in St George the Martyr, Southwark, on 31 January 1827.[14] At some point between the baby's birth and death, Lydia had moved to Christopher's Court where she would live with Sheen. The baby had been found at the lodgings, in the house of John and Sarah Pomeroy. Police officer Ebenezer Dalton described how he had found the body:

> on entering the room I saw the child's head on the table, and a quantity of blood – I searched and in the corner of the room was a bed, with the body of the child covered with a counterpane; there was a

great quantity of blood on the floor, as well as on the table; the head appeared as if it had been cut off with a sharp instrument.[15]

According to the evidence of Joseph Corderoy, who had been with Sheen at the King of Prussia public house in Blue Anchor Yard, Rosemary Lane, the accused had been drinking heavily most of the afternoon.[16] At 5.30, his wife came for him, 'he was in a very good humour; they went directly, and I went with them to their house'. This was described as a small upstairs room with a bed. Corderoy left at about 5.45, at which time, 'his boy was in her arms [his wife] alive and well'. At 7.30 Sarah Pomeroy was called to the room by Lydia, where she found the baby's body. She and the mother immediately went for assistance to Lambeth police office, bringing Dalton back with them.

At the trial, Sheen's father William gave evidence about the marriage and child, 'he had been married about five weeks – I suppose his wife had had the child about two or three months before ... I did not know the name of the child till after it was dead'. Describing Lydia as a 'bad character', Sheen senior seemed unconcerned about the death of his grandchild. He did supply more information about his son's movements. He had last seen him at eight o'clock in the evening. He had told his father that he had been fighting some Irishmen, one of whom he had stabbed, presumably to explain his appearance. Together they went to the house of Joseph Pugh in Carnaby market, off Oxford Street, in order to borrow some money and some clean clothes, and to get rid of a clasp knife which Sheen said he had used in his fight with the Irishmen. He then went 'on the run', travelling to Radnorshire, Wales (where he had relatives).[17] There seems to have been little doubt amongst the officers who attended the scene, Dalton and Robert Davis, that Sheen was guilty. A manhunt was raised; Davis followed Sheen's trail to Radnorshire, where he found the accused staying in a farm in Llanbadarn Fawr on the morning of the 17 May, 'I had made a complete search of that house, at three o'clock in the morning of that day, and did not find him; the prisoner said, when I went in, "O, Davis. Is that you? I shall go any where with you"'.[18] According to Davis, Sheen did not deny culpability for the murder. On the journey back from Radnorshire to London, Sheen was described as saying, 'Oh my poor mother, when she knows I am taken it will break her heart'.

The case went to trial on 31 May 1827, when it was noted that the victim, Charles William Beadle, had been born illegitimately, yet the indictment was drawn in the name of Charles William Sheen.[19] However, Sheen was charged by the Coroner's Inquisition for the 'Wilful Murder of Charles William Beadle'. Mr Clarkson (the court counsel for defence) contended that because of this confusion, a fresh indictment was called for:

> the deceased child having been born out of wedlock had, in law, no name, consequently, if it had not by reputation acquired the name stated either in the indictment or inquisition, the case could not be supported, and that the certificate produced was not sufficiently shown to have been that of the deceased.[20]

The court found Sheen 'not guilty' because of a legal technicality, he was ordered to be detained and a fresh indictment to be preferred. In between the trials, concern was expressed about the adjournment and the possible outcomes. *The Times* commented on the general anxiety that Sheen would 'escape the hands of justice'.[21] These worries were not unfounded. The next trial took place at a very crowded Old Bailey on 12 July.[22] The prosecution had worked hard to present the case against Sheen in such a way as to meet any possible legal objections, presenting 13 differently worded counts in the indictment.[23] At this point Sheen seems to have had no legal counsel (Mr Clarkson was described as being 'out of town'). However, he had clearly been advised between the previous trial and this one, since after the indictment was read he submitted the following written plea:

> That he has been before indicted, tried and acquitted, as well on that Indictment as on the Coroner's Inquest, at the last Session held in this place, for the murder of the same child as described in the present indictment; and that the same child was as well known by the name and description as contained in that Indictment and Inquest, as it is in the present Indictment.[24]

Sheen had presented a plea of *autrefois acquit* (previously acquitted) to the court. Despite being informally written and presented on 'a small piece of paper', the court was minded to give him the time to prepare a more formal plea.[25] The case was adjourned until the next day in order for the plea to be more formally presented and for a counsel to be found for Sheen (at least two of the bar members approached for the task excused themselves). The trial continued the following day with much of the time spent on establishing the identity of the victim. The jury eventually concluded, 'We find that the child was as well known by the name of Charles William Beadle, as any other name' and Sheen was discharged.[26] Naturally, this was not a popular verdict. The evidence pointed to Sheen's guilt and the police did not consider looking for anyone else. Moreover, this had been a ferocious murder. As the writer Emily Eden wrote to her friend, Miss Villiers, 'I am so disgusted with our foolish laws which could not hang, could not even punish, that William Sheen'.[27] The *Examiner* devoted its front page to an outraged, if satirical, commentary on the trial and its outcome. It noted, 'A BALL has been given in Rosemary Lane in Honour of the Law of England, on the occasion of the acquittal of Sheen, who lately cut his child's head off'.[28]

The Community

The extended Sheen family ran into trouble in their local community almost immediately and Sheen would be committed to the Clerkenwell House of Correction as a result of an incident that took place shortly after his discharge.[29] *Jackson's Oxford Journal* described how upon his release in July 1827 Sheen had 'collected a mob around the dwelling of his father, who had given a dance with music in celebration of his son's discharge'.[30] A neighbour, Mrs Roberts, took exception to this. Sheen threatened her, resulting in his being bound over to keep the peace, with a fine of £100 and two sureties for behaviour of £30.[31] It is likely that William could not afford to pay his fines and so was imprisoned. *The Times* described the collection of Sheen from his home to be taken to Clerkenwell, 'On the prisoner making an appearance, the most discordant yells were set up, and degrading epithets applied to him, to which he seemed to pay little attention'.[32] Upon his release from custody in January 1828, Sheen and his father visited a woman named Sarah Robinson at her fish stall and violently threatened her and attacked her stall.[33] Sheen senior was charged with threatening language and William Sheen was again bound over to keep the peace after telling the officer, Ebenezer Dalton, '"Well, if my father goes to Clerkenwell for her, I'll go to Newgate"; suggesting that he would inflict such serious injury on the complainant as would lead to his apprehension and committal to Newgate'.[34]

There had also been confrontations between Ann Sheen and her neighbours and the case had caused significant ill feeling in the local area. The *Examiner* reported, 'It appeared in evidence, that an opinion of Sheen's having a kind of patent for cutting off heads prevails among his neighbours, as they point to the house, and say, "Don't go in there, for if you do, *you will be sure to have your head cut off*"'.[35] In November 1827, Ann brought a prosecution of assault against three of her neighbours,

John Robins, Sarah Robins and Solomon Chambers.[36] They were acquitted by the Chair of the Middlesex Sessions, who found little evidence of assault. It is likely that Sarah Robinson, Mrs Roberts and Sarah Robins were the same person, suggesting the strain on the community that the murder had caused. Ann Sheen emerges as a significant figure at this point. Evidence in the courtroom refers to her having employed William's defence counsel. And whilst she admits that she was not actually struck, she was very clear about her rights 'not to be insulted by these people because of my son's unfortunate conduct'.[37] However, during the murder trial Ann herself had been charged at Lambeth Street for threatening her daughter-in-law (Lydia Sheen nee Beadle) if she gave evidence, 'if she persevered in her intentions to give evidence, she would have such a mob collected at the Old Bailey, on the day of the trial, as would "Serve her out properly", and never permit her to return home alive'. Ann Sheen was bound to keep the peace with her daughter-in-law for three months.[38]

The events during and after the murder trial reveal the developing tensions within the local community. The local reaction to the murder is understandable. Less palatable is the behaviour of the Sheen family, suggesting, at the very least, that violence was a not unfamiliar tool for them. Moreover, the case provides a snapshot of policing on the ground in the early nineteenth century; the local Lambeth Street officers, Dalton and Davis, were clearly familiar with the family. The extent to which this was due to an existing relationship prior to the murder is unclear. However, from the 1830s the Sheen family would increasingly be detected on the radar of the local police, both in the context of the apparent criminal enclave that was associated with the Wentworth Street area, but also as individuals, through their frequent appearances in the metropolitan courts.

The Notorious Sheens

To find out more about this particular family network we need to turn to the 1830s, when the family would develop their reputation as 'the notorious Sheens'.[39] References to William Sheen, his mother, Ann, and his brother, John, span two decades. There are also references to another brother, George, and to his father, William Sheen senior. Some of these cases refer to involvement in actual felonies, others to members of the family appearing as witnesses in trials. In the latter case there are marked similarities to the family network of Mary Harvey a century or so earlier; certainly Ann Sheen is directly accused of giving evidence in return for financial remuneration. By the mid-1830s there is clear evidence that William Sheen had an established criminal reputation, including the Society for the Suppression of Juvenile Prostitution bringing him to trial for brothel keeping. Throughout this period, the Sheen family had significant interactions with both the formal and more informal mechanisms of law enforcement.

Sheen's first traceable appearance in court after the events of 1827 (we know that during early 1828, at least, Sheen was bound over to keep the peace) was at the Old Bailey in 1830. He had been charged at Lambeth Street alongside Robert Lyall, William Stewart and Elizabeth Smith with having been concerned in a robbery in Islington. The men were eventually tried at the Old Bailey with receiving stolen goods; Sheen had been driving the cart that was waiting to receive the goods. James Lee, a Lambeth Street officer, took Sheen from his home in Wentworth Street, Whitechapel, where he lived with his father (the Sheens had moved from the Rosemary Lane area over to Wentworth Street some time between 1828 and 1830).[40] Sheen did not deny that he had been hired to transport some goods in a cart and as this seems to have been his only involvement he was acquitted.[41] Whilst on remand in Clerkenwell, Sheen was noted to be the only prisoner to associate with a baker named John Smith, who had murdered a G-Division policeman, John Long, in August of that year.[42] After his acquittal, in the autumn of 1830, it did not take long for Sheen to get in trouble again. In December 1831 he appeared in front of the Lambeth magistrates charged with drunkenness. Being carried home by a friend, Jeremiah Callahan, Sheen was so intoxicated that witnesses thought that Callahan was 'burking' Sheen's body.[43]

Various members of the Sheen family would also give evidence in criminal trials in this period. Ann Sheen was prominent as a witness, giving evidence in 1831 and at four trials during 1832. In September 1831, Ann gave evidence at the trial of George Bagley, George Forecast and Frances Bagley, who were charged with coining.[44] The accused had been caught with the moulds and other equipment in Dean's Yard, just off Wentworth Street, in a house belonging to William Sheen. They had been taken into custody not by officers of the law, but by William Brummitt, a potter from Lambeth, south London, and Robert Lawrence. It is likely that Brummitt and Lawrence were paid by a parish constable named Gollocker to 'entrap' the accused with the connivance of the landlady, Ann Sheen; although this is denied in court. Frances Bagley defended herself by attacking Ann Sheen's reputation, and accusing her of keeping four brothels. In a final defence, Frances protested, 'Several girls have robbed men in Sheen's house – she is the mother of William Sheen, who cut his child's head off; she is inveterate against us, and said, in the street, she would hang any one she could for money'.[45] The accused were sentenced to death.[46]

The following year members of the Sheen family appeared to give evidence in a further six trials at the Old Bailey. William's daughter Ann gave evidence in the trial of a 13-year-old named Benjamin Stanton in July 1832. Stanton had apparently gone to Sheen's to fence his stolen goods, 'My mother is dead, and my father has three of us to keep; these people buy things, and I went there to sell it'.[47] A local constable, William Law, had seen Stanton go into the Sheen house in Wentworth Street, stating that Sheen was asleep when he went to inquire. Ann said that her father had been out all night on a job, and that they knew nothing of the prisoner. Stanton was found guilty and sentenced to seven years transportation.[48] Given Sheen's criminal record and the local knowledge of the Sheen family's criminality, there was little attempt to question Ann Sheen (although the record is limited, so Ann may have been probed and William may been called in evidence). In the September sessions, William and his mother Ann (senior) would give evidence in two separate trials for theft. Ann gave evidence in the trial of Richard Philip, Thomas Manning and Thomas Rands, who had been accused of entering the shop of one of her neighbours, Leonard Wass.[49] The following month, Ann Sheen (senior) again gave evidence at the Old Bailey. This trial involved an assault upon a Lambeth Street officer named Robert Davis, who was allegedly attacked by James Sutton, Henry Kemp, Thomas Jones and Elizabeth Lawson in the early hours of Sunday 23 September in George Street, off Wentworth Street.[50] According to his evidence, Davis had intervened to break up a fight in the street between two women. Upon apprehending Elizabeth Lawson he was attacked by the three male prisoners, at which point a number of other people came out of a house to rescue her. In this case, Ann Sheen gave detailed evidence for the prosecution. She identified Kemp, Jones and Sutton, who were found guilty of wounding and sentenced to death.[51]

However, the detailed petition shows that the events were not quite as straightforward as this.[52] Sutton's defence was that Davis was mistreating Elizabeth Lawson (whom Sutton lived with), and so he had intervened to help her. According to the petition, he had seen Davis strike Lawson on her back with his truncheon. When Sutton intervened, Davis struck him on the left shoulder and hit him on the head. Sutton hit him back, 'I then crossed the street, he got up and came after me he caught me by the shirts of my coat and tore it right up the back to the collar which of course made me still worse'. Thus, whilst Sutton did not deny beating Davis, he claimed to have been provoked. Moreover, he was particularly concerned about the evidence of Ann Sheen, of whom he stated, 'Sheen is a notorious bad character and all her family it is well known she keeps a Brothel which is resorted to by the lowest of the law and entices young girls and Boys from their Parents to make a property of them'. Sutton was scathing about Ann Sheen's evidence that stated that he had hit Davis on the head with an iron bar repeatedly, since Davis had sustained no severe head injury. Finally he begged that Ann Sheen's character be inquired into. Initially the petition seems to have been unsuccessful. However, shortly after it was considered and a pardon refused, a flurry of correspondence seems to have re-ignited the inquiry into the case.[53]

First a letter (no date) addressed to the Home Secretary, Viscount Melbourne, was received from the police officer concerned, Robert Davis, pleading that Sutton's life be spared, as 'Although nothing could justify his conduct, yet, I am informed, there are some mitigating circumstances'. Perhaps the H Division officers were having some misgivings about their reliance on Mrs Sheen's information on the background of Sutton and his companions, despite what seems to have been common knowledge about her character. She had provided an account of the relationships and criminal pasts of a number of the protagonists involved who lived in and around the Wentworth Street area. On 6 December the case escalated when Commissioner Colonel Rowan wrote to Whitehall to plead on Sutton's behalf, 'the Commissioners are assured that they speak the feelings of every man in the Metropolitan Police Establishment in venturing to request that the Petition of Police Constable Robert Davis may be considered by Viscount Melbourne as the Petition of the whole body'. Finally, on 8 December, the City of London Sheriff Richard Peek wrote to support the petition. Peek gave his opinion that because of the mitigating circumstances and his (Sutton) having been acquitted by the jury of '*any intention* to murder' an execution would be extremely unpopular and claimed that he faced an 'official difficulty', since he could not both attend the execution and preside at the City elections, which apparently took place in the same hour.[54] This seems to have persuaded the Home Secretary, with the outcome that Sutton had his sentence reduced to transportation for life.[55] This case illustrates the troubling links between the Sheens and the local Lambeth police. The evidence suggests that Ann Sheen was not only known to the police but had a co-operative relationship with them. What we cannot know is whether Ann was paid to give evidence or whether there was some sort of negotiation between Ann and the H division constables.

By September 1834, William Sheen was back at the Old Bailey giving evidence at the trial of Elizabeth Harwood for picking the pocket of John Stafford in what was clearly one of the Sheens' disorderly houses (according to William, his mother was the landlady). Harwood claimed to have gone upstairs with the man, drank and presumably had sexual intercourse, since she said:

> the prosecutor then laid the money on the ledge, and it fell down, and he asked me to pick it up, and pay the reckoning – I said it was paid and he laid down on his back – I went and told Mrs Sheen the man was asleep, and I had his money – she said, "You can leave the house, but do not take the money" – I said, "No; I will not leave it, but in his presence" – she then wanted to take the money by force. [56]

Harwood's defence was that the Sheens had turned her over to the police only when she would not give them the money. Harwood was found guilty, and transported for seven years. The relationship between witnesses and the accused in Harwood's trial bore similarities with the trials of Benjamin Stanton and John May, both in 1832, where it seems probable that there was some business disagreement between the Sheens and the accused; who they then turned over to the police and/or gave evidence against.[57]

Inference of a corrupt relationship between the Sheen family and the local Lambeth police during these years can only be speculative. Nevertheless, the public notoriety of this family (and certainly the visibility of 'Sheen the infanticide') and their ability to stay active in Wentworth Street despite considerable interaction with the criminal justice system is significant. It suggests that in these early years of the Metropolitan Police Force's development there were still continuities with the problems of the past and the willingness to use what were effectively informers. These more 'traditional' relationships between law enforcers and informers can be illustrated by Ann Sheen's involvement in the Bagley and Forecast trial. The questionable presence of the 'constable' Gollocker at the Bagley and Forecast trial casts further doubt on Ann Sheen's testimony and arguably provides further evidence for complicity between the Sheen family and the Lambeth street officers. Thus, Ann Sheen gave evidence in at least two cases involving local officers and their associates where there was an implicit suggestion of corruption.

The incidence of corruption was a sensitive topic for the new police. In 1816, the controversial case of the corrupt Bow Street officer George Vaughan had highlighted the inherent tensions in policing.[58] Concerns had circulated in this period around the prevalence of unlicensed public houses, more prosaically known as 'flash houses', and the extent to which police knowledge and familiarity with such institutions was a temptation to corruption. For the police, however, this 'knowledge' was a necessary part of effective policing. According to David Cox, accusations of corruption continued to circulate in the early nineteenth century. However, these tended to be directed at the system more generally, rather than individuals. Other corruption cases did occur. For example, another Bow Street officer, Daniel Bishop, was accused of complicity with thieves in the 1820s.[59] In 1855, in two separate incidents, one police constable, Jesse 'Juicy Lips' Jeaps, was dismissed due to his close association with thieves; another, Charles King, was accused of complicity with thieves, prosecuted and transported for 14 years for larceny from the person.[60] Certainly, concerns about over-familiarity with their home divisions remained after the 1829 Act, and attempts were made to reduce opportunities for corruption.[61] The likely willingness of the Lambeth police to use members of the Sheen family as witnesses reveals glimpses of the negotiation and interaction between police and their local communities in a way that is simply not recoverable on any larger scale. There was no legal impediment to using the Sheens as witnesses. Despite their many appearances in courtrooms of the metropolis they had not been found guilty of any felonies; William had been acquitted of the crimes that he had been accused of. Nevertheless, both William and Ann had been bound over to keep the peace on previous occasions and would have been very familiar faces with the magistrates at Lambeth Street.

Juvenile Offenders

During 1834 Sheen continued to be a familiar face at the police office, appearing twice for incidents of violence and drunken disorder. In late November he had been charged with threatening to kill his father. The *Morning Chronicle* wearily noted in its Police Intelligence column, 'SHEEN AGAIN'.[62] In *The Times*, it was reported that Sheen junior had threatened to bury a knife in his father's gut until his mother had rushed into the house and knocked the knife out his hand. According to Sheen junior, his father had recently taken the benefit of the Insolvent Debtors Act in order to get possession of his (Sheen junior) house, 'he had allowed his father 30s-a-week while in his difficulties, and that now he wanted to turn him out of a house, every thing in which belonged to him'. The magistrate, Mr Walker dismissed the case, stating that father and son were 'quite as bad as the other', dividing the expenses between them, and warning Sheen junior in regards to his future conduct.[63] By February 1835, a possible reference to Sheen appears in the trial of Mary Smith for a burglary in Little George Street in Bethnal Green. The son of Smith's victim claimed to have witnessed an exchange between the accused and a visitor whilst at the police office:

> I heard William Sheen come to her, and he called her Eliza – she asked who it was – he said, 'It is *Bill*' – and he said, 'Eliza, I was surprised to hear you were taken, but never mind, keep your spirits up – when are you sent down for?' – she said, 'I am sent down for Wednesday or Tuesday, I am not certain which' – he said, 'Well, Eliza, do not write to us, whatever you do, or you will *do us all*' – she said, 'Very well' – she called another by name, who was with Sheen, and said, 'Take this money', and some money was shoved under the door – Sheen is a grown-up person – I understand she used to lodge with him.[64]

The east London setting and the reference to this Sheen providing lodgings allow us a glimpse into the life of a man in a pivotal position in local networks of criminal confederacy. Indeed, there is other evidence that Sheen's network extended outside the mean streets of Whitechapel and Spitalfields. In August 1837, the *Standard* would satirically comment: 'Whoever knows anything of Mile-end and Bethnal-Green must be aware of the cruel injustice of not allowing these districts to engross the representation of the metropolitan county. The latest public men that these districts have offered to the notices of the country are ... Mr William Sheen, of Mile-end, who has exhibited remarkably for police reports and Old Bailey reports, and those victims to their zeal for the improvement of anatomical science, Messers, Bishop and Williams, of Bethnal Green'.[65]

The *Standard* may well have been reflecting on events during the previous couple of years, which further support these fragile glimpses of Sheen as a 'career' criminal. In September of 1835, Sheen was again in front of the Lambeth Street magistrates accused of robbing a young man called Robert Taylor who had lodged at Sheen's in Wentworth Street and had been shocked at the numbers of silk handkerchiefs brought in by juvenile thieves. Apparently, on trying to leave, he had been threatened by Sheen and emptied of his pockets.[66] *The Times* described Taylor as a bit of an oddity, a Methodist preacher who was allegedly involved in various schemes such as 'procuring recruits for the Queen of Spain'.[67] According to the account, Sheen could hardly 'contain his feelings' during this testimony and argued that Taylor had owed him money for his lodgings. The magistrate decided that the victim and the accused were cut from the same cloth and dismissed the charge; Sheen, 'on leaving the bar, said it useless for him to make any pretensions to character, but bad as he was the complainant with all his preaching and Methodism was fifty times worse'.[68] The accusations from Taylor that Sheen was effectively 'running' juvenile thieves can be confirmed by evidence given in a series of contemporary interviews with juvenile offenders, taken by the investigator William Augustus Miles on the *Euryalus* prison hulk.[69] Sheen appears in these accounts referred to as a receiver of stolen goods and working with his father. For example, 18-year-old Mary Mause had sold goods to Sheen; another youth, named Hewitt, was much more explicit: 'Sheen always teaching boys – (this is the one who cut the child's head off) his father lives about three doors off – also buys and dosses – walks about & gets boys to buzz him. Sometimes they do it & flare it … & he sends for gin & treats them'.[70]

Miles referred to the incident between Sheen and Taylor in his book, *Poverty, Mendicity and Crime* (1839), which was largely based on the evidence collected for the Constabulary Commission. It is likely that Miles based his account of the incident on press reports, although he did claim to have questioned Whitechapel thieves about Sheen, 'and they all agree he is a thorough villain'.[71] Moreover, the wider culture of violence in which the Sheen family seemed to operate continued to frame their activities. So, when William Sheen senior appeared at Hicks Hall courtroom in Clerkenwell in July 1836 after threatening to 'rip up the bowels of Mary Moore and her man', it was the notoriety of the family that led to the reporting of a relatively minor case.[72] The counsel, Mr Prendergast, pointed out that this was, 'a name well known to that Court, and in all probability by the country generally'.[73] The following month, Sheen junior again appeared at Lambeth Street in a case involving the theft of a blanket from his lodging house. According to the accused, an Irish labourer named William Perry, his wife had gone to visit Sheen's wife, who was imprisoned in Clerkenwell, in order to get a sworn statement that there had not been a blanket on the bed. Sheen tried to deny that he had a wife but then admitted that the woman in prison was his 'woman', who had been committed to prison for a month after threatening a policeman.[74]

During 1837, Sheen's ability to operate relatively unimpeded came to an end. However, it would not be the local Lambeth police office that pushed for a prosecution but a voluntary organisation, The London Society for the Protection of Young Females and the Prevention of Juvenile Prostitution. The organisation had been founded in 1835 in alliance with the London City Mission, with brothel suppression as a specific objective.[75] In March 1837, *The Times* had reported on the abduction of Maria Eagan, a 14-year-old girl from Waterloo Court in Stepney who had been discovered at one of Sheen's Wentworth Street brothels (see Map 5.1). Maria claimed that she had been walking along Commercial Road when an older girl had started talking to her, 'They walked together for some distance, and at length passed up Brick-lane and turned into Wentworth-street. They entered the house No. 77, and she was then immediately taken hold of by another girl, and inmate of the house, and forced into a room, which was instantly locked'. This then led to her being subjected to sexual encounters. She was rescued by her uncle, after which the family 'applied to the London Society for the Prevention of Juvenile Prostitution for advice and protection'.[76] From this point the society worked with local members and police in order to suppress Sheen's brothels. On or around 2 June, a party of H division (Lambeth Street) officers entered Sheen's house in the early hours of the morning.[77] They found nine females and ten males 'lying indiscriminately and three-four, and five in a bed', who they took into custody. The girls were questioned by the magistrate, and evidence was received from H division officers, including Officer Lea (also spelt Lee) who stated that, 'a number of juvenile thieves who infested many of the streets of the metropolis were harboured at the house of Sheen, and that the produce of their plunder passed through his hands'.[78] The next day a warrant was drawn against Sheen and by 10 June he was in custody in New Prison, Clerkenwell. From here he wrote a letter to the Lambeth Street magistrates claiming that he was a reformed character and begging to be allowed to 'get my living in a kindly upright way'.[79] He apologised for having followed such an 'abominable mode of living', but went on to claim 'for, bad as I am, my character has been greatly misrepresented'. He proceeded to describe his 'respectable' relations in Radnorshire who 'would be glad to receive me with open arms', so he could 'seek a refuge among my friends in the country, and endeavour to live a different life for the future'. He seems to have convinced the prison chaplain, David Ruell, who added a postscript supporting the plan.[80]

The society, and presumably the Lambeth Street magistrates, were unimpressed and he stayed in Clerkenwell until his trial at the next Middlesex sessions. According to the evidence at the trial, Sheen's house had been host to as many as 20 boys and ten young girls under the age of 16, 'the boys were encouraged in picking pockets, and the wretched girls were made victims of the greatest depravity'. At one point Sheen interrupted, 'This is too bad; I never refused admission to the police by day or by night to search for any one they might think proper'.[81] The society produced evidence from 16-year-old Ellen McCrawley, a girl under their protection who provided further damning evidence, and Sheen was sentenced to 18 months imprisonment with hard labour.[82] Richard Gregory, the treasurer of Spitalfields parish and a member of the society, briefed the Police Select Committee, giving evidence on 15 June 1837. Gregory, who had been active in the parish affairs of Christchurch and had control of the Watch, described the raid on Sheen's houses: 'we took 18 boys and girls out of those houses, some of them very young, three weeks ago'.[83]

As the earlier case study of Mary Harvey and her associates demonstrated, co-operation between residents, parish officials and reforming societies could be utilised to control local vice, and in this case the local parish worked directly with the society in order to bring Sheen to justice. The magistrate, Mr Prendergast, pointed out at the sessions that the society had 'most properly lent its aid to get rid of a nuisance of the most violent description'.[84] The role of the local police is more ambiguous; certainly they were called upon to break open Sheen's brothels, but to what extent had it been the failure of the local police to deal with Sheen that had led to local residents working with the society? The family's dominance of the local territory meant that the police seem to have been stymied in their ability to control the Sheens. The policing of such communities in this period was likely to have been based on careful negotiations of space and territory. The evidence suggests that the Sheen family were aware of the law and were prepared to use the court system to protect their interests. Moreover, the earlier associations between the Sheen family and the police, and the fact that the Sheens were local property owners (however unsavoury), may also have influenced the police. A fuller account of Sheen's activities was published in 1839 by a doctor and member of the Royal College of Physicians, named Michael Ryan.[85] In *Prostitution in London*, he referred to the suppression of Sheen's houses in Wentworth Street, describing Sheen as a trafficker of juvenile prostitutes.[86] This would certainly explain the proactive strategies taken by the society, 'Parents who had lost their children, were constantly applying to the Police to search these dens of infamy, and in some instances the lost children were there discovered, associated with male and female juvenile thieves'.[87] The only account we have to support this is that of Maria Eagan. However, there is other evidence that homeless children and those children with difficult family situations, gravitated to lodging houses such as Sheen's.[88]

A year later Sheen was still in Clerkenwell, from where he was petitioning the Home Secretary for lighter duties and extra allowances due to his having suffered a 'Rupture'.[89] Whilst he was released from prison some time early in 1839, other members of the Sheen family continued to play an active role in the justice system. By April 1839, William's brother George had joined his mother Ann in bearing witness at the Old Bailey in a trial known as the Gold Dust Robbery. A father and son, Ellis and Lewin Casper (a clerk to a shipping company), had attempted to steal £4,600 worth of gold dust that had been landed at Falmouth from Brazil. The robbery failed and the associated trials and press uncovered an extensive group of associates and family members who were charged in relation to the attempted robbery. George and Ann's role in this seems peripheral. Like William, George drove a 'van and spring cart' that was hired out from Wentworth Street by Ann Sheen.[90] Ostensibly, George gave evidence because he had been employed to move some goods on behalf of a Mrs Levy, the sister of Henry Moss, who had been involved in the robbery but had turned evidence on the Caspers.[91] A number of newspapers reported that George was the brother to 'the notorious Bill Sheen'.[92] In *The Times*, it was noted that when an officer had visited Wentworth Street to make enquiries related to the case, 'William Sheen, who had not long been released from the House of Correction ... was present and on the officer questioning his brother, he (Sheen) cautioned him to be very particular as to what answers he gave, as he would have to repeat them elsewhere'.[93]

Ann Sheen was back in court within a year, this time as the accused; in reporting her charge at Worship Street, the *Morning Chronicle* described the Sheen family as 'infamously notorious'.[94] She was indicted for receiving stolen goods from 16-year-old John Matthew Carter. John had stolen various articles and taken them to Rose Lane, where he sold them to 'William Sheen, who used to live in Wentworth Street'.[95] The boy had then stayed at the Sheens, paying with the money from the goods he had sold (including a squirrel tippet and a velvet waistcoat), 'I had two nights' lodging and food at Mrs Sheen's for them'. John had gone back to his family, who had taken up the matter with the local police at Spitalfields. They had questioned Mrs Sheen who denied knowing about any of the stolen goods. The constable, George Trew, decided to take matters into his own hands and search the house, at which point Ann Sheen tried to escape. Trew found her hidden in a closet. According to *The Times*, the search had produced not only the goods in question, which had apparently been bought by the Sheens in good faith, but also, 'he found 18 silk handkerchiefs, marked with different persons' names, a large number of silver spoons, watches, and other property'.[96] Ann was found guilty and sentenced to 14 years transportation with a recommendation from the Recorder that she served her sentence, 'which was not the usual custom with persons of her advanced age' (she was 59 by this point). This recommendation was not acted upon, and in June 1841, when the census was taken, she was recorded as being resident in Millbank Penitentiary.[97]

Violence

The following year would not be a good one for William Sheen. It is unclear when Ann Sheen was released from Millbank but certainly her time in prison had taken its toll on her health. According to a report from the Prison Discipline Society published in *The Times* on the 12 October 1842, Ann's health had been failing 'Owing, it is said, to the prison discipline'.[98] She was released in late September 1842 and died at William's house. The report clarified some of the questions about Ann's earlier sentence, noting that she had been transferred to Millbank, 'being considered too old to be sent "over the water"'. It also stated that Mrs Sheen's considerable property, which consisted of bank stock and houses, had been signed over to her 'favourite son, "Bill", so as to secure it from the grasp of the sheriff in the event of conviction'.[99] A series of reports from this period suggest that Sheen was becoming increasing unstable. In September 1842 he was charged at Worship Street police office with assaulting a female.[100] The case was dropped for lack of evidence. The melodrama continued in October when Sheen's drunken disorder during the funeral of his mother was reported in the *Examiner* and the *Morning Chronicle*.[101] Ann's funeral procession had taken her body to a private burial ground in Church Lane, Whitechapel that was owned by a member of the extended Sheen family, and was known as 'Sheen's Burial Ground'.[102] Conrad Bulugh (also spelt Buhler and Beuhler), the landlord of the City of Norwich public house and the executor of Ann's will, described how Sheen had conducted himself, 'more like a madman than anything else, and his manner in the burial ground was excessively violent', thumping the coffin, and giving his wife a black eye when she tried to restrain him. Another witness, Samuel Taylor, stated that Sheen had been shouting throughout the procession, despite being a chief mourner. Sheen complained vocally that his mother had been falsely accused and 'murdered', presumably as a result of her ill health from her incarceration in Millbank. Other witnesses described Sheen drunkenly exclaiming that 'he was Bill Sheen, wot murdered his child'. Events deteriorated when the family returned home for the reading of the will and Sheen found that his mother's property had been left to his two younger brothers. He destroyed the will then threatened Taylor with a knife. He was finally taken into custody exclaiming, 'I'm Bill Sheen, the murderer, but Clarkson got me out of it, in spite of all the b— laws in the country'. Not surprisingly at the hearing that followed Sheen had no recollection of his behaviour and the magistrate bound him over.[103]

Ann Sheen's will, which survives, confirms that the executor was her friend Conrad Buhler and that the estate was left to her son John and his family.[104] In 1845, a drink-fuelled Sheen vented his spleen on Buhler, assaulting him and threatening his life with a penknife in his pub, the City of Norwich. He was bailed to keep the peace, and the warrant officer, Rowland, noted that 'when sober (Sheen) was a very quiet and inoffensive man, but he was strongly addicted to habits of intemperance, and when he was intoxicated he was violent and ungovernable'. He also paid a considerable fine of £50, based on his income as the owner of four houses that earned him the rental of £70 per year.[105] He managed to keep the peace for the next two years, although in early 1847 he did take one of his servants, Mary Ryley, to court for theft; perhaps unsurprisingly she was found not guilty.[106]

A few months later his drinking and violence would erupt again, the victim his long-suffering common-law wife, Mary Anne Sullivan. In July 1847 William was charged at Worship Street, at which point it was found that Mary Anne was not in court, and indeed upon leaving the London (Whitechapel) hospital she had declined to appear against the prisoner.[107] The magistrate demanded her attendance and she came to court to tell her story. Mary Anne had lived with William as his common-law wife for 18 years. During this time, according to her testimony, she had been subjected to violence from Sheen and had been in and out of hospitals.[108] On the day in question, they had attended the christening of one of Sheen's brother's children. An argument had brewed on the way home to Keate Street (where they had been living since at least 1841, see Map 5.1), and he had attacked her about the head with a clasp knife, and then kicked and beaten her insensible.[109] Both Sullivan and Sheen had been drinking heavily. Sheen was indicted for assault with intent to murder and the case was adjourned to the next sessions. The trial took place at the Old Bailey in August, with the result that Sheen was found guilty of an aggravated assault and confined for 12 months.[110] In *The Times* report on the trial it was noted that since the murder of his child 20 years previously 'he appears to have pursued a completely reckless career, and he has been repeatedly in custody upon charges of violence and outrage, but has hitherto escaped without any material punishment'.[111]

At this point Sheen all but disappeared from the criminal record. In 1851 his death was registered in the last quarter of the year, on or around 19 December, and was reported in various newspapers. For example, the *Era*, reported: 'THE END OF SHEEN, the INFANTICIDE'.[112] Reports were also printed in the *Examiner*, the *Hampshire Telegraph and Sussex Chronicle*, the *Manchester Times*, the *Preston Guardian*, the *Northern Star* and so on.[113] Whilst to some extent an early form of syndication supplied the news to these provincial papers, it seems likely that Sheen's notoriety had managed to spread beyond the metropolis. Most of the papers recalled details of the 1827 case. Most commented on his notoriety, 'The life so spared, however, has since been a most miserable one'.[114]

The Welsh Fagin?

A final issue remains to be considered: the possibly that some of the fragments of Sheen's life may have stirred the literary imagination of one of his metropolitan contemporaries. Thus, whilst a number of authorities have linked Charles Dickens's characters and descriptions in *Oliver Twist* to the events of Ikey Solomon's life, in later life the author reflected that in Fagin's physical description he had drawn on stereotype, 'it unfortunately was true of the time to which that story refers, that that class of criminal almost invariably *was* a Jew'.[115] The similarities between Solomon and Dickens's character are superficial. However, it is unlikely that Dickens would have been unaware of William Sheen 'the younger'. In the years between 1825 and 1829, when William Sheen was making his name in the dock of the Old Bailey, the young Charles Dickens was shaping his interest in current affairs and the criminal justice system; working for a London paper called the *British Press*, providing what was called 'penny-a-line stuff', notices of accidents, fires and police reports. He was also freelance reporting at Doctors' Commons and clerking for two lawyers.[116] From 1831, a period in which the 'notorious Sheens' would regularly appear in the London press, Charles Dickens was expanding his journalism into the realm of parliamentary reporting, writing first for the *Mirror of Parliament* and then the *True Sun* from March 1832, and finally moving to the *Morning Chronicle* in 1834.[117] Whilst it was at the *Morning Chronicle* that Dickens's literary work started to be recognised, for much of the period up until autumn 1836, when he resigned as a reporter, his parliamentary writing continued.[118] It was during this same period that the reporting of William Sheen expanded beyond the remit of the press and into the parliamentary arena. Dickens was still writing for the *Morning Chronicle* in November 1835, when one wit commented:

> If SHEEN had set up an Infant School, we question whether any parents would have put their off-spring under his hands, however sincerely he may have convinced himself that, all things considered, the sentiment of society, the prejudices of the world, the set of public opinion – it was better to leave children's heads on their shoulders, even when they cried or refused to do what they were bid.[119]

By autumn 1836 Dickens may have been planning *Oliver Twist*, although, according to Burton Wheeler, the first chapters were not completed before January 1837, and the initial *Parish Boy's Progress* was started as a short serial in *Bentley's Miscellany* in February 1837.[120] Fagin and his Field Lane 'nursery of crime' were introduced in the May instalment. Todd Endleman has shown that the association between fencing and Jewishness dates mainly from the later eighteenth century, increasing in the 1810s and 1820s, when, he argues, convictions of Jews at the Old Bailey skyrocketed.[121] This seems to have been based on the proximity of the metropolitan Jewish community to the second-hand trade and dealing, particularly in places like Petticoat Lane and Rag Fair. Sheen was Welsh, probably having lived in London since his late teens. Could Dickens have thought a Jewish Fagin more apposite than a Welsh Fagin? Sheen did not live in Field Lane, which had a notorious reputation for criminality and would have been well known to Dickens. He may have read Thomas Carlyle's *Sartor Resartus*, serialised between 1833 and 1834, with its lines describing, 'Field Lane, with its long fluttering rows of yellow handkerchiefs'. Sheen did live in Whitechapel, the location to which young Oliver would be conveyed after being recaptured by Sikes and Nancy. Indeed, the fictional Sikes lived nearby in Bethnal Green. In June 1837, after introducing Fagin and the Artful Dodger, Dickens broke from writing, in part as a result of the death of his sister-in-law, Mary Hogarth. In July 1837, he introduced Nancy, the young prostitute, as she accuses Fagin in a later chapter, 'I thieved for you when I was a child not half as old as this!'[122] In shifting his focus to the story of Nancy, had Dickens been influenced by events earlier in the year, when *The Times* had reported on the abduction of Maria Eagan from Sheen's Wentworth Street brothel? The raids on Sheen's house and his prosecution at Middlesex Quarter Sessions had taken place that June.

Sheen's career as a 'public' criminal was undoubtedly known and written about in the spheres which Dickens moved: parliament, journalism, criminal justice and the philanthropic sector. By the early 1840s, Dickens would work closely with the London City Mission in his support for the Field Lane Ragged School, which the Mission had established in 1835. And later, in 1851 (Sheen died in December of this year), Dickens would write directly about the Wentworth Street lodging houses. In 'On Duty with Inspector Field', Deputies Green and Black lead an expedition to 'unveil the mysteries of Wentworth Street', and to the house of one 'Bark' lodging-house keeper and receiver of stolen goods, 'Bark's kitchen is crammed full of thieves, holding a CONVERSAZIONE there by lamp-light. It is by far the most dangerous assembly we have seen yet'.[123] Ultimately we can only ever speculate about the extent to which composite elements of Sheen's life were a contemporary source for Dickens characterisation of Fagin and the bully Sikes. However, a telling reference is found in the *Morning Chronicle* in September 1842. Sheen had appeared at Worship Street court to answer a charge from a woman called Ann Raven. Raven, described as 'an "unfortunate" girl', claimed to have been assaulted on Sheen's orders. The evidence was weak and Sheen was discharged, but a moment described in the press account provides a chilling echo of Dickens's characters. Raven described being beaten by two women, one of whom cohabited with Sheen, 'the prisoner encouraged their violence by clapping his hands, and calling out, "Seize her, my bull dogs – go it again," with similar exclamations'.[124]

Conclusion

This chapter has traced fragments of a criminal life. Here I have argued that the detailed study of the life of one offender and his associates enables us to reconstruct the criminal history of a family and the community within which it lived, however antagonistically, from below. The task of recovering plebeian histories is always fraught. Lives are essentially and necessarily assembled through sources produced by governments, criminal justice systems and the agents of historical media. Nevertheless, the press columns of early-Victorian print culture provide surprisingly detailed scenes and vignettes: from the street, the police office and the courtroom. Whilst they remain a mediated source, press narratives can be multi-layered enabling us to trace a form of life history through the series of events in Sheen and his family's life. Layering the press with reports from the Old Bailey and other printed and manuscript materials can, I would argue, provide a reasonably reliable account of the family's interactions with the criminal justice system. The narrative allows us a snapshot into how communities dealt with their offending members. The reaction to the Sheen family, the violence and confrontations, suggest a community whose norms the Sheens had offended against. Understandably, reactions to the murder of 1827 were sharp. In the years that followed, the tensions in the community can be traced. Nevertheless, this was a community in which the Sheens were essentially embedded. They owned property, and family members were spatially tied to the streets that radiated out of Whitechapel: Wentworth Street, Keate Street, Rosemary Lane. In this chapter we have also seen the interactions between the police and their community. Despite the passage of the 1829 Act, in the Lambeth Street office at least, there were clear continuities with the past. Police officers had local knowledge, and may have been inclined to use the Sheen family's willing familiarity with the courtroom despite their poor reputation. Indeed, in 1827 the knowledge of local officers like Dalton and Davis would be crucial to finding Sheen and bringing him back to justice.

Overlapping networks can again be traced. Networks of police officers and former constables overlap with the communities in which they worked and attempted to enforce the law. Moreover, law enforcement networks overlapped with criminal networks; hence, the police and the policed occupied cultures and communities that were far from distinct. Contemporaries would increasingly view the physical and spatial lodging house cultures of Wentworth Street and its environs as the 'underworld', and the Sheen family as a pivot in the nefarious activities with which the area would be associated. Nevertheless, it was, at least in part, the newspaper coverage of the murder and subsequent events in Sheen's life, which would make him a visible 'public' figure. Moreover, Sheen would collude with his public self in the monstrous figure of 'Sheen – the Infanticide'. Thus, in 1842, after being accused of assault, a complaining Sheen told the Worship Street magistrate:

> I declare solemnly that I was not in the house at the time the row took place; but that woman is always casting in my teeth the trouble I got into long ago about the child. Your policemen can all tell you that there's not a more peaceable man alive than I am, if they will only let me alone; but wherever I appear, they call out, 'There goes the murderer!' and I have not had a moment's peace or rest since the hour it happened. It would have been a mercy if they had hung me up at the time, and put an end to me at once; my heart is broken. – [The prisoner here covered his face with his hands, and his muscular frame was apparently convulsed for some minutes].[125]

6

'A new species of swindling': Coiners, Fraudsters, Swindlers and the 'Long-Firm', c. 1760–1913[1]

Introduction

During the long nineteenth century new paradigms of organised and professional crime were framed through the changing prosecution of fraud and forgery, coining and other forms of financial crime. As previous chapters have argued, the records provide only fragmentary evidence of criminal networks and confederacies, suggesting that the existence of organised criminal gangs is far from clear-cut. However, from this period, in the records of the police, the press and the writings of social investigators, a language evolved that described gangs of swindlers, coiners and fraudsters through the rhetoric of criminal organisation, perpetuating an increasingly dramatic shadow world of professional criminals. From the later eighteenth century, financial crimes were seen as increasing in pace with the growth of commerce and banking in the metropolis. Thus, in 1796 Patrick Colquhoun lamented, 'It is not to be wondered at in a country where commerce and manufactures have arrived at such a height, and where from the opulence of the people the interchange of property is so extensive, that forgeries and frauds should prevail in a certain degree.'[2]

Historians have seen frauds linked to the financial innovations of the nineteenth century as 'middle-class' crimes, and such 'white-collar' crimes have often been viewed separately from the great swathe of working-class criminality.[3] However, this dichotomy between middle-class white-collar financial crime and working-class property crime leaves a gap in our understanding of the mass of swindles, frauds and rackets that can be found in the nineteenth-century courtroom.[4] Certainly it can be argued that white-collar crimes proliferated as a result of financial opportunity and development, not least in the banking system. The use of cheques or bills of exchange became more common with the regulation of clearing from 1821 (and the establishment of the Committee of London Clearing Bankers). The Clearing House was set up in 1833 and the new joint stock banks were allowed to join from 1854. The first official chequebook was issued by the Bank of England in 1830, although cheques did not circulate fully until the later nineteenth century.[5] Moreover, as John Locker and George Robb have argued, the growth of joint stock companies during the mid-nineteenth century may also have expanded opportunities for fraud.[6] Yet, closer examination of offences such as fraud, forgery, coining and uttering reveal a picture far from the world of company fraudsters and financial shenanigans that frequently constitute historical definitions of white-collar crime.[7] This chapter explores the increasing visibility of financial crimes that was reflected both in the criminal justice system and in the press. Moreover, the establishment of the Detective Branch in 1842 and practices of surveillance that were developed during the period also had an influence on the rhetorical construction of these crimes. Finally, a detailed case study focuses on a form of fraud that was reported in the press from the mid-nineteenth century: long-firm fraud.

Prosecutions of crimes of deception such as fraud, forgery and embezzlement by groups and individuals (as opposed to companies and businesses) had started to increase from the mid-nineteenth century. Whilst the majority of offences tried at the Old Bailey were forms of theft, this changed from the mid-century with the diversion of many thefts to the lower courts. This process, which had already begun in the previous decades, was to be consolidated from 1855 with the passage of the Criminal Justice Act.[8] Crimes of deception (including fraud, forgery, perjury and bankruptcy) were the most numerous of the remaining crimes at the Old Bailey. In each decade from the 1800s to the 1840s, these sorts of offences accounted for no more than 5 per cent of prosecuted crimes at the court, in the second half of the nineteenth century this was to rise, and by the 1890s they represented 21.22 per cent of all crimes.[9] Moreover, forgery and fraud accounted for the vast majority of these crimes during the course of the nineteenth century, with forgery forming 47.13 per cent and fraud 41.75 per cent of the total.[10] Given that crimes of deception amounted to almost quarter of the business of the Old Bailey by the later nineteenth century, their visibility in terms of the rhetoric surrounding the court, and its reporting in print culture, is not surprising. Indeed, this shift is confirmed in Gatrell's study of the changing landscape of prosecutions in the nineteenth century, where he concluded that prosecutions for white-collar crime, such as swindling, embezzlement, forgery and fraud were probably increasing in real terms.[11]

The forgery of bank notes and other financial documents had exercised the minds of eighteenth-century legislators, and a range of disparate, piecemeal legislation had evolved to deal with it. As Randall McGowen demonstrates, a significant piece of legislation was the 1729 Act that made the forging of private financial instruments a felony (i.e. bills of exchange and such paper instruments that represented money) and hence punishable by death.[12] Subsequently, forgery legislation continued to be passed, with the pace of enactment accelerating after 1760.[13] This may have been in response to cases such as that of the prolific forger William Richardson, who was sentenced to death in October 1765 as a result of falsely forging a counterfeit will and testament. Richardson and various family members (including his wife Elizabeth) and associates, appeared in a number of trials in the early 1760s, although there is evidence that he was active from the 1750s. In 1751, a William Richardson gave evidence in a trial involving a forged mariner's will.[14] From this early appearance Richardson seems to have specialised in the forging of the wills of seamen and mariners, an offence which had been made capital by the 1729 Act.[15] The Sessions Papers reporting his final trial in October 1765 included a long list of trials at which he had appeared as a defendant or witness, spanning more than a decade.[16] However, Richardson's 'gang' were not typical white-collar criminals.[17] Rather they represented the increasing opportunities the new monetary economy was offering to a range of criminals. Over the following decades forgery legislation continued to be passed and by the 1770s John Fielding had been particularly proactive in the prosecution of fraud and forgery.[18] In 1776, Fielding presided over the trial of the brothers Robert and Daniel Perreau and Mrs Rudd for forgery, a crime which had provoked considerable controversy in the 1770s.[19] Indeed, within a couple of months of the Perreaus' execution in January 1776, a 'Society of Guardians for the Protection of Trade against Swindlers and Sharpers' was established.[20]

Later in the eighteenth century there was a further increase in prosecutions when, in 1797, the Bank of England issued low-denomination notes (£1 and £2), which were much easier to forge. The Bank of England's involvement in the prosecution process has been explored by McGowen, who demonstrated the corresponding rise of death sentences leading to executions between 1797 and 1821.[21] Indeed, between 1800 and 1836 at Newgate, of the 523 people executed, 89 were for forgery, 42 for uttering, and four for uttering and forgery together.[22] The seriousness with which these crimes were viewed in this period is demonstrated by the draconian approach to prosecution and punishment. For example, those executed included a number of teenagers such as 18-year-old Joseph Abbott and 19-year-old John Vartie for forgery, and 16-year-old Joseph South for uttering.[23] In December 1819, 17-year-old Dennis Keaton was tried with Edward Voss, an 18-year-old, for uttering.[24] Despite evidence of a pardon for Voss from the Bank of England, *The Times* reported the execution of the boys at the end of March, 'Voss who was only 18 years of age, and Keaton, who had not attained his seventeenth year, and who was of diminutive stature and boyish look, were found guilty of uttering various forged 5*l* notes ... The boy Keaton wept much. He has, it appeared, been a thief since he was tall enough to put his hand in a pocket'.[25] From 1821 forgery prosecutions declined, perhaps as a response to the Bank of England's aggressive pursuance of guilty verdicts and the correspondingly high level of forgery executions.[26] After a substantial pressure movement to repeal the capital sentence attached to the crime, most forgery was made non-capital by an act of 1832.[27] The removal of the death penalty may have contributed to the general increase of forgery and fraud prosecutions at the Old Bailey over the following decades.

The increasing visibility of the various forms of deception may also have been linked to the changes to the Metropolitan Police, and in particular the establishment of the Detective Branch. The branch was founded in 1842, and from this period there is an increasing reference to detectives in cases prosecuted at the Old Bailey. Fraud, forgery and coining cases account for 31 per cent of trials in which detectives were mentioned between the 1840s and 1910s.[28] From the late 1870s, the Detective Branch underwent substantial reorganisation and was renamed as the Criminal Investigation Department (CID).[29] This reorganisation was largely in response to allegations of corruption, particularly those related to what became known as the 'Turf Fraud Scandal'.[30] From 1878, the newly installed Director of Criminal Intelligence, Howard Vincent, expanded the Divisional Detective sections, establishing 60 Divisional Detective Patrols and 20 Special Patrols to be commanded by 159 sergeants and 15 detective inspectors. At Scotland Yard, a superintendent would command three chief inspectors, 20 inspectors, and six sergeants and constables. Thus, as well as increased manpower, new methods of detection would help in identifying the newer technologies of crime.[31]

The Detective Branch made their mark in the mid-nineteenth century with the capture and trial of the 'gang' responsible for the Great Bullion Robbery (also referred to by contemporaries as 'The Great Gold Dust

Robbery') of 1855. This was a very 'modern' robbery, in the sense that it took advantage of the transfer of gold on the South Eastern Railway, which had only been open since 1839 (linking London to Kent), with a regular service to Boulogne operating via paddle steamer from 1843.[32] Edward Agar, described as a 'professional criminal', along with William Pierce, a former railway employee, James Burgess, a train car guard, and William Tester, station master, staged the robbery, replacing a large shipment of gold en route to Paris with two hundredweight of lead shot.[33] The undoing of the protagonists was mainly due to the testimony of Edward Agar rather than to clever detective work.[34] Agar was charged at the Mansion House police court in August 1855 for an unrelated crime of forgery.[35] He was tried at the Old Bailey the following October, for 'forgery and uttering' a banker's cheque, for which he was found guilty and sentenced to transportation for life.[36] Whilst in Pentonville awaiting embarkation to the penal colony, Agar turned evidence against his accomplices resulting in their arrest and trial at the Old Bailey in January 1857.[37] The trial received wide coverage in both the metropolitan and provincial press, and according to *The Times*:

> the court was early besieged by applicants for admission ... the trial evidently excited great interest, owing to the daring nature of the robbery, the ingenuity with which it had been planned and executed, the largeness of the sum involved, and the apparent respectability of some of the persons implicated.[38]

This case represented all that was 'new' about crime in the mid-nineteenth century, with its elements of detailed planning and apparent professionalism. Moreover, the ensuing events seemed to unveil a hidden financial criminal underworld, straddling a line between the criminal class and the respectable class. The crime, according to Dublin's *Freeman's Journal and Daily Commercial Advertiser*, 'shows the deliberateness, professional spirit, and, more than all, the pecuniary resources of the modern offender'.[39] An editorial published in *The Times* the day after the adjournment of the trial on the 14 January (the defendants were found guilty on the 15 January), explored the case of Edward Agar, who in his evidence admitted to having followed crime as an occupation for many years, and revealed that not only was he not 'in want' but that he had invested his 'ill-gotten gains' in government securities.[40] *The Times* found his testimony inexplicable, 'We consider this one of the most extraordinary statements ever made in connexion with the pursuits of crime'.[41] As the editorial noted of crime at the mid-nineteenth century, 'It partakes more of the nature of a profession, is more deliberately adopted as a method of livelihood, is pursued with greater system, and practiced with more signal aids of skill, patience, and capital than we conceive to have been the case in days gone by'.

Coiners

These apparently 'new' crimes had their roots in old-fashioned swindles and currency crimes. As Malcolm Gaskill has argued, coining has 'a history as long as the monetized economy'.[42] During the late seventeenth century, most markedly in the mid-1690s, there was an increase in prosecutions for coining at the Old Bailey.[43] Gaskill suggests that the (general) increase of coining was a consequence of the mechanisation of the minting processes, which led to the increased 'professionalisation' of the crime, one outcome of which was the reform of the coinage in 1696.[44] For much of the eighteenth century prosecutions for coining at the Old Bailey remained fairly low, rarely rising above 1 per cent of prosecuted offences. However, from the later eighteenth century prosecutions started to rise, and by the mid-nineteenth century over 2000 cases of coining were prosecuted at the court (peaking in the 1850s and 60s when they represented over 15 per cent of all offences prosecuted).[45] The explanation for the increasing numbers of coining cases at the higher court is complex and relates to changing practices in prosecution and detection by the Mint; developments in the circulation of currency and the technologies that enabled the counterfeiting of notes and coins; and the shifting focus of the higher court towards financial crime and fraud. This growing focus on monetary crime would be satirised by Sidney Laman Blanchard in Dickens's *Household Words* in 1851 in, 'A Biography of a Bad Shilling'.[46] The article recounted the journey of a 'bad shilling', drawing attention not only to the practice of counterfeiting but also to the circulation of such coins. Indeed, it was charges for the 'uttering' of false coin which constituted the majority of the increasing prosecutions at the Old Bailey. The distinction between coining and uttering rested on the difference between the production and the passing off of bad coins or counterfeit notes. Prosecutions for coining were more difficult to prove, as the prosecution had to produce evidence of the equipment used, such as moulds and presses. On the other hand, uttering required evidence of possession or of putting bad coins or notes into circulation.[47]

In the early nineteenth century, the notion of criminal confederacy was marked in newspaper coverage of coining. Despite frequent references to 'gangs of coiners', accounts of the capture and detection of coining gangs often described what was essentially a household operation. In November 1828, a number of papers reported on the 'Apprehension of a Gang of Coiners', in Mile End, London. According to the *Morning Post*, 'On Friday last, a gang of coiners who have manufactured and circulated an immense quantity of base money, and whose dexterity and vigilance have baffled hitherto every exertion to discover them, were taken into custody, near Dog-row, Mile-end-road, London.'[48] This daring gang consisted of one James Coleman, a costermonger, his wife, daughter and mother-in-law. Coleman and his wife Rhoda were eventually tried at the Old Bailey, where he was found guilty and sentenced to death.[49] Similarly, in 1829 the *Morning Chronicle* reported on the 'Apprehension of a Gang of Coiners', describing how Robert Bradford, Henry Bishop and his wife, Mary Bishop, had been carrying on 'a regular system of coining' from a house in St. Anne's Lane, Westminster.[50] The presence of women in coining cases was significant and was much more marked in the earlier nineteenth century.[51] Coining usually involved the production of coin within an essentially domestic setting, such as that in the Coleman case. The decline of women in coining cases is broadly supported by Lucia Zedner's evidence that women constituted one-third of those tried for uttering in the early nineteenth century, a proportion that dropped to just a quarter in the late nineteenth century. Zedner also showed that the prosecution of women for coining and forgery decreased from the mid-century.[52] A more traditional (and arguably 'pre-modern') model of coining, which encompassed households and thus both genders, has been identified by early modern historians of coining. For example, Gaskill found evidence of 'small-scale production lines with a division of labour and neighbours part of the work force'. He cites the Secretary to the Treasury, William Lowndes, who in 1695 observed that coining was, 'a thing so easie in it self, that even Women and Children (as well as Men) are capable of the Act'.[53] Correspondingly, at the Old Bailey during the late seventeenth and early eighteenth centuries, the ratio of men to women involved in coining cases was much more equal.[54] However, despite the 'domestic' setting of such crimes, coining had frequently been identified as an organised trade.[55]

Contemporary writers drew a relationship between coining offences and at least rudimentary forms of criminal organisation. For example, Mayhew categorised coining under 'Thieves and Swindlers' in a hierarchy of professional crimes.[56] James Grant, John Garwood and Thomas Archer also referred to 'gangs of coiners'.[57] Nevertheless, this association of coining with forms of professional crime may have been superficial. Frederick Wensley and George Cornish, both former CID detectives who were active in London in the late nineteenth and early twentieth centuries, commented on the poor status of coining, 'They are the most wretched of criminals', remarked Wensley in his 1931 autobiography.[58] Cornish noted:

> Coining is, I think, a most despicable crime, for it is almost the very poor who are made to suffer from it; and all better-class criminals regard it with contempt and disgust. It is unprofitable too; I have had any number of coiners through my hands and I have never come across one who has really made much money at the game.

In police memoirs, the criminal elite was more often constituted of swindlers, burglars and housebreakers – a 'professional class' of criminals who were increasingly identified in the late nineteenth and early twentieth centuries.[59] Nevertheless, during the nineteenth century there is some evidence that coiners were moving away from more 'traditional methods' of counterfeiting and taking advantage of new technologies. For example, in 1862, Joseph Jones, his wife, Elizabeth Jones, and William Smith, were charged with making counterfeit florins. According to Police Inspector Brannan, upon searching Jones's house he found:

> on the table, some basins with sand and water in them, and some files with metal in their teeth – on the cupboard were placed two galvanic batteries, charged, and in full work, with seventeen sixpences on the wires, undergoing the process of electroplating – that is a process by which a very thin coating of silver is thrown over the base coin.[60]

Indeed, in volume four of *London Labour and the London Poor*, John Binny provided a useful set of instructions for producing coin. He noted the ease of manufacture, 'Counterfeit coin is manufactured by various classes of people – costermongers, mechanics, tailors, and others – and is generally confined to the lower classes of various ages. Girls of thirteen years of age sometimes assist in making it.'[61]

An increasingly proactive Detective Branch may have some bearing on the identification of groups of individuals in coining cases as 'gangs'. For example, the evidence of Detective Sergeant William Thick in May

1883 at the trial of Evaline Street (18), Albert Howard (21), Philip Garcia (29) and Elizabeth King (18) for possessing counterfeit coins with the intention of uttering them, identified them as a 'gang':

> On 16th April last I had a conversation with Howard in Bishopsgate Street – I knew him before – he said 'Johnny, I can put you on to a gang of counterfeit coiners' – I said 'Very well, meet me in the evening' – I asked him 'Where do they live?' – he said 'On the Seven Dials' – I said, 'Very well, you meet me to-morrow evening at 11 o'clock at this same place; I will introduce you to our chief' … he did not come – I did not see him again till he was in the dock at Leman Street Station.[62]

Police evidence drawing on observation, surveillance and knowledge would help to shape the construction of the 'coining gang' in print culture. In Old Bailey coining cases detectives described watching houses suspected of coining operations for hours, days and weeks. Nowhere is this more notable than in the career of James Brannan (sometimes spelt Brennan), a former Metropolitan Police officer who was employed by the Mint from 1856. As John Binny noted, 'The detection of counterfeit coin in the metropolis is under the able management of Mr Brennan, a skilful and experienced public officer, who keeps a keen surveillance over this department of crime.'[63] Plain-clothed policeman Ambrose Sutton and police sergeant Arthur Elliott watched a house in Hampton Street for several days in February 1866, under the leadership of Mr Brannan. In November 1866 Arthur Elliott stated, 'I am employed by Mr Brannan in watching suspected places.'[64]

Plain-clothes police increasingly appeared in Old Bailey trial accounts from the 1830s, although this seems to have varied over time.[65] For example, in the 1830s and 40s, plain-clothes officers were most often referred to in cases of pickpocketing. With the decline of pickpocketing prosecutions at the Old Bailey, plain-clothes officers were more likely to appear in cases of coining, burglary and robbery.[66] It is not always clear whether these policemen were working undercover, or whether they used the phrase 'plain clothes' simply to refer to their off-duty apparel. In the small number of trials in which both plain-clothed officers and gangs were mentioned (only 53 trials, although none of these are before the 1840s), most are for cases of robbery and wounding or for forms of theft. However, 13 cases involve some sort of fraud or financial crime. In one of the three coining cases that refer to both gangs and plain-clothed police, the court questioned a police constable named John Whitlamb:

Q. Is it authorized by your principals to assume the dress you did? A. They leave it to our discretion. Q. What, to assume every disguise? A. I have not heard that there is any control in that respect – it is all done at our own expense – I have permission to assume disguises – I am a plain-clothes man, that is my duty that I do in general.[67]

The actions of the plain-clothed officer in this case were attacked in *The Times* in December 1845 as essentially opening the police to corruption, the practice described as 'evil means'.[68] These concerns would be dramatically confirmed by the descriptions of the plain-clothed activities of detectives John Meiklejohn and Nathanial Druscovich during the Turf Fraud Scandal of 1877, also known as 'The Trial of the Detectives'.[69] Given the numerical rise of fraud and forgery trials which can be seen from the later 1870s, the subsequent reformation of the Detective Branch and the establishment of the Criminal Investigation Department may have brought a sharper focus to cases of fraud and forgery. Perhaps having learnt from their mistakes, the potential vulnerability of detectives and police officers to involvement in forms of criminal organisation called for a greater vigilance and (hence) visibility of such crimes. Indeed, as Stefan Petrow points out, central detectives 'were not involved "in preventing or arresting the ordinary cases of crime" … Central detectives generally worked on important cases, including swindles and frauds, where the stakes were high.'[70]

Forgery and Swindling Gangs

Swindling was not a new form of crime in the later nineteenth century. References to swindlers, swindler, swindling and swindle found in the Old Bailey date from the late eighteenth century. The first clear reference to swindling is from John Grabham, the prosecutor of Walter Gibbons for Grand Larceny in July 1775. Grabham referred to the accused 'swindling, and robbing people'.[71] At an unrelated trial at the same sessions, John Wilkin was also found guilty of Grand Larceny. In June that year, he had stolen three Bills of Exchange for £50 drawn on the Norwich Bank. As one of the witnesses, a Major Smith, testified, 'he said he belonged to some people, who, I afterwards found were what they call swindlers'.[72] Over half of the Old Bailey prosecutions that referred to the various manifestations of swindling were fraud (46.51 per cent) or forgery (11.09 per cent) trials.[73] The term seems to have developed as a colloquial way of describing crimes involving financial or fraudulent practices of one sort or another.[74] The press eagerly explored this relationship and widely reported swindling and forgery cases as gang crimes. For example, the London papers described, the 'Apprehension of a Gang of Forgers' in March 1828. Similar to the coining cases described above, this case involved a young man (Peter Garling) and his wife (Bridget Garling), an elderly woman (Elizabeth Healey) and her son (Michael Healey), a boy about 12 or 13 years old. They were examined by the solicitor to the Mint, Mr Powell, and committed to trial for uttering counterfeit coin.[75] The 'Conviction of a Gang of Swindlers' reported in the press in July 1857, was another case which involved husbands, wives, sons and daughters: John Jones (55), Harriet Jones (47), John Lewis Jones (17) and Ann Jones (22). In this case the accused had been defrauding tradesmen, yet despite the apparent domesticity of the set-up the reports described a significant scale of fraud:

> From the evidence given it appeared that the prisoners had for years past resided in almost every town near the metropolis and adjoining villages, occupying fashionable residences, and carrying on a most extensive system of plunder. Their mode of operation was for the son to be dressed as a groom, representing his father as his master and a gentleman possessed of large landed estates in Wales, and driving a pair of horses. The mother and daughter were also in the habit of passing and appearing as servants when occasion served.[76]

Such cases demonstrate the ubiquity and problematic nature of press rhetoric relating to gang activity. The collective nature of fraud, forgery and coining offences seems to have lent itself to sensationalist headlines that the press were adopting to describe a range of criminal activity. Indeed, the inference that these activities were the product of far-reaching organised networks was reflected in references to continental gangs of forgers and swindlers from as early as the 1840s.[77] Nevertheless, in the Old Bailey courtroom, specific references to organised forgery and fraud gangs appeared only sporadically.[78]

However, by mid-century the growing problem of swindling and forging, and particularly the belief that they were carried out by professional criminals, was to come more sharply into focus. Edward Agar's testimony at the trial of the bullion robbers in 1857 revealed the involvement of the corrupt barrister, James Townsend Saward, also known as 'Jim (or Jem) the penman'. Portrayed as a remarkable figure by contemporaries, the *Political Examiner* noted, 'James Saward is no ordinary swindler'.[79] Saward was described as the 'mastermind' behind a notorious forgery gang, who had practiced forgeries using forged cheques upon a number of banks in London for some years. Originally tried at the Mansion House court, the prosecutor was a Mr Mullens, solicitor to the Committee of Bankers for Protection from Forgeries and Frauds. Central to the proceedings was the evidence of Henry Atwell and William Salt Hardwicke, who had been tried upon a charge of forgery at the Old Bailey in October 1856.[80] Found guilty of uttering and sentenced to life transportation, the men then turned evidence at Saward's trials at the Mansion House and the Old Bailey the following February and March. According to the *Daily News* of 12 February 1857, Hardwicke described his relationship with Saward:

> with whom I first became acquainted about 25 or 26 years ago. He was always known as 'Jem the penman'. I do not want to make myself appear better than I am; but Saward was known, for years after I first became acquainted with him, to be carrying skeleton keys through the City for a gang of burglars when they wanted them for the night.[81]

In a series of trial reports and articles throughout early 1857, the extent of Saward's activities was revealed. As well as apparently having 'masterminded' various forgeries, Saward had also given evidence at a number of forgery trials. According to Salt Hardwicke, Saward had 'helped' transport 11 forgers; for example 28-year-old James Allen, found guilty of uttering and sentenced to transportation for life in September 1839, and 80-year-old William Wilkinson, who was transported for life after being found guilty of forging and uttering at the sessions on 9 April 1849.[82] Moreover, it was not long before pointed comments about Saward's apparent ability to 'get away with' so much, were aired. For example, in the *Freeman's Journal* of February 14 1857, an editorial asked:

> what are we to think of the London police, who never lit on Jem the Penman, during the quarter of a century over which his 'business' extended? ... The frauds on the City Banks, ranging over such a length of time and within the knowledge of the police, speak little for the detective capacity of that body. Where a body of men were associated for the purposes of forgery, and almost every week for a length of time some of the banks had been defrauded by forged checks, it is hard to conceive, with ordinary vigilance, how the criminals could remain so long undetected ... but where so large a body pursued their

'business', and with such successful activity for such a length of time in the heart of London, until their existence was discovered by a mere accident wholly unconnected with the acts of forgery, we entertain no high idea of the efficiency of the London police.[83]

Whilst the attack on the police may have been motivated by broader commentaries on the inefficiency of the Metropolitan Police, that Saward had his fingers in a number of pies seems to have been generally accepted by a wide press and public. In 1859, *The Times* reported on a forgery trial involving the 'Wagner gang', who they claimed were the remains of Saward's gang, Wagner having filled the breach after Saward was caught.[84]

Public knowledge of Saward's criminal 'career' was based effectively on hearsay and upon the evidence of convicted criminals. Thus, 'Jim the Penman' was retrospectively constructed through the lens of press reporting and sensationalism. In September 1857, the London and provincial press reported on the embarkation of the *Nile* transport, with Agar, Tester and Saward on board; in October 1859, they reported on the arrival of Saward and co. in Western Australia.[85] Over the following years, the occasion of a forgery would bring comparisons to the notoriety of 'Jim the penman'. For example, in 1860 when William George Pullinger, the chief cashier of the Union Bank of London, was charged at the Mansion House for stealing £263,000 from his masters the trial attracted a substantial crowd:

> the justice-room was crowded to an extent unequalled, since the time when it was the scene of the convict Agar's revelations on the subject of the great gold robbery, and the equally extraordinary and quickly succeeding revelations which attended the prosecution of Saward (better known as 'Jim the Penman') for the great bank forgeries that had so long defied detection.[86]

In 1863, the Reverend J. Davis, a witness to the Commission on Penal Servitude, relayed prison gossip about Saward, suggesting that the man who informed on him had saved the 'bankers of London ... 10,000*l* a year since he was convicted'.[87] By the mid-1860s, Saward seems to have been largely forgotten. However, in the 1880s he was to be given a second 'career' as a theatrical production. Written by Sir Charles L. Young, 'Jim the Penman' had its debut at the Haymarket Theatre on 3 April 1886, and later played at Madison Square Theatre in New York.[88] The play was described by contemporaries as a detective melodrama, with the character of Saward connected to an international forgery ring. The manipulation of both the criminal law and the legal profession by 'Jim the penman' mean the Saward case is far from typical of the forgery trials prosecuted during the nineteenth century. Nevertheless, the idea that financial and legal networks could overlap with more 'traditional' criminal confederacies seemed to suggest a worrying new dimension to the organisation of crime.

Long-Firm Fraud

The final sections of this chapter will focus on a form of fraud that combined the worlds of theft and illegality with that of work and respectability, which would be identified by commentators from the later nineteenth century. Long-firm fraud has tended to be most strongly associated with post-Second World War family firms, but can be found described in the Old Bailey from 1874 and in the press from the 1850s.[89] Close examination reveals often complicated cases which show how criminals were taking advantage of the new opportunities provided by changing economic and financial structures. For example, in August 1880 merchant William John Griffith gave evidence in a case involving eight men aged between 32 and 62 who had been charged with unlawfully obtaining goods and conspiracy to defraud. He told the court, 'I had heard that there was a gang of them trading as a long firm'.[90] The definition of long-firm fraud has been most extensively explored by the criminologist Michael Levi.[91] Essentially the crime involved obtaining goods on credit then disappearing before paying and selling the goods on to make an illegal profit. In the case described above, the eight defendants had set up in business premises, calling themselves 'H. Lawrence and Co., the Accidental and General Arbitration Company'. From this address they made orders for various goods, including starch and tea. The traders who supplied them were never paid and the goods were sold on. Upon raiding the premises the police found business stationary and papers. CID Inspector Matthew Fox described the shop-front store on Long Lane in Bermondsey:

> It was a baker's shop, with the name of Holmes outside, and arranged on shelves round the shop inside were 23 empty butter firkins, 20 empty cheese boxes, 14 empty biscuit boxes, and some dummy cheeses arranged carefully on the shelves round the shop – I did not find the smallest particle of butter, cheese, bacon, or anything else.[92]

Levi identified three sub-types of long-firm fraud: pre-planned frauds, which are businesses set up with the intention from the beginning of defrauding suppliers; intermediate frauds, which occur when people decide to turn a formerly legitimate business into one which defrauds its suppliers; and slippery-slope frauds, which occur when businessmen continue to trade and obtain goods on credit although there is a high risk that, unless their business situation improves greatly, they will be unable to pay for the goods.[93] He suggests that similar frauds can be identified in relation to prosecutions for obtaining goods by false pretences as early as the sixteenth century, and also refers to a legal case of 1782, Rex. v. Hevey, Beatty and McCarthy.[94] John Hevey was indicted three times at the Old Bailey, twice for forgery and once for fraud. The trial for fraud, where he was prosecuted with Richard Beaty, involved a fictitious banking house named 'Smith, Moore and Co'. A witness described going to the address in Bath given to him by Hevey and finding 'no Banking-house in Westgate-Street'.[95] Hevey's methods anticipated those that would be identified in the later nineteenth century.

The first Old Bailey cases to refer to long-firm fraud as a specific criminal event appear in 1874 and involve a fraud and a perversion of justice, with the defendants charged with being criminally involved in firms (a brokers and a solicitors) which were accused by witnesses of being 'long firms'.[96] In the press there were references to 'the long firm' (as opposed to long-firm fraud) in various midland and northern towns from 1858, with the first clear reference in the *Bradford Observer* in March 1858.[97] This initial case seems to have been the first to be labelled publicly as a 'long firm', with reports linking it to the Salford and Manchester region. Indeed, until the mid-1860s all the references refer to 'The Long Firm', singular, and all link the gang to northern towns, particularly those in the Manchester conurbation, which may reflect the density of lower-middle class workers in the area. As Geoff Crossick points out, it was the commercially important cities such as Manchester that had the largest white-collar workforces.[98] The Manchester cases came to a head in 1862 when a number of overlapping prosecutions caught the attention of the press. These included the case of the 'Manchester forger' Edmund Ashworth Acton.[99] Ashworth Acton, the son of the manager of a local mill, was a yarn agent and manager of a printworks near Stalybridge before becoming the manager of Kennedy's Mill upon his father's death. According to the newspaper reports, 'For the last two years the prisoner has been known to the police as a member of the notorious "Long Firm," and a very successful swindler'.[100] Long firms in this area were notable enough to merit a chapter in the biography of the Manchester detective Jerome Caminada, published in 1895.[101] References to long firms in northern and midland towns would continue throughout the period, presumably reflecting their growth as industrial and commercial centres and hence lands of rich opportunity.[102] The reportage of the long firm suggested a shadowy omniscience. The *Birmingham Daily Post* noted in May 1866, 'Most of our readers have become familiar with the title of this firm, which trades on the credulity of honest people in all parts of the country. The members of the firm are confined to no one particular city or town, but send their orders from all parts of the kingdom.'[103] This was the swindling underworld with the organisation, networking and ability to communicate their nefarious schemes across 'the kingdom', echoing modern paradigms of organised crime.

By the later 1860s references to long-firm frauds can be found scattered throughout government papers, reflecting the emergence of long firms in the metropolis.[104] The metropolitan long-firm references of the late 1860s predominantly refer to a group of frauds connected to the 'Bristowe gang', based in the Southwark area of the city. George Bristowe, a middle-aged former coffee-house keeper who was 'victimising tradesmen' across the metropolis, was first described as one of the leaders of the long firm in the spring of 1866.[105] Over the next few years a number of cases would link the Bristowe gang, or 'the long firm'.[106] The son of George Bristowe, George Brittain Bristowe, was tried at the Old Bailey in January 1868 with having attempted to prevent George William Day in giving evidence against George Gould. Gould was the alias of George Bristowe senior, who under this name had been tried the previous December with fraud, but found not guilty. At the January trial, despite evidence from a witness named William Robson of violent threats from Bristowe junior, Day was confused, and claimed to have been drunk and as a result not able to remember what had happened.[107] The evidence suggests that Brittain had suborned the witness. Bristowe senior was eventually prosecuted under the name of George Foreman in May 1875, and found guilty of fraud, although at a separate trial it was considered that there was not enough evidence against him for a conviction. According to the *Morning Post* the judgment was respited against Foreman/Gould/Bristowe; however, at the age of 67 these were the last references to this leader of the long firm.[108] The Bristowe long-firm conspiracy would run from c. 1866 to c. 1875 and the involvement of police officers who would specialise in such frauds can also be noted. Thus, from 1868, Inspector Thomas Ambrose Potter of the G Division (King's Cross, Finsbury) was investigating the Bristowe gang for long-firm crimes. In May 1868, he gave evidence at the Southwark hearing of William Barnes, a retired dairyman, Samuel Israel, a marine store dealer, and David Morgan, a labourer, who were charged with involvement in a conspiracy. In his evidence, Potter remarked that, 'he had been for some time on the watch to discover the "long firm", or Bristowe gang of swindlers'.[109] The evidence at the hearing provides some inkling into the apparent scale of these frauds, which in this case extended to Yorkshire. Potter noted that the gang had obtained more than a thousand pounds worth of property, and 'had agents and partners in all parts of London and the large towns in the kingdom'.[110] The case went to the Old Bailey in August, with witnesses from as far afield as Weymouth, Leeds and Brotherton in Yorkshire. The defendants, Barnes, Israel and Morgan, were found guilty.[111]

This case demonstrates the importance of the expanding railway network in crimes of these types, and it may be that concerns about the way in which the railway created networks of opportunity led to the press portrayal of a monolithic 'long firm'.[112] The railway network provided a mobile spatial environment in which crime could start to be organised in a way that can be seen as significantly 'modern'. As Alan Wright notes of the twentieth-century globalisation of organised crime, 'The internationalization of organised crime ... increased during the twentieth century in parallel with the globalization of transport and communications'.[113] In Victorian England it would seem that transport also enabled the reach of the long firm. The *Pall Mall Gazette* would encapsulate this reach in an article from 1878:

> The swindlers are tried, convicted and sent to punishment; and the public, seeing no more of the 'long firm' in question, thinks that nothing more is to be known concerning it. This may be correct now and then; but in most cases that part of the long firm which appears in the criminal courts bears about the same relation to the body as the severed feeler of an octopus bears to the rest of the animal.[114]

The idea of the insidious nature of the long firm was also marked by the involvement of criminals who were decidedly not of the traditional 'criminal class' as regards age, occupation and class.

The Long Firm at the Old Bailey

The final section of this chapter will explore these issues in more detail by focusing on a small group of long-firm frauds which were tried under various formulations such as 'unlawfully conspiring to defraud', 'unlawfully obtaining' and 'false pretences'. Not all of the cases at the Old Bailey described as 'long firms' were tried as frauds (and some allegations of long-firm fraud are clearly the result of hearsay from witnesses).

However, more than three-quarters of the trials where a long firm was referred to were tried as forms of fraud.[115] Examination of the 40 fraud cases (there were 167 individual charges), from 1874 to 1911, where there is a reference to a long firm, has enabled some close work on the individuals involved.[116] Whilst occupations are not given systematically until 1906, by cross-referencing with newspaper accounts of the trials occupational information can be found in most cases. By looking more closely at this group of frauds it is possible to draw some conclusions about the broader patterns in the committal of such financial crimes in the period.[117] The mid-1870s seems to be a key point in terms of increasing references to all forms of deception. As we have seen, fraud prosecutions at the Old Bailey had been increasing, rising from 2.27 per cent of prosecutions in the 1840s to 7.44 per cent of prosecutions in the 1870s and 10.27 per cent by the 1890s.[118] From 1869 there was also an increasing reference to detectives at the Old Bailey, reflecting the move towards reform in the following decade. Detectives played a significant role in long-firm investigations. For example, in May 1876, at the trial of James Humphries, Henry Smith, Edward Houghton and Mary Robinson for fraud, Detective Sergeant Daniel Morgan, referred to the 'late Inspector Fay' (Pay) with whom he had been involved for some years, 'making inquiries about the long firm'.[119] Inspector James Pay had indeed been a key officer in the Bristowe long-firm cases the previous year.[120] Similarly, in Manchester, Jerome Caminada described how he had been employed by the victims of long firms, who requested him to make enquiries, going so far as paying him to travel to London to search for one of the fraudsters.[121]

Another clue to the increased visibility of frauds in general, and long-firm frauds more specifically, may be explained by the perceived involvement of foreigners. According to Levi, a number of international long-firm frauds can be identified by the latter half of the nineteenth century. Certainly, in House of Commons papers from 1894, reviewing the Prosecution of Offences Acts, a number of long-firm frauds were singled out, including one case in which a group of foreigners were moving falsely obtained goods between Amsterdam, Coventry and Bristol, which was tried at the Old Bailey in March 1893.[122] Two years later, the London correspondent of the *Koelnische Volkszeitung* (the *Cologne People's Gazette*), Rollo Reuschel, wrote extensively about long firms in his 1895 book, *The Knights of Industry: Revelations about Long-Firms in London*.[123] Reuschel's 'revelations' had prompted a libel case that was tried at the Old Bailey in March 1895, relating to a series of articles in which he charged the manager of a London Enquiry Office,

Lothair Lehnert, with long-firm fraud.[124] Nevertheless, whilst there are some foreign offenders in the group of long-firm frauds, most were home grown.[125]

The cases of long-firm crime share features. For example, a typical long-firm fraud from October 1907 involved seven defendants, all were men, most were middle aged and they roughly occupied a class spectrum poised between the upper working class and the middle class: John William Clifton (48, hosier), James Harry Vincent (43, traveller), Alexander Doig (39, accountant), John Martin (24, agent), John Ralli (43, clerk), William Roger Caldwell Moore (50, accountant) and Joseph Goodman (50, merchant).[126] Using Levi's definition, this case would seem to be somewhere between an 'intermediate' and 'slippery-slope' fraud. Despite the associations of long firms with gang organisation and professionalisation that were made in print culture, many of the swindles and long-firm frauds are cases whereby a combination of opportunity and greed may have prompted the shift into illegal activity. There is some evidence of pre-planned fraud. For example, in September 1894 William Trautz (36, agent), Emile Trautz (35, agent) and Alexander Joseph (42, licensed victualler) were charged with fraud and obtaining goods by false pretences, and George Charles Fruhling (45, tutor) receiving the goods knowing they had been unlawfully obtained. The former had set themselves up as a firm in the name of Walden & Co, apparently dealing in fancy goods. Detective Inspector William Oldhampstead had been making inquiries about the men since October 1892, and described Walden & Co as 'nothing but a long firm'.[127] In a case from April 1909, the defendants, John Harvey (37, merchant) and Benjamin Fletcher (26, dealer), had used false names to obtain goods, 'This was a long-firm case presenting the usual features. Prisoners obtained premises upon references written by themselves in different names, ordered in goods and moved out before quarter day.'[128]

Long-firm cases usually involved large numbers of defendants. For example, in the 40 cases of fraud associated with long-firm crime, the average number of individuals involved in a trial was three defendants. However, in 10 of the trials there were more than five defendants, and in one trial there was a staggering 13 defendants. This case was tried in December 1892 and all the defendants were found guilty.[129] The high proportion of males involved in these offences was most likely related to proximity to business opportunity.[130] The age range of the men was very different from the normal run of criminal offenders. Just over 40 per cent all offenders between 1870 and 1914 were aged 25 and under.[131] In contrast, for the long-firm cases (where the age was identified) the average age of the male defendants was 41, and nine of them were aged in their 60s.[132] According to Rob Sindall, in his 1983 study of middle-class crime in the nineteenth century, the most common age range was between 30 and 35. This corresponds with the median age for crimes of deception at the Old Bailey, which was 30 (78 per cent were aged over 25).[133] Sindall suggests that this is the age range when marriage generally occurred and when the potential criminal would have risen to an occupational position that would make the commission of crime easier.[134] The higher age range of offenders in long-firm cases is likely to relate to the positions of the defendants in commercial occupations.

The most represented occupational group in the long-firm frauds were commercial travellers (21), agents (14), and clerks (nine). Other significant groups were those allied to the trade in provisions, including shopkeepers, grocers, merchants and dealers. The highest-status occupations represented were one journalist and one surveyor.[135] The travellers, agents and clerks noted here were far from high-status criminals, and the multi-defendant crimes in which they were involved could more usefully be described as cross-class confederacies. Along with the occupations already listed, we find mention of trades such as bakers, drapers, hatters, engineers, publicans, builders, a bricklayer, a printer, a tailor, a druggist, a butcher and a carpenter. Also represented are a labourer, a cabman, a shop-worker, and a lodging-house keeper. There are problems in defining these occupations in simple class terms, and considering them out of the context of the trial reveals little about the particular individual's status and respectability. These occupations arguably suggest that the concentration on the high-end of business illegality and company fraud in accounts of the historical development of white-collar crime may have its limitations. The focus of historians of middle-class crime on what George Robb characterises as the 'great criminal capitalists', tells us little about the range of defendants travelling through the later-nineteenth-century courts, both individually and in multiple groups.[136] Moreover, high-end business and corporate offenders are arguably the least visible criminals. Thus, it may be that the white-collar crime that started to appear in the nineteenth-century courtroom was more likely to involve the lower middle class strata; or more broadly involve cross-class confederacies, simply because they were more likely to be prosecuted.

Closer examination of two of the long-firm frauds suggests complex relationships between the defendants, witnesses and (occasionally) the police. False pretences, usually aliases, were common, and much store was set on being able to appear 'respectable'. For example, in a case involving

11 defendants from March 1877, witnesses frequently referred to their belief that the defendants were respectable, particularly if they had been able to provide references. Thus, Alfred Manning, a clerk giving evidence, described how he had approached one defendant, a clerk named William Wood, who had provided him with a reference to another defendant, a tailor named Alexander Gardner, he said:

> 'I [have] known him a long time, and believe him to be a respectable man and a suitable tenant for a house of that kind' – he asked if Anderson had referred to anybody else – I told him 'Yes, Prendergast and Co, of Bow' – he said 'They are very respectable people; that is a good reference'.[137]

Reputation and respectability were common currency in these long-firm cases. The ability to provide written references and letters of introduction could be crucial for the successful perpetration of a fraud. This suggests that cross-class connections were not only desirable, but essential. Francis Dorset Sim, a witness in a case from December 1892, testified against the defendant William Taylor, a clerk to whom he had let a house. Sim had written to a Mr Holmberg, who was apparently 'connected with a Swedish banking firm' and who had written that Taylor's family *'were very respectable, and had the reputation of being very wealthy ... –* we rather gathered that he was the financial agent to the firm'. After moving his wife, sister and two children into the house, Taylor paid rent up to July and then went away, apparently setting up the house as an address for receipt of correspondence.[138] The ability to play the card of respectability, without being a bona fide member of the 'respectable' classes, may explain the large numbers of travellers and clerks involved in these frauds.

It is important to consider the dynamics of the later Victorian lower-middle class. The fortunes of clerks and commercial travellers changed considerably over the course of the later nineteenth century.[139] In particular, the economic position of the clerk would vary substantially between c. 1870 and c. 1914.[140] However, upwards mobility and aspiration would remain important to the Victorian clerk, whose working life was changing in the last third of the century as a result of various technological and structural changes that impacted on business. On the one hand, clerking expanded as an occupational role, which may be why they appear in so many long-firm frauds and swindles. There were just more of them.[141] Anderson's study of clerking argued that, despite these increasing numbers, clerical workers between 1870 and 1914, suffered socioeconomic pressures and decline.[142] This might also provide some explanation for the presence of clerks; was their eroded economic position rendering them more vulnerable to criminal opportunities? On the other hand new promotion structures and the expanding commercial sector meant that many clerks were earning more, had steady jobs and were making modest progress. Michael Heller described clerks as 'the backbone of this new social grouping'; in other words, their membership of the lower middle class reflected the importance of aspiration and mobility and points to the high levels of affluence and consumption amongst this group.[143] The position of the commercial traveller would also change as a result of the new opportunities, expanding markets and growth in technology.[144] Roy Church has argued that the ability to appear 'gentlemanly' was an essential qualification to the aspirant traveller.[145] The important role of 'respectability' is illustrated by the case of Frederick Hiscock, a 39-year-old commercial traveller who was charged alongside nine other men in a long-firm fraud at the Old Bailey in August 1880. As one of the victims, Henry Beveridge, testified:

> I received such a satisfactory reference of Hiscock from Mr Buxton, and I said I would trust to his honour in selling only to respectable men, and if he got an order from any man he did not know, if he would bring me the references I would make inquiry – he was paid by commission – the result of his employment is that I am out of pocket about 600*l*.[146]

Moreover, like the clerk, the commercial traveller was also vulnerable to fluctuating fortunes in status and job security. As Crossick noted, 'Commercial travellers and clerks shared in different ways the common problems of the aspirant and unorganised white-collar worker in the late Victorian economy.'[147] Nevertheless, the ability to emulate their social betters, the skills and literacy needed to produce letters, references as well as counterfeited documents, and the incorporation of sales techniques into illegal transactions, may make the explosion of the lower-middle-class workforce during the last third of the nineteenth century significant to the corresponding rise of long firms and other frauds.

A focus on occupational information might tend to mask the existence of 'career criminals'. Michael Levi has argued that it was only in the 1950s that long-firm frauds became more organised, arguing that in the post-war period the long firm became part of syndicated crime, which previously had its main interests in prostitution, gaming and extortion.[148] Nevertheless, it is clear that in the later nineteenth and early twentieth centuries the court and the police did not simply view all long-firm frauds as opportunistic crimes. Many of the defendants had previous convictions for fraud and in a number of trials the police exhibit a long familiarity with the individuals involved. Thus, when Harry Stone, a 42-year-old traveller, and Frederick Brooks, a 37-year-old journalist, were charged along with Mark Gage, a 37-year-old dealer, of conspiring together by means of false pretences in July 1911, the court noted that 'The police evidence showed that Brooks and Stone had been for a considerable time connected together in long firm frauds'.[149] Similarly, in 1905, in the case of William Milne, a 45-year-old described as a builder and decorator, and Charles Smith, a 40-year-old collector to an insurance company, the court noted that the police had 'stated that the prisoners were well known in the City as associates of long firm swindlers'.[150] A complicated cluster of cases that were tried in the spring of 1877 could apparently be connected to the earlier Bristowe gang trial, suggesting a persistent network of offenders. As one detective officer, Thomas Roots, testified, 'I was engaged in some of these cases last summer when Shaw was sentenced to two years hard labour – Randall was Shaw's son-in-law – Gardner is Bristow's son, who is now undergoing ten years penal servitude – he is the founder of the long firm – I do not know Hayho, but I have heard of him as a swindler.'[151] These cases were widely reported and depicted as organised criminal activity, with Bristowe and his gang presented as the originators of the long firm. Hence, in a column in *Lloyd's Weekly Newspaper* headed 'The End of the Long-Firm', the paper noted:

> The chief members of the Long Firm have at length found their way to the Old Bailey and thence to penal servitude. That many of them were shrewd fellows is manifest by the enormous number of transactions in which they figured; and by the success with which, for a considerable time, they eluded justice. The Long Firm was of a shadowy, mysterious kind; apparently disconnected but in reality well-kneaded together, with ostensibly independent offices and agencies, but intertwined by invisible threads of rascality.[152]

Conclusion

This chapter has considered the evolution of forms of what can loosely be described as 'financial organised crimes' from the late eighteenth until the early twentieth century. Arguably, these crimes became more visible and hence subject to wider prosecution at the Old Bailey due to a combination of factors. Amongst the most important of these is the development of financial instruments and the accessibility of these to a much broader spectrum of society during the course of the nineteenth century. Moreover, the increasing reportage of such cases in the burgeoning nineteenth-century press would also afford such cases more publicity. The changing practices of prosecution and the legal evolution of laws involving forgery, fraud and counterfeiting also had an impact. It has further been suggested that the establishment of the Detective Branch in 1842, and the reorganisation of this branch into the Criminal Investigation Department in 1878 with its specific remit of dealing with what modern investigators would define as organised crime, is crucial to understanding the increase of prosecutions. However, continuities with older forms of criminal activity remain. Despite the tendency to present swindling and fraud as 'modern', eighteenth-century offenders, like the forger William Richardson, blended suspicious legal practices with criminal illegality. The 'witnessing' of Richardson in the 1750s and 60s, and of James Townsend Saward in the mid-nineteenth century, show that practices of informing continued to be entrenched in the justice system. Moreover, small-scale coining operations, despite being 'criminalised' by the language of the court, were characterised by the community and kinship networks that we have seen elsewhere in this book.

A close consideration of a set of long-firm frauds has enabled insight into the structure of this type of fraud and the characteristics (in relation to age and occupation) of the individuals involved. Hence, the importance of cross-class readings of crime has been highlighted here. In particular, from the later nineteenth century, the involvement of clerks, commercial travellers and agents suggests that lower-middle-class and aspirational Mr Pooters were to be increasingly implicated in crimes of this type. Of course outside of the Old Bailey, and other higher courts, the serious frauds and swindles described here have less significance (although uttering cases were prosecuted at the petty sessions).[153] Nevertheless, the visibility of crimes of this nature in print culture, and the tendency to linguistically construct groups of swindlers, coiners, forgers and fraudsters as constituting organised criminal gangs, reflected a growing belief in the ubiquity of 'professional' and 'career' criminals in the nineteenth century. Arguably the birth of more modern forms of organised crime can be pinpointed to this period.[154]

7
'A London Plague that must be swept away': Hooligans and Street Fighting Gangs, c. 1882–1912[1]

As Geoffrey Pearson memorably noted in 1983, 'The word hooligan made an abrupt entrance into common English usage, as a term to describe gangs of rowdy youths, during the hot summer of 1898.'[2] Nevertheless, the behaviour that would preoccupy the press and public in 1898 was far from novel. Descriptions of youth gang fighting in the metropolis had been circulating from the early 1880s. Moreover, street-based youth gang conflicts had already been identified as a significant problem in three key English cities from the 1870s, and the fights between gangs of youths that can be found in London from the 1880s were remarkably similar to those that had troubled Manchester and Salford, Birmingham and Liverpool since a decade or so earlier.[3] The extent to which such conflicts represented new forms of youthful delinquency and/or street violence is debatable: there are significant continuities with the older models of street disorder as well as with the descriptions of 'organised gangs' of ruffians that would follow in the early twentieth century.[4] In this chapter the intention is not to simply revisit the hooligan 'panic', but rather to place it within a longer trajectory of concerns about street violence and disorder. Thus late-Victorian and Edwardian depictions of young men (and in some cases women) 'holding the street', what Pearson describes as a 'violent ritual of territorial supremacy', echo the crowds of hustling thieves and pickpockets who 'pushed', 'pulled', 'jostled', 'surrounded' and 'hustled' the crowds and pedestrians of the earlier nineteenth-century metropolis.[5] Despite these apparent continuities, from the later nineteenth century gang-related youth violence would increasingly be informed by spatial connections to metropolitan territory. The intention here is to start to trace the origins of territorial crime, the lines of which would become embedded in the development of gang crime in the early twentieth century.

This case study of the London hooligan trials, a relatively small number of which were tried at the Old Bailey from the 1880s, and some
additional trials gleaned from the contemporary press and police court
records, will enable an extended consideration of territorial gang activity in the metropolis. Extending beyond the evolution of the language
of hooliganism in print culture, the focus will be on the make-up and
character of these groupings: the occupation and social class of the
youths and victims involved, the extent and nature of the violence,
and the forms of weapons deployed. A recurring theme in this chapter will be the problematic deployment of 'gang' and what we might
broadly think of as organised crime rhetoric by the authorities and by
other contemporary commentators. The hooligan was fundamentally
constructed as a member of the underclass, and street fighting, hustling
and robbery were perceived as providing a training ground for the
youthful members of the 'criminal class'. As *The Times* noted in 1900,
'Our "Hooligans" go from bad to worse; they do not starve and they
do not work; they hustle and waylay solitary old gentlemen with gold
watches; they hunt in packs too large for a single police-man to cope
with. Many of them mature into the professional criminal.'[6] Thirty
years earlier, in a *Quarterly Review* article on crime and policing in the
metropolis, the author focused on the policing of the 'criminal class',
and the battle for control of the streets between the Metropolitan Police
and the 'heterogeneous mass of roughs, thieves, and desperate characters which constitute the scoundrelism of great cities'.[7] Indeed, policemen would not infrequently be the victim of attacks from roughs and
hooligan gangs, and contemporaries would unsurprisingly link youth
street violence and membership of gangs with the broader spectrum of
criminal activity.[8] Thus, a key theme in this chapter, connecting to the
previous chapters, examines how plebeian and working-class Londoners
were 'policed' in their daily lives, by law enforcers, but also by the press
and civil society.

Changing Street Violence

Like the other short-term panics about street violence, there is little
evidence to suggest that the rising reportage of hooliganism and youth
gang violence reflected any real rise in violent crime.[9] At the Old
Bailey, where most of the cases that feature in this chapter were prosecuted, there had been an increase in the prosecution of some forms of
interpersonal violence. For example, in the 1840s, wounding offences
had accounted for an average of 2.55 per cent of prosecuted crimes.

By the 1900s, they accounted for 8.95 per cent of prosecuted crimes. Combined with assaults, assaults with intent and violent robbery, such crimes of interpersonal violence accounted for 17.43 per cent of all prosecutions.[10] How meaningful were these increases? The increased visibility of wounding prosecutions at the Old Bailey may have been in part a reflection of legal changes. Some violent crimes that previously may not have reached the Old Bailey would be prosecuted at the higher courts in the later nineteenth century. The laws dealing with forms of assault had been subject to revision throughout the early and mid-nineteenth century, culminating in the 1861 Offences Against the Person Act (24 & 25 Vict. c. 100) that consolidated existing law and statutes into a single act to deal with interpersonal violence.[11] It also attempted to clarify the differences between assault, wounding and the inflicting of grievous bodily harm, an offence punishable by life imprisonment.[12] The Act established the difference between common assault and serious, non-fatal assault, and also the abolition of the death penalty for these offences. Such legislation can in part be seen as a bureaucratic response to changing social and cultural attitudes to violent crime, usually explained by historians as the 'civilising process'.[13] During the nineteenth century, this was reflected in the appearance of a more distinct language to describe forms of violence both in print culture and in the courtroom.[14]

Hence, prosecutions for wounding may also have risen in response to contemporary preoccupations of the press with the figure of the 'rough'. References to roughs initially emerged in connection with the anxieties about street violence that have been identified as the 'garotting panics' of 1856 and 1862.[15] Nevertheless, whilst the rough was present at the Old Bailey from the 1860s it was really in the 1880s that he made his mark. In that decade there were 43 Old Bailey cases with references to roughs, 20 of these were in prosecutions for robbery.[16] In these cases victims were 'surrounded by a crowd of roughs', 'surrounded by a lot of roughs', 'surrounded by 20 roughs', though rarely did they describe gangs of roughs. Whilst these threatening epithets resonate with earlier concerns about street robbery, from the mid-Victorian period a collective language developed to describe the masculine street life of the 'criminal classes'. 'Roughs', 'ruffians' and later the 'hooligan' seemed to reflect a disorderly and insubordinate metropolitan underclass which was forever threatening to disturb the daily life of the upper class.[17] Moreover, the rough was increasingly adopted as part of the stock language of journalism, reflected in newspaper editorials throughout the second half of the century which referred to such diverse groups as

'Election Roughs', 'Tory Roughs', 'Gentlemanly Roughs', the 'Lambeth Rough' and 'Our Roughs'.[18]

Whilst wounding prosecutions may have increased at the higher court, the pattern of prosecution at other courts is unclear. Offences where lethal (or potentially lethal) weapons had been used were generally dealt with by the higher courts; in London this was at the Old Bailey. Less serious offences, involving disorderly behaviour, were prosecuted at the police courts or at the Quarter Sessions at Clerkenwell and Newington (later the County of London Sessions (north and south)). The majority of youth gang confrontations that were extensively reported involved significant use of weapons, including knives and revolvers. There are a number of issues to consider in relation to these events. Firstly, what was the extent of gang conflict, how far did the prosecuted crimes reflect street level incidence of disorder? It may be that low-level affrays not involving significant weapons such as pistols, revolvers and knives were less likely to be prosecuted, or at least less likely to be reported in the press. Secondly, what factors instigated these conflicts? Or were they simply now reported by the press and subsequently prosecuted in a way that they had not been previously? Certainly, there is evidence of earlier cases both at the higher and lower court that have similar hallmarks to the later gang cases.[19] Descriptions of 'gangs of young roughs' and 'youths behaving in a disgraceful manner' can be found in the press before the late nineteenth century. However, whilst these occasionally refer to fights amongst boys, most frequently they describe youths responding to the attempts of police to stymie their activities – playing pitch and toss, stone throwing and other disorderly past-times.[20] Thus definitions of youth gangs need to be considered carefully here. Moreover, metropolitan accounts of gangs of youths engaged in internecine territorial conflict date from the early 1880s, a period in which there had already been significant reporting of similar events in Manchester, Liverpool and Birmingham, suggesting the possibility that metropolitan observers may have been identifying street gangs as a response to this.[21] Nevertheless, Andrew Davies concluded that despite exaggeration and distortion, street gangs in Victorian Manchester and Salford were not an invention of the press. Thus the gang functioned as a way of achieving status, masculinity and a reputation for 'hardness', 'gang conflicts provided an alternative arena for displays of masculine prowess'.[22] This echoes criminological analysis of street gangs which focus on place, opportunity, power, identity and masculinity as key constructs determining gang membership, 'Place-based attachments, postcode identities and group-centered bonds assume, perhaps as they always have, profound significance for young people whose opportunities, aspirations and horizons are stultified and thwarted by structural disadvantage.'[23] Thus, the transition from the 'rough' to the 'hooligan' would be closely associated with territory.

Youth, Disorder and Territory

Increased reporting of gangs of disorderly youths emerged across the nation from the 1870s. Reporting of youths involved in stone-throwing incidents, of youths 'holding the street', and generally causing a nuisance to 'respectable' passers-by can be found in any number of towns in this period. Stone throwing had originated as part of the sectarian violence in Ireland, but it seems to have been picked up as a past-time by groups of youths from around the mid-century. The *Liverpool Mercury* reported on the 'practice of stone throwing by lads' in April 1855; in Meltham, near Huddersfield, in June 1861, the magistrate spoke of the dangers of stone throwing at the trial of a youth named Tom Bower, 'it is a mischievous custom with the boys at Meltham to throw stones at every vehicle that passes'.[24] At least some of these concerns seem to have been related to youthful misbehaviour on a Sunday. For example, in 1865, a distressed reader from Edgbaston wrote to the editor of the *Daily Post* to complain about 'gangs of youths and lads who throng the towing path of the Worcester and Birmingham Canal'; in 1872 in Knostrop, near Leeds, there had been complaints about gangs of youths gambling and confronting the police on a Sunday; in 1874, the *Nottinghamshire Guardian* asked, 'Where Are The Police?' in response to reports about youths who assembled on Milton Street to obstruct and insult passers-by, which had come to a climax on Sunday; in 1878, in Sheffield, the Reverend T. W. Holmes was moved to sermonise about the problem: 'The gangs of youths who hang about the lamp posts at our street corners, who make our suburbs hideous by their orgies at pitch and toss, who disturb quiet streets by their quarrelsome clamour, and who alarm the timid by their noisy horse-play, are, one may fear, beyond the reach either of remonstrance or of reason.'[25]

In these accounts, it is difficult not to recognise the long-heard voice of adult authority complaining about youth disorder on urban streets.[26] Nevertheless, the reports of face-to-face youth conflict that emerge around the same time were qualitatively different from other accounts of youth disorder. The first consistent reporting of street gang confrontations as a problem related to the gangs located in the northern conurbation of Manchester and Salford. Territorial clashes between working-class youths came to the attention of the press from the early 1870s when gangs of boys were reported as violently re-enacting the conflict of the Franco-Prussian war. From these initial stone-throwing conflicts, territorial allegiances developed which collectively became identified as 'scuttling'.[27] Manchester and Salford were not alone in being subject to street gang activity and other industrial cities had identified their own street gang problem. Liverpool suffered the depredations of the 'High Rip gang' in the mid-1880s and Birmingham was subject to the 'Peaky Blinders' in the mid-1890s.[28] Arguably, the sheer scale of the internecine gang conflicts in Manchester and Salford was unique. In the first significant outbreak of scuttling, during the twelve months leading up to October 1871, the police had made more than 500 arrests.[29] It may have been the combination of factors in Manchester and its environs, not least the specific role of the local press and attitude of the magistracy, which made scuttling a particularly visible issue. In contrast to Manchester and Salford, the geographical size of London and the number of offences of violent disorder that appear across the many police courts, make it very difficult to systematically identify specific incidents of youth violence as gang-related.[30]

The historicisation of London's street gang culture has tended to be limited to the flurry of headlines that accompanied the arrival of the hooligan in 1898. In fact, the street gangs that comprised the 'hooligan menace' in 1898 had long roots in the working-class districts of London. The hooligan was first referred to in 1894, when newspapers reported on the gangs of youths known as the 'Hooligan Boys' in Southwark and the south-eastern districts of London. In April *Reynolds's Newspaper* reported on the 'Hooligan Boys' when they described an assault that had taken place in a theatre; a policeman gave evidence that the accused (19-year-old Charles Clarke) was the 'king of a gang of youths known as the O'Hooligan boys'.[31] As Pearson suggested, there may have been a link with music halls. In 1891, the *Era* reported on a new programme at the Elephant and Castle Theatre. One of the acts was 'The O' Hooligan Boys', a tenor song by Sinclair and Davies.[32] Certainly by October 1894 events had escalated; according to the *Illustrated Police News*, 'a tradesmen's committee has been formed in this district of the metropolis. It has been decided that a representative deputation should wait on the Home Secretary on the subject.'[33] However, it would be in the summer of 1898 that the press adoption of the hooligan became particularly pronounced, when problems with street disorder in south London were apparently exacerbated by a heat wave.[34] From the height of the hooligan crisis in July and August 1898, any sort of disorderly behaviour including robbery, stone throwing, pushing or shoving passers-by, gambling and playing pitch and toss, was likely to be labelled hooliganism. As one writer to the *Reynolds's News* asked, 'Who are the Hooligans?' For this letter writer, the hooligan 'may be defined as a member of a gang of roughs whose object it is to assault peaceful citizens in the street as a playful amusement or for purposes of robbery'.[35] The adoption of the language of hooliganism reflected many contemporary concerns about juvenile crime and disorder, ruffianism and the declining standards of behaviour amongst young working-class men and youths. The ubiquity and force of this language tends to cloud our understanding of the actual incidence of youth gang crime at the time. As Michael Livie has pointed out, the limited evidence that we have suggests that there was no 'spike' in juvenile violence during the 'hooligan crisis' of 1898.[36]

London's Street Gangs

In this study, the focus is mostly limited to the trials at the higher court, all of which involve the use of severe violence and/or weapons. The cases were sent to trial at the Old Bailey from various metropolitan police courts including: Worship Street, Bow Street, Westminster, Clerkenwell, Marylebone, Southwark, Lambeth, the London Police Court, the South Western Police Court, the West London Police Court and the North London Police Court. However, detailed accounts of the trials are limited to the press reports and to the Old Bailey. The trial reports from the Old Bailey have been compiled along with a small number of related cases (i.e. associated with named gangs) that were identified in the newspaper reports of the London police courts from the period 1882 to 1912. Identification of youth gang incidents was achieved by searching the combined press databases and the Old Bailey Online for both named gangs but also for references to 'gangs of youths', 'gang of roughs, 'gangs of young roughs' and similar phrases. For the courts, there are few surviving records relevant to the London cases discussed here, thus systematic analysis of the police court records across the period is not possible.[37] Whilst press reports could provide a more systematic approach, the coverage is inconsistent, and (as noted above) low-level disorder between youths was not always reported. For example, by the early twentieth century, despite a cluster of significant cases in 1907, the reporting of hooligan crime and youth gang violence is marginal compared to the 1880s and 90s.[38]

The database evidence used here refers to 41 events that are described in a way that can be identified as gang-related affrays and confrontations.[39]

Here 'gang-related' crimes are defined as those involving a predominance of young men (aged from mid-teens to early 20s), who were engaged in fighting a targeted group or individual, and where there was some evidence (often from police and/or witnesses) of territorial identity. The majority of the events were prosecutions for wounding (29), of which some involved multiple charges, including riot and assault. There were four murder trials, two of which related to the same death, one trial for manslaughter, three for rioting, two for assault and two for disorderly behaviour. Altogether there were 62 youths charged with some sort of wounding offence. Looking more closely at the 41 events, all but six of these cases were tried at the Old Bailey; 97 individuals were involved, and only one defendant was female. This was 15-year-old Eliza Walters, who was prosecuted in June 1897 as part of a group of youths who were tried for the manslaughter of 12-year-old Margaret Jane Smith who had been caught in the crossfire of a gang affray.[40] Despite the scarcity of convictions of girls, young women were present in a number of cases, often as witnesses but also as friends of the accused or victim. As in scuttling cases, a perceived slight to a young woman could provide the spark for a fight.[41] In July 1898 Benjamin Morgan, a G Division detective, had commented to Booth's investigators, that there had been a slight 'recrudescence' of violence that year, 'which has taken the form of pistol gangs. Gangs of lads get together and they insult one another's Lady Loves and then comes trouble.'[42] In 1907, a fight outside the London Assurance pub on the City Road that ended in the death of porter Garrett William Dundon, started because of an insult to a female friend of the accused boys. Florence Fairhead, a 16-year-old coffee shop worker, described how 'They came pushing along and one of them put his arm round my neck and I pushed it off. Jim Ashton looked at the man who put his arm on me. The man hit Ashton in the face with his fist.'[43]

Despite the eruption of the hooligan crisis in 1898, youth gang activity in London can be traced back at least to the early 1880s. It is from this period that problems between street gangs first started to escalate in a way serious enough to bring it to the attention of the press and the higher court. In the spring of 1882, in a series of commentaries on the 'fighting gangs of London', the *Pall Mall Gazette* would editorialise on the causes of the outbreaks of 'ruffianly lawlessness' on the streets of the metropolis.[44] The *Gazette* characterised the gangs as ill educated, ill formed and unemployed, 'the new generation of the savages of the slums is more combative and more inclined to organisation that its predecessor'.[45] Their textbook for crime had been the penny dreadful published in the 1860s, *The Wild Boys of London*, and they were 'utterly ignorant and untrained'.[46] Moreover, the *Gazette* was of the opinion that the gangs were not a new phenomenon; on the contrary they had existed for years as 'regular feeders of the vast criminal population of London'.[47] These articles appeared in response to two Old Bailey trials of February that year. These were the first trials involving boys and young men that had a visible public profile identifying them as gang related. Both trials were in connection with the murder of a 19-year-old carman named Frederick Wilmore during a confrontation on the Thames Embankment on 18 December 1881. Wilmore had been left gravely injured and died in the New Year. It was only after the coroner's inquest the following January that any arrests were made, with the trial of the accused Thomas Galliers and James Casey taking place at the Old Bailey in late February.[48] Even before the trial the press called attention to the problem of the 'fighting gangs'. The *Pall Mall Gazette* noted on the 2 February that the Worship Street magistrate, Mr Wontner, had remarked that, 'he had heard something of street-fighting but this was positive terrorism'.[49] The involvement of lethal weaponry here is significant as the majority of the cases that went to the Old Bailey did involve some sort of lethal weapon, such as knives and, from 1897, pistols and revolvers. These cases may represent the tip of a metaphoric iceberg. However, the limited number of Old Bailey cases, and those related cases found in the press, may more realistically reflect a periodic bubbling over of tensions between local youths rather than an endemic youth gang problem.

Those crime events that involved named gangs overwhelmingly went on to be prosecuted at the Old Bailey. It is perhaps significant that the references to named gangs derive most frequently from police evidence or from that given by witnesses or the prosecutor. Thus, in one of the trials of February 1882, a police constable named John Gilbert stated, 'I know a number of persons called the "Dove Row gang"; they number from 100 to 200, more or less'. The brother of one of the defendants, 18-year-old William Hubbard, also gave evidence since the accused was staying with him and his wife, 'I have heard of the Dove Row gang, I don't know any of them – I never heard that my brother belonged to it, or Jennings.' Another police constable, William Shee, testified that another of the defendants, 19-year-old John Collins, had told him that 'I used to belong to the street-fighting gang when old Nichol street used to fight Dove Row.'[50] In unpublished witness statements there were also references to local gangs, including the Green Gate Lads, the Fan Street Lads and the Lambeth Chaps.[51] Moreover, clusters of events involving youths engaged in disorderly behaviour seemed to lead to witnesses, and particularly the police, drawing relationships that may or may not have been meaningful. Thus, it is not always clear how far events were actually part of some broader street gang culture or whether gatherings of youths were labelled by a shared language developed by the police, prosecutors, witnesses and the press. It may have been this process which led to the vilification of a street (or small area), as much as any real territorial violence. For example, in 1896 Arthur Morrison published *A Child of the Jago*. In this thinly disguised account of the Old Nichol area in Bethnal Green, Dove Row metamorphosed into 'Dove Lane', 'The Jago and Dove Lane were districts ever at feud, active or smouldering, save for brief intervals of ostentatious reconciliation, serving to render the next attack on Dove Lane the more savage – for invariably the Jagos were aggressors and victors.'[52] Dove Row and the Old Nichol lay either side of the Hackney Road, which provides the boundary between Haggerston to the north of the road and Bethnal Green to the south. Whilst it is perfectly plausible that territorial incidents between the two areas occurred, the only clear press reference to a 'Dove Row gang' are those related to the trial described above, in early 1882.

The cross-fertilisation of evidence between police, witnesses and other court officials is also apparent from surviving correspondence between CID Director Howard Vincent and the Sessions clerk at the Old Bailey, to whom the former wrote in March 1882 in order to obtain the shorthand notes of the presiding Justice Hawkins's 'observations as to the prevalency of organized gangs of roughs in the metropolis'. The notes did not survive, but the clerk recalled that two gangs had been mentioned at the trial, the 'Dove Row Fighting Gang' and the 'Green Gate Gang'.[53] This suggests, as Hallsworth found in accounts of contemporary gangs, that overlapping narratives (from police, from court officials, from press, from defendants and witnesses, from social investigators and authors of fiction) could interweave to create a metanarrative in which (in this case) territorial gang conflict was terrorising the streets of north-east London.[54] What is certain is that for at least 16 years before the outbreak of the hooligan crisis, youth street gangs were noted as being a problem in metropolitan streets. Moreover, the earliest coverage very quickly noted the territorial associations of the fighting gangs. As the *Gazette* noted in 1882, 'It not unfrequently happens that one set, bent on the extension of its territory, invades the district of another. Then there has to be some sort of rectification of frontier, brought about by the usual process.'[55] Whilst the problem of gangs of young roughs may not have been a new one, the association with territory, at least its identification in the courtroom and subsequently the press, may have been.

Territory

The issue of territoriality is a key indicator in definitional studies of gang culture. Thus territorial rivalry may shape the experience of young working-class people. As one study has noted, 'Mostly, conflict occurred on the boundaries of territories – typically defined by roads, railway lines or other physical markers – or where there were incursions into another group's territory.'[56] In the later Victorian period, territory would also be a defining factor in the identification of gang-related youth affrays, although these territorial alignments were arguably more fluid and less fixed than the associations of crime with the 'rookeries', 'dens', 'dives' and 'sinks' of the earlier period. In Manchester, from the 1870s, confrontations broke out between adjacent districts, as Davies noted, proximity bred resentment. However, youths would also travel signifi-cant distances in order to face rival gangs, crossing major thoroughfares or canal bridges which could be seen as a form of provocation.[57] Indeed, there are dangers in assuming that gangs operated from clearly defined territories. Structural factors may have precipitated certain areas into close associations with criminal activity and disorder; a process ampli-fied by press and police identification of problem areas. As we will see, there were specific territories that reoccurred in the reporting of gang-related offences in London. The extent to which such areas were stigmatised by police, and moreover the possibility that youths in such areas engaged in confrontations as a response to that stigmatisation, is difficult to measure. Many of the areas were those traditionally asso-ciated with urban poverty and disorder. For example, in 1861, John Hollingshead commented on Lisson Grove, an area which would later be associated with the 'Lisson Grove Lads', and dismissively charac-terised it as densely crowded and 'low', 'Somers Town, Shoreditch, and the New Cut, Lambeth, are here repeated in their principal fea-tures, and the whole place looks like a flourishing branch of some great central bank of costermongers, dingy brokers' shops, and Irish labourers'.[58] Dense populations of costermongers and manual work-ers, and the designation of the area (or parts of the area) as a slum, characterised many of the areas associated with gang-related crime. Nevertheless, as Davies found in Manchester and Salford, simple cor-relations between slum life, unemployment and criminality are not borne out by the evidence.

Overwhelmingly the young men and youths involved in these conflicts were workers: costermongers, printers' boys, capsule makers, van guards, machine hands. The areas in which they lived were characterised by proximity to manufacture, markets and opportunities for employment. Moreover, whilst some of the areas were associated with slums, other areas were characterised by a broader class demographic. For example, by the time of Booth's poverty map (1898–99), the area to the west of Lisson Grove contained a mixture of black, dark blue, light blue and purple streets – although it was surrounded by a density of red and yellow streets representing the middle class, upper-middle class and the wealthy. Similar patterns characterised areas many of the areas associated with gang-related activity such as Clerkenwell, Hoxton, Islington, Somers Town and Lambeth. Roads and streets that apparently gave their names to specific gangs reflected a range of social groups as can be seen in the instance of the Bemerton Street Gang (purple), the White Lion Gang (pink), the Dove Row Gang (light blue), the Duckett Street Gang (named Edward Street in 1898–99, light blue) and the Abbey Street Boys (purple).[59] Other roads associated with conflicts were similarly designated: for example, Chapel Street, Islington (pink), City Road (a mixture of pink, purple and light blue) and Rendlesham Street (most likely Rendlesham Road, pink and purple). These were not 'savages of the slums', but working-class youths from poor to respectable working-class areas.[60]

A number of street and area names can be identified over time. The earliest Old Bailey trials of February 1882 would establish early territorial patterns. The confrontation on the Thames embankment, for which Galliers and Casey would eventually be charged, was between the City Road Boys (who were also known as the Green Gate Lads, the Green Gate Tavern being a public house on the junction of the City Road and Bath Street) and the Lambeth Boys or Chaps.[61] This was clearly a territorial conflict, with the youths identifying themselves as belonging to either the Lambeth Lads or to City Road: 'You say you come from Lambeth; we don't come from Lambeth, we come from the City Road, and we are going to pay the Lambeth *chaps.'*[62] The *Pall Mall Gazette* editorials that appeared as a response to this event identified a number of named gangs: the 'Bow-commoners, the Millwallers, the Dove-row gang, the Golden-lane Gang, the New-Cut Gang, the Drury-lane Gang, the Lambeth Lads, and sundry others with equally unprepossessing designations'.[63] At Worship Street in early February 1882, a group of youths were placed on remand after being concerned in cutting and wounding William Shenstone and two other men, with intent. The eight men (aged between 17 and 20) were described as being from 'the costermonger class'. The men went to trial at the Old Bailey during the February Sessions, charged with actual bodily harm. The youths were identified with the Hackney area around Rendlesham Street and Lower Clapton, and there seem to have been connections here with the Dove Row Gang. Moreover, one of the accused, Patrick Kennedy, was referred to by both police and witnesses at Gallier and Casey's trial, the latter of whom had apparently told his employer that the assailant had been 'Patsy Kennedy', who had at that point been 'at large'.[64] These cases are suggestive in drawing the topography and networks of street gangs in this period. Many of the gangs described came from a relatively contained triangle from Lambeth and Southwark in the south, north to Islington and King's Cross, and then to Clerkenwell and Hackney in the north east. Moreover, the 'chaps' and 'lads' of City Road seem to have been reasonably mobile in pursuing their vendettas, walking the two miles or so to the embankment to meet the 'Lambeth lads'.

Despite the dominance of narratives about the north-eastern and south-eastern clusters, Chelsea and Marylebone were also identified as having a problem with street gangs. In 1882, the prosecutor at Worship Street, Mr St John Wontner, commented on the problem of fighting gangs:

> He thought, however, sufficient would be proved to show the public that London, even at this civilised period, was infested, not only at the East-end, but at West also, by gangs of men who appeared to be banded together for the purpose of fighting other gangs, and using the most lawless violence, not only to those they called their enemies, but to the public.[65]

As Wontner suggested, there were gangs identified with west London, or at least what might be called broadly west central London. In these areas, however, conflict seemed to be reasonably self-contained. Confrontations were played out within close neighbourhoods and adjacent streets. For example, the Fitzroy Place and Lisson Grove Lads, from the Marylebone area, came to grief in 1888 when eight youths aged between 15 and 18 sought revenge for an attack upon one of their female friends, Cissy Chapman, who had been attacked with Francis Cole (one of the accused) on a May evening, and had received a black eye. The youths armed themselves with knives the following evening and went to the Marylebone Road, where at least some of the youths caught up with another young man, 22-year-old Joseph Rumbold, who was stabbed in Regent's Park.[66] The press presented the events as 'A London Vendetta', drawing on the hot-blooded stereotype of the foreign criminal.[67] Other gang formations to be associated with west central London were gangs described in the Chelsea area, living and fighting on streets off the King's Road. In 1893, 1894 and 1900 there were reports of fighting between boys in the Manor Street, Arthur Street and College Street area. This was another mixed area according to Booth, a number of the streets were home to middle-class residents, despite the proximity to the Chelsea workhouse. Perhaps significantly, press reports of proceedings at the Westminster police court in May 1893 described the fights as undertaken by 'Rival Gangs of Schoolboys'. One of these, 14-year-old William Cadle, had stabbed a newspaper boy named Frederick Eaton in the face on College Street.[68] The prosecutor described Cadle as one of the 'Manor-street boys', claiming that he had been a participant in on-going warfare between the 'Manor-street boys', 'Arthur-street boys' and 'Oakum Building Warriors'.[69] These roads were extremely close to each other, lying north and south of a short section of the King's Road, centred around the parish of St Luke's, Chelsea. Conflict between groups of youths continued for at least another three years, when 16-year-olds John Proud and Charles Key would be prosecuted at the Old Bailey after attacking two cousins, Frederick and Peter Platt, who lived in Oakum [Oakham] Street.[70] The accused belonged to the Manor Street boys, to the south of the King's Road. Detective John Richardson presented a letter as evidence, which was described in court as 'a challenge from the boys to the "Bay" boys and the "Sands End" boys to come down and fight'.[71]

The emphasis in evidence and witness statement (and particularly police accounts) was on associating street gangs with very clearly defined spatial territory. Nevertheless, other evidence suggests that these youthful alliances were much more disorganised. Groups could redefine their allegiance based on the type of affray or confrontation that unfolded. Like the scuttlers, youths from specific areas fought each other but were also willing to fight together against a common enemy, as we have seen in the case of the fights between youths from north and south London. Moreover, a number of the Old Bailey events were focused on key institutions on the spatial map of working-class communities. The City Road, Islington, King's Cross, Clerkenwell, Hoxton, Shoreditch and Lambeth contained networks of streets in which music halls and public houses helped form the landscape over which territorial allegiances were played out and fought. A number of historians have commented on the central role that the music hall had in working-class culture, particularly for young men.[72] The importance of the music hall to youth cultures in the late-Victorian and Edwardian period can be seen from one trial in 1907. Several of the witnesses to the murder of Garrett William Dundon on the City Road were travelling from music halls. Twelve-year-old schoolboy Thomas Holdsworth had been to the Britannia in Hoxton; Florence Fairhead, the girlfriend of one of the accused youths, had been to the Empire Music Hall in Islington; 17-year-old Elizabeth Wakefield and 16-year-old May Collard had been to Sadler's Wells.[73] Other Old Bailey and police court cases also involved conflicts near or in music halls.[74] For example, in October 1891 17-year-old James Bassett was found guilty of wounding John Moore, stabbing him in the head as he left the Sadler's Wells Theatre. Further evidence revealed that an altercation between two groups of boys, containing the victim and the accused, had broken out inside the theatre with witnesses suggesting this was a fight between the Somers Town boys and Clerkenwell Lads.[75] In June 1912, Harry Silvester, a newspaper vendor, quarrelled with an acquaintance, John Jenkins, whilst he was at the Empire Music Hall in Shoreditch. The argument escalated into 'general fighting' involving a large group of youths. Silvester was shot at, receiving a bullet wound in his right arm. John Jenkins (18), one of four defendants, cross-examined Silvester, asking him about his membership of the 'Abbey Street Boys', which Silvester denied. Further suggestions that this was a 'gang' affray came from Chief Inspector Frederick Wensley who 'said that during the last nine months there had been five cases of use of revolvers in this district. The police had the greatest difficulty in obtaining evidence, as various gangs of lads had become a terror to the neighbourhood.'[76]

Whilst territory may have been fluid rather than fixed, and 'gang' identification with particular streets questionable, longer territorial continuities can be found by looking at the reporting of two of the main gangs described between 1882 and 1908. The Lambeth Lads were to re-emerge in the 1898 hooligan panic, when most of the street violence initially designated as hooliganism took place in Lambeth and parts of Southwark. As we have seen in 1894 and 1896, the hooligan gangs had already been identified with districts south of the river. By July 1898, the hooligans were being described as waging a 'Reign of Terror in South London'.[77] In August, an 18-year-old labourer named Frederick Dockrell was arrested in Battersea and charged at the South Western Police Court. Police constable Carter stated that, 'he saw the prisoner and some dozen other lads with sticks and belts, all wearing velvet caps, and, known as the "Velvet Cap gang", walking along Plough and York Roads, Battersea, pushing people off the pavement, knocking at shop doors, and using filthy language'.[78] This was the Lambeth described in Clarence Rook's novel of working-class life, *Hooligan Nights*, published in 1899; his protagonist, Alf, living on the mean streets of Lambeth and the Elephant and Castle.[79]

Despite the strong connection being made between hooliganism and south London, the north London gangs were tarred with the same brush. In August 1898, *The Times* reported on 'four young fellows of the Larrikin type ... all hailing from Somers Town' having wilfully damaged an ice-cream 'feeder' belonging to Andrea Bascean, an Italian ice-cream vendor of Clerkenwell, the boys were chased by the police, who reported people shouting, 'Look out for the Hooligan gang'.[80] The Somers Town gang were one of a number of gangs (whose membership may well have overlapped) who had been active in the Islington and Clerkenwell area at least since the 1870s. Over the years the gangs included, as well as the Somers Town Boys, the Clerkenwell Boys, the Bemerton Street Boys and the White Lion Street Gang. The territorial allegiances of these gangs are not particularly clear-cut. Whilst in 1882 City Road Lads had marched on the Lambeth Lads; in the 1890s fights were breaking out within fairly small areas. Thus affrays between the Somers Town Boys and the Clerkenwell Boys were reported as early as 1891 and were still a problem by 1907/8. At the Old Bailey in 1908, Harry Jarvis, a 19-year-old labourer who fired shots at two women, was described as belonging 'to the Somers Town gang of lads who employed their spare time in faction fights with others'.[81]

In summary the evidence suggests that some areas had long roots as sites of territorial conflict. Street proximate gang activity can be identified as existing spatially over time. Gangs in Hackney were identified in 1882, 1897 and 1911 (reports of Dove Row and Hackney Road); gang activity in Somers Town was mentioned in 1891 and 1908; the City Road in 1881/2 and 1908; Clerkenwell in 1885, 1891, 1897 and 1903. Even before the reporting of street gang conflicts began, reports of disorderly conduct by youths can be identified in broadly similar areas. Thus, in 1870 youths from Somers Town were described as 'larking' and 'hustling'. Complaints had been received of the nuisance of the 'gangs of young men parading the Pentonville-hill on a Sunday night'.[82] Early reporting from Clerkenwell, Islington, Marylebone and Lambeth also focused on the disorderly conduct of groups of youths. For example, in 1871, *Lloyd's* described Marylebone youths, 'who go in gangs of five or six, arm-in-arm, pushing everyone off the pavement'.[83] These reports bring to mind the depiction of working-class youth engaged in the time-honoured tradition of the monkey parade.[84] Long held identities associated with place and specific location are suggested by these traces over time. Moreover, as criminologists have noted in studies of contemporary youth street gangs, 'it was apparent that territoriality was deeply ingrained and cross generationally embedded', and 'The history of settlement patterns in the localities exerted an important influence on such traditions'.[85] As we have already seen, the areas were mixed in relation to class, though many area could be described as broadly working class. Indeed, like Davies's scuttlers, the youths were not the slum-dwelling residuum but worked in semi-skilled and unskilled occupations. It is to work that we now turn.

Occupations and Age Profiles

Of the 97 individuals in the Old Bailey and related cases, 71 were described as having occupations, either in the court proceedings or in the press (occupational descriptions were provided formally in the Sessions papers from April 1906). Perhaps unsurprisingly 20 of the defendants were described simply as labourers. However of the remaining 51, semi-skilled and manual workers predominated: thus a glassblower, a French polisher, a stickmaker, a fishmonger, a beer bottler, a confectioner and a wood chopper were amongst the single occupations given. Perhaps more unusual was the single sailor. This was 17-year-old Peter Lee, one of the youths charged with the Regent's Park murder in 1888, who was described in court as having 'come from sea'. Their victims were largely of the same constituency, including a greengrocer, two labourers, a printer's boy, a van guard, a tailor and a printing machine attendant. The manual and semi-skilled nature of many of the youths involved can be seen in the earliest case at the Old Bailey, the murder of Frederick Wilmore (see p. 149 and note 48). Thomas Galliers was a packing-case maker who worked for a Mr Benjamin, who had a shop in Shoreditch. James Casey was a stoker in a biscuit factory on Shepherdess Walk, off the City Road. His employer, Thomas William Barrett, and his wife, Ellen Barrett, both appeared to give evidence. The victim, Frederick Wilmore, was a carman living in Lambeth. Another trial involved seven youths described as costers and reflects the high number of young men employed in the capital's food markets and street selling trades. As well as costermongers, there were six porters; other related trades included, 'carman', 'carriers boy', 'general dealer', 'van boy', 'van guard' and 'fishmonger'.[86]

The preponderance of occupations related to street and market selling may confirm the significance of the proximity to metropolitan markets. According to Mayhew, in 1849, the largest weekend street markets could be found in Lambeth, at the New Cut and in Somers Town, where the market was known as the 'Brill'. He also pointed to the large numbers of costermongers near the Bethnal Green Road.[87] Whilst many of the street markets were in decline by the later nineteenth century, street trading remained an important source of income of young Londoners. In Arthur Harding's memoirs, street markets and street trading were presented as a key element of working-class life in the late-Victorian and Edwardian East End.[88] These were the occupations open to working-class youths in the metropolis. Few of these boys could be described as having apprenticeships, and in contrast can be seen as belonging to the large urban proletariat upon which, as a result of mechanisation and de-skilling in industry, employers would increasingly rely. As Michael Childs has noted in relation to the growth of the transport and distributive trades, delivery boys, van boys and errand boys were needed to drive these developing sectors.[89] Efforts would be made to regulate the working conditions of young workers and legislation sought to protect child street traders.[90] However, legislation focused mostly on those aged under 14 (and girls aged under 16). To all intents and purposes, our youth gang members were young men.[91]

Age is given for all but three of the 97 individuals who were charged. The majority were aged between 16 and 19 (76 youths), and the most common age was 17 (26 youths). This range is comparable to the age range of scuttlers in Manchester and Salford identified by Davies.[92] The youngest boys involved in the Old Bailey and related events were aged 14, the oldest was 25-year-old Samuel Harrison, charged at the Old Bailey in May 1901 for wounding 21-year-old Daniel Winn, a carman, outside the Ship Aground pub in Lea Bridge Road, Hackney. Harrison was found not guilty.[93] The two 14-year-olds were William Cadle and Frederick Leader. Cadle was remanded in May 1893 after being charged with stabbing another boy in the face, but it is not clear that the case went any further, possibly because the victim had not recovered enough from his ordeal to prosecute.[94] Leader appeared on a charge of wounding at the Old Bailey in November 1897. Along with another boy, 15-year-old William Bond, he had been accused of shooting at Alfred Webb, a 15-year-old errand boy from Pentonville. Leader was found not guilty, probably because of the poor credibility of one of witnesses, Charles Read, another boy whom the jury noted 'should have been in the dock'.[95] This case prompted some worrying column inches as to where the boys had been able to obtain their pistols. Sensational headings worried about 'The Revolver Mania', 'A London Plague that must be Swept Away', 'The Pistol Plague in London' and 'A London Plague

Spot'.[96] The *Illustrated Police News* linked the shooting to the activities of what it called the Clerkenwell Pistol Gang, noting, 'The shooting arose out of a feud between young lads hailing from Clerkenwell and Islington'. The report noted the significant disquiet of the jury, who called for 'more stringent measures than at present exist for the protection of the public against the prevalent reckless use of fire-arms'.[97]

Weapons

In *Hooligan*, Geoffrey Pearson argued that the repeated alarms about pistol gangs were a reflection of 'the depth of fears surrounding working-class youth at this time' rather than evidence of any real surge in the use of pistols, revolvers or 'toys' such as air pistols.[98] Indeed, like the scuttlers, the London fighting gangs were described as using belts, sticks, fists and feet to inflict violence, as well as more lethal weaponry such as knives and daggers. However, gun crime was an issue, and arguably it was more of an issue in the London gangs that it had been in Manchester and Salford.[99] Davies has described the rapid decline of scuttling from the late 1890s; the point at which emerging concerns about gun crime can be identified in the London cases. In the 41 London cases, 19 involved the use of pistols or revolvers, one involved both a pistol and a knife, nine involved a knife or a dagger, two involved belts, one involved a stick, six involved fists and kicking and three involved disorderly behaviour. The majority of the crimes involving pistols and revolvers date from the later 1890s, only one case before 1897 allegedly involved a pistol. This was the case of 16-year-old William Brown and 18-year-old Harry Foxcroft who were found guilty of wounding, their victims were three 'lads' named Arthur Hobbs, James Page and John Ayres.[100] In the sessions report and in the press, revolver shots were mentioned and one of the victims, John Ayres, claimed to have seen the 'butt end of a pistol', although he was subsequently stabbed in the arm. Whilst the case was described as a shooting, no pistol or revolver seems to have been found. From 1897, the number of cases involving pistols and revolvers increased. How significant this increase was is difficult to assess since the fact that they involved lethal weaponry made them much more likely to be reported and tried at the higher court.

Interestingly a similar shift towards firearms can also be seen in Birmingham. Whereas the scuttlers were in decline by the 1890s, in Birmingham, conflicts between armed youths and the city's police seem to have been escalating. Thus Philip Gooderson has noted the increased frequency of incidents and assaults involving firearms from 1897, noting contemporary comments about the cheapness and easy access to firearms.[101] Indeed, in London, a correspondent to the *Morning Post* in December 1907 referred to the problems in Birmingham in a letter that the paper titled, 'The Epidemic of Revolvers'. This was from an individual named Ellis Lever who claimed to have written to the Home Secretary about the 'indiscriminate sale of firearms to mere youths'. Lever noted that his concerns about the 'revolver nuisance' had been voiced back as far as April 1882, the point at which the London gang affrays first emerged in the press (although the most visible of these early cases had not involved firearms).[102] There were concerns about the use of firearms in the 1890s. In the Commons the debate about a Pistol Bill had been circulating since 1893.[103] When the bill was first introduced in July 1893, the focus was specifically on pistol use by young people. *The Times* reported that the bill was not aimed at interfering with the legitimate sale or possession of pistols, and a new regulation was proposed, 'No boy or girl under 18 may carry a pistol, and no persons may sell pistols to them'.[104] The bill was thrown out in September, in the face of interventions by Charles Hopwood, Member of Parliament for South East Lancashire.[105] Hopwood, in a letter to *The Times*, claimed that his objections to the bill were that it was an ineffective measure. He also suggested that the measure was not justified by recent statistics for firearms use.[106] The bill was reintroduced in the spring of 1895, when again it seemed to focus on the use of pistols by young people, and again was attacked by Hopwood.[107] Discussion of the bill was still on-going by early summer, where it was frequently met with derision, and it would not be until 1903 that a Pistols Act came into force.[108] Specific provisions were made to restrict sales to persons aged under 18. Young people who brought, hired or carried a pistol could also be fined 40 shillings.[109]

In this case, it seems noteworthy that the bill was not reintroduced at the time when the press were reporting on the 'Pistol Plague' and 'Revolver Mania', from the autumn of 1897.[110] There had been some coverage from early 1896, with the *Daily News* reporting on 'The Cheap Pistol Nuisance' in February in reference to two cases involving boys purchasing and using pistols.[111] However, from 1897, reports of revolver and pistol crime were increasingly linked to youths. This coverage was occasionally seen as a London problem. For example, in June 1897, the *Hampshire Advertiser* reported on the 'Revolver Boys', noting that despite the presence of young ruffians in Southampton, the problem was not as in London, 'There the boy roughs appear to have been developing a love for the revolver, which has made the crowded district of Clerkenwell a terror and a trouble to the police'.[112] The article particularly referred to the shooting of an innocent bystander in June 1897.[113] In a terrible tragedy, two groups of youths known as the Chapel Street and Lion gangs (Chapel Street and White Lion Street both ran off Pentonville Road, close to the Angel, Islington) fought. 'Lads' and 'girls' were described as marching in a gang armed with sticks, pieces of iron and one lad, 17-year-old labourer George Robson, with a revolver. Robson shot into the crowd, aiming for an adversary, and hit instead a by-passer, a 12-year-old girl named Margaret Jane Smith. Robson and another of the boys, 17-year-old John Goodey, were charged with manslaughter to which they pleaded guilty at the Old Bailey.[114] One of the witnesses to these events, a local carman named Alfred Smith, provided a detailed account of the gangs.[115] He described how the accused youths belonged to the 'Chapel Street gang', who carried revolvers, iron, sticks and belts as weapons. According to Smith, George Robson carried two revolvers and had a belt made to carry them. He described how there were two layers to the Chapel Street gang, the 'large boys' and the 'small boys', suggesting some sort of graduation between younger and older youths. Smith's account described the involvement of female gang members ('the girls came out to have a fight with Hannah Brown') as well as descriptions of the youths 'playing mouth organs and singing'.[116] This shooting brought to a head a series of problems with 'armed roughs' in the previous year. As reported in *Lloyd's Weekly Newspaper*, the shooting was 'the culminating horror of a state of terrorism that is a disgrace to London itself'. It was noted that some of the most fearful fights were amongst young girls, and according to the father of one of the girls in the gangs, they had recently graduated from toy pistols to revolvers.[117]

There is some evidence of an increase in firearm crime amongst youths in 1907 and 1908, which may have been linked to the passage of the Pistols Act in 1903 and an increased willingness to prosecute such cases. Nevertheless, of the 14 revolver-wounding cases involving youths under 20 at the Old Bailey in 1907, all but two of the cases were linked to youth gang affrays. Arguably, something akin to gang warfare broke out between gangs from the City Road, Somers Town, Clerkenwell and parts of the East End. This phase of violence started in the spring of 1907 when armed youths (boys and girls) in Hoxton were reported as marching on each other. Then in April fighting on the City Road (near the London Assurance pub), a knife claimed the life of William Garrett Dundon.[118] In June a letter writer to the editor of *The Times*, wrote, 'Sir, – The murder in the City-road – savage and hideous – by a boy of 16 has once again staggered London by the sight of the hooligan whom it creates.'[119] Whilst at court the police described this affray as a 'disturbance' rather than a faction fight, the depositions suggest that the victims may have run into one of the local hooligan gangs.[120] For example, William Sewell, a 24-year-old cabinet-maker who had been amongst the group of lads accompanying the murdered youth, described one of the defendants as wearing a black velvet cap. According to Pearson, velvet caps were a badge of identity for some youth gangs.[121] James Ashton pleaded his innocence at Old Street Magistrates Court, protesting that another lad had said, 'I've chived two of 'em, Jim boy'.[122] Another witness, 12-year-old Thomas Holdsworth who lived on the City Road, described the defendants as the 'Nile chaps'.[123] From September, events seem to have escalated with a series of incidents involving revolvers. At the September Old Bailey Sessions three prosecutions involved youths fighting with firearms. All three events took place in East London (on the Mile End Road, Cartwright Street, off Royal Mint Street, and in Limehouse).[124] On first view, the case of Robert Wannell, a 19-year-old labourer who shot at Harry Hall outside a lodging house in Cartwright Street, seems to be a personal altercation between the victim and accused, who had known each other for some years. Both perpetrator and victim passed off the shooting as an accident, however, Wannell was found guilty of unlawful wounding. Inspector Wensley noted at the trial that, 'this revolver business had become an intolerable nuisance in the East End, and that he had receive no end of complaints of people having been shot'. He also noted that the Wannell 'was mixed up with a lot of youths who fought amongst each other with pistols'.[125] By November 1907 events had escalated with the case of ten young men aged between 17 and 19, described variously as costermongers, van guards, a paperhanger and a brass finisher, who were charged with feloniously shooting at people on the public highway in Copenhagen Street, Islington.[126] According to the prosecution evidence, the King's Cross neighbourhood was infested by three gangs of young lads known as the Bemerton Street Gang, the White Lion Street Gang and the Clerkenwell Gang, whose internecine struggles had become such a nuisance that the magistrate at Clerkenwell had decided to commit the defendants to trial, 'in order that they might be severely dealt with'.[127] The witnesses and police described scenes of violence involving '40 or 50 lads'. A revolver, a knife and a belt were amongst the weapons used. In June 1908, George Askew (17) shot Charles Dorsett and George Etherington, who were described as members of the Duckett Street Gang (off the Mile End Road in Shoreditch); in the same month, 19-year-old Roger Hellen knifed 18-year-old George White – White was accused of being involved with a gang of boys called the 'Forties', who had previously pulled a revolver on the prosecutor.[128]

Criminal Careers

The extent to which belonging to a street gang reflected involvement in more sustained criminal activity is difficult to measure with any certainty. Whilst contemporaries frequently portrayed the fighting gangs as 'organised' and as part of the broader landscape of the metropolitan underworld, it is likely that for many of the boys and men, involvement in street gangs and fighting did not lead to a criminal career. In Manchester and Salford, both Davies and Gooderson noted the recidivism of some scuttlers, however, charges seem to have predominately related to scuttling activities rather than to broader criminal activities.[129] In London some boys were noted by the court as having previous convictions, and by the turn of the century at the Old Bailey those convictions were more systematically recorded. Thus from 1899, 12 youths were described as having been charged or convicted previously. However, as in Manchester and Salford, most of these charges and convictions seem to have been related to disorderly conduct or violence of some sort or another. For example, 19-year-old John Harmond, was found guilty of shooting at William Churchwood (also 19) in Charlotte Street, off the Caledonian Road, in October 1907. According to the evidence of detective constable William Herbert, Harmond had been fined for stealing money at Clerkenwell in September 1906, he had also been charged with disorderly conduct in June and September 1907.[130] However, his victim William Churchwood was himself convicted the following month for his involvement in a shooting in the street near Copenhagen Street.[131] Unsurprisingly, some of the youths with numerous previous convictions were amongst the oldest in the sample. For example, 13 previous convictions dating from 1902 were proved against Charles Goddard, a 22-year-old stoker, convicted alongside 20-year-old machinist Harry Goldsworthy for shooting an unknown person with the intent to do bodily harm in April 1911. Goddard had spent nine months in Borstal. Goldsworthy was also described as having 'a number of previous convictions proved', and had been previously convicted as a rogue and vagabond.[132] In many of the cases where previous charges and convictions were referred to, these had been dealt with at the police courts. Given the relatively minor nature of the offences and the poor survival of police court registers, it is unlikely that these would be possible to trace.

On the other hand, two of the youths who continued to offend after their prosecution at the Old Bailey can be traced. Henry Rye, aged 19, was prosecuted with Alfred Jewell in September 1899. Both were charged with wounding, shooting at John Chandler with intent to do grievous bodily harm. The accused were described as being involved in a gang called the Pimlico Lads, although the victim, Chandler, was also accused of having been involved in street fighting. Both youths were found guilty and both youths admitted to previous convictions. Alfred Jewell was already serving a sentence of six months hard labour for another offence. The police stated that 'they were the associates of a gang of thieves'.[133] Whilst there is no record of Jewell other than his Old Bailey appearance, Rye appeared a number of times at the Old Bailey over the next decade or so: convicted for larceny in 1902 and 1904 and then for uttering a forged cheque in 1912.[134] In May 1907, 17-year-old Philip Murty was one of the boys tried at the Old Bailey for the murder of Garrett William Dundon (aged about 24). Charged along with Patrick Chapman (a 16-year old printer) and Thomas Allen (a 15-year-old stick-man), he was discharged. Another boy, James Ashton, was charged separately and found guilty of manslaughter.[135] Within a few short months, Murty was in trouble again. This time he had been found trespassing in an enclosed property and was suspected of being there for the intention of committing a felony. Murty's case was reported because of the efforts that had been made to reform him after the murder trial. *Lloyd's Weekly News* noted that 'After a few weeks spent in a home a situation was got for him on a farm near Swanley, Kent. The work did not please him, and the absence of control made it difficult to deal with him ... he left the farm and came back to his old haunts in Hoxton.'[136]

The defendants in this case were from the closely-knit streets around Hoxton and in particular seem to have been linked to the infamous Nile Street. Indeed, Murty was described as a 'Nile boy' by James Ashton's girlfriend, Florence Fairhead.[137] According to Arthur Harding, 'mobs' from the streets of Hoxton, Nile Street (off the City Road in a cluster of streets including Shepherdess Walk and Westmoreland Place) particularly, were involved in illegalities. For example, he refers to the Titanic mob, from Nile Street, as pickpockets and burglars.[138] Harding's account seems to suggest that there were overlaps between the forms of territorial violence described here and lower levels of organised theft and petty crime. Perhaps unsurprisingly, contemporaries were quick to make connections between hooliganism and petty criminality, in turn linking it to the employment problems of the young in a *Times* editorial titled, '"Hooliganism" In Shoreditch'.[139] Nevertheless, it may be that for many of the boys a guilty verdict at the higher court nipped their criminal careers in the bud, and most of the boys and youths were sent to prison or, in the more serious cases, sentenced to penal servitude. There were five sentences for penal servitude, ranging between three and ten years. Thomas Galliers received the ten-year sentence for the murder of Frederick Wilmore in 1882.[140] Only one boy, William Bond, was sentenced to the reformatory, and from 1908, three youths were recommended to Borstal.[141] One death sentence was handed out, to George Galletly for the murder of Joseph Rumbold in 1888; he was recommended to mercy and a petition was got up on his behalf, eventually he received a reprieve on Monday 13 August.[142]

Conclusion

This study of youth street violence in the late-Victorian and Edwardian period has sought to place the boys and youths involved within the broader context of their communities. Whilst these were undoubtedly working-class youths, their communities were not simply slums. For the most part these youths lived in mixed class communities, in which they also worked, drank and socialised. The rhetoric of the Victorian press may well have labelled the 'hooligan' as a member of the 'criminal class', but in reality membership of and identity with street gangs was probably more disorganised, more flexible and more fleeting than contemporaries believed. The 'gang' may have offered youths a place of refuge. As this chapter has demonstrated, many of the youths did work but mostly in low-level and low-skilled occupations. It may be that these youths, on the cusp of manhood, felt socially marginalised and that the badge of identity linking them to the small area in which they lived their life, had meaning. It remains to be considered to what extent the territorial gangs of this period were a new phenomenon. As we saw in Chapter 4, in the mid-nineteenth century the press had frequently commented on the depredations of the swell mob. As a report from the *Morning Post* noted in 1855, 'several complaints have been of late made by ladies that they have been robbed of watches, money, &c., by a gang of youths who infest the neighbourhood, and who daily alter their style of dress'.[143] The collectivity, identity and style of the swell mob may provide some precedent for the youth gangs that would emerge in the following decades. The specific associations with territory, however, were not part of the tool-kit used by police, press and witnesses with which to describe these youths. On the other hand, a hundred years earlier, in 1757, constables had entered a field near Cold Bath Fields, 'where a Gang of Youths have for some Months assembled on the Sabbath-day, and diverted themselves in Gaming, by tossing up, &c. and took several into Custody, some of whom were Apprentices'.[144] Presumably these were youths who lived and worked in the surrounding Clerkenwell streets.

However, the areas in which the street gangs fought from the 1880s were changing. Whilst Jerry White noted the insularity of one East End community, 'The boundaries of the area were clear cut and some people strayed outside them hardly at all', the geography of east London was re-configured in this period.[145] Slum clearance and rebuilding, the erection of new tenements and model dwellings had changed the landscape in areas such as Bethnal Green, Hoxton, Clerkenwell and Islington. The passage of the Artisans' and Labourers' Dwellings Improvements Act in 1875 had a significant impact on many of the areas associated with street gangs. In these areas new model dwellings would jostle for space with older buildings and arguably create cleavages in communities. For example, with the demolition of the Old Nichol area in the early 1890s, residence in the Boundary Estate that replaced it was beyond the reach of most of its original inhabitants.[146] Arthur Harding's family were typical of this experience, born in Boundary Street on the borders of the Old Nichol, after the clearance the family moved to Hoxton and then to Bethnal Green.[147] Moreover, slum clearance in the centre of London displaced large numbers and working-class communities swelled. For example, in Somers Town, the railway developments at St Pancras undertaken by the Midland Railway Company from the 1860s resulted in significant overcrowding.[148] In Clerkenwell, the impact of slum clearance and rebuilding was also supplemented by the tensions created by the arrival of newer communities. Whilst the Italian community was already established in Holborn by the mid-nineteenth century, in the later nineteenth century it would move further north, settling into the streets between Farringdon and Grays Inn Road. Moreover, from the 1880s, new emigrants from the northern and central regions of Italy supplemented the existing Italian community.[149] Arguably these spatial and population changes contributed to the manifestation of territorially based youth street culture from the 1880s. The extent to which these territorial street cultures merged with new forms of criminal organisation by the interwar period will be considered in the next chapter.

8

'The Terror of the People': Organised Crime in Interwar London[1]

In the 1920s and 1930s the London and national press reported extensively on what appeared to be outbreaks of gang crime bearing a similarity to the forms of organised crime that had recently been reported in Italy and North America. At the start of the 1920s, home-grown gang violence had been mainly confined to the racecourses and cast largely as an unwelcome development of traditional forms of racecourse criminality. By the middle of the decade the incursions of the racing men onto the London streets provoked intense report-age.[2] In London, violent street conflicts were characterised by press, police and politicians as a form of terrorism. The *Evening Standard*, for instance, described a tense search for 'racecourse terrorists' in the West End, 'While Scotland Yard is thus rigorously engaged in hunting down the terrorists, the "enemy" is employing a sort of secret service to ascertain the movements of detectives.'[3] The *Daily Mail* presented the conflicts as an underworld threat, levying fear on the lives of civilians, 'There are many people walking about London maimed because they fell foul of the gangs.'[4] Moreover, 'terrorism' and organised crime would be linked in reports of illicit gambling economies and violent street gangs in other British cities in this period.[5] Most notably, from the later 1920s, the 'reign of terror' associated with the violent conflicts between Glasgow's street fighting gangs would lead to inauspicious comparisons with Chicago.[6] Despite the connections made by the press, the gang violence of the 1920s was largely territorial and limited in its impact. These were internecine battles with the battle lines, at least superfi-cially, drawn on the competition over dominance of the south-east racecourses. The activity on the racecourses gave the men an identity in the press, and the conflicts involved groups of men from different parts of the country with confrontations frequently taking place on the racecourse, or in close proximity to them. Nevertheless, many of the events described and further investigated by the police took place in local pubs, clubs and streets in London. Indeed, despite the connection to the racecourse, the violence was overwhelmingly perceived as metropolitan.

This chapter will focus on the development of the forms of racecourse-related crime in London and the south-eastern courses in the interwar period. The first part of the chapter will consider the debates about modern definitions of British organised crime cultures in relation to the racecourse wars and provide a brief chronological account of the key events and individuals associated with the gangs. The most well known of the racecourse gangs, the Sabinis, were a family-based organisation from the Anglo-Italian community of Clerkenwell. Whilst our understanding of the involvement of the Sabini family is unavoidably shaped by press and police construction of these events, a core focus of the chapter will be an exploration of kin, residence and occupations, revealing how the racing men were anchored into local communities and economies. Thus, despite the presentation of 'racecourse ruffianism' as something unprecedented and external (for example, as an incursion of 'alien' and 'foreign' criminals), the familial, ethnic and criminal networks which shaped the racing men (or at least versions of them) had long been part of metropolitan working-class and plebeian culture.[7] The final part of the chapter will focus in more detail on the issue of territory. The reach of the racecourse gangs from their customary metropolitan territories to the outer environs of London and the south east was arguably one of the factors which led to extensive press reporting of the racecourse wars. Thus, the racing men might have come from areas that had older traditions of territorial street conflicts, but it would be their ability to move beyond the confines of the streets of London that troubled contemporaries. The Sabini gang, their confederates and rival gangs arguably had much in common with the 'traditional' street gangs of Victorian and Edwardian London. Not least in the shared topography of streets with which the racecourse gangs would be associated in the interwar period. Nevertheless, these 'new' criminal communities combined the territorial street violence of the Victorian and early-Edwardian gangs with a criminal career that took advantage of the black economies that would flourish after the First World War. Whilst the racketeering, protectionism and gambling that were bread and butter to the interwar gangs were not an innovation of this period, the combination of the traditional street fighting gangs with organised forms of these activities arguably were.

Organised Crime

The question of whether British gang violence represents a moment of modernisation is central to this chapter. Historically informed criminologists, such as Dick Hobbs and Alan Wright, have seen the events of the interwar period as looking back to older models of criminal confederacy. Thus, Wright questions 'the extent to which these gangs were organised in terms of their structures and objectives'.[8] Nevertheless, the modern development of organised crime is, at least in a North American context, closely connected to this period when the reporting of North American 'gangsterdom' was increasingly visible in the British press. The early reporting of the Sicilian Cosa Nostra and Neapolitan Camorra was largely conducted in terms of organised political crime and violence.[9] However, from the interwar period, comparisons would increasingly be drawn between the gangs of Chicago and the problems in Britain's cities. Gang warfare had arrived on British shores, and contemporaries were quick to draw parallels with international events. As Andrew Davies has noted, 'The American Underworld provided the most compelling demonstrations of crime in the modern age, in which the methods of big business were infused with lethal violence, and the methods of the racecourse gangs were almost axiomatically accused of bringing American crime methods to Britain'.[10] Certainly, by the 1930s, the police biographies that came to proliferate in the interwar period as a result of the retirement of some of the earliest CID detectives would draw on 'gangster' rhetoric to describe their policing of the gangs.[11]

However, the comparison between British organised crime in this period and American and Italian crime groups is far from straightforward. In North America and Italy the reach of organised crime into enterprises other than racketeering, gambling and prostitution had been evident from the nineteenth century.[12] Moreover, the era of prohibition in the USA enabled extensive penetration into political and economic organisations. Arguably, it would not be until post Second World War in Britain that similar penetration occurred. Even then, as Jenkins and Potter have argued, the 'family firms' of the 1960s may have had more in common with their interwar predecessors than the American crime families to which they aspired to.[13] The growth of gangs engaged in loosely organised illegalities in North America in the early twentieth century was studied by subcultural theorists like Frederick Thrasher (1927) and William Foote Whyte (1943), who wrote about the development of gangs within local communities in Chicago and Boston.[14] As Wright points out, 'Thrasher's study of gangs followed the Chicago

School of Criminology in seeking to understand gang life as part of the ecology of local neighbourhoods'.[15] Whyte's famous study of first- and second-generation Italian immigrants focused on the social and spatial worlds of the 'corner boys', or gang members, in Boston's North End slum. The role of immigrant groups was a key theme in North American gangs and organised crime, represented most significantly by Ianni's 'ethnic succession thesis'.[16] However, this model has been subject to substantial revisionism, not least in relation to the demonisation of ethnic groups by the press, police and politicians.[17] In Britain during the 1920s, the 'racecourse wars' can be seen as one of the first tabloid engagements with what would later be referred to as 'an organized crime wave'.[18] Contemporary commentators were often writing in a climate of anti-alienism and as such tended to focus on what was perceived to be a connection between 'foreigners' and crime. Despite such sensational rhetoric about the alien criminal, in the more mundane reporting of the racecourse wars immigrant communities played a limited role. Whilst a shared topography resulted in confrontations between Italian community and local street gangs, evidence for other ethnic tensions is limited.[19] Jewish, Italian, English and Irish communities would all contribute members to the shifting demographics of post-First World War gangland.

A number of popular crime authors have covered the series of events broadly described as the 'racecourse wars' which took place from the early 1920s through to the mid-1930s and involved individuals (such as William Kimber and Edward Emmanuel), family networks (such as the Sabinis and the Whites) and criminal networks (such as the Elephant and Castle gang, the Hoxton gang, and Camden Town gang).[20] These accounts broadly concur, and have contributed to and moulded a shared history and mythology of the interwar metropolitan underworld. The aim of such true-crime texts would seem to be to provide a genealogy and context to the development of the traditional post-war family firm.[21] They place the racecourse wars firmly in the context of chronological histories of organised crime, stretching forward to the present day. In addition, personal connection to the events or some sort of legacy association is important. Thus, Darby Sabini's biographer, Edward Hart, was a Fleet Street reporter in the 1950s and 60s. He apparently worked closely with Scotland Yard Detective Jack Capstick, one of the founding members of 'The Special Duty Squad' or 'Ghost Squad' which was set up to deal with organised crime after the Second World War.[22] True-crime authors are similarly 'connected'. James Morton is a former criminal solicitor with family links to the East End and Brian McDonald is the nephew of the McDonald brothers, who were apparently members of the Elephant and Castle gang. McDonald's family connection has enabled him to narrate the family's place into gangland history. These retellings of the events of the racecourse wars are fundamentally informed by 'inside knowledge' and 'machismo', as are the earlier 'histories' available in police memoirs and biography.

Chronology of Events

The criminal activity to which the 'racecourse wars' was collectively applied has some features of organised crime as it has been defined by modern criminologists.[23] Whilst the evidence suggests that the gangs were involved in a variety of illegal practices, activities related to protectionism and gambling predominated. The most lucrative protection rackets were concerned with bookmaking and betting, which enjoyed a surge of popularity in the post-war period.[24] The rackets essentially rested on control of the right to operate as a bookmaker and to run a stand. Thus the race gangs offered protection to bookies and controlled the allocation of pitches.[25] Confrontations occurred over the control of these pitches and, according to Thomas Dey who wrote about his experience as a bookmaker in the 1920s, the gangs were seen as a necessary evil.[26] Tom Divall, the ex-CID man who was employed as a racecourse steward after his retirement in 1913, noted that the need for protection had originally arisen because of the threats to bookmakers with the resumption of racing after the First World War, 'This sort of thing went on for a while until it became unbearable, and the Sabinis took up the cudgels in defence of the bookies' (presumably in exchange for substantial payments).[27] Nevertheless, swindles and rackets had long been familiar to the racing fraternity.[28] So why had racecourse crime become perceived as such a problem by 1920? To a large part this is due to the shifting fortunes of the racecourses and gambling industry. Attendance at racecourses increased after 1918 and, as Mike Huggins has pointed out, there was a parallel rise in racecourse crime.[29] Moreover, despite attempts to control working-class gambling in the pre-war Street Betting Act of 1906, the anti-gambling lobby, and particularly its mouthpiece the National Anti-Gambling League (NAGL) that had had such an impact in the late nineteenth century, was much less influential in the post-war period.[30] The combination of growing popularity and declining opposition to gambling provided fertile ground for the growth of gambling-related crime.

The earliest references to conflicts specifically associated with racecourse crime start in the aftermath of the First World War, with references

to fights between individuals who would become prominent members of the racecourse gangs. Brian McDonald attributes a number of
pre-war fights and affrays to the racecourse gangs, in particular two
related incidents of wounding in Soho in 1910 which he connects to
William Kimber, the leader of the Birmingham Gang and associate of
the Elephant and Castle Gang.[31] By the early 1920s the events linked
to the 'racecourse wars' are described in a number of different sources,
including a Metropolitan Police file dealing with charges of conspiracy,
assault and demanding money with menaces from between 1922 and
1924. A number of witness statements dated antagonisms between
some of the protagonists back to 1920 when there had been reports of
a shooting incident on the Caledonian Road, involving a Fred Gilbert
and two brothers named George and Trixie Droy.[32] Gilbert, a member of
the Camden Town Gang but affiliated to the Elephant and Castle Gang,
was described by the police in 1922 as a steward of The Bookmakers
and Backers Racecourse Protection Association, which had been set
up as a response to extortion and protection rackets.[33] There are also
reports of a fight between Charles 'Darby' Sabini and Thomas 'Monkey'
Benneworth (described by James Morton as a leader of the Elephant
and Castle Gang) in 1920. According to Morton, 'Benneyworth [*sic*]
deliberately tore the dress of an Italian girl serving behind the bar of the
Griffith public house in Saffron Hill'.[34] These traces are difficult to verify
through the ambiguous and sometimes muddled narratives that have
collectively told the story of the racecourse gangs. The police dated the
beginning of the 'feud' to March 1921, when Darby Sabini, 'instigated
by [Edward] Emmanuel and [Gurchan] Harris, shot at a man'.[35] In an
account compiled by the police as a response to allegations made by the
pseudonymous writer 'Tommy Atkins' in December 1922, an attempt
was made to provide a narrative of key events in the racecourse wars.
This account describes the confrontation between Darby Sabini and the
Birmingham Gang (also known as the 'Brummagem Boys'), headed by
George 'Brummy' Sage. Apparently Sabini fired the revolver in order
to frighten the Birmingham men off. Sabini was charged with shooting with intent, but acquitted of the offence and fined for possessing a
revolver without a permit.[36]

These early events set the scene for the territorial confrontations
between various overlapping groups. The battle lines were broadly
drawn between the Sabinis (or Italian Gang), from Clerkenwell, and
the Jewish bookmakers on one side, and the Elephant and Castle Gang,
Birmingham Gang and Camden Town Gang on the other. One of the
most significant events was the Battle of Epsom, or the Ewell affray,

which took place in June 1921 when, on returning from a race meeting, the Birmingham men attacked a charabanc carrying bookmakers from Leeds, having mistaken them for the Sabinis.[37] In July and August 1922, the violence escalated, and events increasingly moved from the racecourse and on to metropolitan streets.[38] On Good Friday 1922, Fred Gilbert was slashed at the New Raleigh Club in Jermyn Street, allegedly by members of the Italian Gang. Sabini associate Alfred Solomon was detained, but no further proceedings were taken. According to the pseudonymous writer 'Tommy Atkins', a member of the Metropolitan Police was present. In July 1922, a confrontation between the Birmingham Gang and the Italian Gang broke out on Gray's Inn Road. A Detective named Rutherford 'happened to be in and about the vicinity ... and endeavoured to effect their arrest'.[39] Rutherford was shot at and arrests were made of a number of men who were charged with feloniously shooting at a policeman with intent to murder. In August 1922, a further confrontation involving firearms between the Italian Gang and George Sage and Frederick Gilbert, in Mornington Crescent, resulted in a number of arrests. By the late summer of 1922, several of the key protagonists from both sides, including Joseph Sabini, Harry (also known as Harry Boy) Sabini, Joe Jackson, Alfred White, Alfred Solomon, George Sage, George West and Fred Gilbert, had been arrested. Events reached a climax on the evening of 20 November 1922 when Darby and Harry Sabini were shot at by Augustus and Enrico Cortesi in the Fratellanza Social Club in Clerkenwell. This event was widely covered by the press who could not resist the elements of drama it provided. As well as feuding 'Italians' and smoking guns, the headlines sensationally described the actions of Louisa Doralli, the daughter of the club proprietor, who had bodily placed herself in front of Harry Sabini when a pistol was aimed at him.[40] After the Old Bailey trial of the Cortesi brothers, in January 1923, confrontations and affrays continued, however, press coverage of the events was much less vigorous.[41]

It may be that after the events of 1922, some sort of truce was reached between the groups involved, or at least the violence was more contained than it had been. Indeed, Darby Sabini was preoccupied with an accusation of libel against the *Topical Times*. An edition published on 12 April 1924 had made allegations about Sabini's involvement in organised crime.[42] Violence would erupt again in September 1924, when Sabini man Alfred Solomon was charged with the murder of a bookmaker or bookie's runner named Barnett Blitz in a club shooting. He was defended by QC Sir Edward Marshall Hall (who had apparently been hired by Darby Sabini).[43] The case was presented as essentially self-defence, with Solomon's attack on Blitz coming after a struggle in which Blitz had violently attacked Solomon's associate Edward Emmanuel. Solomon was eventually found guilty of manslaughter and sentenced to three years penal servitude. Violence would flare again during 1925. In August the *Daily Express* announced that the Home Secretary, William Joynson Hicks, had declared war on the race gangs and published a list of 'gang outrages', which had allegedly occurred in London and other parts of the country between March 1924 and August 1925.[44] Events came to a head on the evening of 20 August when 50 men fought with razors in East London. The *Express* reported:

> One of the greatest race-gang fights of recent years occurred at Aldgate East last night. It began in a tavern at the corner of Aldgate and Middlesex Street with a dispute about Lewes races. Suddenly, without warning, about fifty men split up in two rival sections, razors were drawn, and the two gangs began fighting. Other people joined in, and a scene of astonishing confusion followed. A mass of struggling and excited men surged out of the tavern into the street, where they were joined by about one hundred more people.[45]

As a response to the *Daily Express* reports the Commissioner of Police held talks with the Secretary of State, which would lead to a full police investigation into the London affrays. This investigation, however, largely concluded that the *Express* had exaggerated the events and no further action was to be taken.[46] As former Flying Squad officer Ted Greeno remarked in his 1959 autobiography, *War on the Underworld*:

> Their deeds needed no magnifying, but they got it. A vividly reported battle in Shaftesbury Avenue turned out never to have happened at all. A running fight with razors was simply two pickpockets chasing a third through a barber's shop; but what prompted 'Jix's' ultimatum was, I am sure, the mythical battle of Petticoat Lane when fifty mobsters fought with razors, stopping the traffic and terrifying the citizens.[47]

According to Greeno, the Home Secretary's ultimatums did little to stop the racecourse violence, and documents from the National Archive's collections of Metropolitan Police and Home Office files, indicate that there were continuities in gang activity after 1925.[48] However, the sensational headlines of the earlier 1920s were largely absent in the press; coverage of racecourse violence was much thinner. In part this might have been connected to the less visible presence of the Sabini gang. Darby Sabini had been threatened with bankruptcy, probably as the result of his failed libel action the previous year.[49] It may be that Sabini's financial problems stymied the family's activities by the later 1920s. Possibly the gangs themselves scaled back their confrontations as a response to the media interest. Darby Sabini had consolidated his interests in the south-eastern racecourses by taking up residence in Hove from 1926. Whilst his brothers remained in London, it may be that removal of the enigmatic Italian gang leader from the metropolis meant that the press had lost interest.[50] Moreover, after 1925 the Bookmakers Association and the Jockey Club would take more effective measures to get its house in order.[51] This may have thwarted some of the more excessive violence that had peaked by 1925.

It would not be until 1936 that press coverage of the 'racecourse wars' re-emerged with any vigour. In this year events on racecourses in Lewes and at Wandsworth would once again focus the lens of the press on the race gangs. In June 1936, a group of 16 men, described as mostly coming from the Shoreditch, Bethnal Green, Hackney and Dalston districts, were charged with frequenting the racecourse to commit felonies.[52] The men were tried at the Sussex Assizes and found guilty of wounding Mark Frater, a bookmaker's clerk, and assaulting both Frater and his employer, the bookmaker Alfred Solomon. Both the accused and victims were men closely connected to the London racing fraternity. Moreover, this attack had connections to earlier events in which Solomon had been involved, as one of the attackers was 24-year-old Albert Blitz, the brother of Barnet Blitz whom Solomon had killed in 1924. According to film historian Steve Chibnall, it was this event on which Graham Greene loosely based his novel, *Brighton Rock*, published in 1938.[53] The second widely reported event was a murder that took place at the Greyhound Stadium in Wandsworth. This was a fight between two Italian brothers named Camilo and Massimino Monte-Columbo, who was killed, and a number of others described by the press as 'racing men' from the Clerkenwell district. The men arrested and charged with the murder were Bert Marsh (also known as Papa Pasquale) and Herbert Wilkins; they were found guilty of manslaughter at the Old Bailey on 17 November.[54] In the press the fight was presented as a result of a quarrel within the Italian gang.[55] These were the last widely reported confrontations of the gangs, but despite the tendency in the press to isolate the events as the 'racecourse wars' it is clear that they have to be understood as part of a broader evolving set of networks in and around London. During 1936 in London, Jack 'Spot' Comer was (allegedly) taking part in the

Battle of Cable Street, and Billy Hill was sentenced to four years penal servitude for robbery. Moreover, notorious burglars and robbers like George Ingram and Ruby Sparks had pursued their 'criminal careers' in the 1920s and 30s, in between frequent terms of imprisonment.[56] Thus, criminal networks overlapped and, arguably, new forms of criminal organisation encompassed the more formal structures that were developing in relation to metropolitan territory and the gambling and associated protection industry. The next part of the chapter will focus on gang membership, residence and occupation, adopting a loosely demographic approach. By considering the Sabinis and their associates in the context of overlapping networks of kinship and community and by tracing their spatial footsteps, the aim is to provide a more nuanced account of the lives of those individuals and family groups who were involved in racecourse crime and to demystify their public reputation as gangsters.

Family, Community and Gang Membership

Whilst many individuals weave in and out of the 'racecourse war' narratives, at the centre of the accounts are the confrontations between the 'Italian Mob' and the Birmingham Gang. The Sabini gang included members of an Anglo-Italian family from Little Italy, in Clerkenwell (see Map 8.1). The Birmingham Gang were a mixed group of men from Elephant and Castle and from Birmingham, under the leadership of Billy Kimber, a bookmaker from Bordersley Green, who was described in 1929 by ex-CID Inspector Tom Divall as 'one of the best'.[57] Another loose grouping of mainly Jewish gang members came from the East End. According to one popular account of the gangs, the Birmingham men, also known as the Elephant Boys, were allied to the Camden Town Gang.[58] As well as Kimber, the gang included George Sage, George Baker and Fred Gilbert, and a number of other members who were either allied with the Birmingham or Camden Town Gangs. The pattern was similar for the other groupings. The Hoxton Gang was also apparently home to Fred Gilbert, and to Sandy Rice (alias Alexander Tomasso) who was also connected with the Sabinis.[59] The Clerkenwell Gang included Alf White, who had also apparently been a member of the Hoxton Gang, as well as the Sabinis and other associates, many of whom were from the Anglo-Italian community. These included Pasqualino Papa, George Fagioli, Paul Boffa and Antonio Mancini, who was also a member of the East End Gang which included Alfred Solomon, Edward Emmanuel and Harry Margulas. Amongst the other associates of this

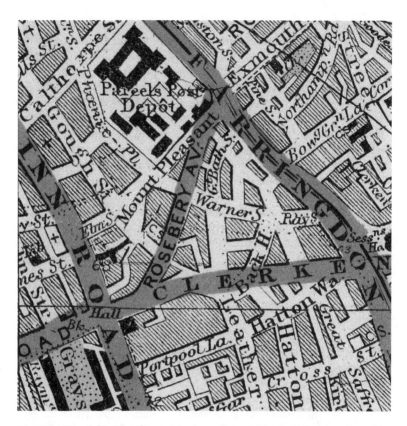

Map 8.1 'The Sabini family were far from the outsiders or 'aliens' portrayed by the press ... In 1891 there were three Sabini families living in 'Little Italy'; in Warner Street, Back Hill and Summer Street... In 1901, there were two Sabini families in Clerkenwell, in Mount Pleasant and Gough Street.' J. Bacon, *Atlas of London and Suburbs* c. 1923 (4 inches to the mile, detail). (Courtesy London Metropolitan Archives.)

gang was apparently Arthur Harding, although evidence of the relationship between Harding and the Sabinis seems tenuous. Certainly Edward Emmanuel does seem to have been as important as Harding suggests.[60] Much less visible than the Sabinis, there is evidence of Emmanuel in a 'leadership' role, and there were allegations that Emmanuel had suborned police officers.[61] In many ways these can be described as loose alliances, with 'members' switching allegiances or combining forces when required. Thus the East End and Sabini gangs formed a rough alliance against the Birmingham gang, who were connected to the Hoxton

and Camden Town gangs. Hence, the gangs seem to be largely structured around identification with a particular territory, or set of territories, accompanied by the overlapping networks of community, family
and neighbourhood.[62] Examination of the records compiled about the
race gangs by the Metropolitan Police at the time reveals some brief references to the organisation of the gangs. For instance, a report from the
investigation into the attempted shooting of Fred Gilbert and George
'Brummy' Sage of the Elephant Mob, in Mornington Crescent in August
1922, noted that, 'There would seem to be little doubt that an organized
gang, consisting of 12 or more men took part in this affray'.[63] However,
for the most part the police tended to be less interested in structure and
organisation and more concerned with specific incidents and the criminal 'careers' of particular individuals. Not surprisingly, the police version of events had focused largely on the activities of key protagonists
or actors. Thus Charles 'Darby' Sabini was a central figure in the police
narrative, and the 'Italian Gang' or 'Sabini Gang' were often referred to
collectively in connection to racecourse crime.[64]

Nevertheless, the most enduring 'structure' connecting the Sabini gang
was family and kinship. Resident in the Clerkenwell area since at least
the 1890s, the Sabini family were far from the outsiders or 'aliens'
portrayed by the press and by anonymous letter writers in the 1920s
(see Map 8.1).[65] However, the specific family structure is difficult to
untangle. In the 1891 census there were three Sabini families living in
the area known as 'Little Italy'; in Warner Street, Back Hill and Summer
Street.[66] In Warner Street, Italian born Joseph Sabini, his London born
wife, Eliza, their three sons, Frederick, Charles and Thomas, aged
respectively ten, eight and three, and their five-month-old daughter,
Mary, lived with four other families.[67] In Back Hill, there was a family
of four Sabinis; in Summer Street, a family of five.[68] With only initials
for these family members it is difficult to say with any certainty which
household the child who would grow up to be Darby Sabini belonged
to. The adult Sabini was known to use a variety of first names, including those of his brothers, and in the Home Office document reviewing
his internment as an enemy alien in 1940, he is named Octavius Sabini,
alias Darby Sabini, alias Frederick Handley.[69] Eliza, nee Handley, is usually described as his mother. However, the order of family relationships
remains ambiguous. Warner Street, Back Hill and Summer Street literally led off each other. It is possible that the households were related,
and that siblings and cousins may have lived shared lives across the
three residences. Thus, in the 1920s the references to the Sabini family
and brothers may have included individuals from these three families.

In 1901, there were two Sabini families living in Clerkenwell, in Mount Pleasant and Gough Street. At Mount Pleasant, 45-year-old Octavia [*sic*.] Sabini is listed as the head of the household, with his wife Eliza and children Mary (ten), Joseph (eight), George (six) and Harry (four months). Octavia is described as a carman, working on his 'own account'.[70] It is not clear whether this is the Octavio Sabini who appeared as a witness in a murder case at the Old Bailey in September 1890. Described as living in Little Bath Street, he had helped to carry the murdered man, Ugo Milandi, to the Royal Free Hospital.[71] It is only from the 1911 census that Darby Sabini can be identified with any certainty. This Sabini family lived in Bowling Green Lane, Clerkenwell, and included the widow and head of family, Mary Sabini (possibly a mistake, since her age fits with Eliza), described as a coal dealer; a daughter Mary, aged 20 by this time; and four sons: Octavio aged 22, Joseph aged 18, George aged 16 and Harry aged ten.[72] Octavio, Joseph and Mary are all described as assisting in business at home, presumably in coal dealing.[73] From what we know of the Sabinis' later career, Octavio was 'Darby', and the ages of Joseph and Harry fit with other evidence. It is likely that this is the same family who are in Warner Street in 1891 and Mount Pleasant in 1901, but Darby and his aliases remain elusive.[74] In December 1922, when he was being interviewed after the incident in the Fratellanza nightclub, Darby's statement noted that he had told the police, 'I have used the name Frank Handly, also Ottavio Sabini. My name is *not* Charles Sabini'. Again in 1940, at the committee to consider his appeal against interment, Darby stated, 'My real name is Ottavio Sabini'.[75]

In the 1940 internment appeals, the police counted six brothers. As well as Darby and Harry, there was Frederick (aged 59), Charles (aged 57), Joseph (aged 48) and George (aged 45).[76] During the 1920s, the Sabini Gang included at least Frederick, Darby, Joseph, George and Harry. In 1925, one of the peak years in the coverage of the Sabinis' affairs, the men were aged between 23 and 44. The most villainous according to contemporary accounts, Darby, Joseph and Harry, were aged respectively 36, 33 and 23.[77] This pattern of ages is fairly consistent in the case of other men active in the violent conflicts of these years.[78] Family and community networks remained important and kinship may have been a particular feature of the groups from immigrant communities. Thus, when the Sabinis clashed with their former allies the Cortesis at the Fratellanza Club in Clerkenwell, the two sets of kin brought their conflict into the heart of the community.[79] In a dramatic fight, Darby Sabini was attacked and Harry was shot by Enrico and Augustus Cortesi.[80] The Fratellanza, in Great Bath Street, was a club for the Italian community of which the Sabinis were members and the Cortesis former members (see Map 8.1). The Cortesis, who also lived in Great Bath Street, were a French-Italian family, consisting of four brothers, Henry (Enrico), Augusto, George and Paul. The Cortesi boys were living in Little Saffron Hill in 1901, with their widowed father Angelo. They were described as Italian subjects, born in France. The boys were aged between 16 and nine. By 1911 they were living in Great Bath Street. August, George and Paul were present the night of the census; as was an older brother, Albert (aged 31), described as a bookmaker.[81] Other Sabini allies were two sets of Jewish brothers from the East End Mob, Alfred and Harry Solomon, and Edward and Philip Emmanuel. The Emmanuel brothers were born in Bermondsey, where their father Alfred had been a fruit salesman.[82] Alfred and his wife Adelaide were born in Whitechapel.[83] By 1901, the Emmanuels were living in Queen's Block, Artizans' Dwellings off Gravel Lane, in the City of London. By 1911, Edward Emmanuel was living in Thoydon Road (probably Theydon), Bethnal Green, aged 29 and was described as a retail fruit salesman. This is supported by Arthur Harding who noted that Emmanuel 'started off as a market porter in Spitalfields'.[84] Whilst the racing men were resident in local ethnic communities, including in Clerkenwell, Whitechapel and Bethnal Green, spatial and class contexts are as important in thinking about the development of these gangs and the overlaps with local networks. As Dick Hobbs has shown, British organised crime has tended to be 'enacted within the cultures of the urban working class, and localised organised crime, often in the form of "family firms", has long been central to the economies and cultures of traditional working-class communities'.[85]

Occupations

Members of the gangs are described as pursuing a variety of occupations. Thus, as well as their identity as gang members and criminals, they were also members of the metropolitan working class. As we have seen, Edward Emmanuel worked for at least some of his working life in the family fruit trade business. Alfred Solomon, who was found guilty of the manslaughter of Barnett Blitz (alias Buck Emden) at the Eden Club in 1924, was a close associate of Emmanuel and was also referred to as a fruit salesman, although he was living in Gerrard Street off Shaftesbury Avenue by this point, rather than East London.[86] It is likely that Emmanuel and Solomon were connected as early as 1909, when Emmanuel was a witness in the case of Joseph Goldsmid at the Old Bailey. This was a long-firm fraud where Goldsmid had brought fruit from a number of suppliers, 'in each case with intent to defraud'. As far as can be ascertained, a man named Solomon was working with Goldsmid and they passed on some of the fraudulently obtained goods to Emmanuel.[87] In 1935, Alfred White senior is described as a bookmaker, and his sons, Alfred junior and William (known as Billy) are described as florists.[88] Newspaper reports from 1923 describe White senior as a florist when he was on a charge of conspiracy, accused of trying to convey letters to Joseph Sabini, who at that point was being held in Maidstone prison for the shooting of Fred Gilbert.[89] In the 1922 Gray's Inn Road shooting, the accused, Joseph Jackson, Arthur Phillips, William Edwards and George Fagioli, were described as a dealer, a fruiterer and two labourers.[90] Amongst the Birmingham men involved in the Epsom Affray of 1921, as well as labourers and manual workers, there were three casters, two capstan operators, a wire drawer, a millwright, a polisher, a mechanist and an asphalter.[91] Given that these men lived in Birmingham, it is unsurprising that there was a higher number of men involved in forms of industrial manufacture than there were amongst the London men, who were mostly involved in some form of market trading. Nevertheless, in Birmingham five of the men were involved in the fruit trade, either as fruiters or hawkers of fruits. The extent to which the men worked in a sustained way in these industries and trades is unclear. Certainly, it may be that some of these trades, such as the fruit trade (or at least market trading and costermongering), may have provided opportunities and networks that overlapped with the broader illicit cultures with which the men were involved.[92] As we have seen in the previous chapter, markets were at the centre of working-class communities and were often been perceived as spaces in which the disposal of illegal goods could be easily managed, for instance via the costermongers barrow.[93]

Many of the men involved in the race gangs are, unsurprisingly, described as involved in some sort of employment either in bookmaking or on its fringes. Certainly, during the 1920s, there seemed to be a blurred line between villains and employees within the bookmaking fraternity. The Sabinis had attempted to use more formal mechanisms to secure their place on the racecourses. When the Racecourse Bookmakers and Backers Protection Association was formed in August 1921, Darby Sabini, Alf White and Edward Emmanuel were employed as stewards. Moreover, in CID files from 1922 dealing with the Mornington Crescent shooting it was explained that:

> Alfred White was employed as Chief Steward of the Race Course Bookmakers and Backers Protection Association; Sabini obtained

his living as a bookmakers clerk; George West as a 'Tick Tacker' on race courses and Mack, as, what is termed, 'a Number Caller' on the course.[94]

By 1940, when the Sabini brothers were being investigated by the Home Office Advisory Committee (Italian), those blurred boundaries can be seen even within the family. Thus Frederick Sabini was described as having worked as a bookmaker for the previous 12 years under the name of Bob Wilson at Harringay and White City greyhound stadiums. Joseph Sabini is described as having been a bookmaker for 14 years, in the name of Harry Lake, again at Harringay. Neither were said to be involved in the violence associated with Darby and Harry, despite Joseph Sabini having had previous convictions. Charles (Darby's older brother) and George were described as being at least peripherally involved with rackets. For example, it was noted of Charles Sabini that 'For the past 15 years he has been engaged at West Ham Greyhound Stadium supplying bookmakers' lists, stools, betting forecast tissues, sponges etc., under the charge of Joseph Levy. This business, it will be appreciated, can be aptly described as a racket.'[95] On the other hand, neither Charles nor George had been previously convicted. Indeed, Charles was described as being 'slightly mentally deranged'.[96]

Criminal Records and Criminal Careers

The criminal records of race-gang members suggest that violent offences were the predominant activity for which they were charged, or which brought them to the attention of the police. Both Home Office and CID investigations provide details of previous convictions. The majority of the men who came into contact with the police had Criminal Record Office numbers, and many, although not all of them, had criminal records.[97] In many cases, previous offences were closely related to the racing affrays. For example, Alfred Solomon was mainly charged with racecourse related offences. Thus in 1924, in the police file dealing with the murder of Barnett Blitz, it was noted that Solomon had been 'once convicted of Welshing, 11 cases, and twice indicted at the Central Criminal Court for causing grievous bodily harm and acquitted upon each occasion'.[98] Minor convictions for drunkenness and loitering whilst on the racecourse also occurred, and it is likely that the police were using stop and search powers to arrest men for loitering in a suspicious way as a means of managing racecourse crime. When Thomas 'Monkey' Benneworth, the Elephant Gang enforcer, was arrested in

1925 his record showed that he had been charged previously with loitering, once at Marlborough Police Court, receiving a three-month sentence, and once at Epsom Petty Sessions, as 'Suspected person loitering
(attempting to pick pockets)'.[99]

Other offenders had been involved in a much greater range of criminal activities. According to the police file, Edward Emmanuel 'has been
nine times convicted of various offences including assault, larceny and
keeping and managing gaming houses'.[100] George Drake, a Sabini man
who was charged with conspiracy in 1923, had previously been convicted of robbery with violence at Norwich County Assizes for which he
was sentenced to Maidstone prison for three years; then in 1920 he was
again convicted at Norwich, and received two sentences of two years
and two years with hard labour, to be served concurrently, for receiving
stolen goods and conspiracy.[101] The Birmingham men who were investigated in the Epsom Affray had various previous convictions, including
manslaughter, shopbreaking, stealing from the person, housebreaking,
wounding, stealing, receiving stolen goods and uttering counterfeit
coins. Certainly, the evidence available suggests that many of the men
involved in these events could be described as 'career criminals', and a
number of them had significant reputations for violence. Fred Gilbert,
of the Elephant Gang, was seen as a violent offender of long standing. In
the Metropolitan Police Return of Convictions included in the investigation into Gilbert's involvement with blackmail cases, the witness Frank
Droy provided a statement about an attack Gilbert had made upon him
and his brother 'Trixie' Droy, 'I have known Gilbert for a number of
years, and I know him to be a very dangerous & violent man'.[102] Unlike
many of his associates, Darby Sabini seems to have steered remarkably
clear of the law. As he noted in a statement provided in December 1922,
'I am a quiet peaceable man. I never begin a fight myself'.[103]

In contrast to the scuttlers examined by Andrew Davies, most of
whom retired from gang fighting upon reaching maturity, the men
involved in the race gangs were adult offenders.[104] It is not possible to
ascertain in any systematic way whether there was a direct graduation
from youth street gangs to older fighting or criminal gangs. The extent
to which they had honed their fighting skills and violence as street fighting youths is far from clear. Moreover, at least some of the race-gang
men came of age during the war, which may have had an impact on
juvenile records and youth offences. One of the bookmakers who was
a victim of the Epsom Affray, Woolf Schwartz, had started as a juvenile
at Old Street Police Court, in 1911, 'Stealing 4 watches', accruing a list
of convictions for theft and loitering, until September 1919, when he

was charged at Thames Police Court with 'Army Desertion'.[105] Indeed, in some cases whilst the war had provided a break from (recorded) criminal activities, it is evident that the men had simply returned to their criminal careers once it had ended.[106] Other racing men also started their criminal lives at an early age. A decade before the fight at the Fratellanza Club, 20-year-old George Cortesi and his companion Vincent Sabini (aged 24), were tried at the Old Bailey in January 1910 for an attack on another Italian, Francisco Pacifico, in Little Gray's Inn Lane.[107] Cortesi was found guilty of common assault and much was made of his previous criminal record. He had been previously convicted on 20 April 1899 of warehouse breaking, around the age of nine, and he had been sent to a reformatory until he was 16 years of age. A further list of convictions followed: 9 June 1904 at Clerkenwell Police Court, he received six months imprisonment for stealing £1 and 12s from a shop; 29 July 1907, again at Clerkenwell, he received three months for loitering; on 18 February 1908 he received one month's hard labour for an assault on the police; and at the North London Police Court, 12 January 1909, he received 14 days for obtaining credit by fraud. George Fagioli, one of the Clerkenwell gang who was charged with possession of a firearm after the Gray's Inn Road shooting in July 1922, started his criminal record at the age of 11 in 1911, when he was convicted at Bow Street of office-breaking and sent to Werrington Industrial School until October 1918. George seems to have stayed out of trouble, or at least was not convicted, until the early 1920s when he started 'associating with undesirables'.[108] Certainly, further research may show that many of these men had juvenile records. As Billy Hill, who generously described himself as 'The Boss of Britain's Underworld', boasted in the mid-1950s, 'I've been crooked since I was thirteen years of age'.[109]

Territory and Mobility

Whilst the police were overwhelmingly concerned with the escalation of racecourse violence, both on the courses and in London streets, there is also evidence that the gangs were extending their territory in the 1920s, and this may have been one of the factors that contributed to the increased press coverage in this period. Certainly we know that the confrontations between the different gangs occurred at least in part due to the attempts by gang leaders to 'colonise' and extend their operations. Thus, Billy Kimber was accused of using his connection with London to gain dominance over the south-eastern racecourses, away from his usual midlands and northern territories.[110] Moreover,

there is some limited evidence to suggest that the gangs were attempting to extend their territory into the West End: a number of incidents
occurred in west-central London, in places such as Shaftesbury Avenue,
Coventry Street and Tottenham Court Road.[111] On Good Friday 1922,
Fred Gilbert was attacked by the Italians, who slashed him about the
legs, in the New Raleigh Club in Jermyn Street.[112] It is debatable how
much success the Sabinis had with transplanting their activities into the
West End clubland. In this period the nightclub business was booming;
the 'Queen of the Nightclubs', Kate Meyrick arguably aimed at a rather
more elevated crowd than the Sabinis, though both would catch the
beady eye of the crusading Home Secretary, William Joynson-Hicks, in
1925.[113] However, by the later 1920s it was apparent that if any protection money was being paid in the West End, it was to the Metropolitan
Police rather than the Sabinis.[114] Nevertheless, the Sabinis did have connections to the club world, or at least to local clubs like Fratellanza's in
Clerkenwell or the Eden Club (off the Hampstead Road), and, through
Edward Emmanuel, to gambling dens. According to an anonymous
letter received by the police 11 June 1923, Emmanuel ran a gambling
den on the Edgware Road, known as the Titchbourne Club.[115]

The ability and willingness of the post-war gangs to move out of their
immediate territories may well explain why the policing of such gangs
became more intensive in the post-war period. Whilst, the pre-war
gangs were not completely geographically limited, the apparent new
reach into the West End and to the various southern racecourses clearly
alarmed the police. For example, the movements of Barnett Blitz, before
Alf Solomon shot him at the Eden club, give some indication of the
topography of gang members:

> About this time Harry Moss, of 17, Newcastle Place, Aldgate, a Clerk,
> a friend of Blitz, was in Eden Street, and saw Blitz at the door of
> the Eden Club. Apparently Blitz had seen Moss approach from the
> window of the Club and went downstairs to meet him. Blitz and
> Moss then went together to Coltans [*sic*] Restaurant, in Aldersgate
> Street, and had some dinner, after which they went to the Ring in
> Blackfriars Road, to see some boxing bouts which were in progress
> that night. They remained at the Ring throughout the evening, and
> about 11 p.m. went to the Club in Eden Street, Hampstead Road.[116]

Arguably a major feature of the racecourse gangs' geographical distribution or spread was their use of transport.[117] Significantly, many of the
West End incidents occurred in close proximity to points of departure

and arrival in central London and particularly to key transport hubs like Euston, King's Cross and Paddington. Moreover, the association between the criminal and the car was increasingly noted after the war, with 'motor bandits' the subject of numerous headlines and letters to the press during the 1920s and 30s.[118] The Flying Squad had originally been formed in 1919 as the 'Mobile Patrol Experiment' in part due to concerns that the villains were themselves becoming much more mobile.[119] Thus, in August 1922, according to their statements, Alfred White and Darby Sabini had driven to the Red Bull public house, where they sat quietly drinking and minding their own business whilst shots were fired across the Gray's Inn Road, 'Darby Sabini and I returned from Goodwood Races by motor car and arrived at the "Prince of Wales" Public house, Northdown Street, King's Cross, about 9.30pm ... We then went by the same motor car to the "Red Bull" Public house, Gray's Inn Road.'[120]

However, whilst the police and press may have been concerned about the mobility of the racing men and the apparent escalation of racecourse-related violence, closer examination of the residential territories with which they were associated are marked by striking elements of spatial continuity with earlier areas of gang conflict. Thus, in the interwar period confrontations between the racecourse gangs would be played out once again on the streets of Clerkenwell, Hoxton and King's Cross; moreover, their main adversaries were from the Elephant and Castle and other mean streets of Southwark and Lambeth.[121] As we saw in the previous chapter, streets in these areas were often the frontline for the youths involved in street fighting. The territories over which gangs fought contained mixed working-class communities, overlapping with the Italian and Jewish families who had arrived in the past couple of decades. Both recent arrivals and more established residents worked as semi-skilled manual workers, costermongers and traders; a community of families who were not quite respectable enough to move to the more salubrious parts of Hackney, Islington and Camden. By the post-war period, this geography had not shifted a great deal. The Sabinis hailed from Clerkenwell, Fred Gilbert from Camden Town and Mornington Crescent, Alfred White from King's Cross and Hoxton, north of the City Road, still within the same metropolitan boroughs. Moreover, the main Sabini rivals for the racecourses outside of the south east, the Birmingham Gang, were allied to the Elephant and Castle Gang in Lambeth.

It is possible that the Sabinis and other gangs of the 1920s had roots in the territorial street fighting gangs that had long been a feature of these areas. Rather than the gang genealogy implied by true-crime writers like McDonald, this reflects a continuing history of terrain and communities that were contested. Thus, whilst the Sabinis were part of the close-knit community of Little Italy from the later-Victorian period, they also shared their terrain with the fighting gangs. It is possible that these confrontations may have been provoked by territorial tensions linked to the arrival of new immigrant groups. Humphries noted the racial tensions between street gangs and Jewish settlers, and Pearson described hooligan attacks on Italian food vendors.[122] From the 1880s, Sabini family members appeared in a number of trials at the Old Bailey, mostly on or near to Eyre Street Hill, in the triangle of 'little Italy'. Most of these trials involved victims, accused and witnesses from within the community. In 1894, Eyre Street Hill was the location for an attack on Ottavio Sabini, described as an ice-cream vendor from Biggs Road, Clerkenwell; his attacker was a 60-year-old hawker named Thomasso Casella.[123] In 1910, Vincent Sabini and George Cortesi were involved in an affray in Little Gray's Inn Lane, their victim a fireman named Francisco Pacifico.[124] However, there is some evidence of trials involving the Italian community in this period responding to provocation from local youths. For example, Augustus Sabini was attacked by 16-year-old Alfred Smith in May 1898. Sabini, who was with a friend, James Dunks, testified, 'I saw a gang of boys, who asked us if we wanted to fight – we said "No," and walked away – I saw Smith fire two shots, and saw a pistol in his hand.'[125] In a similar confrontation involving youths and the Italian community, five Italian men were charged with wounding and assaulting a group of youths in September 1902. In sentencing the jury considered that the 'prisoners had provocation'.[126]

Could it be that the networks that constituted the later Sabini gang had their roots in the forms of defence that the Italian community drew on to protect themselves against the incursions of local youths? In September 1907, there was significant gang activity in the Clerkenwell, City Road and King's Cross area; two Italian boys were charged with wounding John Tower, a trace-horse boy, at Clerkenwell Police Court. The Italians were an 18-year-old mosaic layer named Dominic Marini and an 18-year-old wire-frame maker named George Cortesi, later to become an associate and subsequently, adversary, of the Sabinis. According to the report in the *News of the World*, fights had been proceeding amongst a number of gangs, including the 'Somers Town and Hoxton gangs of hooligans' and 'others, some comprised of English roughs and some of Italians', for 12 months.[127] In the same month, Augustus and Ottavio Sabini, aged 21 and 18 respectively, were fined at Clerkenwell for using obscene language.[128] Ottavio would reinvent himself as 'Darby' Sabini by the interwar period. The presence of Sabinis and Cortesis in cases linked to street gang fighting underline the important continuities in the development of territorial criminality and delinquency and its relationship to metropolitan spaces. Arguably, these areas had developed a reputation for street fighting during the late nineteenth century, and perhaps only naturally, the bonds of these working-class communities and territorial identification would be sustained by the next generation.

Conclusion

If the post-war gangs shared topographical roots with the late-Victorian gangs, they also represented a shift in the taxonomy of criminal types. In the new 'gangster', the older forms of territorial street crime and crim-inal confederacy had blended with the new opportunities afforded in the post-war world. The growth of racecourse and dog-track gambling, combined with an increased mobility, shaped the gangs. Moreover, in other cities as well gambling provided structure and organisation to fighting gangs. For instance, the Mooney Gang and Park Brigade Gang in Sheffield also combined around gambling and, according to Bean, by the mid-1920s the *Sheffield Mail* was reporting links between the Sheffield and London gangs. Indeed, looking back from 1940, Darby Sabini would point to the urban identity of the gangs present on the racecourses, 'There were several gangs: there was the Sheffield gang, the Birmingham gang, and at the finish there was the London gang'.[129] Moreover, the combination of street fighting with protectionism, swin-dling and gambling rackets would mark the borders of British gangland for the following generations: the black economy of underworld boss Billy Hill, active from the late 1920s, and the Kray Twins in the post-Second World War period. Also important was the coincidence of these developments with the emerging cultural language of gangsterdom, which was being exported from North America, recording the growing problems of Chicago's Italian gangsters. This was to provide a handsome parallel for British journalists and commentators, who as we have seen, turned to the community of London's 'Little Italy'. They largely ignored the mixed character of the 1920s gangs, which included English, Irish and Jewish Londoners, as well as Italians. Charles 'Darby' Sabini would be portrayed as the key mastermind of the racecourse wars. Moreover, police autobiography played fast and loose with the gangster stereotype in their retellings of the racecourse wars. Tom Divall would graphically describe the Italians as violent hotheads and the bookmakers involved in the feud working, 'to cool the heated blood coursing through the veins of these half-raving men'.[130] Ted Greeno's portrayal of the 'Italian mob' echoed the cheap pulp fiction that was popular from the interwar period.[131] Describing an attack on Darby at Greenford Trotting Track, 'Darby zigzagged backwards like a cornered hero in a Western film and a pistol appeared in his hand'. In the middle of another affray, Greeno stepped in, 'I grabbed him from them, pushed him up the stairs ... with his coterie of assorted thugs tagging on behind ... "Darby", I said, "there's a train back to town in five minutes and I want you on it"'.[132]

Both geographic and social mobility also made the racecourse gangs more distinct. Either real or imagined attempts to move westwards may have caused alarm. Thus, when local gangs and crime networks started to have aspirations beyond their immediate and neighbouring communities, policing became more assertive and the rhetoric of organisation employed more forcibly. Criminal mobility, and indeed aspiration, was not something new. In the nineteenth century, the swell mob were characterised by their mobility, following the opportunities of the turf and the fair. Moreover, in the nineteenth century, long-firm swindles or major events such as the Great Bullion Robbery (1855) had required both organisation and mobility. However, in the 1920s, increased mobility also meant the driving of cars, the hiring of charabancs, enabling Billy Kimber to turn his ambitious eyes to the south and Darby Sabini to patrol the south-east racecourses. Whilst the move from their north-east London territories may have been limited to gambling dens and drinking clubs, the night time economy would be a key characteristic of the following generations of metropolitan hard men, as demonstrated by Billy Hill's association with John Aspinall and the Clermont Club, and the Kray twins' venture, Esmeralda's barn in Knightsbridge.[133] Moreover, mobility was not only geographic. Thus some members of the post-war gangs would significantly improve their social status. When he was interned in 1940, Darby was living in Hove, where he apparently worked as a bookmaker. A mythology has grown around Darby's life in Brighton, where he is said to have been the inspiration for the character of the wealthy gangster Colleoni in Graham Greene's *Brighton Rock*.[134] According to Morton, when Sabini died in 1950, his family were surprised that he left so little money, although his clerk, Jimmy Napoletano, may have been stopped leaving the country with £36,000 (there is no firm evidence for this).[135] Harry Sabini was living in Hamilton Park, Highbury Barn, by the time of his appeal against interment. The house was described (presumably by the officers who had arrested him) as 'palatially furnished'. Harry referred to himself as a 'professional backer of horses', a trade at which he had apparently succeeded. As he noted to his interviewers when faced with accusations about this past, he told them, 'When you try to climb the ladder and you get on a little, you have always enemies to write about you and get you into trouble. That is all I can put it down to – nothing else.'[136]

Arguably, the 'racecourse wars' represented a cipher through which the press, the police and politicians variously constructed the landscape of crime using a collection of metaphor, sensation and rhetoric. Nevertheless, the extent to which the public was actually troubled by the 'racecourse wars' is hard to determine. Unlike other surges in concern about violent crime, such as the garotting panics of the previous century, the victims of the gangs were mainly each other; the public was largely incidental, though they were occasionally caught in the fray by being in the wrong place at the wrong time. Nevertheless, these events do represent a break with the past, and tell us something about the changing ways in which criminal activity would come to be organised from the mid-twentieth century. Thus, after the Second World War, the Special Correspondent of *The Times* would look back to the gang violence of the interwar years, 'The aftermath of the two wars produced gangsterdom on a large scale and, significantly, the racecourse in the early twenties provided the spring-broad for the black-mailing and, so, for the beginning of gang warfare.'[137]

Conclusion

In 1930, a columnist writing in *The Times* ruminated on the challenge of the modern 'underworld':

> There men and women devote themselves openly to battening upon other people's sins and vices. They form a separate nation; and the author of 'Sybil' never dreamed of so sharp a cleavage between two nations in one country. They live under laws of their own, not the laws of the State; and the first of their laws is the law of force. Few though they are, they seem to have little to fear from the State. They openly defy or deride or suborn it; and now and then, at any rate, the bitterest enemies among these people of the underworld will combine against the authorized powers of the dwellers aboveground.[1]

Seeking explanations for the modern underworld, the author drew on the past in order to draw comparisons with the contemporary problem, 'One cause may be that there is not enough excitement in modern life for these neurotically restless creatures; another that a lust for power is more quickly and easily satisfied through firearms than even through finance; another that it was only yesterday when, in many parts of the country, the law of the pistol was the only law current.' The column ended with an exhortation to learn from the past, 'As England knew in her smuggling days, every failure of the forces of the law awakes the ridicule which is the best friend of the lawless. From our own past, indeed, we may learn the danger of joining in the laugh'.[2] By 1930 the underworld was fully established in criminal justice, press and public understanding. Moreover, it had a history, a genealogy, which stretched back into the 'smuggling days'. The underworld had become a cipher not only for the activities of the criminal and deviant, but for the street dwellers and those marked by poverty and idleness. Whilst this vision of the underworld had its literary roots in the social investigation and journalism of the previous century, by 1930, international events meant that it was no longer only the purview of writers, journalists, policemen and reformers. By the late 1920s and early 1930s the impact of 'gang wars' in North America was inexorably changing the debate about organised crime.[3] After this pivotal point, the underworld was less often cloaked in the slang of Mayhew and his contemporaries and much more often clothed in the rhetoric of 'gangsterism'. As a rueful Assistant Commissioner Wembury remarks in Edgar Wallace's 1932 novel, *When the Gangs Came to London*, 'God how we used to laugh when we got the news through from Chicago that their police couldn't deal with their racketeers and gangsters! And now we know why. We're fighting guns with feather-dusters.'[4]

When I started the research for this book quite a few years ago my aim was to write a history of the underworld. Most books that attempt to do this tread the common path taken by those authors whose histories are shaped by the classic genealogies of organised crime. I originally set out to write a history that would straddle the two forms: the sensationalised true-crime account and the more careful historical studies of crime. Eventually, trying to uncover or reconstruct something that does not exist in a concrete form led me to think much more laterally about the meanings and perceptions of criminal confederacy in the past. Moreover, a long-held commitment to trying to understand the lives of the marginal and the 'other' from below, to identify agency, fundamentally influenced this research.[5] Hence, whilst many stories are told through this book, the core narratives which focus on the sisters Mary Harvey and Isabella Eaton, the Sheen family and the Sabini family are my attempt to reconstruct, through what might be described as 'thick description', the relationships, networks and spaces inhabited by these groups and individuals. The result is, I hope, very different from those usual histories of the underworld. Nevertheless, for some readers, it may be too far from that established path. Thus, key events and periods for some readers may be seen to be lacking here. The book barely touches on the 'Outcast London' so strongly evoked by Mearns and his contemporaries and memorably researched by authors such as Gareth Stedman Jones and Judith Walkowitz.[6] Whilst robbery is partly surveyed here in the early eighteenth and early nineteenth century, the crime wave following the end of the American war in 1783 is not. The 1780s were a decade in which the highest ever proportion of highway robbers were prosecuted at the Old Bailey.[7] Also lacking from my cast are the burglars and housebreakers who, as scholars like William Meier and Eloise Moss have recently demonstrated, played a key role in the Victorian and early twentieth-century making of the underworld.[8] Thus, the detailed reconstructions that form a substantial part of this book have resulted in a selectivity that is ultimately highly personal.

Despite this selectivity I have tried to identify a set of themes that, to a great or lesser degree, can be traced through the chapters and case studies. Expanding print culture, the interactions between the public and the publicity of crime, and the evolution of networks and territory underpin the development of modern understandings of criminal organisation and confederacy. In this book I have argued that this evolution can be seen most markedly between the early eighteenth century and the interwar period of the twentieth century, the point when the underworld and the gangster became absorbed by mass culture.[9] The first theme explored print culture and its escalation into a force which contributed to the ways in which crime was perceived, understood and responded to from the early eighteenth century. As we saw in Chapters 2 and 3, the way in which the press presented criminal activity strongly influenced contemporary responses to crime. Despite the fact that the press often concentrated on a relatively small number of offenders, a familiar process took hold in which portrayals of crime played out in the public sphere prompted social fears amongst a populace seemingly eager to recognise the folk devils amongst them. By the later eighteenth and into the nineteenth century, swindlers, hustlers, the swell mob and hooligans were similarly constructed through an alliance between print culture, criminal justice and the public desire to transmit knowledge about crime. The publicity of crime had the potential to make ordinary, if chaotic, plebeian lives into extraordinary and often self-destructive lives. As we saw in Chapter 3, Mary 'Moll' Harvey spent a significant portion of her life in conflict with the law and her reforming neighbours. In Chapter 5, the life of William Sheen was both self-destructive and destructive for his victims and community. Whilst the Sabinis, discussed in Chapter 8, did not fare so poorly from their lives as public criminals, the contemporary portrayal of the brothers as an 'organised crime family' was not always welcome.[10]

Harvey, the Sheens and the Sabinis were members of communities as well as criminal networks. For working-class and plebeian people, those most vulnerable to the law, blurred boundaries existed between their networks of friends, family, associates, workmates and neighbours. As Matt Neale has argued, 'it is difficult to detect the presence of networks which were either stable over time or to a significant degree separated from normal economic activity'.[11] This does not mean that forms of confederacy, networks if you will, cannot be identified. Thus, networks were characterised by flexibility and fluidity, and criminal organisation was perhaps better characterised by disorganisation. However, this book has argued that such networks fundamentally overlap with the other communities, associations and relationships that structure people's lives. Hence, we saw in Chapter 6 men who formed their criminal confederacies through the shared business of work, such as clerking, which provided opportunities for illegality. The communities defined by the authorities and in print culture as belonging to the underworld had multiple identities based on kinship, ethnicity, territory, neighbourhood and work. Moreover, none of these communities were mutually exclusive socially, spatially or indeed in class terms. In the metropolis, some of these communities shared space and territory over time. Thus areas on borders and the edges of districts like the City of London were inherently contested. The cluster of streets in Clerkenwell were defined and redefined in territorial terms by many generations of Londoners; as were the dense areas of poverty and manufacture to the east of the city. Other territorial hubs are significant. As we have seen in Chapter 3, Mary Harvey and her associates contested the streets around the Haymarket, an area with long associations with prostitution. In the early nineteenth century, as described in Chapter 4, pickpockets and robbers hustled their victims on the contested streets of the ceremonial City. In Chapter 5, William Sheen and his family owned properties, fought with their neighbours and consorted with the police on the borders of the City, on Wentworth Street. In the late nineteenth century, as we saw in Chapter 7, gangs of young men and women would fight over territory on the streets of Clerkenwell, and parade on public streets like the Pentonville Road. In the early twentieth century, the Sabini gang, their associates and their enemies would fight over territory on the streets of Clerkenwell, and fight in public streets like Gray's Inn Road.

The metropolis and particularly its most famous courtroom, the Old Bailey, have fundamentally shaped the research for and writing of this book. Without the *Old Bailey Sessions Papers* the reconstruction of the lives that I have attempted here would be much less rich and nuanced. Many hours (indeed years) of absorption in the *Sessions Papers* has unlocked the stories found in this book. Whilst the research for this book was grounded in the archive, the creation of online archives has undoubtedly assisted this attempt to reconstructed London's criminal underworlds. The ability to piece together lives that were often lived marginally has been enabled by this increasing digitisation of primary sources, including legal, census and press records.[12] The metropolis and the Old Bailey have brooded over the book – however, criminal lives that echo those that have been detailed here can be found in other towns and cities. Indeed, historians have focused on reconstructing criminal careers and criminal activity in such diverse places as Bristol, Cheshire, Manchester and Glasgow.[13] Like this book, Godfrey, Cox and Farrall's work on Cheshire combined traditional archive work with digitisation. They used both types of archive to generate life-course data that could be systematically interrogated. Davies's detailed reconstruction of gangs in Manchester, Salford and Glasgow were undertaken largely without digital records, producing careful and nuanced accounts of criminal lives.

The aim of this book has been to explore a series of snapshots, moments and episodes in the making of the modern 'underworld' and in the often marginalised stories of Londoners who lives have been captured in the records. It has not sought to be a history of the underworld. As historians from below have long argued, the underworld IS constructed: through the media, through the enforcement of law, through the lives of criminals, witnesses, and victims. Thus the underworld does not exist after all. It is a collection of fragmentary experiences of and understandings about criminality, a jumble of cultural and social practices that have been shaped by magistrates, police, writers, reformers, and journalists whose purpose was not only to control crime but also to define it in a way that separated it from the lives of 'respectable' citizens. Ultimately, the discursive power of the 'underworld' was (and remains) in its function as a shorthand for commentators who sought (and seek) to describe the worlds of the criminal, deviant and the poor, and to keep them at arm's length.

Notes

1 Introduction

1. *Old Bailey Proceedings* (hereafter *OBP*), December 1732, Jane Murphey (t17321206-38). See also *Ordinary of Newgate's Account* (hereafter *ONA*), January 1733 (OA17330129).
2. *OBP*, February 1847, Mary Ryley (t18470201-479).
3. *Empire News*, 3 September 1922.
4. R. Evans (1998), *Tales from the German Underworld: Crime and Punishment in the Nineteenth Century* (New Haven: Yale University Press), p. 159.
5. D. Hobbs (2013), *Lush Life: Constructing Organized Crime in the UK* (Oxford: Oxford University Press), pp. 58–88.
6. S. Slater (2009), 'Prostitutes and Popular History: Notes on the "Underworld", 1918–1939', *Crime, Histoire et Sociétés*, 13, 1, pp. 25–48.
7. A. Davies (2007), 'The Scottish Chicago?: From 'Hooligans' to 'Gangsters' in Interwar Glasgow', *Cultural and Social History*, 4, 4, pp. 511–27.
8. P. Griffiths (2000), 'Overlapping Circles: Imagining Criminal Communities in London, 1545–1645', in A. Shepard and P. Withington, *Communities in Early Modern England: Networks, Place, Rhetoric* (Manchester: Manchester University Press), pp. 115–33.
9. Some of the ideas in the following sections were first explored in H. Shore (2007), '"Undiscovered Country": Towards a History of the "Criminal Underworld"'. *Crimes and Misdemeanors: Deviance and the Law in Historical Perspective*, 1, 1, pp. 41–68.
10. G. Ellington (pseud., 1869), *The Women of New York* (New York: New York Book Co.); H. Campbell (1899), *Darkness and Daylight* (Hartford, Connecticut: Worthington & Co.).
11. For example, T. Allen (1931), *Underworld* (London: Grant Richards); C. G. Gordon (1929), *Crooks of the Underworld* (London: Geoffrey Bles); B. Hill (1955), *Boss of Britain's Underworld* (London: Naldrett Press); T. Holmes (1912), *London's Underworld* (London: J. M. Dent & Sons).
12. *The Times*, 9 December 1864. This is based on searches of the *C19 British Library Newspapers* and *The Times Online* on the 23 May 2013.
13. *The Times*, 9 December 1864. In the 1860s, Longfellow published a hugely popular translation of Dante's *The Divine Comedy*. Dante Alighieri (1867), *The Divine Comedy, translated by Henry Wadsworth Longfellow* (Boston: Ticknor & Sons).
14. William Harrison Ainsworth published his gothic romance *Rookwood* (Richard Bentley, London) in 1834 and then *Jack Sheppard* was published in *Bentley's Miscellany* between 1839 and 1840. G. W. M. Reynolds *The Mysteries of London* was published between 1844 and 1846 as a penny dreadful, following the influence of Eugène Sue's *Les Mystères de Paris*, which had been published serially in the *Journal des débats* between 1842–43.
15. See R. Crone (2012), *Violent Victorians: Popular Entertainment in Nineteenth Century London* (Manchester: Manchester University Press), pp. 78, 146,

173, 177–8; R. McGowen (1990), 'Getting to Know the Criminal Class in Nineteenth Century England', *Nineteenth Century Contexts*, 14, pp. 33–54.

16. R. Shoemaker (2013), 'Celebrating Criminality? Print Culture and the Creation of Criminal Celebrities in Eighteenth-Century London', paper given at conference on Cultural Representations of Crime and Policing: Scottish and International Perspectives, Past and Present (Dundee University, 16–17 April), see podcast: http://www.sipr.ac.uk/downloads/RSE_160413/Shoemaker.mp3, accessed 16 September 2014.

17. See A. Croll (2004), 'Who's afraid of the Victorian underworld?', *The Historian*, 84, pp. 30–5.

18. Griffiths, 'Overlapping Circles'; J. McMullan (1984), *The Canting Crew: London's Criminal Underworld, 1550–1700* (New Brunswick: Rutgers University Press); A. Brown (2013), *Interwar Penal Policy in England: The Dartmouth Convict Prison Riot, 1932* (Basingstoke: Palgrave Macmillan), pp. 96–128; Slater, 'Prostitutes and Popular History'.

19. Evans, *Tales*, pp. 1–10.

20. A. McKenzie (2007), *Tyburn's Martyrs: Execution in England, 1675–1775* (London: Hambledon Continuum); A. McKenzie (1998), 'Making Crime Pay: Motives, Marketing Strategies, and the Printed Literature of Crime in England, 1670–1770', in G. Smith, A. May and S. Devereaux (eds.), *Criminal Justice in the Old World and the New: Essays in Honour of J. M. Beattie* (Toronto: University of Toronto Press), pp. 235–69; Crone, *Violent Victorians*; J. Flanders (2011), *The Invention of Murder: How the Victorians Revelled in Death and Detection and Created Modern Crime* (London: Harper Press).

21. E. Snell (2007), 'Changing Discourses of Crime: Representations of Criminality in the Eighteenth-Century Newspaper Press', *Continuity and Change*, 22, 1, pp. 13–47; R. Ward (2012), 'Print Culture, Moral Panic and the Administration of the Law: The London Crime Wave of 1744', *Crime, Histoire et Sociétés*, 12, 1, pp. 5–24; J. C. Wood (2010), '"The Third Degree": Press Reporting, Crime Fiction and Police Powers in 1920s Britain', *Twentieth Century British History*, 21, 4, pp. 464–85; M. Houlbrook (2013), 'Fashioning an Ex-crook Self: Citizenship and Criminality in the Work of Netley Lucas', *Twentieth Century British History*, 24, 1, pp. 1–30; M. Houlbrook (2013), 'Commodifying the Self Within: Ghosts, Libels, and the Crook Life Story in Interwar Britain', *Journal of Modern History*, 85, 2, pp. 321–63.

22. See K. Chesney (1970), *The Victorian Underworld* (London: Temple Smith); D. Low (2005), *The Regency Underworld* (Stroud: Sutton); D. Thomas (1998), *Victorian Underworld* (London: Murray, 1998); D. Thomas (2003), *An Underworld at War* (London: Murray).

23. B. McDonald (2000), *Elephant Boys: Tales of London and Los Angeles Underworlds* (Edinburgh: Mainstream); B. McDonald (2010), *The Gangs of London: 100 Years of Mob Warfare* (Wrea Green: Milo Books); J. Morton (1994), *Gangland, vol. 2: The Underworld in Britain and Ireland* (London: Little Brown); J. Morton (2000), *East End Gangland* (London: Little Brown).

24. R. Barthes (1972 edn.), *Mythologies* (New York: Farrar, Strauss & Giroux), p. 137.

25. J. Wiltenburg (2004), 'True Crime: The Origins of Modern Sensationalism', *The American Historical Review*, 109, 5, pp. 1377–404.

26. A. Wright (2006), *Organised Crime: Concept, Cases, Control* (Cullompton: Willan), p. 3.

27. D. Hobbs (1994), 'Professional and Organized Crime in Britain', in Mike Maguire, Robert Morgan and Robert Reiner, *The Oxford Handbook of Criminology* (Oxford: Clarendon Press) pp. 441–68, p. 457.
28. Hobbs, *Lush Life*, pp. 13–14, 18.
29. P. Reuter (1983), *Disorganized Crime: Illegal Markets and the Mafia – The Economics of the Visible Hand* (Cambridge, MA: MIT Press).
30. See A. Davies (1998), 'Street Gangs, Crime and Policing in Glasgow During the 1930s: The Case of the Beehive Boys', *Journal of Social History*, 32, 2, pp. 349–69. A. Davies (2013), *City of Gangs: Glasgow and the Rise of the British Gangster* (London: Hodder & Stoughton).
31. Such flexibility and disorganisation can be gleaned from the key work on Wild by G. Howson (1970), *The Thief-taker General: The Rise and Fall of Jonathan Wild* (London: Hutchinson).
32. A. Davies (1998), 'Youth Gangs, Masculinity and Violence in Late Victorian Manchester and Salford', *Journal of Social History*, 32, pp. 349–69, pp. 363–4.
33. S. Hallsworth (2011), 'Gangland Britain? Realities, Fantasies and Industry', in B. Goldson (ed.), *Youth in Crisis? 'Gangs', Territoriality and Violence* (London: Routledge), pp. 20–37, pp. 183–197, p. 185.
34. M. Clayton (2008), 'The Life and Crimes of Charlotte Walker, Prostitute and Pickpocket', *London Journal*, 33, 1, pp. 3–19; T. Hitchcock and R. Shoemaker (2007), *Tales from the Hanging Court* (London: Hodder Arnold); T. Hitchcock and R. Shoemaker, (2015), *London Lives: Poverty, Crime and the Making of a Modern City, 1690–1800* (Cambridge: Cambridge University Press); H. Shore (1999), *Artful Dodgers: Youth and Crime in Early Nineteenth Century London* (Woodbridge: Boydell Press); J. C. Wood (2012), *The Most Remarkable Woman in England: Poison, Celebrity and the Trial of Beatrice Pace* (Manchester: Manchester University Press).
35. M. Harris (1987), *London Newspapers in the Age of Walpole: A Study of the Origins of the Modern English Press* (London: Associated University Presses).
36. R. Shoemaker (2009), 'Print Culture and the Creation of Public Knowledge about Crime in 18th-Century London', in P. Knepper, J. Doak and J. Shapland (eds.), *Urban Crime Prevention, Surveillance and Restorative Justice: Effects of Social Technologies* (Boca Raton, FL: Taylor and Francis).
37. Shoemaker, 'Print Culture', p. 18.
38. McKenzie, 'Making Crime Pay', pp. 259–65; L. B. Faller (1987), *Turned to Account: The Forms and Functions of Criminal Biography in the Late Seventeenth and Early Eighteenth Century England* (Cambridge: Cambridge University Press).
39. R. Ward, 'Print Culture and Responses to Crime in Mid-Eighteenth-Century London' (University of Sheffield, 2011, Ph.D thesis), p. 6.
40. R. B. Shoemaker (2006), 'The Street Robber and the Gentleman Highwayman: Changing Representations and Perceptions of Robbery in London, 1690–1800', *Cultural and Social History*, 3, pp. 381–405; G. Spragg (2003), *Outlaws and Highwaymen: The Cult of the Robber in England from the Middle Ages to the Nineteenth Century* (London: Pimlico).
41. Beattie, J. M. (2003), *Policing and Punishment, 1660–1750: Urban Crime and the Limits of Terror* (Oxford: Oxford University Press), p. 373.
42. See J. Warner and F. Ivis (2001), 'Informers and their Social Networks in Eighteenth-Century London: A Comparison of Two Communities', *Social Science History*, 25, 4, pp. 563–87, p. 570. For reporting on Gonson and De

Veil see, *Daily Journal*, 13 November 1731, 8 September 1732; *Grub Street Journal* 19 August 1731; *Daily Gazetter*, 4 February, 16, 22 March 1738. Also, T. Hitchcock (2003), 'You Bitches ... Die and Be Damned', Gender, Authority and the Mob in St. Martin's Roundhouse Disaster of 1742', in T. Hitchcock and H. Shore (eds.), *The Streets of London: From the Great Fire to the Great Stink* (London: Rivers Oram Press), pp. 69–81.

43. See R. Paulson (1991), *Hogarth, Vol. 1, The 'Modern Moral Subject' 1697–1732* (New Brunswick: Rutgers University Press), especially pp. 241–52; J. Uglow (1997), *Hogarth: A Life and a World* (London: Faber & Faber) pp. 193–7, pp. 202–6, p. 209.

44. Shoemaker, 'Print Culture', p. 18.

45. See J. C. Reid (1971), *Bucks and Bruisers: Pierce Egan and Regency London* (London: Routledge).

46. See C. Hindley (1878), *The Life and Times of James Catnach* (London: Reeves and Turner).

47. See P. D. James and T. A. Critchley (1971), *The Maul and the Pear Tree: The Ratcliffe Highway Murders, 1811* (London: Constable).

48. Crone, *Violent Victorians*, p. 92.

49. Ainsworth, *Rookwood*; Ainsworth, *Jack Sheppard*; E. Bulwer-Lytton (1830), *Paul Clifford* (London: Richard Bentley); C. Dickens (1838), *Oliver Twist; Or the Parish Boy's Progress. By "Boz."* (London: Richard Bentley).

50. See J. Marriott (1999), 'Introduction', in J. Marriott and M. Matsumura (eds.), *The Metropolitan Poor: Semi-Factual Accounts, 1795–1910, Vol. 1* (London: Pickering and Chatto), pp. xi–l.

51. A. Tomkins, 'Greenwood, James William (*bap.* 1835, *d.* 1927)', *Oxford Dictionary of National Biography* (Oxford: Oxford University Press, May 2010, http://www.oxforddnb.com/view/article/41224, accessed 8 September 2014).

52. J. Greenwood (1869), *The Seven Curses of London* (London); *Era*, 1 August 1869.

53. A. Mearns (1883), *The Bitter Cry of Outcast London* (London: James Clarke & Co.); A. S. Wohl, 'Mearns, Andrew (1837–1925)', *Oxford Dictionary of National Biography* (Oxford: Oxford University Press, 2004, http://www.oxforddnb.com/view/article/56012, 8 September 2014).

54. For example see the report on 'The Treatment of Criminals' in *The Times*, 23 October 1908.

55. H. Shpayer Makov (2011), *The Ascent of the Detective: Police Sleuths in Victorian and Edwardian England* (Oxford: OUP), p. 279.

56. T. Divall (1929), *Scoundrels and Scallywags, and Some Honest Men* (London: Ernest Benn), p. 208; F. P. Wensley (1931), *Detective Days: The Record of Forty-two Years' Service in the Criminal Investigation Department* (London: Cassell); F. D. Sharpe (1938), *Sharpe of the Flying Squad* (London: John Long).

57. Sharpe, *Flying Squad*, p. 213.

58. From the *Sheffield Mail* in reference to the Sheffield gang problem in 1926, cited in J. P. Bean (1981), *The Sheffield Gang Wars* (Sheffield: D & D Publications), p. 125.

59. *Empire News*, 6 August 1922.

60. K. E. Meyrick (1933, 1994), *Secrets of the 43 Club* (Dublin: Parkgate Publications), p. 17.

61. A. Davies (2007), 'Glasgow's Reign of Terror: Street Gangs, Racketeering and Intimidation in the 1920s and the 1930s', *Contemporary British History*,

21, 4, pp. 405–27. See H. Shore (2011), 'Criminality and Englishness in the Aftermath: The Racecourse Wars of the 1920s', *Twentieth Century British History*, 22, 4, pp. 474–97.

62. G. Greene (1938), *Brighton Rock* (London: Heinmann); P. Cheney (1944), *Making Crime Pay* (London: John Long).

63. E. T. Hart (1993), *Britain's Godfather* (London: Forum).

64. Davies, 'Scottish Chicago?', p. 513.

65. *Empire News*, 3 September 1922.

66. P. Rogers (1980), *Hacks and Dunces: Pope, Swift and Grub Street* (London: Metheun & Co). Applebee and Defoe would produce two accounts of John Sheppard and a life of Jonathan Wild, as well as other pamphlets. See P. N. Furbank and W. R. Owens (1988), *The Canonisation of Daniel Defoe* (New Haven: Yale University Press).

67. J. Sharpe (2004), *Dick Turpin: The Myth of the English Highwayman* (London: Profile Books).

68. W. A. Miles (1839), *Poverty, Mendicity and Crime* (London: Shaw & Sons).

69. TNA: HO73/16: Select Committee on Gaols (secret), box 3, 8. Shore, *Artful Dodgers*, pp. 155–7.

70. Crone, *Violent Victorians*, pp. 77–8.

71. *OBP*, June 1810, Joel Joseph and Isaac Solomon (t18100606-89). Solomon was identified by contemporaries as the 'Prince' of fences, see the *Morning Chronicle*, 10 July 1829. J. J. Tobias (1974), *Prince of Fences: The Life and Crimes of Ikey Solomons* (London: Valentine Mitchell), pp. 18–19, 147–8.

72. See *OBP*, July 1830, Isaac Solomon (t18300708-16); *OBP*, July 1830, Isaac Solomon (t18300708-17); *OBP*, July 1830, Isaac Solomon (t18300708-63); *OBP*, July 1830, Isaac Solomon (t18300708-140); *OBP*, July 1830, Isaac Solomon (t18300708-141); *OBP*, July 1830, Isaac Solomon (t18300708-177); *OBP*, July 1830, Isaac Solomon (t18301209-107); *Morning Chronicle*, 28 May 1827, July 10 1829.

73. Tobias, *Prince of Fences*, pp. xiii–xiv.

74. See, Anon. (1829), *Adventures ... of that Notorious Fence, and Receiver of Stolen Goods, Isaac Solomons* (London: J. Knight); M. Hebron (1829), *The Life and Exploits of Ikey Solomons* (London); Anon. (1830), *The Life and Adventures of Ikey Solomons* (London).

75. Hobbs, *Lush Life*, pp. 86–7.

76. McDonald, *Elephant Boys*.

77. Hill, *Boss*; J. Pearson (1973), *The Profession of Violence: The Rise and Fall of the Kray Twins* (St Albans: Panther); J. Pearson (2001), *The Cult of Violence: The Untold Story of the Krays* (London: Orion).

78. A. Harding (ed. by R. Samuel, 1981), *East End Underworld: Chapters in the Life of Arthur Harding* (London: Routledge), pp. 182–6, see p. 183. Also S. Newens (2007), 'The Genesis of *East End Underworld: Chapters in the Life of Arthur Harding* by Raphael Samuel', *History Workshop Journal*, 64, 1, pp. 347–53; *Report of the Royal Commission upon the Duties of the Metropolitan Police*, vol. 1, 1908 (4156), pp. 338–50.

79. For family networks in offending histories see B. Godfrey, D. Cox and S. Farrall (2007), *Criminal Lives: Family Life, Employment and Offending* (Oxford: Oxford University Press).

80. M. Neale (2011), 'Making Crime Pay in Late Eighteenth-Century Bristol: Stolen Goods, the Informal Economy and the Negotiation of Risk', *Continuity and Change*, 26/3, pp. 439–59, p. 453.
81. P. Linebaugh (1991), *The London Hanged: Crime and Civil Society in the Eighteenth Century* (London: Allen Lane), p. 141.
82. P. Griffiths (2008), *Lost Londons: Change, Crime and Control in the Capital City, 1550–1660* (Cambridge: Cambridge University Press), p. 172.
83. Griffiths, *Lost Londons*, p. 177.
84. *OBP*, October 1744, Thomas Wells, Theophilus Watson, Joshua Barnes, Thomas Kirby, Ann Duck (t17441017-6).
85. E. Sutherland (1949), *White Collar Crime* (New York: Dryden Press), p. 2; G. Robb (1992), *White-Collar Crime in Modern England: Financial Fraud and Business Morality, 1845–1929* (Cambridge: Cambridge University Press).
86. J. H. Langbein (2003), *The Origins of the Adversary Criminal Trial* (Oxford: Oxford University Press), pp. 143–5.
87. M. Galeotti (2005), 'Global Crime Today', in M. Galeotti (ed.), *Global Crime Today: The Changing Face of Organised Crime* (Abingdon: Routledge), pp. 1–7.
88. For example see F. Egmond (1993), *Underworld: Organised Crime in the Netherlands* (London: Polity); D. V. Jones and A. Bainbridge (1979), 'The Conquering of China: Crime in an Industrial Community, 1842–64', *Llafur The Journal of the Society for the Study of Welsh Labour History*, 2, 4, pp. 7–37.
89. C. Emsley (2005 edn.), *Crime and Society in England, 1750–1900* (Harlow: Pearson), pp. 128–9.
90. T. Henderson (1999), *Disorderly Women in Eighteenth-Century London: Prostitution and Control in the Metropolis, 1730–1830* (London: Longman), p. 41; R. Trumbach (1998), *Sex and the Gender Revolution, Vol. 1: Heterosexuality and the Third Gender in Enlightenment London* (Chicago: University of Chicago Press), pp. 71, 116, 125.
91. S. Gunn (2001), 'The Spatial Turn: Changing Histories of Space and Place', in S. Gunn and R. Morris (eds.), *Identities in Space: Contested Terrains in the Western City since 1850* (Aldershot: Ashgate), pp. 1–14, p. 7.
92. S. Herbert (1998), 'Policing Contested Space: On Patrol at Smiley and Hauser', in N. R. Fyfe (ed.), *Images of the Street: Planning, Identity and Control in Public Space* (London: Routledge), pp. 225–35, p. 226.
93. *OBP*, September 1820, Thomas Shaw (T-18200918-235).
94. *World*, 3 October 1788.
95. Griffiths, 'Overlapping Circles', p. 115.
96. *Jackson's Oxford Journal*, 4 November 1820.
97. *OBP*, July 1888, George Galletly, Peter Lee, William Joseph Graefe, William Henshaw, Charles Henry Govier, Francis Cole, William Elvis, Michael Doolan (t18880730-759). See D. Gray (2013), 'Gang Crime and the Media in Late 19th Century London: The Regent's Park Murder of 1888', *Cultural and Social History*, 10, 4, pp. 559–75.
98. F. Barker and P. Jackson (1990), *The History of London in Maps* (London: Guild Publishing), pp. 66–7.
99. M. J. Halvorson and K. E. Spierling (2008), *Defining Community in Early Modern Europe* (Aldershot: Ashgate), p. 7.
100. Halvorson and Spierling, *Defining Community*, p. 7.

101. Karl Bell has argued that parish boundaries are often sites where legends and myths cluster. K. Bell (2012), *The Legend of Spring-Heeled Jack: Victorian Urban Folklore and Popular Cultures* (Woodbridge: Boydell Press), pp. 158–9.
102. T. Beames (1850), *The Rookeries of London* (London: Thomas Bosworth), pp. 57–8.
103. J. C. Wood (2007), 'Locating Violence: The Spatial Production and Construction of Physical Aggression', in K. D. Watson (ed.), *Assaulting the Past: Violence and Civilization in Historical Context* (Newcastle: Cambridge Scholars Publishing), pp. 20–37, p. 28.
104. Hitchcock and Shoemaker, 'Introduction', *London Lives*.
105. *Second Report from the Committee on the State of the Police of the Metropolis*, 1817 (484), p. 349 (p. 29 online version).
106. E. Reynolds (1998), *Before the Bobbies: The Night Watch and Police Reform in Metropolitan London, 1720–1830* (Hampshire: Macmillan), p. 34.
107. See J. Marriott (2008), 'The Imaginative Geography of the Whitechapel Murders', in A. Werner (ed.) *Jack the Ripper and the East End* (London: Chatto and Windus), pp. 31–63. On the policing of the area during the murders, see D. Gray (2010), *London's Shadows: The Dark Side of the Victorian City* (London: Continuum).
108. Reynolds, *Before the Bobbies*, p. 33; D. George (1966 edn.), *London Life in the Eighteenth Century* (Harmondsworth: Penguin).
109. L. Sponza (1988), *Italian Immigrants in Nineteenth Century Britain: Realities and Images* (Leicester: Leicester University Press).
110. Wood, 'Locating Violence', p. 24.
111. M. Gaskill (2000), *Crime and Mentalities in Early Modern England* (Cambridge: Cambridge University Press), p. 17.
112. P. Burke (2005 edn.), *History and Social Theory* (New York: Cornell University Press), p. 40.
113. Evans, *Tales*, p. 214. Also, D. Nash and A. M. Kilday (2010), *Cultures of Shame: Exploring Crime and Morality in Britain, 1600–1900* (Basingstoke: Palgrave Macmillan).
114. *Standard*, 17 July 1827. It was also reported in the *Morning Post* the following day, 18 July 1827.
115. On the relationship between London and representations of crime, deviance and the poor see S. Joyce (2003), *Capital Offenses: Geographies of Class and Crime in Victorian London* (Charlottesville: University of Virginia Press); S. Koven (2004), *Slumming: Sexual and Social Politics in Victorian London* (Princeton, NJ: Princeton University Press).
116. T. J. Gilfoyle (2006), *A Pickpocket's Tale: The Underworld of Nineteenth-Century New York* (London: W. W. Norton & Co.); J. Schlör (1998), *Nights in the Big City: Paris, Berlin, London, 1840–1930* (London: Reaktion Books).
117. Neale, 'Making Crime Pay', p. 454.
118. T. Hitchcock (2013), 'Confronting the Digital, Or How Academic History Writing Lost The Plot', *Cultural and Social History*, 10, 1, pp. 9–23; R. B. Shoemaker (2008), 'The Old Bailey Proceedings and the Representation of Crime and Criminal Justice in Eighteenth-Century London', *Journal of British Studies*, 47, pp. 559–80. Also see, T. Hitchcock and R. B. Shoemaker (2006) 'Digitising History From Below: The Old Bailey Proceedings Online, 1674–1834', *History Compass*, 4, pp. 1–10.

2 'Now we have the Informing Dogs!': Crime Networks and Informing Cultures in the 1720s and 1730s

1. *OBP*, January 1722, Edward Vaughan, Philip Cholmley (t17220112-43).
2. Howson, *Thief-Taker*; L. Moore (1998), *The Thieves' Opera: The Remarkable Lives and Deaths of Jonathan Wild, Thief-taker and Jack Sheppard, House-breaker* (London: Penguin).
3. Not least by his most famous contemporary biographer, D. Defoe (1725, 2004 edn.), *The True and Genuine Account of the Life and Actions of the Late Jonathan Wild* (London: Harper Perennial).
4. Howson, *Thief-Taker*, p. 115.
5. For example, see Faller, *Turned to Account*, p. 272.
6. Griffiths, *Lost Londons*; McMullan, *Canting Crew*.
7. *Daily Journal*, 3 November 1730, 10 November 1731, for references to Moll Harvey's gang.
8. Apprehension of Highwaymen Act, 4 & 5 William & Mary, c. 8 (1692), Coining Act, 6 & 7 William III, c. 17 (1695); 10 & 11 Wm III, c. 23 (1699).
9. Beattie, *Policing*, p. 371.
10. Shoemaker, 'Street Robber'.
11. *OBP*, Tabulating offence subcategory, between 1700 and 1749 Counting by offence; Tabulating offence subcategory against punishment category, between 1700 and 1749 Counting by punishment (there is incomplete data for the period 1700–1714).
12. See R. Clark (2014), Capital Punishment UK, http://www.capitalpunishmen-tuk.org/tyburn.html
13. J. M. Beattie (1986), *Crime and the Courts in England, 1600–1800* (Princeton, NJ: Princeton University Press), pp. 136–7. For the decline of highway robbery in criminal biography, etc., see McKenzie, *Tyburn's Martyrs*, pp. 115–20; Shoemaker, 'Street Robber'.
14. Sharpe, *Dick Turpin*.
15. E. Mackie (2009), *Rakes, Highwaymen and Pirates: The Making of the Modern Gentleman in the Eighteenth Century* (Baltimore: John Hopkins University Press), p. 98.
16. Ward, 'Print Culture'; Hitchcock and Shoemaker, *London Lives*.
17. R. Paley (1989), 'Thief-takers in London in the Age of the McDaniel Gang, c. 1745–1754', in Douglas Hay and Francis Snyder (eds.), *Policing and Prosecution in Britain, 1750–1850* (Oxford: Clarendon Press), pp. 301–41. See also, Beattie, *Policing*, pp. 406–14.
18. Paley, 'Thief-Takers'. For De Veil and the Black Boy Alley Gang, see Beattie, *Policing*, p. 407; T. Deveil (1748), *Memoirs of the Life and Times of Sir Thomas Deveil, Knight* (London: M. Cooper), p. 66.
19. M. Madan (1785), *Thoughts on Executive Justice, with Respect to Our Criminal Laws* (London: J. Dodsley), pp. 127–8.
20. Shoemaker, 'Print Culture', p. 18; Faller, *Turned to Account*; P. Linebaugh (1977), 'The Ordinary of Newgate and his Account', in J. Cockburn (ed.), *Crime in England 1550–1800* (London: Methuen); A. McKenzie (2005), 'From True Confessions to True Reporting? The Decline and Fall of the Ordinary's *Account*', *London Journal*, 30, 1, pp. 55–70; McKenzie, *Tyburn's Martyrs*; G. Morgan and P. Rushton (2007), 'Print Culture, Crime and Transportation in the Criminal

Atlantic', *Continuity and Change*, 2, 1, pp. 49–72; P. Rawlings (1992), *Drunks, Whores and Idle Apprentices: Criminal Biographies of the Eighteenth Century* (London: Routledge). On distribution, M. Harris (c. 1984), 'Trials and Criminal Biographies: A Case Study in Distribution', in R. Myers and M. Harris (eds.), *Sale and Distribution of Books from 1700* (Oxford: Oxford Polytechnic Press), pp. 1–36.

21. *OBP*, C. Emsley, T. Hitchcock and R. Shoemaker, 'Publishing History of the Proceedings', http://www.oldbaileyonline.org/static/Publishinghistory.jsp, accessed 16 September 2014.
22. Faller, *Turned to Account*.
23. Shoemaker, 'Street Robber'.
24. Shoemaker, 'Street Robber', p. 311–12.
25. I. A. Bell (1991), *Literature and Crime in Augustan England* (London: Routledge), pp. 67–8, 80–4.
26. B. Mandeville (1725), *An Enquiry into the Causes of the Frequent Executions at Tyburn* (London: J. Roberts). See also D. Defoe (1728), *Street Robberies Consider'd* (London: J. Roberts); D. Defoe (1731), *An Effectual Scheme for the Immediate Preventing of Street Robberies* (London).
27. Shoemaker, 'Street Robber', p. 384.
28. *OBP*, Tabulating decade against offence category. Counting by offence.
29. Searching 01/01/1723 to 31/12/1723, 'gang' OR 'gangs', *17th and 18th Century Burney Collection Newspapers*.
30. *Evening Post*, 24 January 1723; *Daily Post*, 14 May 1723.
31. *OBP*, Based on searching 'Violent Theft' from 1715 to 1799, counting by offence per decade.
32. Benjamin Child was tried in Aylesbury, Buckinghamshire, and executed on the 9 March 1722 (*Daily Post*, 10 March 1722); *OBP*, July 1722, James Carrick (t17220704-51), *ONA*, July 1722 (OA17220718); *OBP*, May 1722, John Hawkins and George Simpson (t17220510-3), *ONA*, May 1722 (OA17220521); *OBP*, August 1724, Joseph Sheppard (t17240812-52), *ONA*, September 1724 (OA17240904); Edward Burnworth (alias Frazier) was executed in Kingston, Surrey, 6 May 1726; *OBP*, February 1728, Martin Bellamy (t17280228-44), *ONA*, March 1728 (OA17280327); *OBP*, April 1730, James Dalton, (t17300408-61), *ONA*, May 1730 (OA17300512); *OBP*, January 1729, Thomas Neeves (t17290116-21), *ONA*, February 1729 (OA17290207).
33. See chapters XVII and XVIII in Howson, *Thief-Taker*, pp. 171–203. For Burnworth and Wild see the *Weekly Journal or British Gazetter*, 26 February 1726.
34. *Weekly Gazetter or British Journal*, 3 March 1722.
35. *Daily Post*, 10 March 1722. B. Child (1722), *The Whole Life and History of Benjamin Child, Lately Executed for Robbing the Bristol Mail, etc.* (London: J. Peele).
36. Howson, *Thief-Taker*, p. 176.
37. *OBP*, May 1722, John Hawkins and George Simpson (t17220510-3); R. Wilson (1722), *A Full and Impartial Account of all the Robberies Committed by JOHN HAWKINS, GEORGE SYMPSON (Lately Executed for Robbing the Bristol Mail) and their COMPANIONS* (London: J. Peele); *Weekly Journal or Saturday Post*, 5 May 1722; *St. James's Journal*, 24 May 1722.
38. Accounts from William of his brother John's 'Life' and of his own robberies were later published in A. Smith (1726), *Memoirs of the Life and Times of the Famous Jonathan Wild* (London: Sam. Briscoe), pp. 49–64, 65–98.

39. *ONA*, March 1728 (OA17280327); M. Bellamy (1728), *The Life of Martin Bellamy; with an Account Of all the Several Robberies, Burglaries, Forgeries, and other Crimes by him Committed, etc.* (London: J. Applebee). Rawlings, *Drunks*, pp. 83, 108–7. *OBP*, February 1728, Martin Bellamy (t-17280228-44).

40. *OBP*, May 1725, Jonathan Wilde (t17250513-55). The List is detailed in Howson, *Thief-Taker*, pp. 306–11.

41. *London Gazette*, 19 January 1720.

42. Beattie, *Policing*, p. 379.

43. F. Dabhoiwala (2007), 'Sex and Societies for Moral Reform, 1688–1800', *Journal of British Studies*, 46, pp. 290–319, p. 290; J. Hurl-Eamon (2004), 'Policing Male Heterosexuality: The Reformation of Manners Societies' Campaign Against the Brothels in Westminster, 1690–1720', *Journal of Social History*, 37, 4, pp. 1017–35.

44. Hurl-Eamon, 'Policing', p. 15; R. B. Shoemaker (1991), *Prosecution and Punishment: Petty Crime and the Law in London and Rural Middlesex, c. 1660–1725* (Cambridge: Cambridge University Press), particularly chapter nine; R. B. Shoemaker (1992), 'Reforming the City: The Reformation of Manners Campaign in London, 1690–1738' in L. Davison et al. (eds.), *Stilling the Grumbling Hive: The Response to Social and Economic Problems in England, 1689–1750* (Basingstoke: Palgrave Macmillan), pp. 99–120.

45. Shoemaker, 'Reforming the City', p. 100.

46. Dabhoiwala, 'Sex and Societies', p. 299.

47. Shoemaker, 'Reforming the City', p. 106.

48. Anon. (1691), *Antimoixeia* (London).

49. G. V. Portus (1912), *Caritas Anglicana* (London: Mowbray & Co), pp. 46–9.

50. Dabhoiwala, 'Sex and Societies', p. 304.

51. Beattie, *Policing*, particularly Chapter 8, pp. 370–423; L. Radzinowicz (1956), *A History of the English Criminal Law and Its Administration from 1750. Vol. 2: The Clash Between Private Initiative and Public Interest in the Enforcement of the Law* (London: Stevens and Son); T. Wales (2000), 'Thief-Takers and Their Clients in Later Stuart London', in P. Griffiths and M. S. R. Jenner (eds.), *Londonopolis: Essays in the Social and Cultural History of Early Modern London* (Manchester: Manchester University Press), pp. 67–84.

52. Plate 3 of 'A Harlot's Progress' (paintings, 1731; engravings, 1732). Paulson, *Hogarth: Vol. 1*, pp. 241–52. H. Shore, 'Gonson, Sir John (1676/7–1765)', *Oxford Dictionary of National Biography* (Oxford: Oxford University Press, May 2012, http://www.oxforddnb.com/view/article/96892, accessed 8 September 2014); P. Sugden, 'Veil, Sir Thomas de (1684–1746)', *Oxford Dictionary of National Biography* (Oxford: Oxford University Press, 2004, http://www.oxforddnb.com/view/article/38735, accessed 8 September 2014).

53. R. Paulson (1993), *Hogarth: Vol. 2, High Art and Low, 1732–1750* (Cambridge: Lutterworth Press), pp. 131–2, 140, 146, 147.

54. *London Lives* (hereafter *LL*), MS/SP, Justices' Working Documents, 31 December 1721, LMSMPS501960007.

55. Shoemaker, *Prosecution*, pp. 257–8. See examples of disorderly prosecutions involving Railton and Blackerby in the Justices' Working Papers (*LL*), WJ/PS, October 1722, LMWJPS653630006; SM/PS, April 1730, LMSMPS502670134; WJ/PS, 10 February 1731–8 July 1731, LMWJPS653920033; WJ/PS, 10 February 1731–8 July 1731, LMWJPS653920035.

56. *OBP*, July 1729, William Rowland (t17290709-23); *London Journal*, 9 August 1729.

57. R. Norton (1992), *Mother Clap's Molly House: The Gay Subculture in England, 1700–1830* (London: GMP Publishers), pp. 54–69.

58. *London Journal*, 9 August 1729.

59. See J. Gonson (1730), *Five Charges to Several Grand Juries ... Third Edition* (London).

60. A. Pope (1735), *The Works of Alexander Pope, Esq; vol. II.* (London: L. Gilliver), p. 147.

61. *Daily Journal*, 7 November 1730. *OBP*, July 1731, Luke Powell (t17310714-9); *London Evening Post*, 25 August 1730.

62. P. King (2000), *Crime, Justice and Discretion in England, 1740–1820* (Oxford: Oxford University Press); Langbein, *Origins;* G. Morgan and P. Rushton (2003), 'The Magistrate and the Community and the Maintenance of an Orderly Society in Eighteenth Century England', *Historical Research*, 76, 191, pp. 54–77; D. Palk (2006), *Gender, Crime and Judicial Discretion, 1780–1830* (Woodbridge: Royal Historical Society).

63. S. Webb and B. Webb (1906), *English Local Government from the Revolution to the Municipal Corporations Act: The Parish and the County* (London: Longmans, Green and Co.), p. 328. For the 'trading justice' see J. Beattie (2007), 'Sir John Fielding and Public Justice: The Bow Street Magistrates' Court, 1754–1780', *Law and History Review*, 25, pp. 61–100; N. Landau (1984), *The Justice's of the Peace, 1679–1760* (Berkeley: University of California Press); N. Landau (2002), 'The Trading Justices Trade', in N. Landau (ed.), *Law, Crime and Society, 1660–1830* (Cambridge: Cambridge University Press), pp. 46–70.

64. Landau, 'Trading', p. 46.

65. Shoemaker, *Prosecution*, pp. 225–33.

66. Beattie, *Policing*, pp. 244–7.

67. J. Innes (2009), *Inferior Politics: Social Problems and Social Policies in Eighteenth-Century* (Oxford: Oxford University Press), pp. 279–341 for William Payne. See also J. Innes, 'Payne, William (1717/18–1782)', *Oxford Dictionary of National Biography* (Oxford: Oxford University Press, 2004, http://www.oxforddnb.com/view/article/70400, accessed 8 September 2014).

68. E. Ward (1709), *The London-Spy Compleat in Eighteen Parts* (London: J. How, London), pp. 365–7.

69. C. Walker (1723), *Authentick Memoirs of the Life, Intrigues and Adventures of the Celebrated Sally Salisbury* (London), p. 59.

70. City of London Sessions (*LL*), SL/PS, 29 June 1733, LMSLPS150440071. Langbein, *Origins*, pp. 140–1.

71. *OBP* (t17220112-43); *Daily Post*, 15 January 1722. The year before they had been seized by a mob whilst they were on their way from the Round House to the Court House in Bloomsbury, Middlesex Sessions (*LL*), SM/PS, 31 July 1721, LMSMPS501960006.

72. Cholmley (also spelt Cholmondley) and Vaughan are described as constables for the society by Dabhoiwala, 'Sex and Society', p. 304, fn. 75; see also LMA: MJ/SP/1721, August 1721, affadavit: 'Philip Cholmondly & Edward Vaughan re their apprehension on the oath of a disorderly woman'. Shoemaker notes that they were particularly active in the early 1720s, *Prosecution*, p. 242.

73. *OBP*, February 1722, Charles Mac-Cave, Edward Dun and Edward Galloway (t-17220228-65). See *Daily Post*, 16 February 1722, and *Weekly Journal or British Gazetter*, 17 February 1722, for details of the £50 reward offered for MacCave's apprehension.

74. Anon. (1733), *A Looking Glass For Informing Constables* (London: J. Wilford); for Dent see Shoemaker, *Prosecution*, pp. 180, 241, 261, 262. Philip Cholmondley gave information about this case, Middlesex Sessions (*LL*), SM/PS, 19 March 1709, LMSMPS501050015; see also the information of Thomas Lovett, 12 March 1709, LMSMPS501050012; Foulk Withers, 18 March 1709, LMSMPS501050018. See also the case of Thomas Cook for the murder of John Cooper, a Constable, as he was in the Execution of his Office, in *ONA*, August 1703 (OA17030811). Cook was apparently 'a sworn Enemy to those who were employ'd in the Reformation of Manners'.

75. *OBP*, January 1721, Edward Arnold (t17210113-35).

76. For example see *Daily Journal*, 13 November 1729; *Weekly Journal or British Gazetter*, 15 November 1729.

77. See *British Journal or Censor*, 8 November 1729. Also *Daily Journal*, 3 November 1729.

78. *Fogs Weekly Journal*, 8 November 1729.

79. For example, see Sir John Gonson's requests for the protection of constables, in TNA: SP36/18, Folios 197–8, 13 May 1730, and similar in SP 36/59, Folio 222, 8 December 1742.

80. For social networking theory see J. S. McIllwain (1999), 'Organized Crime: A Social Network Approach', *Crime, Law and Social Change*, 32, pp. 301–23.

81. J. Warner, F. Ivis and A. Demers (2000), 'A Predatory Social Structure: Informers in Westminster, 1737–1741', *Journal of Interdisciplinary History*, 30, pp. 617–34.

82. Howson, *Thief-Taker*, p. 233.

83. There are 14 references to Thomas Willis, mostly working on his own, once working with Robert Willis. There are also two further references to Robert Willis and one to Michael Willis. All these refer to arrests of disorderly persons and all but two are arrests of women. For example see Bridewell Royal Hospital, Minutes of the Court of Governers (*LL*), 22 February 1717, BBBRMG202040287; 8 June 1722, BBBRMG202040546; 12 November 1725, BBBRMG202050092; 21 November 1729, BBBRMG202050228.

84. CLRO: SF 652, Sessions File, Indictments and Recognizances, August 1725, Mary Kirkham, Lydia Close, Abraham Pound. Mary Clayton has found references to the Willises on bloody money certificates from 1726 and 1728, TNA: E407/29. My thanks to Mary for generously sharing her research and sending me copies of the certificates.

85. *OBP*, April 1725, Sarah Field and William Field, Receiving (t17250407-33); Howson claims that the charge was made by Abraham Mendez Ceixes, and that the recognizance is signed by Robert Willis amongst others. Howson, *Thief-Taker*, p. 243.

86. *OBP*, January 1730, John Everett (t17300116-35); *OBP*, May 1728, William Russell, William Holden and Robert Crouch (t17280501-22); *OBP*, May 1728, Christopher Rawlins, Isaac Ashley and John Rowden, Highway Robbery (t17280501-30), *ONA*, May 1728 (OA17280520).

87. *OBP* (t17280501-30).

88. Anon. (1728), *Villany Exploded* (London: T. Read), p. 40.

89. Anon., *Villany Exploded*, p. 43.
90. *London Evening Post*, 14 May 1730; *Daily Journal*, 16 May 1730. An affidavit from Charles Ge(e)ry survives, TNA: KB1/3/3. For the trial see *Country Journal or, the Craftesman*, 11, 18 December 1731; *Daily Journal*, 13 December 1731; *Gentleman's Magazine*, 11 December 1731. Also Anon., *Looking Glass for Informing Constables*.
91. *Daily Journal*, 13 December 1731; *Country Journal or, the Craftesman*, 18 December 1731.
92. *OBP*, July 1726, William Brown (t17260711-77).
93. Norton, *Mother Clap's Molly House*, pp. 57–8; *OBP*, April 1736, Gabriel Lawrence (t17260420-64).
94. The Blood Money certificate for the arrest of John Rowden states that the informants were rewarded £40. Presumably the reward was divided between the 14 men named on the certificate, see TNA: E407/29.
95. Ward, *London Spy*, p. 276.
96. *Daily Journal*, 13 November 1729.
97. Blood Money certificates give us some idea of how the money was divided. For example, for the conviction of Edward Wentland who was tried for Highway Robbery at the Old Bailey in April 1732, the victim, the beadle and four watchmen divided up £40 between them. *OBP*, April 1732, Edward Wentland (t17320419-9); CLRO: MISC MSS/152/5 – Blood Money Certificates for Highwaymen, Newgate Gaol Delivery for City of London.
98. Langbein, *Origins*, p. 160.
99. CLRO: SM 112, Marshall mayor, 1744–45, rewards; The main trials associated with Harper are in December 1744: *OBP* (t17441205-34), (t17441205-35), (t17441205-37), (t17441205-48).
100. CLRO: SM 112, Marshall mayor, 1744–45, rewards. *OBP*: October 1744, Ann Duck and Ann Barefoot (t-17441017-23).
101. *Gentleman's Magazine*, 29 December 1731, p. 539; *ONA*, December 1731 (OA17311220).
102. Langbein, *Origins*, p. 164.
103. *OBP*, May 1722, John Hawkins and George Simpson (t17220510-3). Wilson, *A Full and Impartial Account*. For Wilson's evidence see *Evening Post*, 26 April 1722; *Daily Post*, 27 April 1722.
104. *OBP*, December 1721, Butler Fox (t17211206-41); *OBP*, December 1721, James Wright (t17211206-66); *Weekly Journal or Saturday's Post*, 11 November 1721; *Applebee's Original Weekly Journal*, 16 December 1721. Also see Howson, *Thief-Taker*, pp. 172–4, 178–82, for Hawkins gang.
105. CLRO: CLA/047/LJ/19/005, 'Pardons of prisoners convicted at Newgate, many of condition of transportation', 26 February 1727/8, 30 April 1728 (Dalton & Neeves). *OBP*, July 1728, Supplementary Material, James Dalton and Thomas Neaves Pardon (O17280717-1).
106. *OBP*, May 1728, William Russell, William Holden and Robert Crouch (t17280501-22); *OBP*, May 1728, Christopher Rawlins alias Thomas Rawlins, Isaac Ashley alias Ashby, and John Rowden alias Hulks (t17280501-30). See *ONA*, May 1728 (OA17280520); A. L. Hayward (1927), *Lives of the Most Remarkable Criminals* (London: Routledge), pp. 438–44.
107. J. Dalton (1730), *The Life and Actions of James Dalton* (London: R. Walker), p. 43.

108. *OBP*, May 1728, Richard Nichols and John Perkins (t17280501-8).

109. Dalton, *Life and Actions*, p. 44.

110. Howson, *Thief-Taker*, pp. 139, *OBP*, March 1720, James Dalton and John Pindar (t17200303-45); *OBP*, March 1721, James Dalton (t17210301-61).

111. Hayward, *Lives*, p. 533. For a discussion of Dalton's 'career' in the early 1720s see the commentary in Rawlings, *Drunks*, pp. 79–109.

112. Hayward, *Lives*, p. 533.

113. CLRO: SF 673, 'James Dalton committed by...R. Hopkinson on the 4 day of March 1727 he having made a voluntary confession of his being concerned in several robberies with divers other persons who he hath given information of, and him in your said custody safely keep till discharged by due course of law'. The list which Dalton is on contains examples of other 'informations' being kept safe in the Compter. CLRO: SP 807, session roll, calendar of persons committed to Wood street Compter.

114. *Daily Journal*, 17, 21 January 1730. See Paulson, *Hogarth: Vol. 1*, pp. 244, 373. For the events in Dalton's life leading up to the attack on Dr Mead see Dalton, *The Life and Actions*.

115. *Daily Courant*, 17 January 1730.

116. *Daily Journal*, 17 Saturday January 1730. The following Wednesday (21 January) it was reported that Dalton had been found guilty and sentenced to three years imprisonment and a fine of 40 marks.

117. *OBP*, April 1730, James Dalton (t17300408-61). See also John Waller (1732), *The Life and Infamous Actions of That Perjur'd Villain John Waller, etc.* (London).

118. *Daily Journal*, 12 May 1730; *Country Journal, or Craftsman*, 16 May 1730. See also, *ONA*, May 1730 (OA17300512).

119. *OBP*, April 1724, Edward Joire (probably Joice/Joyce) (t17240415-10).

120. *OBP*, December 1744, Mary Kemp (t-17441205-47), evidence of Joseph Copp.

121. T. Neaves (1729), *The Life of Thomas Neaves, the Noted Street-Robber* (London: R. Walker). For the trials at which Neaves informed see *OBP*, May 1728, John Hornby (t17280501-26); *OBP*, May 1728, Edward Benson, alias Brown, alias Boyston, George Gale, alias Kiddy George and Thomas Crowder (t17280501-35); *OBP*, May 1728, James Toon (t17280501-37).

122. *ONA*, February 1729 (OA17290207). He was tried under the spelling Neeves in January: *OBP*, January 1729, Thomas Neeves (t17290116-21). See also McKenzie, *Tyburn's Martyrs*, p. 20.

123. *Flying Post or the Weekly Medley*, 8 February 1729; *Daily Post*, 10 February 1729.

124. Langbein, *Origins*, pp. 157, 291–310; J. Langbein (1999), 'The Prosecutorial Origins of Defense Counsel in the Eighteenth Century: The Appearance of Solicitors', *Cambridge Law Review*, 58, pp. 314–65; Beattie, *Policing*, p. 376.

125. For more on Waller and Dalton see Hitchcock and Shoemaker, *Tales*, pp. 316–24.

126. Waller, *Life*, pp. 6–7.

127. 'Act for the better regulation of attorneys and solicitors', 2 Geo. II, ch. 23 (1729). See Langbein, 'Prosecutorial Origins'. Dalton, *Life*, pp. 6–12.

128. *Daily Journal*, 14 February 1728; *London Journal*, 17 February 1728.

129. Waller, *Life*, p. 13.

130. This seems to have been during the Anglo-Spanish War of 1727–1729, since the peace with King Philip (Treaty of Seville, 1729) is referred to. Waller, *Life*, p. 14.

131. *OBP*, January 1730, James Dalton (t17300116-13); *OBP*, April 1730, James Dalton (t17300408-61); *London Evening Post*, 25 April 1730.
132. *OBP* (t17300408-61).
133. Waller, *Life*, p. 17. This seems to be confirmed in *ONA* (OA17300512).
134. *OBP*, May 1730, Charles Ditcher, John Wells (t17300513-8).
135. This was obviously Ditcher, Wells and Dalton; it is unclear who the fourth person was. Dalton would be tried in April: *OBP* (t17300408-61). *London Evening Post*, 25 April 1730.
136. Two witnesses with the unlikely names of George Ozenbrook and Mr Twatcher are recorded in the session papers. *OBP* (t17300513-8).
137. *Parker's Penny Post*, 31 January 1726.
138. There is some confusion in the indictments and recognizances since they seem to suggest that Waller and Robert Willis were unjustly imprisoning Preston and Watkinson [sic]. Although in the Sessions papers it refers to John Waller as Robert Willis, suggesting impersonation. See LMA: MS/SP, Justices' Working Papers (*LL*), 11 December 1725 (LMSMPS502310079).
139. *Parker's Penny Post*, 31 January 1726. CLRO: SF 62: Sessions File, Indictments and Recognizances.
140. CLRO: SF 62: Sessions File, Indictments and Recognizances.
141. There are several references in the CLRO file to individuals who were called to the sessions to 'answer the complaint' of either Thomas or Robert Willis for being 'idle and disorderly' or 'a lewd woman'. CLRO: SF 62: Sessions File, Indictments and Recognizances: Mary Kirkham (August 1725), Lydia Close (July 1725), Abraham Pound (nd).
142. *ONA*, May 1730 (OA17300512).
143. Waller, *Life*, pp. 15–16. This probably refers to the 1729 trial of Mary Macartny and Mary Wild for grand larceny in the December sessions, over which Sir Richard Brocas presided. *OBP*, December 1729, Mary Macartny and Mary Wild (t17291203-35). According to an advertisement for the Sessions Papers, Mary Wild was the wife of Jonathan Wild's brother, *OBP*, Old Bailey Proceedings Advertisements, 16 January 1735 (a17350116-1).
144. Hitchcock and Shoemaker (2007), *Tales*, pp. 210–15; Langbein, *Origins*, pp. 152–5. For his appearances at the Old Bailey see, *OBP*, August 1730, Robert Newel (t17300828-52); *OBP*, October 1731, Charles Knowles and Sarah Harper (t17311013-47); *OBP*, December 1731, William Garret and Samuel Cole (t17311208-81); *Daily Courant*, 8 June 1730, 'John Sheffield was committed to Newgate, on the oath of John Waller' (this is also referred to in Waller, *Life*, p. 17). In the *Daily Advertiser* (27 September 1731), there is a report that Waller was paid £100 by the Treasury, 'for that service', and had now 'enter'd himself a Cook on board an East-India Man'. *Life* does not mention this, but does describe his involvement in a number of other cases out of London, Waller, *Life*, pp. 18–19.
145. *OBP*, May 1732, John Waller (t17320525-69).
146. *Read's Weekly Journal, or British Gazette*, 3 June 1732; *Daily Courant*, 10 June 1732.
147. *OBP*, September 1732, Edward Dalton, Rich. Griffith and William Belt (t17320906-69); *The Daily Journal*, 14 June 1732; See also Waller, *Life*, pp. 22–30.
148. *ONA*, October 1732 (OA17321009).

149. E. P. Thompson (1975), *Whigs and Hunters* (Pantheon: New York), p. 196.
150. A. Pepper (2011), 'Early Crime Writing and the State: Jonathan Wild, Daniel Defoe and Bernard De Mandeville in 1720s London', *Textual Practice*, 25, 3, pp. 473–91, p. 473.
151. J. Beattie (1995), 'Crime and Inequality in Eighteenth-Century London', in J. Hagan and R. D. Peterson (eds.), *Crime and Inequality* (California: Stanford University Press), p. 133.
152. T. Hitchcock, S. Howard and R. Shoemaker, 'Vexatious Prosecutions', *London Lives, 1690–1800*.
153. D. Lemmings (2009), 'Introduction: Law and Order, Moral Panics, and Early Modern England', in D. Lemmings and C. Walker (eds.), *Moral Panics, the Media and the Law in Early Modern England* (Basingstoke: Palgrave Macmillan), pp. 1–21, p. 7.

3 'A Noted Virago': Moll Harvey and her 'Dangerous Crew', 1727–1738

1. *Evening Post*, 29 August 1730.
2. S. Devereaux (1996), 'The City and the Sessions Paper: "Public Justice in London, 1770–1800"', *Journal of British Studies*, 35, 4, pp. 466–503; S. Devereaux (2002), 'The Fall of the Sessions Paper: Criminal Trial and the Popular Press in Late Eighteenth-Century London', *Criminal Justice History*, pp. 57–88.
3. Hitchcock and Shoemaker, *London Lives*, 'Introduction'.
4. See also Clayton, 'Charlotte Walker'.
5. For example, *Fog's Weekly Journal*, 2 December 1729; *Grub Street Journal*, 3 September 1730; *British Journal*, 4 July 1730; *Daily Courant*, 22 December 1734.
6. *Daily Journal*, 31 August 1730. On pre-modern gender and crime see J. M. Beattie (1975), 'The Criminality of Women in Eighteenth-Century England', *Journal of Social History*, 8, pp. 80–116; G. Walker (2003), *Crime, Gender and Social Order in Early Modern England* (Cambridge: Cambridge University Press).
7. F. Dabhoiwala (2012), *The Origins of Sex: A History of the First Sexual Revolution* (London: Allen Lane), p. 65; L. Gowing (1998), *Domestic Dangers: Women, Words, and Sex in Early Modern London* (Oxford: Oxford University Press).
8. On defining communities see A. Macfarlane, with S. Harrison and C. Jardine (1977), *Reconstructing Historical Communities* (Cambridge: Cambridge University Press), pp. 1–4; see also, P. Withington and A. Shepard (2000), 'Introduction: Communities in Early Modern England', in Shepard and Withington, pp. 1–15.
9. Withington and Shepard, 'Introduction', p. 6.
10. *OBP*, December 1721, Mary Harvy and Ann Parker (t17211206-33); 'Felons transported from London by the *Gilbert*, Capt. Darby Lux in January 1722 and registered in Annapolis in July 1722', 'London: Harvey alias Coates, Mary', TNA: T53/29/451. P. W. Coldham (1988), *The Complete Book of Emigrants in Bondage, 1614–1775* (Baltimore: Genealogical Publishing), p. 368.
11. G. Morgan and P. Rushton (2003), 'Running Away and Returning Home: The Fate of English Convicts in the American Colonies', *Crime, Histoire et Sociétés*, 7/2, pp. 61–80.
12. Howson, *Thief-Taker*, pp. 127–8, 243, 251, 287.
13. Howson, *Thief-Taker*, p. 128.

14. John Eaton and Mary Stanley (alias Sullivan) gave evidence for the defence. *OBP*, December 1727, Richard Savage, James Gregory and William Merchant (t17271206-24); LMA: MJ/SR/2494; MJ/SR/2497. S. Johnson (1744), *An Account of the Life of Mr Richard Savage* (London: J. Roberts).
15. LMA: MJ/SR/2497, folio 3.
16. *OBP*, February 1728, Mary Harvey, John Eaton and Arabella Eaton (t17280228-76); LMA: MJ/SR/2497.
17. *OBP*, February 1728, Mary Harvey and John Eaton (t17280228-78); LMA: MJ/SR/2498, folio 47.
18. *OBP*, December 1727, Henry Wilcox (t17271206-38); LMA: MJ/SR/2494. See also LMA: MJ/SP/1727, May, Instructions, etc. File 3. Copies of commitments to New Prison, of Henry Willcox, for various causes. [no ref. or dates].
19. *OBP*, Punishment Summary 28 February 1728. See also LMA: MJ/SP/1727, May, Instructions, etc. File 3.
20. *OBP* (t17280228-78); LMA: MJ/SR/2498.
21. Henderson, *Disorderly Women*, pp. 16–18.
22. A significant number of cases involving a 'reckoning' feature at the Old Bailey (although not all refer to a sexual reckoning). *OBP*, Tabulating decade against offence subcategory where the transcription matches 'reckoning'. Counting by offence.
23. T. Brown (1730), *The Third Volume of The Works of Thomas Brown, Being Amusements Serious and Comical, Calculated for the Meridian of London* (London: Edward Midwinter), p. 67.
24. Henderson, *Disorderly Women*, p. 93.
25. See LMA: Middlesex Sessions, Orders of Court: WJ/OC/01, f. 127d (April 1728); MJ/OC/003, f. 167d (Dec. 1728); WJ/OC/002, ff. 101d–105d (April 1731).
26. See Shoemaker, 'Reforming'. For co-operation between the societies and the Westminster Justices see T. B. Isaacs (1979), 'Moral Crime, Moral Reform, and the State in Early Eighteenth Century England: A Study of Piety and Politics' (Rochester, Ph.D), p. 257.
27. Shoemaker, *Prosecution*, p. 319.
28. *Fog's Weekly Journal*, 27 December 1729.
29. Shoemaker, *Prosecution*, p. 264. LMA: Middlesex Sessions, Orders of Court: WJ/OC/002, ff. 69d–70 (26 October 1728), 87–87d (July 1730), 89–89d (Aug. 1730); MJ/OC/003, f. 157d (Nov. 1729); WJ/SP/1728, October.
30. LMA: Middlesex Sessions, Orders of Court: WJ/OC/002, ff. 69d–70 (26 October, 1728).
31. Sherrard, or Sherwood Street, ran south of Golden Square, running into Shug Lane, which then ran into Piccadilly and the Haymarket (see Map 3.1).
32. *British Journal or Censor*, 29 August 1729. Mary Salawen (Sullivan) was arrested in April 1729, but the bill was not found (LMA: MJ/SR/2518, folio. 65); in the same sessions there is an indictment for David Harvey (folio 66) and references to John and Arabella Eaton. David Harvey and Maria Harvey were next indicted in July 1729 (LMA: MJ/SR/2521). The women can also be traced through the Sessions Books over the course of 1729 in the volume for that year (LMA: MJ/SBB/B/0086).
33. *Daily Post*, 10 October 1729; *London Journal*, 11 October 1729.
34. *Daily Journal*, 1 November 1729.
35. J. Hurl-Eamon (2005), *Gender and Petty Violence in London, 1680–1720* (Columbus: Ohio State University Press), pp. 99–100.

36. Hurl-Eamon, *Gender*, p. 98.
37. *Daily Journal*, 4 November 1729.
38. *Daily Journal*, 26 November 1729. See the Gaol Delivery records for December 1729, LMA: MJ/SR/2525, folio 41.
39. *OBP*, January 1730, Mary Sullivan and Isabella Eaton (t17300116-19). The Sessions Peace roll for December 1729 is missing. However, the administration of the trials can partially be traced in the Gaol Delivery Rolls for the same month. LMA: MJ/SR/2525.
40. LMA: MJ/SR/2525, Mary West alias Ryley is mentioned on the wrapping of this roll as being 'committed ... for being an evidence against Mary Sulavan als Stanley Mary Harvey als Phillips, Isabella Eaton also Gwinn, they being now in custody for several felonies by them committed ...'.
41. LMA: MJ/SR/2525.
42. Ibid. *London Evening Post*, 17 January 1730; *Daily Journal*, 19 January 1730.
43. *OBP*, April 1730, Mary Sullivan and Isabella Eaton (t17300408-26).
44. *British Journal*, 4, 22 July 1730; *Fog's Weekly Journal*, 4 July 1730.
45. *Daily Journal*, 26 November 1729.
46. For malicious prosecution against constables see Shoemaker, *Prosecution*, pp. 264–5, and by constables see Hurl-Eamon, *Gender*, pp. 99–100.
47. *OBP* (t17280228-76).
48. *OBP*, August 1730, Thomas Willis and Michael Willis (t17300828-76).
49. *British Journal*, 19 September 1730.
50. J. White (2012), *London in the Eighteenth Century: A Great and Monstrous Thing* (London: Bodley Head), pp. 158–60.
51. Linebaugh, *London Hanged*, p. 288, and on the Irish in London more generally, pp. 288–326.
52. *Daily Gazetter*, 2 August 1736. On Rosemary Lane see J. Turner (2013), 'Ill-favoured sluts'? – The Disorderly Women of Rosemary Lane and Rag Fair', *London Journal*, 38/2, pp. 95–109; Hitchcock and Shoemaker, *Tales*, pp. xx–xxi.
53. Uglow, *Hogarth*, p. 202.
54. Uglow, *Hogarth*, pp. 193–7, 204–6, 209.
55. Paulson, *Hogarth: Volume 1*, pp. 241–52.
56. R. Penfold-Mounce (2009), *Celebrity Culture and Crime: The Joy of Transgression* (Basingstoke: Palgrave Macmillan), p. 98.
57. *Grub Street Journal*, 1 October 1730.
58. F. Dabhoiwala (1995), 'Prostitution and Police in London, c. 1660–1760' (Oxford, Dphil.), pp. 191–2.
59. LMA: Order to Court: WJ/OC/2, ff. 85d–86d (June, 1730).
60. LMA: Order to Court: WJ/OC/2, ff. 85d–86d (June, 1730).
61. LMA: Orders to Court: WJ/OC/2, folio 102.
62. For example, the *London Journal* of Saturday 18 July 1730 gave a full account of the meetings. See earlier references in the *Daily Journal*, 16 May 1730; *London Journal*, 23 May 1730, 13 June 1730, 18 July 1730, 1 August 1730, 8 August 1730; *Grub Street Journal*, 23 July 1730, 30 July 1730, 6 August 1730.
63. For example, *Daily Journal*, 16, 23, 26 September 1730, 11, 16, 18 November 1730, 3, 19, 23, 29 December 1730; *Daily Post*, 4, 24 September 1730, 10 October 1730, 5, 11 November 1730, 17, 21, 27 December 1730; *Grub Street Journal*, 7, 14 January 1731.
64. LMA: Orders to Court: WJ/OC/2, ff. 101d–105d.
65. LMA: Orders to Court: WJ/OC/2, f. 103.

66. LMA: Orders to Court: WJ/OC/2, ff. 101d–105d.
67. LMA: Orders to Court: WJ/OC/2, ff. 89–90d. *Daily Journal*, 18 August 1730.
68. *Daily Post*, 18 August 1730; *Daily Journal*, 18 August 1730.
69. *Daily Post*, 18 August 1730; *Daily Journal*, 18 August 1730.
70. By this time the Westminster justices were meeting twice a week mainly in the vestry room of St Paul's, Covent Garden, or St Martins. For example, *London Journal*, 1, 8, 29 August 1730; *Grub Street Journal*, 6 August 1730; *Daily Journal*, 21 August 1730; *Daily Post*, 25 August 1730.
71. *Daily Post*, 21 August 1730.
72. *Universal Spectator and Weekly Journal*, 22 August 1730. Harvey was tried along with Mary Sullivan and Isabel Eaton for receiving stolen goods in October 1730, *OBP*, October 1730 (t17301014-70).
73. Hitchcock and Shoemaker, *London Lives*.
74. A. Wood (2006), 'Subordination, Solidarity and the Limits of Popular Agency in a Yorkshire Valley, c. 1596–1615', *Past and Present*, 193, pp. 41–72.
75. *OBP*, August 1730, Thomas Willis and Michael Willis (t17300828-76). For the administration of the trial see LMA: MJ/SR/2537, folio 66, Maria Phillips (alias Harvey), William McCage and Maria Johnson (an alias of Mary Sullivan's) are named on the back of the indictment; *Evening Post*, 29 August 1730; *Daily Journal*, 31 August 1730. Eaton was not charged until 14 September 1730 (*Evening Post*, 15 September 1730; LMA: MJ/SR/2543, folio 60).
76. *Evening Post*, 29 August 1730.
77. See Chapter 2, pp. 38–9. At the trial Mary Harvey in her evidence refers to '*Thomas Willis*, who now says his name is *John*' (*OBP* (t17300828-76)). In the indictment he is named as Thomas Willis (LMA: MJ/SR/2537, folio 66).
78. *OBP* (t17300828-76).
79. *OBP* (t17300828-76).
80. *OBP* (t17300828-76). See also, *Daily Journal*, 31 August 1730; *Grub Street Journal*, 3 September 1730.
81. For example, *Daily Journal*, 1, 23, 26 September 1730 (the latter for the reference to Hedge Lane); *Daily Post*, 4, 5, 16 September 1730; *London Journal*, 5 September 1730; *Grub Street Journal*, 10, 17, 24 September 1730.
82. LMA: MJ/SR/2543, 'Mary Sullavan' is named on the wrapping of the Sessions Roll.
83. *OBP*, October 1730, Mary Hall, Mary Harvey and Isabel Eaton (t17301014-70); LMA: MJ/SR/2543, folio 60.
84. *Evening Post*, 17 October 1730; *London Evening Post*, 31 October 1730. See the Sessions Roll for December 1730 (LMA: MJ/SR/2545, folio 53). This includes an indictment for Maria Sullivan alias Hall alias Stanley and Isabella Eaton alias Gwin.
85. There are several forms of the habeas corpus writ. The more well-known writ was used in cases of illegal imprisonment, but there was also a habeas corpus writ which was used to remove people from one jurisdiction to another, or to bring them up to testify. It is unclear which form of the writ is being used in this case. My thanks to Ruth Paley who explained this issue. Unfortunately, the affidavits for the terms in which Mary Harvey first appeared at the King's Bench are missing (TNA: KB1/3/2/12, 4 Geo. II Mich. 1730; 4 Geo. II Hil. 1730/31). A search of the other terms through 1731–32 (TNA: KB1/3/2 and KB1/3/3, and KB2/1 'Miscellaneous affidavits

1727–37) drew a blank. Moreover, there are no King's Bench prison records for this period. Maria Harvey alias Philips, Willus Harvey and Isabella Eaton (also listed as Gwin) can be found in the indexes to London and Middlesex defendants (TNA: IND1/6672).

86. *Daily Post*, 2 November 1730; *Daily Journal*, 2 November 1730.
87. King's Bench Prison was in Southwark, off Borough.
88. *Daily Journal*, 2 November 1730; *Daily Post*, 3 November 1730.
89. Henderson, *Disorderly Women*, p. 29.
90. *Daily Journal*, 28 November 1730; *Grub Street Journal*, 3 December 1730. This writ is referred to in the report discussed above (LMA: WJ/OC/2, ff. 101d–105d), in the context of accusations about the legality of the warrants, f. 103.
91. *Daily Post*, 13 November 1730.
92. LMA: MJ/SR/2545.
93. *Daily Journal*, 27 November 1730.
94. *Daily Journal*, 5 December 1730.
95. *OBP*, December 1730, Mary Sullivan and Isabella Gwyn (t17301204-72). *Daily Journal*, 9 December 1730. See LMA: MJ/SR/2545, folio 53.
96. *Daily Journal*, 10 December 1730. An indictment survives for Isabella Gwin alias Hambledon in the Sessions Roll for January 1731, LMA: MJ/SR/2547, folio 32.
97. *Daily Journal*, 31 December 1730.
98. *London Evening Post*, 14 January 1731; *Daily Journal*, 15 January 1731.
99. *London Evening Post*, 6 February 1731; *Daily Journal*, 8 February 1731: *Daily Post*, 8 February 1731.
100. King's Street was a main thoroughfare near to Westminster Hall. In other sources the Fountain is described as being in Tothill Street. *London Evening Post*, 11 February 1731; *Daily Post*, 13 February 1731.
101. *Daily Journal*, 15 February 1731; *Grub Street Journal*, 18 February 1731.
102. *Daily Journal*, 16 February 1731; also reported in *Daily Courant*, 12 February 1731; *Daily Journal*, 13 February 1731; *British Journal or the Traveller*, 20 February 1731.
103. *Daily Courant*, 20 May 1731; *Daily Journal*, 20 May 1731; *Daily Post*, 20 May 1731; *Country Journal or, the Craftesman*, 22 May 1731; *Fog's Weekly Journal*, 22 May 1731; *Read's Weekly Journal or British Gazetter*, 22 May 1731; *Universal Spectator and Weekly Journal*, 22 May 1731.
104. Ward, 'Print Culture', p. 204.
105. *Daily Post*, 20 May 1731. The report was also printed in the *Daily Courant*, 20 May 1731 and the *Universal Spectator and Weekly Journal*, 22 May 1731. Rasp House (*Rasphuis*) had been established in 1596 in Amsterdam. T. Sellin (1994), *Pioneering in Penology: The Amsterdam Houses of Correction in the Sixteenth and Seventeenth Centuries* (Philadelphia: University of Pennsylvania Press), p. 31.
106. Rawlings, *Drunks*, p. 71; Ward, 'Print Culture', pp. 204–5.
107. *Universal Spectator and Weekly Journal*, 22 May 1731. Mackeig's committal was also noted by the *Daily Advertiser*, 21 May 1731 and Mackeig's and Eaton's committals in the *Daily Courant*, 21 May 1731.
108. *London Evening Post*, 25 May 1731; *Daily Journal*, 27 May 1731; TNA: IND1/6672.
109. TNA: IND1/6672.

110. *Daily Courant*, 26 May 1731; *Daily Journal*, 27 May 1731.
111. *London Evening Post*, 15 June 1731; *Daily Journal*, 17 June 1731; *London Evening Post*, 19 June 1731.
112. Either on Friday 18 or Monday 21 May. *London Evening Post*, 19 June 1731; *Daily Journal*, 22 June 1731.
113. *London Evening Post*, 26 May 1731; *Grub Street Journal*, 1 July 1731.
114. The debates between the counsel can be traced through the press in November: *London Evening Post*, 20 November 1731; *Fog's Weekly Journal*, 20 November 1731; *Daily Post*, 23, 26 November 1731; *Daily Journal*, 25 November 1731; *Daily Advertiser*, 26 November 1731.
115. *London Evening Post*, 27 November 1731; *Daily Journal*, 29 November 1731.
116. *Daily Journal*, 5 December 1730.
117. Hedge Lane was still associated with prostitution in 1750 (see *OBP*, February 1750, Mary Maschal (t17500228-40)) and 1770. See John Fielding's evidence in 'Committee to Enquire into the Several Burglaries and Robberies', *Commons Journal*, 1770, vol. XXXII, 881. See also Henderson, *Disorderly Women*, p. 50, 57.
118. Defoe, *Effectual Scheme*. Also P. N. Furbank and W. R. Owens (1994), *Defoe De-attributions* (London: Hambledon Press).
119. Defoe, *Effectual Scheme*, pp. 60, 61–2.
120. *Craftsman*, No. 316, 22 July 1732, p. 186.
121. *Gentleman's Magazine*, 11 December 1731; *Daily Journal*, 13 December 1731; *Country Journal or, the Craftesman*, 18 December 1731.
122. Defoe, *Effectual Scheme*, pp. 14, 24.
123. *OBP*, July 1732, Mary Sullivan (t17320705-12); LMA: MJ/SR/2578, folio 19. Her sentence of transportation is also recorded on the indictment. For Isabella Eaton see MJ/SR/2579, folio 37.
124. 'Felons transported from London to Virginia by the *Caesar*, Capt. William Loney, in October 1732', 'Middlesex: Sullivan *als* Johnson', TNA: T53/36/423. See Coldham, *Emigrants*, p. 833.
125. *Grub Street Journal*, 6 July 1732; LMA: MJ/SR/2577, folio 51.
126. In January 1733 she was indicted for assaulting the Under Keeper of Tothill-Fields Bridewell, *London Evening Post*, 6 January 1733. For the reference to Dublin see *Daily Courant*, 22 December 1733. She is not on Coldham's lists of Irish Transported Felons under any of her aliases. Coldham, *Emigrants*, p. 975.
127. *OBP*, December 1732, Jane Murphey (t17321206–38).
128. *General Evening Post*, 31 July 1735; *Grub Street Journal*, 7 August 1735. A Mary and John Eaton are named in the calendars for the Sessions Peace for August 1735, LMA: MJ/SR/2640, folio 28.
129. *London Evening Post*, 31 July 1735. *OBP*, December 1735, Elizabeth Walker (t17351210-74).
130. *London Evening Post*, 17 January 1736. See also *Daily Gazetter*, 17 December 1735.
131. CLRO: CLA/047/LJ/13/1737/010, Petitions of Isabella Eaton, condemned to 12 months in prison in Jan 1736, at least 8 months overdue for release. n.d.
132. *London Evening Post*, 20 June 1738; *Daily Post*, 22 June 1738; *Read's Weekly Journal or British Gazetter*, 24 June 1738; *Old Common Sense or the Englishman's Journal*, 1 July 1738; *Daily Gazetter*, 22 June 1738. The indictment survives in LMA: MJ/SR/2700, folio 39, however it was 'not found'.
133. *Daily Post*, 27 October 1738.

4 'The pickpockets and hustlers had yesterday what is called a *Grand Day*': Changing Street Theft, c. 1800–1850

1. *Morning Post*, 22 June 1810.
2. *Jackson's Oxford Journal*, 9 December 1820.
3. P. King (2003), 'Moral Panics and Violent Street Crime, 1750–2000: A Comparative Perspective', in B. Godfrey, C. Emsley and G. Dunstall (eds.), *Comparative Histories of Crime* (Cullompton: Willan Publishing), pp. 53–71; Ward, 'Print Culture'; J. Davis (1980), 'The London Garotting Panic of 1862: A Moral Panic and the Creation of a Criminal Class in Mid-Victorian England', in V. A. C. Gatrell, B. Lenman and G. Parker (eds.), *Crime and the Law: The Social History of Crime in Western Europe since 1500* (London: Europa), pp. 190–213.
4. Shoemaker, 'Street Robber', p. 383. Based on the period 1723–1763.
5. Shoemaker, 'Street Robber', p. 403.
6. *OBP*, Tabulating year against offence subcategory where offence category is violent theft, after 1750. Counting by offence.
7. J. M. Beattie (2012), *The First English Detectives: The Bow Street Runners and the Policing of London, 1730–1840* (Oxford: Oxford University Press), p. 211.
8. J. Stevenson (1979), *Popular Disturbances in England, 1700–1870* (London: Longman), p. 200.
9. *Lloyd's Weekly Newspaper*, 2 June 1844.
10. *OBP*, Tabulating year against offence subcategory where the transcription matches 'hustled hustling hustle', between 1815-25. Counting by offence.
11. *OBP*, Tabulating year against offence subcategory where the transcription matches 'hustled hustling hustle', between 1815 and 1825. Counting by defendant.
12. Beattie, *First English Detectives*, p. 212.
13. Palk, *Gender*, pp. 81–6.
14. W. Hawkins (1787), *A Treatise of the Pleas of the Crown* (London: His Majesty's Law Printers), p. 490, cited in Palk, *Gender*, p. 70.
15. P. King (2006), *Crime and the Law in England, 1750–1840: Remaking Justice From the Margins* (Cambridge: Cambridge University Press).
16. Beattie, *First English Detectives*, pp. 212–22.
17. Shore, *Artful Dodgers*, pp. 17–29.
18. *OBP*, September 1820, William Sidney Smith and Frederick Hopkins (t18200918-36).
19. T. Smollett (1751, 1964 edn), *The Adventures of Peregrine Pickle* (Oxford: Oxford University Press), p. 11.
20. *OBP*, October 1762, Francis Jones (t17621020-11).
21. *OBP*, April 1784, Michael Lee (t17840421-39); *OBP*, February 1785, James Coyle (t17850223-13); *OBP*, April 1785, John Foster (t17850406-3).
22. *General Evening Post*, 22 March 1785.
23. *Morning Post*, 29 October 1813.
24. *Select Committee on the State of the Police of the Metropolis*, 1816 (510), p. 228.
25. *Select Committee on the State of the Police of the Metropolis*, 1817 (484), p. 409.
26. Anon. (1818), *The London Guide and Stranger's Safeguard, etc.* (London: J. Bumpus), p. 16.
27. J. H. Vaux (1819), *Memoirs of James Hardy Vaux* (London: W. Clowes, 1819), p. 213.

28. *OBP*, February 1819, Hyam Alexander and John Phillips (t18190217-83); October 1819, Lewis Green and William Farmer (t18191027-50).
29. *OBP*, Tabulating year against offence subcategory where the transcription matches 'hustled hustling hustle', between 1815 and 1825. Counting by defendant.
30. *OBP*, December 1815, William Collins, William Adolphus Thompson, Francis Allsop (t18151206-40).
31. *OBP*, Tabulating decade against offence subcategory where the transcription matches 'hustling hustle hustled'. Counting by offence; Tabulating decade against offence subcategory where the transcription matches 'hustling hustle hustled' and defendant gender is female. Counting by offence.
32. Palk, *Gender*, pp. 81–7.
33. *OBP*, June 1820, Eliza Brown, Lucy Saunders and Edward Crispin (t18200628-22).
34. Shore, *Artful Dodgers*, p. 59. *OBP*, Tabulating decade against offence subcategory where the transcription matches 'hustling hustle hustled', defendant age is at least one and defendant age is at most 16. Counting by offence.
35. *OBP*, January 1819, Thomas Thompson and Robert Rose (t18190113-46).
36. *OBP*, Tabulating year against defendant age where the transcription matches 'hustle hustling hustled', defendant age is at least one and at most 120, between 1815 and 1825. Counting by defendant.
37. *OBP*, July 1836, John Wilson, John Nelson (t18360713-1382).
38. *The Times*, 17 December 1820.
39. *Morning Chronicle*, 28, 29, 30 July 1819. Also reported in the *Annual Register*, 'Chronicle for July 1819' (1820), p. 55. On disturbances at fairs see B. Heller (2010), 'The "Menu Peuple" and the Polite Spectator: The Individual in the Crowd at Eighteenth-Century London Fairs', *Past and Present*, 208, 1, pp. 131–57.
40. *Morning Chronicle*, 16, 18 September 1819.
41. *Morning Chronicle*, 29 July 1819; C. R. Elrington et al. (1989), *A History of the County of Middlesex, Vol. 9* (Oxford: Oxford University Press, http://www.british-history.ac.uk/report.aspx?compid=22648, accessed 9 September 2014).
42. *OBP*, September 1819, William Carter and Philip Cameron (t18190915-170); *Morning Chronicle*, 29 July 1819; *Morning Post*, 4 August 1819.
43. *OBP*, September 1819, John Henley (t18190915-7); *Morning Post*, 29 July 1819.
44. *Morning Post*, 2 August 1819.
45. *Bury and Norwich Post*, 1 December 1819; *Morning Post*, 27 November 1819; *OBP*, September 1819, Edward Cassidy (t18190915-73); September 1819, John Henley (t18190915-06; t18190915-07); September 1819, William Fletcher (t18190915-5); September 1819, Henry Lovell (t18190915-51).
46. Elrington, *Middlesex*.
47. H. Cunningham (1977), 'The Metropolitan Fairs: A Case Study in the Social Control of Leisure', in A. P. Donajgrodski (ed.), *Social Control in Nineteenth Century Britain* (London: Croom Helm), pp. 163–84, pp. 164–5.
48. *OBP*, Tabulating year against offence subcategory where the transcription matches 'hustle hustling hustled', between 1815 and 1825. Counting by defendant.
49. Stevenson, *Popular Disturbances*, p. 193.

50. There is some discussion of the Caroline processions in S. H. Palmer (1977), 'Before the Bobbies: The Caroline Riots of 1821', *History Today*, October, 27, pp. 637–44. For crowds and processions otherwise see M. Harrison (2002), *Crowds and History: Mass Phenomena in English Towns* (Cambridge: Cambridge University Press); R. McWilliam (1998), *Popular Politics and Protest in Nineteenth Century England* (London: Routledge); M. White (2008), '"Rogues of the Meaner Sort"?: Old Bailey Executions and the London Crowd in the Early Nineteenth Century', *London Journal*, 33, 2, pp. 135–53.

51. J. Belcham (1985), *"Orator" Hunt: Henry Hunt and English Working Class Radicalism* (Oxford: Clarendon Press), p. 123; *OBP*, September 1819, Felix Henry Miller (t18190915-12); September 1819, Daniel Huffman (t18190915-65); September 1819, Abraham Davis (t18190915-206).

52. *OBP*, September 1819, Daniel Huffman (t18190915-65).

53. *OBP*, April 1820, John Fitzgerald (t18200412-213).

54. *Morning Post*, 7 April 1820.

55. T. W. Laqueur (1982), 'The Queen Caroline Affair: Politics as Art in the Reign of George IV', *Journal of Modern History*, 54, pp. 417–66; J. Stevenson (1977), 'The Queen Caroline Affair', in J. Stevenson (ed.) *London in the Age of Reform* (Oxford: Blackwell), pp. 117–48.

56. *OBP*, Tabulating decade against offence subcategory where the transcription matches 'procession processions', before 1913. Counting by offence.

57. I. J. Prothero (1981), *Artisans and Politics in Early Nineteenth Century London: John Gast and his Times* (London: Methuen), pp. 133–6, 140.

58. *OBP*, Tabulating offence subcategory where the transcription matches 'queen procession', between June 1820 and December 1820. Counting by offence.

59. *OBP*, October 1820, Thomas Dorset (t18201028-36).

60. *OBP*, October 1820, Lewis Lazarus (t18201028-31); October 1820, William Penn (t18201028-135).

61. *Jackson's Oxford Journal*, 4 November 1820.

62. *Morning Post*, 11 October 1820.

63. A. T. Harris (2004), *Policing the City: Crime and Legal Authority in London, 1780–1840* (Columbus: Ohio State University Press), p. 105.

64. See 'WEEKLY RETROSPECT' 13 October, in *The Loyalist and Anti-Radical* (Loyalist Association Magazine), 1820, p. 87.

65. *Morning Chronicle*, 30 November 1820.

66. *Morning Post*, 1 December 1820.

67. *The Times*, 14 December 1820; *John Bull*, 17 December 1820.

68. *Morning Chronicle*, 16 August 1821. See also TNA: HO44/10, ff. 220-231, 'Disturbances at Queen Caroline's funeral: statements of members of police dismounted horse patrol', September 1821. See also folios in TNA: HO44/9, 10 and 48 for disturbances at Queen Caroline's Funeral.

69. Reynolds, *Before the Bobbies*, pp. 114–5, 116–7.

70. *Report of the Select Committee on the Police of the Metropolis*, 1822 (440), pp. 8, 19, 23, 32.

71. Reynolds, *Before the Bobbies*, pp. 114–15.

72. 2 Geo. IV. – Sess. 1821. A bill for the more effectual administration of the office of a justice of the peace in and near the metropolis; and for the more effectual prevention of depredations on the River Thames and its vicinity;

3 Geo. IV. – Sess. 1822. A bill [as amended by the committee] for the more effectual administration of the office of a justice of the peace in and near the metropolis, and for the more effectual prevention of depredations on the River Thames and its vicinity (find Acts). TNA: HO44/8, ff. 630-631, 'Coronation of George IV: Lord Gwydir, requesting police officers to attend at north door of Westminster Hall, where pickpockets are troublesome', 27 July 1821.

73. TNA: HO61/1, Charles Stable to Lord Sidmouth, 3 May 1821, cited in Reynolds, *Before the Bobbies*, p. 117.
74. Emsley (2005), *Crime and Society*, p. 27.
75. L. Radzinowicz (1948), *A History of the English Criminal Law and Its Administration from 1750, Vol. 1: The Movement for Reform* (London: Stevens & Sons), pp. 497–9.
76. *OBP*, October 1815, John Lane (t18151025-41).
77. *OBP*, December 1815, Isaac Davis and Moss Jacobs, Highway Robbery (t18151206-3).
78. *OBP*, September 1820, Charles Smith and George Mason (t18200918-255).
79. *OBP*, September 1820, Isaac Wolfe, Samuel Wherry and Daniel Edwards (t18200918-251).
80. Radzinowicz, *History, Vol. 1*, p. 499.
81. J. Herring (2012), *Criminal Law: Text, Cases and Materials, Fifth Edition* (Oxford: Oxford University Press), pp. 862–3.
82. Radzinowicz, *History, Vol. 1*, pp. 500–1.
83. *OBP*, January 1821, Michael Harley (t18210110-2).
84. *Glasgow Herald*, 25 December 1820.
85. *OBP*, January 1821, Michael Harley (t18210110-2).
86. *Morning Post* 10, 17 February 1821; *Jackson's Oxford Journal*, 10 March 1821; *The Times*, 12 March 1821.
87. *The Times*, 12 March 1821.
88. *OBP*, September 1820, William Sidney Smith and Frederick Hopkins (t18200918-36).
89. *Morning Post*, 1 March 1822.
90. *OBP*, 20 February, James Edrop (t18220220-96).
91. *Morning Post*, 20 August 1823.
92. *OBP*, September 1820, Joseph Ellinger (t18200918-79).
93. *The Times*, 6 December 1820.
94. Searching the Old Bailey Online for the whole period (1674 to 1913) using the phrase 'stealing from the person only' 86 cases were found. All these came from between 1800–49, 72 (83.72 per cent) came from the 1810s and 1820s; 64 of these had been prosecuted for highway robbery and seven for robbery.
95. King, *Crime and the Law*, pp. 122–3.
96. *OBP*, October 1818, William Knight and Edward Evans (t18181028-21).
97. *Morning Chronicle*, 13 January 1819.
98. The poem was reprinted in J. G. Nichols (1837), *London Pageants* (London: J. B. Nichols).
99. McGowen, 'Criminal'.
100. TNA: MEPO 3/1, 'Miscellaneous Criminal Activities' (1830–1871).
101. Evidence of Mr Chesterton, *First Report of the Commissioners appointed to inquire into the best means of establishing an efficient Constabulary Force in the Counties of England and Wales*, 1839 [169], pp. 205–15, for these quotes p. 213.

102. See also *First report from the Select Committee of the House of Lords appointed to inquire into the present state of the several gaols and houses of correction in England and Wales; with the minutes of evidence and an appendix*, 1835 (438) (439) (440) (441), p. 90

103. C. Random de Bérenger Beaufain (1835), *Helps and Hints How to Protect Life and Property* (London: T. Hurst), p. 124.

104. Bérenger Beaufain, *Helps and Hints*, p. 124.

105. *Chambers's Edinburgh Journal* (1847), p. 312.

106. Pierce Egan (1821), *Life in London or, the Day and Night Scenes of Jerry Hawthorn, esq., and his elegant friend, Corinthian Tom* (London: Chatto and Windus). See Reid, *Bucks and Bruisers*; Gregory Dart (2001), '"Flash Style": Pierce Egan and Literary London, 1820–1828', *History Workshop Journal*, 51, pp. 180–205.

107. E. Partridge (1950, 1989 edn), *A Dictionary of the Underworld* (London: Wordsworth), p. 707.

108. *Standard*, 5 July 1827. Based on a search of the British Library Nineteenth Century newspaper collection.

109. *The Times*, 3 March 1829, p. 4; see also references in the *Morning Chronicle*, 3 June, 12 December 1829.

110. *OBP*, 16 September 1830, John Hemmings (t18300916-320).

111. *OBP*, Tabulating decade against offence subcategory where the transcription matches '+"swell mob"'. Counting by offence.

112. OBP, 15 December 1856, Dennis Bryan (t18561215-166). This was the year of the first garotting panic, see R. Sindall (1987), 'The London Garotting Panics of 1856 and 1862', *Social History*, 12/3, pp. 351–9.

113. Searching for the term in the British Library Nineteenth Century newspaper collection produced 2043 references between 1829 and 1900 (85 per cent between 1829 and 1859), albeit some of these will have been referring to the same set of events.

114. H. Mayhew (1857), *The Great World of London* (London: David Bogue), p. 90.

115. TNA: HO73/16, notebook 3, evidence of W. Johnson (c. 1836).

116. Miles, *Poverty*, p. 137; Nelson is mentioned across a number of documents, for example TNA: HO26/42, Middlesex Criminal Registers, series 1, 1836. William Nelson, aged 23, was sentenced to transportation for seven years at Westminster Sessions on 8 Dec. 1836; also TNA: MEPO3/1, 'Miscellaneous Criminal Activities' (1830–1871). See Shore, *Artful Dodgers*, pp. 60, 61.

117. Goldsmiths Library, University of London, 'Petition to the "swell Mob" from the Tribe of "blacklegs, Prigs, & Pickpockets," Requesting to Enjoy the Same Privileges as Their "brethren" the "millocrats"' (s.n.c. 1834). For millocrats see *Northern Star and Leeds General Advertiser*, 23 January 1841.

118. See 'The Modern Science of Thief-taking' and 'A Detective Police Party', *Household Words*, July 1850, pp. 370–1, 410.

119. 'Lord Chamberlain's Plays, 1852–1866. January–February 1852', p. 27, https://www.royalholloway.ac.uk/dramaandtheatre/documents/pdf/lcp/playslicensedin1852.pdf, accessed 16 September 2014.

120. Davis, 'Garotting', pp. 190–213.

121. Harris, *Policing*, pp. 120–1; Reynolds, *Before the Bobbies*, pp. 113–14.

122. *Report from the Select Committee on the Police of the Metropolis*, 1822 (440), pp. 25, 82–3, p. 9 for this quote. Also C. Emsley (1983), *Policing and its Context, 1750–1870* (Basingstoke: Macmillan), p. 50.

123. M. J. D. Roberts (1988), 'Public and Private in Early Nineteenth Century London: The Vagrancy Act of 1822 and its Enforcement', *Social History*, 13, pp. 237–94.
124. Shoemaker, 'Street Robber'.
125. *The Times*, 17 December 1820.
126. *Jackson's Oxford Journal*, 4 November 1820.
127. *The Times*, 11 March 1831.
128. See Chapter 7.

5   'There goes Bill Sheen, the Murderer': Crime, Kinship and Community in East London, 1827–1852

1. Egan, *Life in London*; Vaux, *Memoirs*.
2. Crone, *Violent Victorians*, pp. 78–9.
3. King, *Crime and the Law*, p. 60.
4. J. Marriott (2011), *Beyond the Tower: A History of East London* (London: Polity Press), pp. 150–73.
5. J. Turner, 'An Anatomy of a Disorderly Neighbourhood: Rosemary Lane and Rag Fair in the Late Seventeenth and Eighteenth Centuries' (Ph.D in progress, University of Hertfordshire).
6. The Lambeth Street Police Office was in Whitechapel and covered a substantial jurisdiction north and northeast of the Tower. White, *London*, p. 236.
7. H. Mayhew (1851), *London Labour and the London Poor*, vol. 1 (London: George Woodfall & Son), p. 252.
8. *Report from the Select Committee on Metropolis Police Offices*, 1837 (451), p. 178, Index, p. 10.
9. *OBP*, May 1827, William Sheen (t18270531-14). See LMA: MJ/SPC, E3304a, for depositions.
10. According to the 1841 census Sheen was born in 1801. TNA: HO107, piece 710, book 10.
11. Lambeth Police Court records only survive from 1877 (held at LMA). A coroner's inquest survives in the Middlesex Sessions records, MJ/SPC, E 3309. The inquest was held at Whitechapel Workhouse on the 12 May, *The Times*, 14 May 1827, p. 3.
12. Bodleian Library, University of Oxford, John Johnson Collection: Broadsides: Murder and Executions folder, 8 (7).
13. *OBP*, July 1827, William Sheen (t18270712-36).
14. The Lombard Street Poor House was in the Mint.
15. *The Times*, 12 May 1827; *OBP* (t18270531-14). See also LMA: MJ/SPC, E3304a.
16. *OBP* (t18270531-14).
17. An account of Davis's 'hunt' for Sheen is found in the Newgate Calendar, 'William Sheen. Tried for the Murder of His Son', http://www.exclassics.com/newgate/ng842.htm, (accessed 12 September 2014).
18. *OBP* (t18270531-14).
19. F. A. Carrington and J. Payne (1827), *Reports of Cases Argued and Ruled at Nisi Prius, in the Courts of King's Bench, Common Please, and Exchequer, Together with Cases Tried on the Circuits and at the Old Bailey* (London: S. Sweet, R. Pheney),

p. 637; W. O. Russell and C. S. Greaves (1843), *A Treatise on Crimes and Misdemeanours*, Vol. 1 (London: Saunders and Benning), pp. 832–4.

20. *OBP* (t18270531-14).
21. *The Times*, 7 June 1827.
22. *OBP* (t18270712-36); *Morning Chronicle*, 14 July 1827.
23. *The Times*, 14 June 1827.
24. *Morning Chronicle*, 14 July 1827.
25. *The Times*, 13 July 1827; *Standard*, 11 July 1827.
26. The child was buried in St Mary's, Whitechapel. The burial can be found in the City of London Burial Index at the LMA, 'Sheen, Charles William, 4 m, Workhouse (Childs head removed from body by the father WILLIAM SHEEN)', May 1827.
27. Letter from Miss Eden to Miss Villiers, from Bigod, Essex, July 1827, *Miss Eden's Letters, Edited by her Great Niece, Violet Dickenson* (London: Macmillan), p. 137.
28. *Examiner*, 22 July 1827.
29. *The Times*, 19 July 1827.
30. *Jackson's Oxford Journal*, 21 July 1827.
31. *Morning Chronicle*, 18 July 1827.
32. *The Times*, 19 July 1827.
33. *Morning Chronicle*, 1 January 1828; *Leicester Chronicle*, 5 January 1828.
34. *Examiner*, 13 January 1828.
35. *Examiner*, 9 December 1827.
36. *Morning Chronicle*, 9 November 1827.
37. *Morning Chronicle*, 9 November 1827.
38. *The Times*, 28 May 1827.
39. *Morning Chronicle*, 4 March 1840.
40. James Lee or Lea would be involved in the investigation into the 'Murder in the Red Barn', the following year. D. Cox (2010), *A Certain Share of Low Cunning: A History of the Bow Street Runners, 1792–1839* (Cullompton: Willan), p. 31. He was also active in the arrest and prosecution of Isaac Solomon in 1830.
41. *The Times*, 13 September 1830; *OBP*, October 1830, William Sheen, Robert Lyall and William Stewart (t18301028-192).
42. *Freeman's Journal and Daily Commercial Advertiser*, September 13 1830. *OBP*, September 1830, John Smith (t18300916-15). Long was the second metropolitan police officer to be murdered.
43. *The Times*, 13 December 1831; *Jackson's Oxford Journal*, 17 December 1831.
44. *OBP*, September 1831, George Bagley, George Forecast and Frances Bagley (t18310908-11).
45. *OBP* (t18310908-11).
46. The Bagleys and Forecast had their sentences respited in October, *Jackson's Oxford Journal*, 22 October 1831.
47. *OBP*, July 1832, Benjamin Stanton (t18320705-293).
48. *OBP* (t18320705-293). In the same month, Phoebe James alias Mary Powell had been charged at Lambeth Street for forging a will. She was described as living with William Sheen, the infanticide, *The Times*, 26 July 1832.
49. William Sheen in *OBP*, September 1832, John May (t18320906-320); Ann Sheen in *OBP*, September 1832, Richard Philip, Thomas Manning and Thomas Rands (t18320906-317). The accused were sentenced to transportation. The

other men, George Carter and Jeremiah Manning, were both found guilty of theft and transported with the help of Ann Sheen's evidence in two later trials, *OBP*, October 1832, George Carter (t18321018-58); November 1832, Jeremiah Manning (t18321129-163).

50. *OBP*, October 1832, James Sutton, Henry Kemp, Thomas Jones and Elizabeth Lawson (t18321018-8).

51. According to *The Times* (4 December 1832) the prisoners had their sentence respited with the exception of Sutton, who was ordered for execution the following Thursday.

52. See, 'List of Capital Convicts to be Reported to His Majesty in Council the 3rd Day of December 1832, October Session', for the outcome of petitions from James Sutton, Henry Kemp and Thomas Jones, TNA: HO6/17.

53. For Sutton's petition and letters from Davis, Rowan and Peek (discussed below), see TNA: HO17/74, no. 35, 18 October 1832, for his petition and HO6/17, 3 December 1832, for the recorder's report.

54. Peek was well known for his dislike of capital punishment, and would frequently appeal to the Home Secretary to obtain a reprieve, 'Richard Peek, Esq., Hazlewood', *Christian Witness and Congregationalist Magazine* (1867), p. 280.

55. See Middlesex Criminal Registers entry, TNA: HO26/38, p. 220; Australian Convict Transportation Registers, HO11/9, 7 March 1834.

56. *OBP*, September 1834, Elizabeth Harwood (t18340904-192).

57. *OBP* (t18320705-293), (t18320906-320).

58. Radzinowicz, *History*, *Vol. 2*, pp. 333–46.

59. Cox, *A Certain Share*, pp. 42–3, 45–8, 48–55.

60. Emsley, *Policing*, p. 128. *Reynold's Newspaper*, 7 January 1855; *Era*, 7 January 1855.

61. Reynolds, *Before the Bobbies*, p. 153.

62. In June 1834, William Sheen was on a charge of being drunk and disorderly, having threatened the woman (described as a 'common prostitute') with whom he cohabited. The magistrates discharged him, having cautioned him to take more care in his conduct. *Examiner*, 22 June 1834. For the attack on William Sheen senior see, *Morning Chronicle*, 29 November 1834.

63. *The Times*, 29 November 1834.

64. *OBP*, February 1835, Elizabeth Smith (t18350202-518).

65. *Standard*, 7 August 1837. John Bishop and Thomas Williams were the 'London Burkers'. S. Wise (2004), *The Italian Boy: A Tale of Murder and Body Snatching in 1830s London* (London: Metropolitan Books).

66. *Examiner*, 13 September 1835.

67. *The Times*, 8 September 1835.

68. *The Times*, 8 September 1835.

69. Shore, *Artful Dodgers*, pp. 76, 78–80. The evidence (from c. 1835–37) was included in the *Select Committee on Gaols and the Houses of Correction* (1835), and the Chadwick directed *Constabulary Committee* (1839).

70. TNA: HO73/2/2, loose papers, interview with reputed thief Mary Mause; HO73/16, notebook 3, evidence of Hewitt.

71. Miles, *Poverty*, p. 101.

72. *The Times*, 27 July 1836. A year later, in a case similarly reported due to the connection to 'Sheen the Infanticide', Sheen's brother-in-law, James Morris, threatened to 'rip open' his mother-in-law Ann. *The Times*, 22 June 1837.

73. When this case was originally heard at the Lambeth police office, a witness described as 'a hoary-headed old Israelite' gave evidence supporting Sheen's version of events. The court dismissed the evidence of this man, who claimed to be a 'scrivener and interpreter of languages at the Old Bailey', as a paid witness. *London Shipping Gazette*, 7 July 1836.
74. *Standard*, 19 August 1836; *Morning Post*, 19 August 1836.
75. Shore, *Artful Dodgers*, pp. 140–1. See M. J. D. Roberts (2004), *Making English Morals: Voluntary Associations and Moral Reform in England, 1787–1886* (Cambridge: Cambridge University Press), p. 159.
76. *The Times*, 25 March 1837.
77. *The Times*, 2 June 1837.
78. *Morning Chronicle*, 2 June 1837.
79. *The Times*, 10 June 1837.
80. *The Times*, 10 June 1837.
81. *Morning Chronicle*, 29 June 1837.
82. *The Times*, 28 June 1837.
83. *Report from the Select Committee on Metropolis Police Officers*, 1837 (451), p. 176. See editorial, *The Times*, 13 November 1838.
84. *The Times*, 28 June 1837.
85. M. Ryan (1839), *Prostitution in London with a Comparative View of that of Paris and New York* (London: H. Bailliere).
86. Ryan, *Prostitution*, pp. 149–50.
87. Ryan, *Prostitution*, p. 150.
88. Shore, *Artful Dodgers*, pp. 75–80.
89. TNA: HO17/111, vy 55, petition of William Sheen, 13 July 1838.
90. *Morning Chronicle*, 11 April 1839.
91. *OBP*, June 1839, Lewin Casper, Ellis Casper, Emanuel Moses and Alice Abrahams (t18390617-1958). See also evidence of George Sheen in *OBP*, March 1840, Lewin Casper (t18400302-909); *OBP*, March 1840, Henry Moss (t18400302-791).
92. *Charter*, 14 April 1839.
93. *The Times*, 11 April 1839.
94. *Morning Chronicle*, 4 March 1840.
95. *OBP*, April 1840, Ann Sheen (t18400406-1132).
96. *The Times*, 10 April 1840.
97. For Ann Sheen in Millbank Penitentiary see 1841 Census, TNA: HO107, piece 737, book 21.
98. *The Times*, 12 October 1842.
99. *The Times*, 12 October 1842. Sheen senior had died sometime between 1836 and 1840. His death was referred to in the *Morning Chronicle*, 4 March 1840.
100. *Liverpool Mercury*, 23 September 1842.
101. *Morning Chronicle*, 14 October 1842; *Examiner*, 15 October 1842.
102. For controversy about Samuel Sheen's burial ground see *The Times*, 21, 26 September, 1846; also *Era*, 2 July 1854.
103. *Morning Chronicle*, 14 October 1842; *Examiner*, 15 October 1842.
104. LMA: X19/38, 'Last will and testament of Ann Sheen, of Wentworth Street, Whitechapel'.
105. *The Times*, 21 May 1845.
106. *OBP*, February 1847, Mary Ryley (t18470201-479). The same month, two women, allegedly prostitutes working for Sheen, accused Charles Andrew

Amos, an H division constable, of (sexual) assault. The case was dismissed. *Morning Chronicle*, 18 February 1847.
107. *The Times*, 27 July 1847; *OBP*, August 1847, William Sheen (t18470816-1856).
108. For example, Sheen had appeared at Worship Street on a charge of violently assaulting his wife in April 1843. *Standard*, 27 April 1843.
109. In the 1841 census, William Sheen was recorded in Keate Street in the Whitechapel Enumeration district, aged 40; his occupation a wheelwright. He was described as not being born in the same country, and was head of a household which included a Mary (25) and John (5) Sheen, probably his wife and child. It also included 11 other occupants: four men; a one-year-old baby boy; and six women, one of whom, Ann Tims, was the mother of the baby. 1841 Census, TNA: HO107, piece 710, book 10.
110. *OBP* (t18470816-1856); *The Times*, 23 August 1847.
111. *The Times*, 23 August 1847.
112. *Era*, 21 December 1851.
113. *Examiner*, 27 December 1851; *Hampshire Telegraph and Sussex Chronicle*, 27 December 1851; *Manchester Times*, 27 December 1851; *Preston Guardian*, 27 December 1851; *Northern Star*, 27 December 1851. He was buried at St Mary's, Whitechapel; see the City of London Burial Index (LMA).
114. *Manchester Times*, 27 December 1851.
115. Tobias, *Prince of Fences*, p. 148. This identification was supported by P. Collins (1962, 1994 edn.), *Dickens and Crime* (Basingstoke: Palgrave Macmillan), p. 262. In the preface to the third edition, Collins noted that he had been mistaken in this identification, p. xvi.
116. J. M. L. Drew (2003), *Dickens the Journalist* (Basingstoke: Palgrave Macmillan), p. 8.
117. Drew, *Dickens*, pp. 14–15.
118. Drew, *Dickens*, pp. 36–7.
119. *Morning Chronicle*, 2 November 1835.
120. B. M. Wheeler (1993), 'The Text and Plan of Oliver Twist', in C. Dickens/F. Kaplan (ed.), *Oliver Twist* (London: Norton), pp. 525–37.
121. T. Endelman (2002), *The Jews of Britain, 1656 to 2000* (Berkeley: University of California Press), p. 82.
122. Dickens/Kaplan, *Oliver Twist*, p. 116.
123. C. Dickens, 'On Duty with Inspector Field', *Household Words*, 14 June 1851.
124. *Morning Chronicle*, 16 September 1842.
125. *Standard*, 16 September 1842.

6   'A new species of swindling': Coiners, Fraudsters, Swindlers and the 'Long-Firm', c. 1760–1913

1. *The Times*, 18 January 1905.
2. P. Colquhoun (1796), *A Treatise on the Police of the Metropolis* (London: H. Fry), p. 142.
3. Robb, *White-Collar Crime*. J. Locker (2005), '"Quiet thieves, quiet punishment": Private Responses to the "Respectable" offender, c. 1850–1930', *Crime, Histoire et Sociétés*, 9, 1, pp. 9–31; R. Sindall (1983), 'Middle Class Crime in Nineteenth-Century England', *Criminal Justice History*, 4, pp. 23–40;

G. Wilson and S. Wilson (2007), '"Getting away with it" or "Punishment enough"?: The Problem of "Respectable" Crime from 1830', in J. Moore and J. Smith (eds.), *Corruption in Urban Politics and Society, 1780–1950* (Aldergate: Ashgate), pp. 57–78; S. Wilson (2003), 'Moral Cancers: Fraud and Respectable Crime', in J. Rowbotham and K. Stevenson (eds.), *Behaving Badly: Social Panic and Moral Outrage – Victorian and Modern Parallels* (Aldershot: Ashgate), pp. 97–111.

4. See B. Godfrey and J. Locker (2001), 'The Nineteenth-Century Decline of Custom and its Impact on Theories of "Workplace Theft" and "White-Collar Crime"', *Northern History*, 38, pp. 261–73.

5. G. Davies (2002), *A History of Money from Ancient Times to the Present Day* (Cardiff: University of Wales Press).

6. Robb, *White-Collar Crime*, pp. 21–2.

7. Robb, *White-Collar Crime*; for definitions see S. Wilson (2010), 'Fraud and White-Collar Crime: 1850 to the Present', in A. M. Kilday and D. Nash (eds.), *Histories of Crime: Britain, 1600–2000* (Basingstoke: Palgrave Macmillan), pp. 141–59.

8. From 1800 to around the mid-century roughly 87 per cent of all crimes tried at the court were some form of theft. *OBP*, Tabulating year against offence category between 1800 and 1849. Counting by offence. Criminal Justice Act (1855), 18 & 19 Vict. c. 126. See HC Deb 06 August 1855 vol. 139, cc. 1866–73.

9. *OBP*, Tabulating decade against offence category between 1800 and 1899. Counting by offence. Deception is a category constructed by the authors of the Old Bailey Online who note the growth of trials for financial crimes after 1834, C. Emsley, T. Hitchcock and R. Shoemaker, 'Currency, Coinage and the Cost of Living', http://www.oldbaileyonline.org/static/Coinage.jsp#coinage (accessed 12 September 2014).

10. *OBP*, Tabulating decade against offence subcategory where offence category is deception, between 1800 and 1899. Counting by offence.

11. V. A. C. Gatrell (1980), 'The Decline of Theft and Violence in Victorian and Edwardian England', in Gatrell, Lenman and Parker, *Crime and the Law*, pp. 238–337, pp. 323–25.

12. R. McGowen (1999), 'From Pillory to Gallows: The Punishment of Forgery in the Age of the Financial Revolution', *Past and Present*, 165, 1, pp. 107–40; Langbein, *Origins*, pp. 166–7.

13. R. McGowen (2002), 'Forgery Legislation in Eighteenth-Century England', in N. Landau (ed.), *Law, Crime and Society, 1660–1830* (Cambridge: Cambridge University Press), pp. 117–38, pp. 131–2.

14. *OBP*, May 1751, Thomas Bride (t17510523-38); April 1757, William Richards (t17570420-58); December 1762, Thomas Goswell (t17621208-39) for early appearances at the court. See also TNA: ADM106/1094/159, 15 June 1751. In 1751 there is a reference to an Elizabeth Richardson, ordered to the Bridewell on 'suspicion of being concerned in publishing Seamens Wills and Powers of Attorneys', *London Daily Advertiser*, 10 December 1751.

15. The first significant press reference to the forging of seaman's wills was in 1744. See the case of Anne Brogden in *London Evening News*, 22 March 1744.

16. *OBP*, October 1765, William Richardson (t17651016-27); December 1763, William Richardson (t17631207-59); September 1765, Jane Care and William Richardson (t17650918-73). By 1763, Richardson was fearing for his life, TNA: ADM106/1128/3, 'William Richardson. Request that he is not prosecuted by Mr Mauger or moved to Newgate where he will be murdered',

5 January 1763. Richardson was executed 13 November 1765, *OBP*, December 1765, Supplementary Material, William Richardson (o17651211-5).

17. TNA: ADM106/1142/178 'John Ross, Poultry. Has sent an account of his expenses (now attached) for the several forgeries committed by William Richardson and his gang (4 October 1765)'; ADM106/1144/129, 'Petition of James Dyson who was instrumental in convicting William Richardson, tried at the Old Bailey, to be paid an allowance'.

18. J. Beattie, 'Sir John Fielding'. Letter from a member of the 'Society of Guardians for the Protection of Trade against Swindlers and Sharpers', in the *European Magazine, and London Review*, vol. 74 (July to December 1818), pp. 311–12.

19. See D. T. Andrew and R. McGowen (2001), *The Perreaus and Mrs Rudd: Forgery and Betrayal in Eighteenth-Century London* (Berkeley: University of California Press).

20. Andrew and McGowen, *Perreaus*, pp. 261–4. See, *The Guardians, Or, Society for the Protection of Trade against Swindlers and Sharpers, established March 25th, 1776* (London); Anon. (1799), *A List of the Members of the Guardians, Or, Society for the Protection of Trade Against Swindlers and Sharpers* (London).

21. R. McGowen (2007), 'Managing the Gallows: The Bank of England and the Death Penalty, 1797–1821', *Law and History Review*, 25, 2, pp. 241–82. See also, R. McGowen (2005), 'The Bank of England and the Policing of Forgery 1797–1821', *Past and Present*, 186, pp. 81–116.

22. Clark, http://www.capitalpunishmentuk.org/new1800.html, accessed 13 September 2014. C. Emsley (2010 edn.), *Crime and Society in England, 1750–1900* (London: Longman), pp. 267–71.

23. *OBP*, January 1800, Joseph-Samuel Abbott (t18000115-38); *OBP*, September 1817, John Vartie (t18170917-56); *OBP*, October 1821, Joseph South (t18211024-51); TNA: HO6/6 Recorders Report, Joseph South 19 November 1821; TNA: HO17/49 Hh 3, HO17/53 Ih 48, Petitions Joseph South, 24 October, 24 November 1821; TNA: HO6/2, Recorders Report, John Vartie, 5 December 1817; John Vartie (1817), *A Memoir of the Unfortunate John Vartie* (London: Effingham Wilson). See McGowen, 'Managing', p. 25 for South's case.

24. *OBP*, December 1819, Edward Voss and Dennis Keaton (t18191201-50).

25. Bank of England (*LL*) (assocrec_309_7495) F2/146, 154, Pardon and witness notes, Edward Voss; TNA: HO6/5, Recorders Report, Edward Voss, 24/03/1820. *The Times*, 30 March 1820; *Examiner*, 2 April 1820; *Annual Register*, April 1820, p. 88.

26. P. Handler (2005), 'Forgery and the End of the "Bloody Code" in Early Nineteenth-Century England', *The Historical Journal*, 48, 3, pp. 683–702, see p. 690.

27. Handler, 'Forgery'. The Act (2 & 3 Will.4 c. 123) repealed the death sentence for all forgery except for forgery of wills and forgery of power of attorney for the transfer of government stock. These remained capital until 1837 (7 Will. 4, and 1 Vic. c. 84).

28. *OBP*, Tabulating decade against offence category where the transcription matches 'detective'. Counting by offence.

29. S. Petrow (1993), 'The Rise of the Detective in London, 1869–1914', *Criminal Justice History*, 14, pp. 91–108. Also M. Fido and K. Skinner (2000), *The Official*

Encyclopaedia of Scotland Yard: Behind the Scenes at Scotland Yard (London: Virgin Publishing), pp. 68–9; Shpayer Makov, *Ascent*, p. 32.

30. G. Dilnot (1928), *The Trial of the Detectives* (London: Geoffrey Bles). See also Shpayer Makov, *Ascent*, p. 38, passim.

31. See 'The Detection of Crime', *The Times*, 12 February 1884; R. M. Morris (2006), '"Crime Does Not Pay": Thinking Again About Detectives in the First Century of the Metropolitan Police', in C. Emsley and H. Shpayer-Makov, *Police Detectives in History, 1750–1950* (Aldershot: Ashgate), pp. 79–102.

32. The fullest account of the robbery can be found in G. Dilnot (1930), *The Trial of Jim the Penman* (London: Geoffrey Bles). A more recent treatment can be found in Thomas, *Victorian Underworld*.

33. Initial reports came in May 1855, for example, *Lloyd's Weekly Newspaper*, 27 May 1855, *Morning Chronicle*, 28 May 1855.

34. Fido and Skinner, *Scotland Yard*, p. 176.

35. *Daily News*, 17 August 1855.

36. *OBP*, October 1855, Edward Agar (t18551022-943).

37. William Pierce and James Burgess were charged at the Mansion House police court in November 1856. William Tester surrendered himself in December. *Daily News*, 22 November 1856; *Morning Chronicle*, 11 December 1856; *The Times*, 27 November, 22 December 1856; *OBP*, January 1857, William Pierce, James Burgess and William Tester (t18570105-250).

38. *The Times*, 14 January 1857; *Daily News*, 14 January 1857.

39. *Freeman's Journal and Daily Commercial Advertiser*, 19 January 1857.

40. *The Times*, 15 January 1857; *Era*, 18 January 1857.

41. *The Times*, 15 January 1857, passim.

42. Gaskill, *Crime*, p. 125; J. Styles (1980), '"Our traitorous money makers": The Yorkshire Coiners and the Law, 1760–83', in J. Brewer and J. Styles (eds.), *An Ungovernable People? The English and their Law in the Seventeenth and Eighteenth Centuries* (London: Hutchinson), pp. 172–249.

43. This was related to the 'Great Recoinage' of the 1690s. A. Macfarlane (1981), *The Justice and the Mare's Ale: Law and Disorder in Seventeenth-Century England* (Oxford: Blackwell).

44. Gaskill, *Crime*, pp. 126–7, 145.

45. *OBP*, Tabulating decade against offence subcategory. Counting by offence. The coining prosecutions in the Old Bailey Online counts cover a range of offences. See C. Emsley, T. Hitchcock and R. Shoemaker, 'Coining offences', http://www.oldbaileyonline.org/static/Crimes.jsp#coining, accessed 13 September 2014.

46. S. L. Blanchard, 'A Biography of a Bad Shilling', *Household Words*, 2/44 January 1851, pp. 420–6.

47. D. Philips (1977), *Crime and Authority in Victorian England: The Black Country, 1835–1860* (London: Taylor & Francis), pp. 228–9.

48. *Morning Post*, 18 November 1828.

49. *OBP*, December 1828, James Coleman and Rhoda Coleman (t18281204-180); TNA: HO6/13: Recorders Report; HO17/93: Petition, Rn. 22. Coleman was executed at Newgate 21 January 1829, C. Hindley (ed.) (1871), 'The Gaol Delivery and the Trials and Sentences of all the Prisoners at the Old Bailey Sessions, together with a full account of the Execution of the Fifteen Unfortunate Convicts', *Curiosities of Street Literature* (London: Reeves and Turner).

50. *Morning Chronicle*, 25 September 1829.
51. *OBP*, Tabulating decade against defendant gender where offence category is coining offences. Counting by defendant.
52. L. Zedner (1991), *Women, Crime and Custody in Victorian England* (Oxford: Clarendon Press), pp. 39, 313, 315.
53. Gaskill, *Crimes*, pp. 138–9; W. Lowndes (1695), *A Report Containing an Essay for the Amendment of the Silver Coins* (London: Charles Bill).
54. *OBP*, Tabulating decade against defendant gender where offence category is coining offences. Counting by defendant.
55. Gaskill, *Crime*, p. 160; Styles, 'Traitorous'.
56. Mayhew, *London Labour, vol. 4*, pp. 29, 30.
57. J. Grant (1838), *Sketches in London* (London: Ward Lock), pp. 401, 402; J. Garwood (1853), *The Million-Peopled City* (London: Wertheim and Macintosh), p. 46; T. Archer (1865), *The Pauper, the Thief and the Convict* (London: Groombridge & Sons), p. 77.
58. Wensley, *Detective Days*, pp. 141–2; G. W. Cornish (1935), *Cornish of the 'Yard'* (London: Bodley Head), pp. 24–7.
59. See W. M. Meier (2011), *Property Crime in London, 1850 to the Present* (Basingstoke: Palgrave Macmillan), pp. 15, 16, 47; Shpayer Makov, *Ascent*, p. 293. See the debate about the extent of professional crime between the High Court Judge Alfred Wills and the Assistant Commissioner of Police, Robert Anderson in *The Times*, 12, 21 February, 22 April, 1901.
60. *OBP*, April 1861, Joseph Jones, Ellen Jones and William Smith (t18610408-319).
61. Mayhew, *London Labour*, vol. 4, p. 378.
62. *OBP*, May 1883, Evaline Street, Albert Howard, Philip Garcia and Elizabeth King (t18830528-581).
63. Mayhew, *London Labour*, vol. 4, pp. 378–80.
64. *OBP*, February 1866, Frederick Clode and Frederick Comyn (t18660226-258); November 1866, John Barrett, Cornelious Barrett and Elizabeth Barrett (t18611119-19).
65. *OBP*, Tabulating decade against offence subcategory where the transcription matches 'plainclothes "plain clothes"'. Counting by offence. The use of the term in Old Bailey cases increases from the 1830s (there are few references before 1830 and none before 1803), reflecting the entrenchment of the Metropolitan Police and, from 1842, the Detective Branch. Shpayer Makov, *Ascent*, pp. 31, 33, 36.
66. In the House of Commons in 1866 the Secretary of State, Sir George Grey, noted that the employment of policeman in plain clothes had been adopted in response to the increase of 'garrotte robberies' of 1862. HC Deb 16 February 1866 vol. 181 c597.
67. *OBP*, November 1845, Catherine Hacket and Robert Doolan (t18451124-182).
68. *The Times*, 2 December 1845. See Morris, 'Crime Does Not Pay', p. 81.
69. *OBP*, October 1877, John Meiklejohn, Nathanial Druscovitch, William Palmer and George Clarke (t18771022-805).
70. S. Petrow (1994), *Policing Morals: The Metropolitan Police and the Home Office, 1870–1914* (Oxford: Clarendon Press), p. 57. See TNA: HO45/9442/66692, 'State, Discipline and Organisation of the Detective Force of the Metropolitan Police. Report of the Departmental Commission and subsequent Rules'.

71. *OBP*, July 1775, Walter Gibbons (t17750712-36); LMA: OB/PS, Justices' Working Documents (*LL*): 6 July 1735, LMOBPS450230305, 12 July 1735 LMOBPS450230288.
72. *OBP*, July 1775, John Wilkin (t17750712-51).
73. *OBP*, Tabulating decade against offence subcategory where the transcription matches 'swindling swindle swindler swindlers'. Counting by offence.
74. The term 'to swindle' apparently came to London with German Jews in the 1760s, *schwindel* meaning 'to cheat', Partridge, *Underworld*, p. 708.
75. *Standard*, 31 March 1828.
76. *Lloyd's Weekly Newspaper*, 26 July 1857.
77. *Morning Chronicle*, 27 May 1840; *The Times*, 6 June 1840.
78. There are 25 references to gangs of forgers in the Old Bailey Proceedings Online. All but five of these date from the 1840s. Two cases in the 1760s are connected to the Richardson case. *OBP*, Tabulating decade against offence subcategory where the transcription matches '+gang +forgery'. Counting by offence. *OBP*, September 1763, William Barlow, Jane Durant (t17300914-66); *OBP*, September 1765, Mary Collins (t17650918-72).
79. *Political Examiner*, 10 January 1857. The 'barrister Saward' was referred to at the trial of Pierce, Burgess and Tester (*OBP*, January 1857, William Pierce, James Burgess and William George Tester (t18570105-250)). Agar had sold him 500oz of the stolen gold. Saward was tried at the Old Bailey in March 1857, on a charge of forgery. *OBP*, March 1857, James Townshend Saward and James Anderson (t18570302-413). See the recent biography by his descendent J. Carnell (2011), *James Townsend Saward, Criminal Barrister* (Hastings: Sensation Press); also D. Donovan (1901), *Jim the Penman: The Life Story of One of the Most Astounding Criminals That Have Ever Lived* (London: George Newnes); Dilnot, *Trial of Jim the Penman*; Thomas, *Victorian Underworld*, pp. 229–37; Fido and Skinner, *Scotland Yard*, p. 177.
80. *OBP*, October 1856, William Salt Hardwicke and Henry Attwell (t18561027-1004).
81. *Daily News*, 12 February 1857.
82. *Daily News*, 12 February 1857. *OBP*, September 1839, James Allen (t18390916-2451); April 1849, William Wilkinson (t18490409-884).
83. *Freeman and Daily Commercial Advertiser*, 14 February 1857.
84. *The Times*, 24 May 1859. *OBP*, May 1859, Andrew Foster, William Wynn Bramwell, Frederick Humphreys and William Wagner (t18590509-497); May 1859, William Wagner, William Wynn Bramwell and Horton Bateman (t18590509-518).
85. *Reynold's Newspaper*, 6 September 1857; *Aberdeen Journal*, 9 September 1857; *Liverpool Mercury etc.*, 3 October 1859; *Birmingham Daily Post*, 4 October 1859; *North Wales Chronicle*, 8 October 1859.
86. *Daily News*, 28 April 1860. *OBP*, May 1860, William George Pullinger (t18600507-466). J. E. Ritchie (1860), *About London* (London: William Tinsley), p. 151.
87. *Report of the Commissioners Appointed to Inquire into the Operation of the Acts (16 & 17 Vict. c. 99. and 20 & 21 Vict. c. 3.) Relating to Transportation and Penal Servitude. Vol. I. Report and Appendix*, 1863 (3190), p. 158.
88. C. L. Young (1886), *Jim the Penman* (New York: S. French). See also 'The History of "Jim the Penman"', *New York Times*, 8 May 1910; J. B. Clapp and E. F. Edgett (1902), *Plays of the Present* (New York: Dunlap Society).

89. Meier, *Property Crime*, pp. 87, 106–7; A. Wright (2006), *Organised Crime: Concept, Cases, Control* (Cullompton: Willan), p. 169.
90. *OBP*, August 1880, Samuel John Holmes, Henry John Dover, Heney Lawrence, William Farrington, Frederick Hiscock, Alfred Vincent, Edward Simmonds and William Phillips (t18800803-449).
91. M. Levi (1981), *The Phantom Capitalists: The Organisation and Control of Long-Firm Fraud* (London: Heinemann).
92. *OBP* (t18800803-449).
93. Levi, *Phantom*, pp. 1–2.
94. Levi, *Phantom*, p. 13. For the Hevey case see, R. N. Gooderson (1952), 'When is a Document False in the Law of Forgery?', *Modern Law Review*, 15, 1, pp. 11–27.
95. *OBP*, January 1782, John Hevey (t17820109-22); February 1782, John Hevey (t17820220-32); February 1782, John Hevey and Richard Beaty (t17820220-63).
96. *OBP*, August 1874, John Churchill (t 18740817-538); December 1874, Charles Barrell and John Henry Rogers (t18741214-100).
97. *Bradford Observer*, 18 March 1858; *Hull Packet and East Riding Advertiser*, 19 March 1858.
98. G. Crossick (1977), 'The Emergence of the Lower Middle Class in Britain', in G. Crossick (ed.), *The Lower Middle Class in Britain, 1870–1914* (London: Croom Helm), pp. 11–60, 19–20.
99. 'Career of a Manchester Forger-The "Long Firm"', *Manchester Times*, 20 September 1862.
100. *Liverpool Mercury*, 20 September 1862.
101. J. Caminada (1895), *Twenty Five Years of Detective Life* (Manchester: J. Heywood), pp. 361–3.
102. *Birmingham Daily Post*, 8 July 1862, 12 August 1865; *Liverpool Mercury*, 10 July 1862; *Manchester Times*, 12 July 1862, 12 November 1864, 5 August 1865; *Derby Mercury*, 16 July 1862. *The Times* reported on 'The Long Firm at Nottingham', 10 October 1862; the *Birmingham Daily Post* reported on 'A Domestic Long Firm in Wolverhampton', 12 August 1865.
103. *Birmingham Daily Post*, 28 May 1866.
104. In giving evidence to the House of Lords at the Select Committee on the Law of Hypothec in Scotland, a Mr A. McNoel-Caird, referred to a customer potentially belonging to a 'long firm'. *Report from the Select Committee of the House of Lords on the law of Hypothec in Scotland, together with the proceedings of the committee, minutes of evidence, and appendix* (1868-9 (367) (367-I) (367-II)), p. 174; *Prosecution of Offences Acts, 1879 and 1884. Return to an address of the Honourable the House of Commons, dated 13 April 1894*, 1894 (73). From 1868 to 2001/2 there were 73 records which produced references to 'long firm'; 44 of these are from the pre-First World War period (and at least some of these early Committees and Report contain multiple references), see http://parlipapers.chadwyck.co.uk/home.do, accessed 13 September 2014. Wright, *Organised Crime*, p. 168.
105. *Morning Post*, 20 February 1866; *Standard*, 5 March 1866.
106. For example, see *OBP*, February 1867, James Bradshaw (t18670225-296). The accused is described as having been a waiter at Bristowe's coffee house; also *Daily News*, 28 February 1867. The case of John Lockwood, tried at Southwark, was reported in the *Illustrated Police News*, 20 April 1867. Later

he was tried at the Old Bailey for forgery of a promissory note, *OBP*, June 1867, John Lockwood (t18670610-563).

107. See related trials: *OBP*, January 1868, George Brittain Bristowe (t18680106-132); December 1867, George Gould (t18671216-75); May 1875, George Foreman (t18750503-335); May 1875, George White, Walter Carruthers, Alfred Carruthers, Florence North, George Foreman, Richard Browning, Charles Harrison Barker and Samuel Jacobs (t18750503-336); May 1875, Richard Browning, Charles Harrison Barker and Samuel Jacobs (t18750503-330).

108. *Morning Post*, 7 May 1875.

109. *Daily News*, 21 May 1868.

110. *Daily News*, 21 May 1868.

111. *OBP*, August 1868, Samuel Israel, William Barnes and David Morgan (t18680817-754); *Standard*, 19 August 1868; *Lloyd's Weekly Newspaper*, 23 August 1868.

112. Potter would go on to become the superintendent of police at the South Western Railway, dying in service in November 1875. *OBP*, June 1870, William Steele, John Simmonds (t18700606-536); *Hampshire Advertiser*, 20 November 1875.

113. Wright, *Organised Crime*, p. 22.

114. *Pall Mall Gazette*, 29 April 1878.

115. *OBP*, Tabulating year against offence subcategory where the transcription matches 'long firm'. Counting by offence. There are 67 offences where a long firm is mentioned, of these 76.12 per cent are for prosecutions of fraud.

116. In determining actual numbers the count function on www.oldbaileyonline. org (accessed 13 September 2014) has some limitations. Manual counting of individuals and trials was used to confirm the numbers. Whilst 167 people were charged in 40 trials, there were some individuals who were tried more than once, so the actual number of distinct individuals would be lower.

117. Whilst I have focused on the frauds here, long firms are also referred to in cases of larceny, forgery, bankruptcy, etc. Moreover, many other cases which would fit the long-firm model can be found (for example, see the Bristowe gang cases above, which are not specifically referred to as long firms in the courtroom). Levi, *Phantom*, pp. 16, 28.

118. *OBP*, Tabulating decade against offence subcategory, after 1800. Counting by offence.

119. *OBP*, May 1876, James Humphries, Henry Smith, Edward Houghton and Mary Robinson (t18760529-389). Pay was also involved in raiding and prosecuting disorderly houses, see TNA: HO45/9511/17216, Police Report, 'C' Division, by James Pay, Inspector (1863, not dated), cited in H. Cocks (2003), *Nameless Offences: Homosexual Desire in the Nineteenth Century* (London: I. B. Tauris), p. 206.

120. *OBP*, May 1875, George Foreman (t18750503-335); May 1875, George White, Walter Carruthers, Alfred Carruthers, Florence North, George Foreman, Richard Browning, Charles Harrison Barker and Samuel Jacobs (t18750503-336); May 1875, Richard Browning, Charles Harrison Barker and Samuel Jacobs (t18750503-330).

121. Caminada, *Twenty Five Years*, p. 363.

122. Prosecution of Offences Acts, 1879 (42 & 43 Vict. c. 22) and 1884 (47 & 48 Vict. c. 58). *Return to an address of the Honourable House of Commons dated 13 April 1894* (1894 (73)), p. 3. *OBP*, March 1893, Leon Block, Augustus Tallett,

Ernest Chevallier, George Auguste Bondet Dusan-Lier and Marius Oudet (t18930306-255).

123. Levi, *Phantom*, p. 20, more generally pp. 19–28. R. Reushel (1895), *The Knights of Industry* (London).

124. *OBP*, March 1895, Stanilaus Reuschel (t18950325-304); see related trials, *OBP*, February 1895, Stein Semansky (t18950225-258); May 1895, Gustav Opitz (t18950520-469). P. Knepper (2009), *The Invention of International Crime: A Global Issue in the Making, 1881–1914* (Basingstoke: Palgrave Macmillan); P. Knepper (2007), 'British Jews and the Racialisation of Crime in the Age of Empire', *British Journal of Criminology*, 47, pp. 61–79.

125. For example see *OBP*, September 1894, William Trautz, Emile Trautz, Alexander Joseph and George Charles Fruhling (t18940910-716); December 1892, William Haydon, William Borrows, Hugh Jarvis, Albert Hennessey, Robert Bell Salisbury, Henry Adolphus Rice, George Staab, William Robert Jackson, William Harland, Henry George Morris, William Robert Taylor, Karl Adrian Wassenaar and Samuel Nightengale (t18921212-140). Whilst both of these trials had foreign connections, there is no specific evidence that the Trautz's, Fruhling or Wassenaar were foreigners.

126. *OBP*, October 1907, John William Clifton, James Harry Vincent, Alexander Doig, John Martin, John Ralli, William Roger Caldwell Moore and Joseph Goodman (t19071021-27).

127. *OBP* (t18940910-716).

128. *OBP*, April 1909, John Harvey and Benjamin Fletcher (t19090420-34).

129. *OBP* (t18921212-140).

130. Only seven long-firm defendants were women. *OBP*, Tabulating year against defendant gender where the transcription matches 'long firm', after 1874. Counting by defendant.

131. *OBP*, Tabulating defendant age against offence subcategory where defendant age is at least 1, after 1870. Counting by defendant.

132. *OBP*, Tabulating defendant age against offence subcategory where the transcription matches 'long firm'. Counting by defendant.

133. *OBP*, Tabulating defendant age against offence subcategory where offence category is deception and defendant age is at least 1, after 1870. Counting by defendant.

134. Sindall, 'Middle-Class', p. 35.

135. M. Woollard (1999), 'The Classification of Occupations in the 1881 Census of England and Wales', Historical Censuses and Social Surveys Research Group, University of Essex, http://privatewww.essex.ac.uk/~matthew/Papers/Woollard_1881Classifications_no%20illustration.pdf, accessed 13 September 2014), Appendix 5, p. 42 passim.

136. Robb, *White-Collar Crime*, p. 10.

137. *OBP*, March 1877, Alexander Gardner, Charlotte Trayford, William Alexander Wood, John Laurie, James Parker, Edward Batson, Joseph Ord, Richard Jackson, Samuel Waite Moore, John Richard Burden and Morris Cohen (t18770305-318).

138. *OBP*, December 1892, William Haydon, William Borrows, Hugh Jarvis, Albert Hennessey, Robert Bell Salisbury, Henry Adolphus Rice, George Staab, William Robert Jackson, William Harland, Henry George Morris, William Robert Taylor, Karl Adrian Wassenaar and Samuel Nightengale (t18921212-140).

139. This group has been neglected in the expansion of middle-class historiography. P. Bailey (1999), 'White Collars, Gray Lives?: The Lower Middle Class Revisited', *Journal of British Studies*, 38, pp. 273–90; Crossick, *Lower Middle Class*.

140. G. L. Anderson (1977), 'The Social Economy of Late-Victorian Clerks', in Crossick, *Lower Middle Class*, pp. 113–33; M. Heller (2008), 'Work, Income and Stability: The Late Victorian and Edwardian London Male Clerk Revisited', *Business History*, 50, 3, pp. 253–71.

141. Anderson suggests that in 1861, 91,733 men were engaged as clerks; by 1911 this number had risen to 561,155, 'Late-Victorian Clerks', p 113.

142. Anderson, 'Late-Victorian Clerks'; Heller, 'Work', p. 254.

143. Heller, 'Work', pp. 268–9.

144. R. Church (2004), 'The Rise and Changing Role of Commercial Travellers in Britain between 1870 and 1914', unpublished paper given at EBHA Conference, http://www.econ.upf.edu/ebha2004/programme2.html, accessed 16 September 2014; M. French (2005), 'Commercials, Careers and Culture: Travelling Salesmen in Britain, 1890s-1930s', *Economic History Review*, 58, 2, pp. 352-77; M. French and Popp, A. (2008), '"Ambassadors of Commerce": The Commercial Traveler in British Culture, 1800-1939', *Business History Review*, 82, pp.789-814.

145. Church, 'Rise', p. 7.

146. *OBP* (t18800803-449).

147. Crossick, *Lower Middle Class*, p. 23.

148. Levi, *Phantom*, p. 59.

149. *OBP*, July 1911, Harry Stone, Frederick Brooks and Mark Sidney Gage (t19110717-48).

150. *OBP*, March 1905, William John Milne and Charles William Smith (t19050306-271).

151. *OBP*, March 1877, Joseph Ord, Samuel Waite Moore and James Holmes (t18770305-320); *OBP* (t18770305-318); March 1877, Richard Jackson, Joseph Ord, James Parker, Edward Batson, Samuel Waite Moore, Robert Alfred Welham, Beauchamp St. John Mootham, Thomas Brandon Terry and George Law (t18770305-321).

152. *Lloyd's Weekly Newspaper*, 25 March 1877.

153. A first offence of uttering was a misdemeanour but a second offence was a felony. See *Report of the Commissioners Appointed to Inquire into the Constitution, Management, and Expense of the Royal Mint, from the Select Committee on the Royal Mint* (1849), p. 248.

154. Dick Hobbs has explored some of these firms in a slightly later chronology, in D. Hobbs (2001), 'The Firm: Organisational Logic and Criminal Culture on a Shifting Terrain', *British Journal of Criminology*, 41, pp. 549–60.

7 'A London Plague that must be swept away': Hooligans and Street Fighting Gangs, c. 1882–1912

1. *Illustrated Police News*, 13 November 1897.

2. G. Pearson (1983), *Hooligan: A History of Respectable Fears* (London: Macmillan), p. 74.

3. A. Davies (2008), *The Gangs of Manchester: The Story of the Scuttlers, Britain's First Youth Cult* (Preston: Milo Books); P. Gooderson (2010), *The Gangs of Birmingham:*

From the Sloggers to The Peaky Blinders (Preston: Milo Books); M. Macilwee (2007), *The Gangs of Liverpool* (Preston: Milo Books); McDonald, *Gangs*.

4. *The Times*, 17 July 1920, 5 April 1921. S. Slater (2012), 'Street Disorder in the Metropolis, 1905–39', *Law, Crime and History*, 2, 1, pp. 59–91.

5. G. Pearson (2011), 'Perpetual Novelty: Youth, Modernity and Historical Amnesia', in Goldson, *Youth in Crisis*, pp. 20–37, p. 27.

6. *The Times*, 30 October 1900.

7. *Quarterly Review*, Volume 129, no. 257 (1870), p. 91.

8. See the attack on Constable William Kitch, *OBP*, November 1884, Alfred Hickson, George Barnes, James Kevill, George Francis and Cornelius Fitzgerald (t 18841117-56); and attack on Constable Charles Collins, *OBP*, November 1897, Thomas Tool and Michael Small (t18971122-49).

9. Davis, 'Garotting'; R. Sindall (1990), *Street Violence in the Nineteenth Century: Media Panic or Real Danger?* (Leicester: Leicester University Press).

10. *OBP*, Tabulating decade against offence subcategory, between 1800 and 1913. Counting by offence.

11. P. Handler (2007), 'The Law of Felonious Assault in England', *Journal of Legal History*, 28, 2, pp. 183–206; P. King (1996), 'Punishing Assault: The Transformation of Attitudes in the English courts', *Journal of Interdisciplinary History*, 27, pp. 43–74.

12. M. J. Allen (2001), *Textbook on Criminal Law*, 6th edn. (Oxford: Blackstone Press), pp. 356–62.

13. N. Elias (1978), *The Civilizing Process: The History of Manners* (New York: Urizen Books).

14. For a recent discuss of this 'process' in relation to the Old Bailey courtroom see, S. Klingenstien, T. Hitchcock and S. DeDeo (2014), 'The Civilizing Process in London's Old Bailey', *Proceedings of the National Academy of Sciences of the United States of America*, 111, 26, pp. 9419–24.

15. Davis, 'Garotting'; Sindall, *Street Violence*.

16. *OBP*, Tabulating decade against offence category where the transcription matches 'roughs'. Counting by offence.

17. J. Welshman (2005), *Underclass: A History of the Excluded, 1880–2000* (London: Bloomsbury).

18. *Bristol Mercury*, 25 June 1870; *Liverpool Mercury*, 26 November 1868; *Lloyd's Weekly Newspaper*, 16 November 1873; *Daily News*, 10 April 1890; *Illustrated Police News*, 12 June 1897.

19. See *OBP*, September 1866, Joseph Gairdelli, Timothy Nolan, Edward Cane (t18660917-798).

20. For example, in 1878, the *Pall Mall Gazette* (29 April) reported on a gang of youths throwing missiles at the congregation of St Alban's church in Holborn; also *Lloyd's Weekly Newspaper*, 9 July 1876.

21. Scuttling was reported in the *Pall Mall Gazette*, 10 September 1878. The first 'slogging' death in Birmingham was reported in the *Reynolds's Newspaper*, 8 March 1874.

22. Davies, 'Youth Gangs, Masculinity', pp. 363–4.

23. B. Goldson (2011), 'Youth in Crisis?', in B. Goldson (ed.), *Youth in Crisis?*, pp. 1–19, p. 11.

24. *Liverpool Mercury*, 15 April 1855; *Huddersfield Chronicle and West Yorkshire Advertiser*, 29 June 1861.

25. *Birmingham Daily Post*, 12 June 1865; *Leeds Mercury*, 4 June 1872; *Nottinghamshire Guardian*, 1 May 1874; *The Sheffield and Rotherham Independent*, 17 September 1878.

26. P. Griffiths (1996), *Youth and Authority: Formative Experiences in England, 1560–1640* (Oxford: Oxford University Press).

27. Davies, *Gangs of Manchester*, p. 74.

28. Sindall, *Street Violence*, pp. 66–70; Pearson, *Hooligan*, pp. 96–7.

29. A. Davies (2011), 'Youth Gangs and Late Victorian Society', in Goldson, *Youth in Crisis?*, pp. 38–54, p. 40.

30. Davies, 'Youth Gangs, Masculinity', p. 351.

31. *Reynolds's Newspaper*, 29 April 1894. For other references see *Liverpool Mercury*, 26 December 1896; *Bristol Mercury and Daily Post*, 16 August 1898; *Penny Illustrated Paper and Penny Illustrated Times*, 16 November 1907.

32. Pearson, *Hooligan*, pp. 74–5; *Era*, 24 October 1891.

33. *Illustrated Police News*, 20 October 1894. See also *Daily News*, 24 April 1894.

34. M. Livie (2010), 'Curing Hooliganism: Moral Panic, Juvenile Delinquency, and the Political Culture of Moral Reform in Britain, 1898–1908' (University of Southern California, Ph.D), pp. 20–2.

35. *Reynolds's Newspaper*, 6 November 1898.

36. Livie, 'Curing Hooliganism', p. 6.

37. The survival of metropolitan police court records is poor. Clerkenwell and Worship Street Police Court records survive from 1905; South Western Police Court from 1919; Westminster Police Court from 1897; Lambeth Police Court from 1906; and Bow Street Police Court from 1895 (surviving records are held at the London Metropolitan Archives).

38. Searches of *Daily Graphic, Daily Mail, Evening News, Evening Standard, Islington Daily Gazette and North London Chronicle, Lloyd's Weekly News, Manchester Guardian* and the *Pall Mall Gazette* for 1907 turned up only a few references to the most serious hooligan crime, the murder of William Garrett Dundon in April of that year.

39. *OBP*: (t18820227-312); (t18820227-328); (t18841117-56); (t18850727-740); (t18850727-741); (t18880730-759); (t18911116-59); (t18970405-307); (t189 70628-473); (t18970726-528); (t18971122-34); (t18971122-49); (t18980620-453); (t18990912-607); (t19001119-47); (t19010204-178); (t19010513-393); (t19020210-215); (t19030518-483); (t19061022-35); (t19070528-11); (t1907 0528-12); (t19070910-83); (t19070910-82); (t19070910-81); (t19071021-84); (t19071119-32); (t19080428-28); (t19080623-10); (t19080623-26); (t19080623-37); (t19080721-27); (t19110425-43); (t19120611-35). The cases reported in the press but tried in other courts were: William Cadle, Westminster, *Illustrated Police News*, 20 May 1893; Charles Clarke, Southwark, *Reynolds's Newspaper*, 29 April 1894; Edward Holt, Edward Smith, Lambeth, *Illustrated Police News*, 19 May 1894; John Chandler, Southwark, *Standard*, 30 January 1897; Michael Connell, George Skeffington, Clerkenwell, *Daily News*, 27 November 1897; Frederick Dockrell, South Western, *Standard*, 15 August 1898; Charles Nunn, Thomas Wyatt, Thomas Pullen, William Canty, South Western, *Morning Post*, 9 January 1899.

40. *OBP*, June 1897, John Goodey, Michael Reed, George Robert Robson, James Beaumont, Eliza Walters (t18970628-473).

41. Davies, 'Youth Gangs, Masculinity', p. 356.

42. Charles Booth Archive Online, Booth B353, pp. 214–15, 4 July 1898.
43. TNA: CRIM1/107/4, 'evidence of Florence Fairhead', May 1907.
44. *Pall Mall Gazette*, 'The Lawlessness of London', 6 March 1882. See also 'The Fighting Gangs of London', 3 February 1882; 'The Fighting Gangs of London', 14 March 1882; 'The Fighting Gangs on the Embankment', 17 March 1882.
45. *Pall Mall Gazette*, 6 March 1882.
46. On the *The Wild Boys of London*, see John Springhall (1994), '"Pernicious Reading"? "The Penny Dreadful" as Scapegoat for Late-Victorian Juvenile Crime', *Victorian Periodical Review*, 27, 4, pp. 326–49.
47. *Pall Mall Gazette*, 14 March 1882.
48. *OBP*, February 1882, Thomas Galliers and James Casey (t18820227-328). For the inquest report see *Daily News*, 20 January 1882. Thomas Galliers was charged at Bow Street on the 31 January; *Pall Mall Gazette*, 31 January 1882. James Casey was arrested later and charged along with Galliers at Bow Street in early February, *Standard*, 8 February 1882. The related trial is: *OBP*, February 1882, Trial of William Hubbard, David Jennings, Henry Kirby, Frederick Ball, Patrick Kennedy, David Williams and John Collins (t18820227-312).
49. *Pall Mall Gazette*, 2 February 1882.
50. *OBP* (t18820227-312).
51. See evidence of Arthur Thompson and of Sarah Williams, TNA: CRIM1/13/6, Defendant, Galliers, Thomas, February 1882.
52. A. Morrison (1896, 2012 edn.), *A Child of the Jago* (Oxford: Oxford University Press), p. 85.
53. TNA: CRIM8/14, 'Request from the Director of Criminal Investigations, Metropolitan Police Office for a transcript of Mr Justice Hawkin's remarks at the trial of Galliers and Casey alleging the existence of street gangs', 8 March 1882.
54. Hallsworth, 'Gangland Britain?', p. 191.
55. *Pall Mall Gazette*, 14 March 1882.
56. K. Kintrea, J. Bannister and J. Pickering (2011), '"It's just an area – everybody represents it": Exploring Young People's Territorial Behaviour in British Cities', in Goldson, *Youth in Crisis?*, pp. 55–71, p. 59.
57. Davies 'Youth Gangs', p. 44.
58. J. Hollingshead (1861), *Ragged London in 1861* (London: Smith, Elder and Co.), p. 147.
59. Light blue, purple and pink respectively equated to: Poor, Mixed and Fairly Comfortable. Streets located using the searchable digital version of the *Maps Descriptive of London Poverty, 1898–99* made available at the Charles Booth Online Archive, http://booth.lse.ac.uk/, accessed 14 September 2014.
60. *Pall Mall Gazette*, 6 March 1882.
61. See 'Plan of City Road at Shepherdress Walk', in TNA: CRIM1/107/4.
62. *OBP* (t18820227-328). TNA: CRIM1/13/6, Defendant: Galliers, Thomas: Charge, Murder. *Reynolds Newspaper*, 22 January 1882, *Lloyd's Weekly Newspaper*, 29 January 1882.
63. *Pall Mall Gazette*, 14 March 1882. See also, 'The Lawlessness of London', 6 March 1882; 'London Brigands and Their Methods', 25 March 1882.

64. *Daily News*, 2 February 1882; *OBP* (t18820227-312). The youths were found guilty of riot.
65. *Daily News*, 2 February 1882.
66. *OBP*, July 1888, George Galletly, Peter Lee, William Joseph Graefe, Wiliam Henshaw, Charles Henry Govier, Francis Cole, William Elvis and Michael Doolan (t18880730-759); TNA: CRIM1/29/9, 'Defendant: GELLATLY, George ELVIS, William COLE, Francis LEE, Peter GRAEFE, William Joseph HENSHAW, William GOVIER, Charles Henry DULING, Michael Charge: Murder'.
67. *Penny Illustrated Paper*, 9 June 1888; *Lloyd's Weekly Newspaper*, 10 June 1888. Gray, 'Gang Crime'.
68. *Morning Post*, 15 May 1893; *Berrow's Worcester Journal*, 1 September 1894, p. 3.
69. *Illustrated Police News*, 20 May 1893. Oakum Street buildings was probably on Oakham Street, now Lucan Place.
70. Westminster Police Court Register, 9, 16, 22, 23, 30 October 1900, LMA: PS/WES/A1/19.
71. *OBP*, November 1900, John Proud, Charles Key (t19001119-47).
72. B. Beaven (2005), *Leisure Citizenship and Working-Class Men in Britain, 1850–1914* (Manchester: Manchester University Press), p. 58; D. Kift (1996), *The Victorian Music Hall: Culture, Class and Conflict* (Cambridge: Cambridge University Press, 1996), pp. 65, 70.
73. TNA: CRIM1/107/4: 'Depositions file, Defendant: Ashton, James, Charge: Murder'.
74. Another affray took place at the South London Palace of Varieties and was tried at the Southwark Police Court. *Daily News*, 24 April 1894.
75. *OBP*, November 1891, James Bassett (t18911116-59).
76. *OBP*, June 1912, John Jenkins, James Bennett, Charles Tompkins and Henry Barker (t19120611-35).
77. *Lloyd's Weekly Newspaper*, 24 July 1898.
78. *The Times*, 14 August 1898.
79. C. Rook (1899), *Hooligan Nights* (London: Grant Richards).
80. *The Times*, 16 August 1898.
81. *OBP*, July 1908, Harry Jarvis (t19080721-27).
82. *Lloyd's Weekly Newspaper*, 6 February 1870.
83. *Lloyd's Weekly Newspaper*, 19 November 1871. See comments about youths in Upper Street, Islington in *Penny Illustrated Paper*, 1 May 1869; *Pall Mall Gazette*, 8 November 1870.
84. J. Birchall (2006), '"The Carnival Revels of Manchester's Vagabonds": Young Working-Class Women and Monkey Parades in the 1870s', *Women's History Review*, 15, 2, pp. 229–52.
85. Kintrea, Bannister and Pickering, 'It's Just an Area', p. 60.
86. *OBP* (t18820227-312).
87. H. Mayhew (1849), 'Labour and the Poor, Letter XII', *Morning Chronicle*, 27 November.
88. Harding, *East End Underworld*, pp. 8, 35, 42, 126, 290.
89. M. J. Childs (1992), *Labour's Apprentices: Working-Class Lads in Late Victorian and Edwardian England* (Quebec: McGill-Queen's University Press), pp. 58–61, 62.
90. H. Shore (2009), 'Street Children and Street Trades in the United Kingdom', in Hugh. D. Hindman, *The World of Child Labor: An Historical and Regional Survey* (New York: M. E. Sharpe), pp. 563–6.

91. Shore, 'Street Children', pp. 564–5. Also E. Hopkins (1994), *Childhood Transformed: Working-Class Children in Nineteenth Century England* (Manchester: Manchester University Press), pp. 203–4.
92. Davies, 'Youth Gangs, Masculinity', p. 352.
93. *OBP*, May 1901, Harry Lewis, Samuel Harrison, Frederick Millard and Joseph Boulton (t19010513-393).
94. *Morning Post*, 15 May 1893.
95. *OBP*, November 1897, William Bond and Frederick James Leader (t18971122-34).
96. *Reynolds's News*, 7 November 1897; *Illustrated Police News*, 13, 20 November, 4 December 1897.
97. *Illustrated Police News*, 4 December 1897.
98. Pearson, *Hooligan*, pp. 105–6.
99. Davies, 'Youth Gangs', p. 50.
100. *OBP*, July 1885, William Brown and Harry Foxcroft (t18850727-741); July 1885, William Brown (t18850727-740). Brown pleaded guilty to a related offence.
101. Gooderson, *Gangs*, pp. 265–6.
102. *Morning Post*, 9 December 1897, p. 8.
103. For discussion of the pistols bill see TNA: HO45/9788/B3145A and HO45/9788/B3145D, 'Pistols Bill, 1893'; also MEPO2/1429, 'Firearms Bill: amending Pistols Act 1903'.
104. *The Times*, 25 July 1893, p. 5.
105. *The Times*, 16 September 1893, p. 9; HC Deb 14 September 1893 vol. 17 c1153.
106. *The Times*, 12 October 1893, p. 12.
107. HC Deb 27 February 1895 vol. 30 cc1657-85.
108. *The Times*, 3 July 1895, p. 6.
109. C. Greenwood (1972), *Firearms Control: A Study of Armed Crime and Firearms Control in England and Wales* (London: Routledge), pp. 27–9.
110. *Illustrated Police News*, 13, 20 November 1897; *Reynolds's News*, 7 November 1897.
111. *Daily News*, 10 February 1896.
112. *Hampshire Advertiser*, 9 June 1897, p. 2.
113. *Morning Post*, 4 June 1897, p. 6.
114. See 'Clerkenwell Pistol Tragedy', *Lloyds Weekly Newspaper*, 6 June, 1897; *OBP* (t18970628-473). See TNA: CRIM1/48/1: 'Defendant: Goodey, John; Reed, Michael; Robson, George Robert; Beaumont, James; Walter, Eliza Charge: Manslaughter and riot'.
115. TNA: CRIM1/48/1: 'Deposition of Alfred Smith, June 1897'.
116. TNA: CRIM1/48/1.
117. 'The Reign of Terror in Clerkenwell', *Lloyd's Weekly Newspaper*, 13 June 1897. A. Davies (1999), '"These Viragoes are no less cruel than the lads": Young Women, Gangs and Violence in Late Victorian Manchester and Salford', *British Journal of Criminology*, 39, 1, pp. 72–89.
118. *The Times*, 26 March, 24 April 1907; *Islington Daily Gazette and North London Chronicle*, 23 April 1907, p. 2; *Daily Mail*, 24, 30 May 1907, p. 4. *OBP*, May 1907, James Ashton (t19070528-11); TNA: CRIM1/107/4, Depositions file, Defendant: Ashton, James, Charge: Murder; Defendant: Allen, Thomas,

Charge: Assault, May 1907. The London Assurance was at 193–5 City Road, on the corner of City Road and Westmoreland Place (now Westland Place).

119. *The Times*, 3 June 1907.
120. *OBP* (t19070528-11); TNA: CRIM1/107/4, Deposition of William Sewell, May 1907. Three other boys were charged on a separate indictment but discharged, *OBP*, May 1907, Philip Murty, Patrick Chapman and Thomas Allen (t19070528-12).
121. Pearson, *Hooligan*, p. 94.
122. TNA: CRIM1/107/4, Deposition of James Ashton, 23 May 1907.
123. TNA: CRIM1/107/4, Deposition of Thomas Holdsworth, 23 May 1907. Nile Street ran off Shepherdress Walk, and would be mentioned by Arthur Harding (see below).
124. *OBP*, September 1907, George Mortimer (t19070910-81); September 1907, Robert Wannell (t19070910-82); September 1907, Alfred Potter (t19070910-83).
125. *OBP*, September 1907, Robert Wannell (t19070910-82).
126. TNA: CRIM1/108/2, Defendant: Francis, Arthur; Lowe, Edward; Churchwood, William; Hunter, Henry; Strettin, Thomas; Francis, Thomas; Keefe, Edward: Charge: Shooting at various people with intent to injure them, November, 1907. *The Times*, 22, 25, 31 October, 1, 23 November 1907.
127. *OBP*, November 1907, Arthur Francis, William Churchwood, Henry Hunter, Thomas Streetin, Edward Keefe, Edward Lowe, Thomas Francis and Frederick James Dyson (t19071119-32); *Daily Graphic*, 21 November 1907.
128. See *OBP*, June 1908, George Askew (t19080623-37); June 1908, Roger Hellen (t19080623-10); June 1908, George Price (t19080623-26). 'The Forties' or the 'Forty Thieves' are described as a gang of youths from around the Limehouse area who worked as fishmongers (*OBP*, April 1908, George Johnson (t19080428-28)).
129. Davies, *Gangs of Manchester*; P. Gooderson (1997), 'Terror on the Streets of Late Victorian Salford and Manchester: The Scuttling Menace', *Manchester Region History Review*, 11, pp. 3–11, p. 6.
130. *OBP*, October 1907, John Harmond (t19071021-84).
131. *OBP* (t19071119-32). See Clerkenwell Police Court Register, 21, 30 October 1907, LMA: PS/CLE/A1/8.
132. The court register at Old Street notes that Goddard and Goldsworthy were charged with 'unlawfully carrying revolvers without a licence', Old Street Police Court Register, 4, 11 April 1911, LMA: PS/OLD/A1/14. *OBP*, April 1911, Charles Goddard and Harry Goldsworthy (t19110425-43).
133. *OBP*, September 1899, Henry Rye, Alfred Jewell (t18990912-607). See also West London Police Court Register, 23, 31 August 1899, LMA: PS/WLN/A1/112. *Morning Post*, 24 August, p. 6, 20 September, p. 2, 1899.
134. *OBP*, February 1902, Henry Rye (t19020210-155); July 1904, Henry Rye (t19040725-546); October 1912, Henry Rye (t19121008-60).
135. *OBP* (t19070528-11).
136. *Lloyd's Weekly News*, 1 September 1907, p. 3. *OBP* (t19070528-12). See also Old Street Police Court Register, 23, 30 April, 7, 14, 21, 23 May 1907, LMA: PS/OLD/A1/5.
137. *OBP* (t19070528-11).
138. Harding, *East End Underworld*, p. 148.

139. *The Times*, 3 September 1908.
140. *OBP* (t18820227-328).
141. *OBP* (18971122-34); (t19080623-26) (t19080623-37) (t19120611-35).
142. *Reynolds's Newspaper*, 12 August 1888; *Daily News*, 15 August 1888, Gray, 'Gang Crime', pp. 564–5.
143. *Morning Post*, 26 April 1855, p. 7.
144. *Lloyd's Evening Post and British Chronicle*, 26 September 1757.
145. J. White (1980), *Rothschild Buildings: Life in an East End Tenement Block, 1887–1920* (London: Routledge and Kegan Paul), p. 137.
146. S. Wise (2008), *The Blackest Streets: The Life and Death of a Victorian Slum* (London: Bodley Head), p. 19.
147. Harding, *East End Underworld*, pp. 2, 53, 54.
148. *Royal Commission on the Housing of the Working Classes*, 1884–85, XXX, 24, p. 616.
149. Sponza, *Italian Immigrants*, p. 19. T. Allen (2008), *Little Italy: The Story of London's Italian Quarter* (London: Camden Local Studies), pp. 6, 11.

8 'The Terror of the People': Organised Crime in Interwar London

1. *Star*, 5 December 1922.
2. See M. Huggins (2000), *Flat Racing and British Society, 1790–1914: A Social and Economic History* (London: Cass), pp. 136–7.
3. *Evening Standard*, 25 August 1925.
4. *Daily Mail*, 26 August 1925.
5. J. P. Bean (1981), *The Sheffield Gang Wars* (Sheffield: D & D Publications).
6. Davies, 'Street Gangs'; Davies, 'Reign of Terror'; Davies, 'Scottish Chicago?'.
7. For references to foreign and alien criminality see *The Times*, 4, 5 April, 26 July 1921. Shore, 'Criminality'. See also S. Slater (2007), 'Pimps, Police and Filles De Joie: Foreign Prostitution in Interwar London', *London Journal*, 32, 1, pp. 53–74.
8. Wright, *Organised Crime*, p. 167. Also D. Hobbs (2006), *Bad Business: Professional Crime in Modern Britain* (Oxford: Oxford University Press), p. 115.
9. H. Shore (2014), '"Rogues of the Racecourse": Racing Men and the Press in Inter-War Britain', *Media History*, 20, 4, pp. 352–367.
10. Davies, 'Scottish Chicago', p. 511.
11. Divall, *Scoundrels*; E. Greeno (1959), *War on the Underworld* (London: Brown, Watson Ltd); Sharpe, *Flying Squad*.
12. Wright, *Organised Crime*, pp. 123–4.
13. P. Jenkins and G. W. Potter (1988), 'Before the Krays: Organised Crime in London, 1920–60', *Criminal Justice History*, 9, pp. 209–30.
14. F. Thrasher (1927), *The Gang: A Study of 1,313 Gangs in Chicago* (Chicago: University of Chicago Press); W. Foote Whyte (1943), *Street Corner Society: The Social Structure of an Italian Slum* (Chicago: University of Chicago Press).
15. Wright, *Organised Crime*, p. 29.
16. F. A. J. Ianni (1974), *Black Mafia: Ethnic Succession in Organized Crime* (New York: Simon & Schuster).
17. Wright, *Organised Crime*, p. 180.

18. 'How the Gangs Work: Risk and Economic Reward of Organized Crime', *The Times*, 20 July 1956.

19. *OBP*, April 1906, George Moore and George Thomas Hyams (t19060402-35). Pearson, *Hooligan*, p. 76.

20. J. Morton (1992), *Gangland: London's Underworld* (London: Little Brown); Morton, *East End Gangland*; B. McDonald, *Gangs of London*. A pulp account of Darby Sabini's life can be found in Hart, *Britain's Godfather*.

21. See Morton, *Gangland*; McDonald, *Gangs of London*. For a definition of the 'family firm' see Hobbs, 'The Firm'.

22. D. Kirby (2011), *The Sweeney: The First Sixty Years of Scotland Yard's Crimebusting Flying Squad, 1919–1978* (Barnsley: Pen and Sword Books), p. 75–81.

23. Jenkins and Potter, 'Before the Krays', pp. 221–3.

24. M. Huggins (2003), *Horseracing and the British, 1919–1939* (Manchester: Manchester University Press), pp. 1–3, passim.

25. R. Murphy (1993), *Smash and Grab: Gangsters in the London Underworld, 1920–60* (London: Faber and Faber), pp. 30–1.

26. T. H. Dey (1931), *Leaves from a Bookmaker's Book* (London: Hutchinson).

27. Divall, *Scoundrels*, p. 199.

28. Chesney, *Victorian Underworld*, pp. 330–41; W. Vamplew (1976), *The Turf* (London: Allen Lane), pp. 141–2.

29. Huggins, *Horseracing*, p. 146.

30. D. Dixon (1980), '"Class Law": The Street Betting Act of 1906', *International Journal of The Sociology of Law*, 8, pp. 101–28; D. Dixon (1991), *From Prohibition to Regulation: Bookmaking, Anti-Gambling and the Law* (Oxford: Clarendon Press), p. 299. *House of Lords Select Committee on Betting*, 1902 (389), v. 2.

31. McDonald, *Gangs of London*, pp. 125–8. OBP, September 1910, Henry Byfield (t19100906-18); September 1910, Michael McCausland and Matthew McCausland (t19100906-17); in *The Times*, 9 September 1910, the events were linked to gang crime in Soho but not specifically to racecourse crime.

32. TNA: MEPO 3/366: 'Various members of a race gang charged at different times with demanding money with menaces, assault, and conspiring together', 1922–24. Morton, *East End Gangland*, p. 127.

33. TNA: HO 144/10430: 'Letter from CID, dated 1 December 1922'; Huggins, *Horseracing*, pp. 88–9.

34. Morton, *East End Gangland*, p. 123.

35. TNA: HO 144/10430: 'Racecourse ruffians: activities of the "Sabini" gang'; 'Memorandum', n.d.

36. TNA: HO 144/10430: 'Metropolitan Police Report', 1 December 1922.

37. TNA: MEPO 3/346: 'Affray at Ewell known as "The Epsom Hold-Up" on 2 June 1921, following race meeting', 1921. See also the reports in the *Epsom Herald*, 10 June 1921, 17 June 1921, 1 July 1921; *Surrey Advertiser and County Times*, 23 July 1921; *Sunday Express*, 24 July 1921. See the Clerkenwell Police Court Register for charges against George Fagioli for possession of a loaded firearm and Joseph Jackson for shooting at Police Constable Rutherford, 31 July 1922, in LMA: PS/CLE/A1/60; charges against William Edwards, Arthur Phillips, Joseph Jackson for feloniously shooting Police Constable Rutherford, 1, 7, 10, 12 August 1922, in LMA: PS/CLE/A1/61. See charges

against Fred Gilbert, Fred Brett and George Sage for demanding money with menaces, 22, 26 August, 2 September 1922, in LMA: PS/CLE/A1/60 and PS/CLE/A1/61; charges against the same for possessing firearms, 2, 9 September 1922, in LMA: PS/CLE/A1/60. See Marylebone Police Court Register for charges against Alfred White, Joseph Sabini, George West, Simon Nyberg, Paul Boffa, Thomas Mack, for unlawfully and maliciously shooting at George Sage and Frederick Gilbert, 30 August 1922, the same for illegal possession of firearms, 6 September 1922, in LMA: PS/MAR/A1/70. See charge against Harry Sabini for threats and assaults against Frederick Gilbert, 6, 20 September 1922, in LMA: PS/MAR/A1/70.

38. See McDonald, *Gangs of London*, pp. 115–280. For the events of the summer of 1922, see pp. 168–77. A detailed account of the events described below and the anonymous letters from 'Tommy Atkins' and other writers, can be found in the Home Office file, TNA: HO144/10430.

39. TNA: HO144/10430, 'Letter from "Tommy Atkins"', 5 October 1922.

40. For example, 'Sabini Drama Heroine', *Daily Express*, 29 November 1922; 'Club Shooting: Girl's Pluck', *Daily Mirror*, 29 November 1922; 'Harry Sabini Tells His Story', *Star*, 13 December 1922; 'Scene In A Club', *Empire News*, 26 November 1922; 'Heroine Of A Club', *Empire News*, 3 December 1922.

41. TNA: CRIM1/209: 'Cortesi, Augustus; Cortesi, George; Cortesi, Paul; Cortesi, Enrico; Tomaso, Alexander, Charge: Attempted Murder', January 1923.

42. According to a report in *The Times*, it was this failed writ which would lead to Sabini's bankruptcy in 1926, 'C. D. Sabini's Affairs', *The Times*, 30 June, 1926.

43. *Morning Chronicle*, 19 November 1924; TNA: MEPO3/374: 'Alfred Solomon charged with the wilful murder of Barnett Blitz'.

44. *Daily Express*, 24 August 1925. For Joynson-Hicks's campaigns see M. Kohn (1992), *Dope Girls: The Birth of the British Drug Underground* (London: Granta), pp. 120, 140, 141, 149. See also, C. Emsley (2005), 'Sergeant Goddard: The Story of a Rotten Apple or a Diseased Orchard', in R. Lévy and A. Gilman Srebnick (eds.), *Crime and Culture: An Historical Perspective* (Aldershot: Ashgate), pp. 85–104, pp. 89–90.

45. *Daily Express*, 21 August 1925.

46. TNA: HO144/10430: 'Minutes, H.O., August 1925'.

47. Greeno, *War*, p. 26.

48. For example, TNA: HO144/10430 covers the activities of racecourse ruffians and the Sabini gang until 1929. TNA: MEPO3/374 covers the murder of Barnet Blitz by Alfred Solomon and its aftermath from 1924 to 1931. TNA: MEPO3/910 covers a charge of GBH by Alfred White and William White in 1935.

49. *The Times*, 16 December 1925, 30 June 1926, 11 June 1926.

50. It has also been suggested that divisions within the Italian community meant that the Sabinis were unable to maintain their dominance on the racecourses. Murphy, *Smash and Grab*, p. 33.

51. C. Chinn (1991), *Better Betting with a Decent Feller: Bookmaking, Betting and the British Working Class, 1750–1990* (London: Harvester Wheatsheaf), pp. 181–4.

52. *The Times*, 10 June 1936; *Empire News*, 14 June 1936; *Empire News*, 21 June 1936.

53. S. Chibnall (2005), *Brighton Rock* (London: L. B. Tauris), p. 17.

54. TNA: CRIM1/882: 'MARSH, Bert; WILKINS, Herbert Charge: Murder, wounding with intent', 10 November 1936. *The Times*, 17 November 1936; *Daily Mirror*, 18 November 1936. McDonald, *Gangs of London*, p. 257.
55. *Daily Mirror*, 18 September 1936. McDonald, *Gangs of London*, p. 257.
56. Murphy, *Smash and Grab*, pp. 156–60; Hill, *Boss*; A. Brown (2011), 'The Smash-and-Grab Gangster', *BBC History*, January, pp. 42–3.
57. Divall, *Scoundrels*, p. 200. For Kimber and Birmingham Gang see Chinn, *Better Betting*, pp. 178–9; Morton, *Gangland, vol. 2*, pp. 247–75. For Alfred Solomon's attack on Billy Kimber see *The Times*, 30 March 1921.
58. McDonald, *Elephant Boys*, p. 81.
59. TNA: HO144/10430, for references to Rice/Tomasso alias.
60. Harding, *East End Underworld*, pp. 182–6. Harding's main brushes with the Clerkenwell and East End gangs seems to have been mainly in the early 1920s when he was still criminally active.
61. Harding, *East End Underworld*, pp. 182, 200, 204–5; TNA: HO144/10430, letter received 11 June 1923; MEPO3/352.
62. Andrew Davies has emphasised the fluid nature of the Glaswegian gangs at this time. Davies, 'Street Gangs', p. 354.
63. TNA: MEPO3/1581: 'Shooting affray between the "Italian or Sabini Gang" and the "Birmingham Gang"', report dated 20 August 1922; Frederick Gilbert, Joseph Sabini, George Sage, 12 October 1922, in TNA: CRIM5/111: *Calendar of Indictments from 5th September 1922 to 16th July 1929*. The indictments are in CRIM4/1451. Marylebone Police Court Register, 30 August 1922, LMA: PS/MAR/A1/71; *Evening Standard*, 21, 27 August 1922; Morton, *East End Gangland*, pp. 127–8.
64. TNA: HO144/10430, 'Memorandum'.
65. TNA: HO144/10430, 'Letter from "Tommy Atkins"', 5 October 1922.
66. This included the area around Saffron Hill and a triangle of streets bounded by the Clerkenwell Road, Farringdon Road and Mount Pleasant. Summer Street, Warner Street, Back Hill, Great Bath Street and Eyre Street Hill were key areas of residence for the Italian community by the early twentieth century. Allen, *Little Italy*.
67. 1891 Census, TNA: RG/12, piece 223, folio 61, p. 14; TNA: HO45/25720: 'Defence Regulation 18B, Harry Sabini', here Harry Sabini notes that Handley is his mother's maiden name.
68. 1891 Census, TNA: RG12, piece 220, folio 69, p. 26 and folio 72, p. 31.
69. For details of Darby and Harry Sabini's internment in 1940 see, TNA: HO45/25720; HO45/23691: 'Octavius Sabini, alias Darby Sabini … Internment'; HO45/25993: 'Cases of Liversidge, Greene, Sabini, and Budd, Judgements of'. In these records 'Darby' is referred to as Frederick Handley and Harry as Harry Handley. Morton, *East End Gangland*, pp. 119–20.
70. TNA: 1891 Census, TNA: RG12, piece 223, folio 61, p. 14; 1901 Census, RG13, piece 141, folio 141, p. 23; piece 247, folio 33, p. 5; piece 253, folio 170, p. 1.
71. *OBP*, September 1890, Marzielli Valli (t18900908-669).
72. According to an interview with Harry Sabini contained in the files that deal with his appeal against internment in 1940, his father died in 1901. The death of an Otavio Sabini, aged 49, was registered in the second quarter of 1902. The dates and ages given in these later records suggest that Octavio

Sabini (senior) and Joseph Sabini were one and the same. TNA: HO45/25720; GRO Death Index, 1837–1915, Otavio Sabini, 1902, Apr-May-June, London City, vol. 1, p. 15.

73. 1911 Census, TNA: RG14, piece 1241.

74. According to Brian McDonald, Darby Sabini was born Otavio Handley in Holborn, in 1888. McDonald, *Gangs of London*, p. 150.

75. TNA: CRIM1/209, Charles Sabini statement, 5 December 1922; HO45/23691.

76. TNA: HO45/25720; together with the census data this gives us the following birth years: Frederick (1881), Charles (1883), Darby/Octavio/Ottavio (1889), Joseph (1892), George (1895), Harry (1901).

77. From TNA: HO45/25720. Morton, *East End Gangland*, pp. 119–20.

78. The Birmingham men who were charged for the Epsom Affray, were aged as follows: 5 men were in their 20s (the youngest 22); 13 men were in their 30s; 8 were in their 40s; and 2 were in their 50s (the oldest 54), TNA: MEPO3/346: 'List of men arrested in connection with wounding affray at Ewell'.

79. Clerkenwell Police Court Register, 21, 28 November, 5, 13, December 1922, LMA: PS/CLE/A1/62-3, chargebook, PS/CLE/B2/44.

80. TNA: CRIM1/209, 'Rex vs. Cortesi and others'. See *Daily Express*, 21 November 1922; *The Times*, 22, 29, November 1922; *Star*, 13 December 1922.

81. 1901 Census, TNA: RG13, piece 248, folio 47, p. 3; 1911 Census, TNA: RG14, piece 1243; *The Times*, 14 December 1922.

82. In CID records from 1930 Alfred Solomon is referred to as one of four brothers who 'obtain their living, as far as I know in a legitimate manner', as Bookmakers. TNA: MEPO3/374, report dated 11 March 1930.

83. 1891 Census, TNA: RG12, piece 376, folio 82, p. 17. In 1891 Edward is aged 11 and Philip is aged 12. There are also three other brothers, Alfred (13), Isaac (10) and Lewis (5), and three young sisters. The family are also in Bermondsey in the 1881 census (TNA: RG11, piece 57, folio 75, p. 25) with Philip aged two and Edward a baby.

84. 1901 Census, TNA: RG13, piece 262, folio 56, p. 22; 1911 Census, TNA: RG14, piece 1410. Morton, *East End Gangland*, pp. 124–6, 132–4; Harding, *East End Underworld*, p. 182. For references to the Emmanuel's fruit business, see *OBP*, November 1909, Joseph Goldsmid (t19091116-82), evidence of Edward Emmanuel; *OBP*, February 1911, George Honeybun, Percy Stiles and David Hart (t19110207-39), evidence of Philip Emmanuel.

85. D. Hobbs (2002), 'Organized Crime Families', *Criminal Justice Matters*, 50, 1, pp. 26–7, p. 26.

86. *The Times*, 19 November 1924. TNA: MEPO3/374. For this and other indictments against Solomon see 26 June 1923, 14 October 1924, in *Calendar of Indictments from 5th September 1922 to 16th July 1929* in TNA: CRIM5/11 (indictments in CRIM4/1460 and 1475).

87. *OBP*, November 1909, Joseph Goldsmid (t19091116-82). In 1931 a Joseph Goldsmid was also involved in the Eden Club Affray, along with Solomon and Emmanuel. See TNA: MEPO3/374.

88. TNA: MEPO3/910: 'Alfred and William White and Others: Causing Grievous Bodily Harm to John McCarthy Defferary'.

89. *Morning Chronicle*, 2 July 1923. The files for the case are in TNA: MEPO3/444.

90. *The Times*, 8 August 1922.

91. TNA: MEPO3/340, 'List'.

92. B. S. Godfrey, D. J. Cox and S. Farrall (2010), *Serious Offenders: A Historical Study of Habitual Criminals* (Oxford: Oxford University Press), pp. 123–9.
93. H. Mayhew and J. Binny (1862, 2011 digital edn.), *The Criminal Prisons of London and Scenes of Prison Life* (Cambridge: Cambridge University Press), p. 47.
94. TNA MEPO 3/1380: 'Shooting affray between the "Italian or Sabini Gang" and the "Birmingham Gang"', report dated 1 December, 1922. For shooting incident see *The Times*, 24 October 1922.
95. TNA: HO45/25720.
96. TNA: HO45/25720.
97. This was the Criminal Record Office number, a listing of convicted criminals, the number stays with a convicted criminal throughout his life.
98. TNA: MEPO3/374, report dated 27 October 1924.
99. TNA: MEPO3/352, 'Race gang affray in Waterloo Road and malicious damage'.
100. TNA: MEPO3/374.
101. He was convicted 1 June 1914, discharged from Maidstone 22 September 1916 and convicted again 28 April 1920. TNA: MEPO3/444, 'Attempts to bribe two Maidstone Prison Warders to convey correspondence to Joseph Sabini', report from Governor of Maidstone, 17 February 1923.
102. TNA: MEPO3/366, statement dated 21 August 1922. The Droy family were well-known boxers from Islington, see http://www.boxinghistory.org.uk/, accessed 15 September 2014.
103. TNA: CRIM1/209, Charles Sabini statement, 5 December 1922. Darby's only major brush with the police seems to have been when he was charged with 'shooting with intent' at the Greenford Trotting Track in Ealing, in March 1921. The case was dismissed. Ealing Police Court Register, 29 March 1921, LMA: PS/B/E/1/2; Morton, *East End Gangland*, pp. 123–4.
104. Davies, *Gangs of Manchester*, p. 306.
105. TNA: MEPO3/346: 'Particulars taken from file of Woolf Schwartz, C. R. O. No. S. 146229', the file notes, 'Since his discharge from the Army, Schwartz has been attending Race Meetings in various parts of the country'.
106. For other examples see Shore, 'Criminality', pp. 16–19.
107. *OBP*, January 1910, George Cortesi and Vincent Sabini (t19100111-46). There is a V. Sabini of the right age, living in Back Hill in the 1891 Census (TNA: RG12, piece 220, folio 72, p. 32).
108. TNA: MEPO3/1579: 'Antecedents of Jackson, Edwards, Phillips and Fagioli'. Clerkenwell Police Court Register, 31 July 1922, LMA: PS/CLE/A1/60.
109. Hill, *Boss*, p. 2.
110. Harding, *East End Underworld*, pp. 182–3; Morton, *East End Gangland*, p. 121. There is some suggestion that Kimber was involved with the Park Brigade in Sheffield, Bean, *Sheffield Gang Wars*, p. 25.
111. For example, see TNA: HO 144/10430, Memorandum dated 8 December 1922; 'Alleged Disturbances by Race Rangs', List of offences, dated 1 September 1925.
112. Morton, *East End Gangland*, p. 126.
113. K. E. Meyrick (1933), *Secrets of the 43* (London: John Long); more generally see H. Shore (2013), '"Constable Dances with Instructress": The Police and the Queen of Nightclubs in Inter-War London', *Social History*, 38, 2, pp. 193–202; J. Walkowitz (2012), *Nights Out: Life in Cosmopolitan London* (New Haven: Yale University Press), pp. 208–29.

114. Emsley, 'Sergeant Goddard'; Shore, 'Constable'.
115. TNA: HO144/10430, letter received 11 June 1923.
116. TNA: MEPO3/374, report dated 27 October 1924.
117. For crime and mobility see A. Brown (2011), 'Crime, Criminal Mobility and Serial Offenders in Early Twentieth Century Britain', *Contemporary British History*, 25, 4, pp. 551–68.
118. For example see *The Times*, 25 November 1924, 12 March 1928, 25 February 1930. See also report on the Flying Squad's, 'Scheme to Check Criminals in Motor-Cars', *The Times*, 7 February 1927.
119. During this period requests were made for ever faster cars in order to catch criminals more effectively (the Lea Francis was introduced in 1927), TNA: MEPO2/1880, '"Flying Squad" cars and tenders...'. See Fido and Skinner, *Scotland Yard*, p. 152.
120. TNA: MEPO3/1579: 'Statement of Witness, Charles Sabini'.
121. McDonald, *Gangs of London*, pp. 115–28.
122. S. Humphries (1981), *Hooligans or Rebels? An Oral History of Working-Class Childhood and Youth, 1889–1939* (Oxford: Basil Blackwell), pp. 190–9; Pearson, *Hooligan*, pp. 76, 82. See also Sponza, *Italian Immigrants*, p. 246.
123. *OBP*, November 1894, Thomasso Casella (t18941119-32). Also *OBP*, September 1890, Marzielli Valli (t18900908-669).
124. *OBP* (t19100111-46). Ottavio Sabini is a defendant at an earlier trial for wounding, at the Clerkenwell Sessions, 3 September 1888. He was acquitted.
125. *OBP*, June 1898, Alfred Smith (t18980620-453).
126. *OBP*, September 1902, Michaelo Rispoli, Crisuge Fariello, Vincenzo Gerrali, Alborghetti Bottista and Andrea Rispoli (t19020909-597).
127. *News of the World*, 8 September 1907, p. 4.
128. Clerkenwell Police Court Register, 2 September 1907, LMA: PS/CLE/A1/7.
129. Bean, *Sheffield Gang Wars*, p. 25. TNA: HO45/23691, here Darby is talking about Greenford Trotting Track in the early 1920s.
130. Divall, *Scoundrels*, p. 204.
131. Greeno, *War*, p. 12.
132. Greeno, *War*, pp. 22, 26.
133. D. Thompson (2007), *The Hustlers: Gambling, Greed and the Perfect Con* (London: Sidgwick and Jackson). Esmeralda's Barn was a Knightsbridge club owned by Ronald and Reginald Kray, D. Thomas (2005), *Villains' Paradise: Britain's Underworld from the Spivs to the Krays* (London: John Murray), p. 408.
134. TNA: HO45/23691; Greene, *Brighton Rock*; Chinn, 'Sabini, (Charles) Darby (1889–1950)', *Oxford Dictionary of National Biography* (Oxford University Press, 2004). See also Chibnall, *Brighton Rock*, pp. 73–4.
135. Morton, *East End Gangland*, p. 140.
136. TNA: HO45/25720.
137. *The Times*, 20 July 1956.

Conclusion

1. *The Times*, 15 October 1930.
2. *The Times*, 15 October 1930.
3. See the column, 'Organized Crime in Chicago', in *The Times*, 22 May 1928.

4. E. Wallace (1932), *When the Gangs Came to London* (London: John Long), pp. 149–50.
5. For a recent discussion of the importance of 'agency' see Hitchcock and Shoemaker, *London Lives*, 'Introduction'.
6. Mearns, *Bitter Cry*; G. Stedman Jones (1976), *Outcast London: A Study in the Relationship Between Classes in Victorian Society* (Harmondsworth: Penguin); J. Walkowitz (1992), *City of Dreadful Delight: Narratives of Sexual Danger in Late Victorian London* (Chicago: University of Chicago Press).
7. Amounting to around 639 trials or the prosecution of around 880 individuals. Indeed, 15.33 per cent of all highway robbery prosecutions at the Old Bailey were in that decade. *OBP*, Tabulating decade against offence subcategory. Counting by offence. Beattie, *First English Detectives*, pp. 9, 138–40.
8. Meier, *Property Crime*, pp. 13–40; E. Moss (2011), 'Burglary Insurance and the Culture of Fear in Britain, 1889–1930', *The Historical Journal*, 54, 4, pp. 1039–64.
9. Davies, 'Scottish Chicago?'; Houlbrook, 'Fashioning'; M. Roodhouse (2011), 'In Racket Town: Gangster Chic in Austerity Britain, 1939–1953.' *Historical Journal of Film, Television and Radio*, 31, 4, pp. 523–41.
10. *Empire News*, 3 September 1922.
11. Neale, 'Making Crime Pay', p. 454.
12. For example, the on-going digitisation of convict records will reassemble the lives of masses of individual offenders who were transported to the Australian penal colonies. This will be undertaken for the AHRC funded project, 'The Digital Panopticon: The Global Impact of London Punishments, 1780–1925' (https://news.liv.ac.uk/2013/09/18/1-7m-award-to-trace-the-lives-of-british-and-australian-convicts/, accessed 15 September 2014).
13. Neale, 'Making Crime Pay'; Godfrey, Cox and Farrall, *Serious Offenders*; Davies, *Gangs of Manchester*; Davies, *City of Gangs*.

Select Bibliography

Primary Sources

Corporation of London Record Office (now administered by London Metropolitan Archives)

CLA/047/LJ/19/005, Petitions
CLA/047/LJ/13/1737/010, Petitions
SF 62; 652; 673, Sessions File, Indictments and Recognizances
SM 112, Rewards
SP 807, Session roll, Calendar
MISC MSS/152/5, Blood Money Certificates

Goldsmiths Library, University of London

'Petition to the "swell Mob" from the Tribe of "blacklegs, Prigs, & Pickpockets,"
  Requesting to Enjoy the Same Privileges as Their "brethren" the "millocrats"'
  (c. 1834).

London Metropolitan Archives

City of London Burial Index
GRO Death Index, 1902

Police Court Registers

PS/WLN/A1/112
PS/CLE/A1/62–3
PS/CLE/B2/44
PS/CLE/A1/60
PS/CLE/A1/60
PS/CLE/A1/61
PS/MAR/A1/70
PS/MAR/A1/71
PS/OLD/A1/14
PS/WES/A1/19
PS/B/E/1/2
PS/OLD/A1/5
PS/CLE/A1/7
PS/CLE/A1/8

Sessions Papers

MJ/OC/003, f. 157d, 167d
MJ/SBB/B/0086
MJ/SP/1721, Affadavit
MJ/SP/1727, May, Instructions, etc. File-3.

MJ/SPC, E 3309; E3304a
MJ/SR/2494; 2497 f.3; 2498, f.47; 2518, f. 65-66; 2521; 2525, f.41; 2537, f.66; 2543, f.60; 2545, f.53; 2547, f.32; 2577, f.51; 2578, f.19; 2640, f.28; 2700, f.39, WJ/OC/002, ff. 69d–70; 127d, 85–87d, 89–90d; 101–105d
WJ/SP/1728, October

Special Collections
SC/PZ/SW/01/439

Wills
X19/38

National Archives, Kew

Admiralty Records
ADM106/1094/159
ADM106/1128/3
ADM106/1142/178
ADM106/1144/129

Central Criminal Court Records, Depositions and Indictments
CRIM1/13/6
CRIM1/29/9
CRIM1/48/1
CRIM1/107/4
CRIM1/108/2
CRIM1/209
CRIM1/882
CRIM4/1451
CRIM4/1460
CRIM4/1475
CRIM5/11
CRIM8/14

Exchequer Records
E407/29

Home Office Records
Commissions: Records and Correspondence
HO73/16
HO73/2
Convict Transportation Registers
HO11/9
Criminal Registers
HO26/38
HO26/42
HO27/210

Domestic Correspondence
HO44/10, ff. 220–231
HO44/8, ff. 630–631
HO44/9, ff. 10, 48
Judges and Recorders Reports
HO6/13
HO6/17
HO6/2
HO6/5
HO6/6
Metropolitan Police Correspondence
HO61/1
Petitions
HO17/49, 53, 74, 93, 111
Registered Papers
HO45/23691
HO45/25720
HO45/25993
HO45/9442/66692–66692A
HO45/9511/17216
HO45/9788/B3145A
HO45/9788/B3145D
HO144/10430
HO144/21/60045

King's Bench

KB1/3/2
KB1/3/3
KB2/1
IND1/6672 (index to KB)

Metropolitan Police Records

MEPO2/1429
MEPO2/1880
MEPO3/1
MEPO3/340
MEPO3/346
MEPO3/352
MEPO3/366
MEPO3/374
MEPO3/444
MEPO3/910
MEPO3/1579
MEPO3/1581

State Papers Domestic

SP36/18, f.197–8
SP36/59, f.222

Treasury Records

T53/29/451
T53/36/423

Census

1841
HO107, piece 737, book 21
HO107, piece 710, book 10
1881
RG11, piece 57, folio 75, page 25
1891
RG12, piece 220, folio 69, page 26
RG12, piece 220, folio 72, page 31
RG12, piece 220, folio 72, page 32
RG12, piece 223, folio 61, page 14
RG12, piece 376, folio 82, page 17
1901
RG13, piece 141, folio 141, page 23
RG13, piece 247, folio 33, page 5
RG13, piece 248, folio 47, page 3
RG13, piece 253, folio 170, page 1
RG13, piece 262, folio 56, page 22
1911
RG14, piece 1203
RG14, piece 1241
RG14, piece 1243
RG14, piece 1410

Archives consulted on www.londonlives.org

Bridewell Royal Hospital Minutes

BBBRMG202040287
BBBRMG202040546
BBBRMG202050092
BBBRMG202050228

City of London Sessions Papers

SL/PS, LMSLPS150440071

Middlesex Sessions Papers

SM/PS, LMSMPS501050012
LMSMPS501050015
LMSMPS501050018
LMSMPS501960006
LMSMPS502310079
LMSMPS502670134

Old Bailey Associated Records
assocrec_309_7495: F2/146, 154

Old Bailey Sessions Papers
OB/PS, LMOBPS450230288
LMOBPS450230305

Westminster Sessions Papers
WJ/PS, LMWJPS653630006
LMWJPS653920033
LMWJPS653920035

Official Documents and Publications

Parliamentary Papers Commons and Lords

'Committee to Enquire into the Several Burglaries and Robberies', *Commons Journal*, 1770, vol. XXXII, 881

Select Committee on the State of the Police of the Metropolis, 1816 (510)

Second Report from the Committee on the State of the Police of the Metropolis, 1817 (484)

Report from the Select Committee on the Police of the Metropolis, 1822 (440)

First Report from the Select Committee of the House of Lords Appointed to Inquire into the Present State of the Several Gaols and Houses of Correction in England and Wales, 1835 (438) (439) (440) (441)

Report from the Select Committee on Metropolis Police Offices, 1837 (451)

First Report of the Commissioners Appointed to Inquire into the Best Means of Establishing an Efficient Constabulary Force in the Counties of England and Wales, 1839 (169)

Report of the Commissioners Appointed to Inquire into the Operation of the Acts (16 & 17 Vict. c. 99. and 20 & 21 Vict. c. 3.) Relating to Transportation and Penal Servitude. Vol. I., 1863 (3190)

Report from the Select Committee of the House of Lords on the Law of Hypothec in Scotland, together with the Proceedings of the Committee, Minutes of Evidence, and Appendix, 1868–69 (367) (367-I) (367-II))

Royal Commission on the Housing of the Working Classes, 1884–85, XXX, 24

Prosecution of Offences Acts, 1879 and 1884. Return to an address of the Honourable the House of Commons, dated 13 April 1894, 1894 (73)

House of Lords Select Committee on Betting, 1902 (389)

Report of the Royal Commission upon the Duties of the Metropolitan Police, vol. 1, 1908 (4156)

Hansard's Parliamentary Debates

HC Deb August 1855 v. 139, cc. 1866–73
HC Deb April 1860, v. 157, c. 1873
HC Deb May 1860, v. 158, cc. 747, 999–1001
HC Deb February 1866 v. 181, c. 597
HC Deb September 1893 v. 17, c. 1153
HC Deb February 1895 v. 30, cc. 1657–85

Websites

http://booth.lse.ac.uk/
http://broadsides.law.harvard.edu/
http://parlipapers.chadwyck.co.uk/home.do
http://www.boxinghistory.org.uk/
http://www.capitalpunishmentuk.org/
http://www.exclassics.com/newgate/ngbibl.htm
http://www.londonlives.org/
http://www.oldbaileyonline.org/
http://www.victorianlondon.org/
17th and 18th Century Burney Collection Newspapers
19th Century British Library Newspapers Database

Oxford Dictionary of National Biography

J. Innes, 'Payne, William (1717/18–1782)', *Oxford Dictionary of National Biography*, Oxford University Press, 2004 [http://www.oxforddnb.com/view/article/70400, accessed 8 September 2014].

H. Shore, 'Gonson, Sir John (1676/7–1765)', *Oxford Dictionary of National Biography*, Oxford University Press, May 2012 [http://www.oxforddnb.com/view/article/96892, accessed 8 September 2014].

P. Sugden, 'Veil, Sir Thomas de (1684–1746)', *Oxford Dictionary of National Biography*, Oxford University Press, 2004 [http://www.oxforddnb.com/view/article/38735, accessed 8 September 2014].

A. Tomkins, 'Greenwood, James William (*bap.* 1835, *d.* 1927)', *Oxford Dictionary of National Biography*, Oxford University Press, May 2010 [http://www.oxforddnb.com/view/article/41224, accessed 8 September 2014].

A. S. Wohl, 'Mearns, Andrew (1837–1925)', *Oxford Dictionary of National Biography*, Oxford University Press, 2004 [http://www.oxforddnb.com/view/article/56012, accessed 8 September 2014].

Australian Dictionary of Biography

'Solomon, Isaac (Ikey) (1787–1850)', *Australian Dictionary of Biography*, National Centre of Biography, Australian National University, [http://adb.anu.edu.au/biography/solomon-isaac-ikey-2678/text3743, accessed 15 September 2014]

Newspapers and Periodicals

Aberdeen Journal
Annual Register
Berrow's Worcester Journal
Birmingham Daily Post
Bradford Observer
Bristol Mercury
Bristol Mercury and Daily Post
British Journal or Censor
British Journal or The Traveller
Bury and Norwich Post
Chambers's Edinburgh Journal

Charter
Christian Witness and Congregationalist Magazine
Country Journal or, the Craftsman
Craftsman
Daily Advertiser
Daily Courant
Daily Express
Daily Gazetteer
Daily Graphic
Daily Journal
Daily Mail
Daily Mirror
Daily News
Daily Post
Daily Telegraph
Derby Mercury
Empire News
Epsom Herald
Era
European Magazine, and London Review
Evening Post
Evening Standard
Examiner
Fog's Weekly Journal
Freeman's Journal and Daily Commercial Advertiser
General Evening Post
Gentleman's Magazine
Glasgow Herald
Grub Street Journal
Hampshire Advertiser
Household Words
Huddersfield Chronicle and West Yorkshire Advertiser
Hull Packet and East Riding Advertiser
Illustrated Police News
Islington Daily Gazette and North London Chronicle
Jackson's Oxford Journal
John Bull
Leeds Mercury
Leicester Chronicle
Liverpool Mercury
Lloyd's Evening Post and British Chronicle
Lloyd's Weekly Newspaper
London Evening Post
London Journal
Loyalist and Anti-Radical
Manchester Times
Morning Chronicle
Morning Post
Newcastle Courant

North Wales Chronicle
Northern Star and Leeds General Advertiser
Nottinghamshire Guardian
Old Common Sense or the Englishman's Journal
Pall Mall Gazette
Parker's Penny Post
Penny Illustrated Paper
Penny Illustrated Paper and Penny Illustrated Times
Quarterly Review
Read's Weekly Journal, or British Gazette
Reynolds's Newspaper
Reynolds's Weekly Newspaper
Sheffield and Rotherham Independent
Standard
Star
Sunday Business Post
Sunday Express
Surrey Advertiser and County Times
The Times
Universal Spectator and Weekly Journal
Weekly Journal or British Gazetteer
Weekly Journal or Saturday Post
World

Printed Primary Sources

Ainsworth, W. H. (1834), *Rookwood: A Romance* (London: Richard Bentley)
Ainsworth, W. H. (1839), *Jack Sheppard: A Romance* (London: Richard Bentley)
Allen, T. (1931), *Underworld: The Biography of Charles Brooks – Criminal* (London: Grant Richards)
Anon. (1691), *Antimoixeia: or, the Honest and Joynt-Design of the Tower-Hamblets for the General Suppression of Bawdy-Houses, as Incouraged thereto by the Publick Magistrates* (London)
Anon. (1698), *A Black List of the Names or Reputed Names of Seven Hundred Fifty Two Lewd and Scandalous Persons who by the Endeavours of a Society Set Up for Promoting a Reformation of Manners in the City of London and Suburbs Thereof, have been Legally Prosecuted and Convicted* (London)
Anon. (1701), *A Sixth Black List of the Names, or Reputed Names, of Eight Hundred and Forty Three Lewd and Scandalous Persons, Who, by the Endeavours of a Society for Promoting a Reformation of Manners ... Have Been Legally Prosecuted* (London)
Anon. (1706), *The Eleventh Black List of the Names, or Reputed Names, of Eight Hundred and Forty Three Lewd and Scandalous Persons, Who, by the Endeavours of a Society for Promoting a Reformation of Manners ... Have Been Legally Prosecuted* (London)
Anon. (1723), *The History of the Blacks of Waltham in Hampshire; and those under the like Denomination in Berkshire* (London: A. Moore)
Anon. (1728), *Villany Exploded: or, the Mistery of Iniquity laid open; In a Faithful Relation of all the Street-Robberies, Committed by the Notorious Gang now in Newgate* (London: T. Read), p. 40

Anon. (1733), *A Looking Glass for Informing Constables. Represented in the Tryal ... for the Murder of Mr. John Dent, Constable, in the Parish of St. Paul's Covent Garden, March 18 1708–9* (London: J. Wilford)

Anon. (1742), *Select Trials at the Sessions-House in the Old-Bailey, for Murder, Robberies, Rapes, Sodomy, Coining, Frauds, Bigamy, and other Offences* (Dublin: S. Powell)

Anon. (c. 1780), *The Guardians, Or, Society for the Protection of Trade against Swindlers and Sharpers, established March 25th, 1776* (London)

Anon. (1799), *A List of the Members of the Guardians, Or, Society for the Protection of Trade Against Swindlers and Sharpers* (London)

Anon. (1818), *The London Guide and Stranger's Safeguard Against the Cheats, Swindlers, and Pickpockets that Abound Within the Bills of Mortality: Forming a Picture of London as Regards Active Life: to which is Added ... a Glossary of Cant Terms. By A Gentleman who has Made the Police of the Metropolis an Object of Enquiry Twenty-Two Years, William Perry* (London: J. Bumpus)

Anon. (1829), *Adventures ... of that Notorious Fence, and Receiver of Stolen Goods, Isaac Solomons ... together with the ... Apprehension, Trial, and Subsequent Transportation of Mrs. Solomons ... By a former Police Officer* (London: J. Knight)

Anon. (1830), *The Life and Adventures of Ikey Solomons, the Notorious Receiver of Stolen Goods, better known as Ikey Solomon's ...* (London)

Archer, T. (1865), *The Pauper, the Thief and the Convict* (London: Groombridge & Sons)

Beames, T. (1850), *The Rookeries of London* (London: Thomas Bosworth)

Bellamy, M. (1728), *The Life of Martin Bellamy; with an Account of all the Several Robberies, Burglaries, Forgeries, and Other Crimes by him Committed, etc.* (London: J. Applebee)

Blanchard, S. L. (1851), 'A Biography of a Bad Shilling', *Household Words*, 2/44 January, pp. 420–6

Brown, T. (1730), *The Third Volume of The Works of Thomas Brown, Being Amusements Serious and Comical, Calculated for the Meridian of London* (London: Edward Midwinter), p. 67

Bulwer-Lytton, E. (1830), *Paul Clifford* (London: Richard Bentley)

Caminada, J. (1895), *Twenty Five Years of Detective Life* (Manchester: J. Heywood)

Campbell, H. (1899), *Darkness and Daylight; or, Lights and Shadows of New York Life ... With Thrilling Personal Experiences ... in the Underworld of the Great Metropolis* (Hartford, CT: Worthington & Co.)

Carrington, F. A., and Payne, J. (1827), *Reports of Cases Argued and Ruled at Nisi Prius, in the Courts of King's Bench, Common Please, and Exchequer, Together with Cases Tried on the Circuits and at the Old Bailey* (London: S. Sweet, Chancery Lane and R. Pheney, Inner Temple Lane)

Cheney, P. (1944), *Making Crime Pay* (London: John Long)

Child, B. (1722), *The Whole Life and History of Benjamin Child, Lately Executed for Robbing the Bristol Mail, etc.* (London: J. Peele)

Clapp, J. B., and Edgett, E. F. (1902), *Plays of the Present* (New York: Dunlap Society)

Collins, R. (1732), *The Friendly Writer and Register of Truth* (London: James Roberts)

Colquhoun, P. (1796), *A Treatise on the Police of the Metropolis* (London: H. Fry)

Cornish, G. W. (1935), *Cornish of the 'Yard': His Reminiscences and Cases* (London: Bodley Head)

Dalton, J. (1730), *The Life and Actions of James Dalton (The Noted Street Robber) containing All the Robberies and other Villanies Committed by Him, Both Alone and in Company, from his Infancy down to his Assault on Dr. Mead* (R. Walker: London)

Dante Alighieri (1867 edn), *The Divine Comedy*, translated by Henry Wadsworth Longfellow (Boston: Ticknor & Sons)

De Bérenger Beaufain, R. (1835), *Helps and Hints How to Protect Life and Property. With Instructions in Rifle and Pistol Shooting, & c.* (London: T. Hurst)

Defoe, D. (1725, 2004 edn.), *The True and Genuine Account of the Life and Actions of the Late Jonathan Wild* (London: Harper Perennial)

Defoe, D. (1728), *Street Robberies Consider'd: The Reason of Their Being so Frequent* (London: J. Roberts)

Defoe, D. (1731), *An Effectual Scheme for the Immediate Preventing of Street Robberies* (London)

Deveil, T. (1748), *Memoirs of the Life and Times of Sir Thomas Deveil, Knight* (London: M. Cooper)

Dey, T. H. (1931), *Leaves from a Bookmaker's Book* (London: Hutchinson)

Dickens, C. (1838), *Oliver Twist; Or the Parish Boy's Progress. By "Boz."* (London: Richard Bentley)

Dilnot, G. (1928), *The Trial of the Detectives* (London: Geoffrey Bles)

Dilnot, G. (1930), *The Trial of Jim the Penman* (London: Geoffrey Bles)

Divall, T. (1929), *Scoundrels and Scallywags, and Some Honest Men* (London: Ernest Benn)

Donovan, D. (1901), *Jim the Penman: The Life Story of One of the Most Astounding Criminals That Have Ever Lived* (London: George Newnes)

Eden, E. (1919), *Miss Eden's Letters, Edited by her Great Niece, Violet Dickenson* (London: Macmillan and Co)

Egan P. (1821), *Life in London: or, The Day and Night Scenes of Jerry Hawthorn, esq., and his Elegant Friend Corinthian Tom, Accompanied by Bob Logic, the Oxonian, in their Rambles and Sprees Through the Metropolis* (London: Jones & Co)

Ellington, G. (1869), *The Women of New York; or, The Under-World of the Great City. Illustrating the Life of Women of Fashion, Women of Pleasure, Actresses and Ballet Girls, Saloon Girls, Pickpockets and Shoplifters, Artists' Female models, Women-of-the-Town, Etc.* ...(New York: New York Book Co.)

Garwood, J. (1853), *The Million-Peopled City* (London: Wertheim and Macintosh)

Gonson, J. (1730), *Five Charges to Several Grand Juries ... Third Edition* (London)

Gordon, C. G. (1929), *Crooks of the Underworld* (London: Geoffrey Bles)

Grant, J. (1838), *Sketches in London* (London: Ward Lock)

Greene, G. (1938), *Brighton Rock* (London: Heinmann)

Greeno, E. (1959), *War on the Underworld* (London: Brown, Watson Ltd)

Greenwood, J. (1869), *The Seven Curses of London* (London: Rivers)

Hawkins, W. (1787), *A Treatise of the Pleas of the Crown* (London: His Majesty's Law Printers)

Hayward, A. L. (1927), *Lives of the Most Remarkable Criminals, Who Have Been Condemned and Executed; From the Year 1720 to the Present Time: vol. 3* (London, Routledge)

Hebron, M. (1829), *The Life and Exploits of Ikey Solomon, Swindler, Forger, Fencer, and Brothel-Keeper...* (London)

Hill, B. (1955), *Boss of Britain's Underworld* (London: Naldrett Press)

Hindley, C. (ed.) (1871), 'The Gaol Delivery and the Trials and Sentences of all the Prisoners at the Old Bailey Sessions, together with a full account of the Execution of the Fifteen Unfortunate Convicts', *Curiosities of Street Literature* (London: Reeves and Turner)

Hindley (1878), *The Life and Times of James Catnach ... Ballad Monger* (London: Reeves and Turner)

Hollingshead, J. (1861), *Ragged London in 1861* (London: Smith, Elder and Co.)

Holmes, T. (1912), *London's Underworld* (London: J. M. Dent & Sons)

Hughson, D. (1817) *Walks Through London Including Westminster and the Borough of Southwark with the Surrounding Suburbs* (London: Sherwood, Neely and Jones)

Jones, E. (1736), *Luxury, Pride and Vanity, the Bane of the British Nation ...* (London: J. Roberts)

Lowndes, W. (1695), *A Report Containing an Essay for the Amendment of the Silver Coins* (London: Charles Bill)

Madan, M. (1785), *Thoughts on Executive Justice, with Respect to Our Criminal Laws* (London: J. Dodsley)

Mandeville, B. (1725), *An Enquiry into the Causes of the Frequent Executions at Tyburn* (London: J. Roberts)

Mayhew, H. (1849), 'Labour and the Poor, Letter XII', *Morning Chronicle*, 27 November

Mayhew, H. (1851), *London Labour and the London Poor*, vol. 1 (London: George Woodfall & Son)

Mayhew, H. (1857), *The Great World of London* (London: David Bogue).

Mayhew, H. (1861–62, 1968 edn.), *London Labour and the London Poor*, vol. 4 (London: Dover)

Mayhew, H., and Binny, J. (1862, 2011 digital edn.), *The Criminal Prisons of London and Scenes of Prison Life* (Cambridge: Cambridge University Press)

Mearns, A. (1883), *The Bitter Cry of Outcast London: An Inquiry into the Condition of the Abject Poor* (London: James Clarke & Co.)

Meyrick, K. E. (1933, 1994 edn.), *Secrets of the 43 Club* (London: John Long, reprinted, Dublin: Parkgate Publications)

Miles, W. A. (1839), *Poverty, Mendicity and Crime; or, the Facts, Examinations, &c., upon which the Report was Founded, Presented to the House of Lords by W. A. Miles, Esq. To Which is Added a Dictionary of the Flash or Cant Language Known to Every Thief or Beggar. Edited by H. Brandon* (London: Shaw & Sons)

Morrison, A. (1896, 2012 edn.), *A Child of the Jago* (Oxford: Oxford University Press)

Neaves, T. (1729), *The Life of Thomas Neaves, the Noted Street-Robber, Executed at Tyburn on Friday the Seventh of February, 1728–9, etc.* (R. Walker: London)

Nichols, J. G. (1837), *London Pageants* (London: J. B. Nichols)

Pope, A. (1735), *The Works of Alexander Pope, Esq; vol. II.* (London: L. Gilliver)

Reushel, R. (1895), *The Knights of Industry: Revelations about Long-Firms in London* (London)

Reynolds, G. W. M. (1844–6), *The Mysteries of London* (London: John Dicks)

Ritchie, J. E. (1860), *About London* (London: William Tinsley)

Rook, C. (1899), *Hooligan Nights: Being the Life and Opinions of a Young and Impertinent Criminal* (London: Grant Richards)

Russell, R. O., and Greaves, C. S. (1843), *A Treatise on Crimes and Misdemeanours*, Vol. 1 (London: Saunders and Benning)

Ryan, M. (1839), *Prostitution in London with a Comparative View of that of Paris and New York* (London: H. Bailliere)

Sharpe, F. D. (1938), *Sharpe of the Flying Squad* (London: John Long)

Smith, A. (1726), *Memoirs of the Life and Times of the Famous Jonathan Wild, Together with the History and Lives of Modern Rogues* (London: Sam Briscoe)

Smollett, T. (1751, 1964 edn.), *The Adventures of Peregrine Pickle: In Which Are Included Memoirs of a Lady of Quality, Volumes 1–2* (Oxford: Oxford University Press)

Stephens, E. (1691), *The Beginning and Progress of a Needful and Hopeful Reformation in England: With the First Encounter of the Enemy Against it, His Wiles Detected, and His Design ('t may be hop'd) Defeated* (London)

Vartie, J. (1817), *A Memoir of the Unfortunate John Vartie, a Youth only 19 Years of Age: Who Was Executed on Thursday, December 11, 1817, for the Crime of Forgery: To Which are Added some Letters Addressed to the Rev. James Rudge, M. A., of Limehouse, Written by Himself, a Short Time Previous to his Execution* (London: Effingham Wilson)

Vaux, J. H. (1819), *Memoirs of James Hardy Vaux, Written by Himself in Two Volumes* (London: W. Clowes, 1819)

Walker, C. (1723), *Authentick Memoirs of the Life, Intrigues and Adventures of the Celebrated Sally Salisbury* (London)

Wallace, E. (1932), *When the Gangs Came to London* (London: John Long)

Ward, E. (1709 edn.), *The London-Spy Compleat in Eighteen Parts. The First Volume of the Author's Writings, part. XV Fourth Edition* (London: J. How, London), pp. 365–7

Weight, G. (1840), 'Statistics of St. George the Martyr, Southwark', *Journal of the Statistical Society of London*, 3/1, pp. 50–71

Wensley, F. P. (1931), *Detective Days: The Record of Forty-Two Years' Service in the Criminal Investigation Department* (London: Cassell).

Wilson, R. (1722), *A Full and Impartial Account of all the Robberies Committed by JOHN HAWKINS, GEORGE SYMPSON (Lately Executed for Robbing the Bristol Mail) and their COMPANIONS.* (London: J. Peele)

Young, C. L. (1886), *Jim the Penman: A Romance of Modern Society in Four Acts* (New York: S. French)

Secondary Sources

Allen, M. J. (2001), *Textbook on Criminal Law*, 6th edn. (Oxford: Blackstone Press)

Allen, T. (2008), *Little Italy: The Story of London's Italian Quarter* (London: Camden Local Studies)

Anderson, G. L. (1977), 'The Social Economy of Late-Victorian Clerks', in Crossick, *Middle Class*, pp. 113–33

Andrew, D. T., and McGowen, R. (2001), *The Perreaus and Mrs. Rudd: Forgery and Betrayal in Eighteenth-Century London* (Berkeley: University of California Press)

Archer, J. (1999), 'The Violence We Have Lost'? Body Counts, Historians and Interpersonal Violence in England', *Memoria y Civilización*, 2, pp. 171–90

Bailey, P. (1999), 'White Collars, Gray Lives?: The Lower Middle Class Revisited', *Journal of British Studies*, 38, pp. 273–90

Barker, F., and Jackson, P. (1990), *The History of London in Maps* (London: Guild Publishing)

Barthes, R. (1972 edn.), *Mythologies, Selected and Translated from the French by Annette Lavers* (New York: Farrar, Strauss & Giroux), p. 137

Bean, J. P. (1981) *The Sheffield Gang Wars* (Sheffield: D & D Publications), p. 125

Beattie, J. (1995), 'Crime and Inequality in Eighteenth-Century London', in J. Hagan and R. D. Peterson (eds.), *Crime and Inequality* (California: Stanford University Press)

Beattie, J. M. (1975), 'The Criminality of Women in Eighteenth-Century England, *Journal of Social History*, 8, pp. 80–116

Beattie, J. M. (1986), *Crime and the Courts in England, 1660–1800* (Oxford: Oxford University Press)

Beattie, J. M. (2003), *Policing and Punishment, 1660–1750: Urban Crime and the Limits of Terror* (Oxford: Oxford University Press)

Beattie, J. M. (2007), 'Sir John Fielding and Public Justice: The Bow Street Magistrates' Court, 1754–1780', *Law and History Review*, 25, pp. 61–100

Beattie, J. M. (2012), *The First English Detectives: The Bow Street Runners and the Policing of London, 1730–1840* (Oxford: Oxford University Press)

Beaven, B. (2005), *Leisure Citizenship and Working-Class Men in Britain, 1850–1914* (Manchester: Manchester University Press)

Belcham, J. (1985), *'Orator' Hunt: Henry Hunt and English Working Class Radicalism* (Oxford: Clarendon Press)

Bell, I. A. (1991), *Literature and Crime in Augustan England* (London: Routledge)

Bell, K. (2012), *The Legend of Spring-Heeled Jack: Victorian Urban Folklore and Popular Cultures* (Woodbridge: Boydell Press)

Birchall, J. (2006), '"The Carnival Revels of Manchester's Vagabonds": Young Working-Class Women and Monkey Parades in the 1870s', *Women's History Review*, 15, 2, pp. 229–52

Brown, A. (2011), 'The Smash-and-Grab Gangster', *BBC History*, January, pp. 42–3

Brown, A. (2011), 'Crime, Criminal Mobility and Serial Offenders in Early Twentieth Century Britain', *Contemporary British History*, 25, 4, pp. 551–68

Brown, A. (2013), *Interwar Penal Policy in England: The Dartmouth Convict Prison Riot, 1932* (Basingstoke: Palgrave Macmillan)

Burke, P. (2005 edn.), *History and Social Theory* (New York: Cornell University Press)

Carnell, J. (2011), *James Townsend Saward, Criminal Barrister: The True Story of Jim the Penman* (Hastings: Sensation Press)

Chesney, K. (1970), *The Victorian Underworld* (London: Temple Smith)

Chibnall, S. (2005), *Brighton Rock* (London: L. B. Tauris)

Childs, M. J. (1992), *Labour's Apprentices: Working-Class Lads in Late Victorian and Edwardian England* (Quebec: McGill-Queen's University Press)

Chinn, C. (1991), *Better Betting with a Decent Feller: Bookmaking, Betting and the British Working Class, 1750–1990* (London: Harvester Wheatsheaf)

Clapson, M. (1992), 'Playing the System: The World of Organised Street Betting in Manchester, Salford and Bolton, c. 1880–1939', in A. Davies and S. Fielding (eds.), *Workers Worlds: Cultures and Communities in Manchester and Salford, 1880–1939* (Manchester: Manchester University Press), pp. 156–78

Clayton, M. (2008), 'The Life and Crimes of Charlotte Walker, Prostitute and Pickpocket', *London Journal*, 33, 1, pp. 3–19

Cocks, H. (2003), *Nameless Offences: Homosexual Desire in the Nineteenth Century* (London: I. B. Tauris)

Coldham, P. W. (1988), *The Complete Book of Emigrants in Bondage, 1614–1775* (Baltimore: Genealogical Publishing Co)

Collins, P. (1962, 1994 edn.), *Dickens and Crime* (Basingstoke: Palgrave Macmillan)

Cox, D. (2010), *A Certain Share of Low Cunning: A History of the Bow Street Runners, 1792–1839* (Cullompton: Willan)

Cressey, D. (1969), *The Theft of the Nation: The Structure and Operations of Organized Crime in America* (New York: Harper & Row)

Croll, A. (2004), 'Who's Afraid of the Victorian Underworld?', *The Historian*, 84, pp. 30–5

Crone, R. (2012), *Violent Victorians: Popular Entertainment in Nineteenth-Century London* (Manchester: Manchester University Press)

Crossick, G. (1977), 'The Emergence of the Lower Middle Class in Britain', in G. Crossick (ed.), *The Lower Middle Class in Britain 1870–1914* (London: Croom Helm), pp. 11–60

Cunningham, H. (1977), 'The Metropolitan Fairs: A Case Study in the Social Control of Leisure', in A. P. Donajgrodski (ed.), *Social Control in Nineteenth-Century Britain* (London: Croom Helm), pp. 163–84

Dabhoiwala, F. (2007), 'Sex and Societies for Moral Reform, 1688–1800', *Journal of British Studies*, 46, pp. 290–319

Dabhoiwala, F. (2012) *The Origins of Sex: A History of the First Sexual Revolution* (London: Allen Lane)

Dart, G. (2001), '"Flash Style": Pierce Egan and Literary London, 1820–1828', *History Workshop Journal*, 51, pp. 180–205

Davies, A. (1998), 'Street Gangs, Crime and Policing in Glasgow During the 1930s: The Case of the Beehive Boys', *Journal of Social History*, 32, 2, pp. 349–69

Davies, A. (1998), 'Youth Gangs, Masculinity and Violence in Late Victorian Manchester and Salford', *Journal of Social History*, 32, 2, pp. 349–69

Davies, A. (1999), '"These Viragoes are No Less Cruel Than the Lads": Young Women, Gangs and Violence in Late Victorian Manchester and Salford', *British Journal of Criminology*, 39, 1, pp. 72–89

Davies, A. (2007), 'Glasgow's Reign of Terror: Street Gangs, Racketeering and Intimidation in the 1920s and the 1930s', *Contemporary British History*, 21, 4, pp. 405–27

Davies, A. (2007), 'The Scottish Chicago?: From "Hooligans" to "Gangsters" in Interwar Glasgow', *Cultural and Social History*, 4, 4, pp. 511–27

Davies, A. (2008), *The Gangs of Manchester: The Story of the Scuttlers, Britains First Youth Cult* (Preston: Milo Books)

Davies, A. (2011), 'Youth Gangs and Late Victorian Society', in B. Goldson (ed.), *Youth in Crisis? 'Gangs', Territoriality and Violence* (London: Routledge), pp. 38–54

Davies, A. (2013), *City of Gangs: Glasgow and the Rise of the British Gangster* (London: Hodder & Stoughton)

Davies, G. (2002), *A History of Money from Ancient Times to the Present Day* (Cardiff: University of Wales Press)

Davis, J. (1980), 'The London Garotting Panic of 1862: A Moral Panic and the Creation of a Criminal Class in Mid-Victorian England', in V. A. C. Gatrell, B. Lenman and G. Parker (eds.), *Crime and the Law: The Social History of Crime in Western Europe since 1500* (London: Europa), pp. 190–213

Davis, J. (1984), 'A Poor Man's System of Justice: The London Police Courts in the Second Half of the Nineteenth Century', *The Historical Journal*, 27, 2, pp. 309–35

Devereaux, S. (1996), 'The City and the Sessions Paper: "Public Justice in London, 1770–1800"', *Journal of British Studies*, 35, 4, pp. 466–503

Devereaux, S. (2002), 'The Fall of the Sessions Paper: Criminal Trial and the Popular Press in Late Eighteenth-Century London', *Criminal Justice History*, pp. 57–88

Dixon, D. (1980), '"Class Law": The Street Betting Act of 1906', *International Journal of The Sociology of Law*, 8, pp. 101–28

Dixon, D. (1991), *From Prohibition to Regulation: Bookmaking, Anti-Gambling and the Law* (Oxford: Clarendon Press)

Drew, J. M. L. (2003), *Dickens the Journalist* (Basingstoke: Palgrave Macmillan)

Egmond, F. (1993), *Underworld: Organised Crime in the Netherlands* (London: Polity)

Elias, N. (1978), *The Civilizing Process: The History of Manners* (New York: Urizen Books)

Elrington, C. R., et al. (1989), *A History of the County of Middlesex, volume 9, Victoria County History* (Oxford: Oxford University Press) [http://www.british-history.ac.uk/report.aspx?compid=22648, accessed 15 September 2014]

Emsley, C. (1983), *Policing and its Context, 1750–1870* (Basingstoke: Macmillan)

Emsley, C. (2005 edn.), *Crime and Society in England, 1750–1900* (Harlow: Pearson)

Emsley, C. (2005), 'Sergeant Goddard: The Story of a Rotten Apple or a Diseased Orchard', in R. Lévy and A. Gilman Srebnick (eds.), *Crime and Culture: An Historical Perspective* (Aldershot: Ashgate), pp. 85–104

Emsley, C. (2010 edn.), *Crime and Society in England, 1750–1900* (London: Longman)

Endelman, T. (2002), *The Jews of Britain, 1656 to 2000* (Berkeley: University of California Press)

Evans, R. (1998), *Tales from the German Underworld: Crime and Punishment in the Nineteenth Century* (New Haven: Yale University Press)

Faller, L. B. (1987), *Turned to Account: The Forms and Functions of Criminal Biography in the Late Seventeenth and Early Eighteenth Century England* (Cambridge: Cambridge University Press)

Fido, M., and Skinner, K. (2000), *The Official Encyclopaedia of Scotland Yard: Behind the Scenes at Scotland Yard* (London: Virgin Publishing)

Flanders, J. (2011), *The Invention of Murder: How the Victorians Revelled in Death and Detection and Created Modern Crime* (London: Harper Press)

Foote Whyte, W. (1943), *Street Corner Society: The Social Structure of an Italian Slum* (Chicago: University of Chicago Press)

French, M. (2005), 'Commercials, Careers and Culture: Travelling Salesmen in Britain, 1890s–1930s', *Economic History Review*, 58, 2, pp. 352–77

French, M., and Popp, A. (2008), '"Ambassadors of Commerce": The Commercial Traveller in British Culture, 1800–1939', *Business History Review*, 82, pp. 789–814

Furbank, P. N., and Owens, W. R. (1988), *The Canonisation of Daniel Defoe* (New Haven: Yale University Press)

Furbank, P. N., and Owens, W. R. (1994), *Defoe De-Attributions: A Critique of J.R. Moore's Checklist* (London: Hambledon Press)

Galeotti, M. (2005), 'Global Crime Today', in M. Galeotti (ed.), *Global Crime Today: The Changing Face of Organised Crime* (Abingdon: Routledge), pp. 1–7

Gaskill, M. (2003), *Crime and Mentalities in Early Modern England* (Cambridge: Cambridge University Press)

Gatrell, V. A. C. (1980), 'The Decline of Theft and Violence in Victorian and Edwardian England', in V. A. C. Gatrell, B. Lenman and G. Parker (eds.), *Crime and the Law: The Social History of Crime in Western Europe since 1500* (London: Europa), pp. 238–337

George, D. (1966 edn.), *London Life in the Eighteenth Century* (Harmondsworth: Penguin)

Gilfoyle, T. J. (2006), *A Pickpocket's Tale: The Underworld of Nineteenth-Century New York* (London: W. W. Norton & Co.)

Godfrey, B. (2003), 'Counting and Accounting for the Decline in Non-Lethal Violence in England, Australia and New Zealand, 1880–1920', *British Journal of Criminology*, 43, pp. 340–53

Godfrey, B., and Lawrence, P. (2005), *Crime and Justice, 1750 to 1950* (Cullumpton: Willan)

Godfrey, B., and Locker, J. (2001), 'The Nineteenth-Century Decline of Custom and its Impact on Theories of "Workplace Theft" and "White-Collar Crime"', *Northern History*, 38, pp. 261–73

Godfrey, B., Cox, D., and Farrall, S. (2007), *Criminal Lives: Family Life, Employment and Offending* (Oxford: Oxford University Press)

Godfrey, B., Cox, D. J., and Farrall, S. (2010), *Serious Offenders: A Historical Study of Habitual Criminals* (Oxford: Oxford University Press)

Goldson, B. (2011), 'Youth in Crisis?', in B. Goldson (ed.), *Youth in Crisis? 'Gangs', Territoriality and Violence* (London: Routledge), pp. 1–19

Gooderson, P. (1997), 'Terror on the Streets of Late Victorian Salford and Manchester: The Scuttling Menace', *Manchester Region History Review*, 11, pp. 3–11

Gooderson, P. (2010), *The Gangs of Birmingham: From the Sloggers to The Peaky Blinders* (Preston: Milo Books)

Gooderson, R. N. (1952), 'When is a Document False in the Law of Forgery?', *The Modern Law Review*, 15, 1, pp. 11–27

Gowing, L. (1998), *Domestic Dangers: Women, Words, and Sex in Early Modern London* (Oxford: Oxford University Press)

Gray, D. (2010), *London's Shadows: The Dark Side of the Victorian City* (London: Continuum)

Gray, D. (2013), 'Gang Crime and the Media in Late 19th Century London: The Regent's Park Murder of 1888', *Cultural and Social History*, 10, 4, pp. 559–75

Greenwood, C. (1972), *Firearms Control: A Study of Armed Crime and Firearms Control in England and Wales* (London: Routledge)

Griffiths, P. (1996), *Youth and Authority: Formative Experiences in England, 1560–1640 (Oxford: Oxford University Press)*

Griffiths, P. (2000), 'Overlapping Circles: Imagining Criminal Communities in London, 1545–1645', in A. Shepard and P. Withington (eds.), *Communities in Early Modern England: Networks, Place, Rhetoric* (Manchester: Manchester University Press), pp. 115–33

Griffiths, P. (2008), *Lost Londons: Change, Crime and Control in the Capital City, 1550–1660* (Cambridge: Cambridge University Press)

Gunn, S. (2001), 'The Spatial Turn: Changing Histories of Space and Place', in S. Gunn and R. Morris (eds.), *Identities in Space: Contested Terrains in the Western City since 1850* (Aldershot: Ashgate), pp. 1–14

Hallsworth, S. (2011), 'Gangland Britain? Realities, Fantasies and Industry', in B. Goldson (ed.), *Youth in Crisis? 'Gangs', Territoriality and Violence* (London: Routledge), pp. 183–97

Halvorson, M. J., and Spierling, K. E. (2008), *Defining Community in Early Modern Europe* (Aldershot: Ashgate)

Handler, P. (2005), 'Forgery and the End of the "Bloody Code" in Early Nineteenth-Century England', *The Historical Journal*, 48, 3, pp. 683–702

Handler, P. (2007), 'The Law of Felonious Assault in England', *The Journal of Legal History*, 28, 2, pp. 183–206

Harding, A. (ed. by R. Samuel). (1981), *East End Underworld: Chapters in the Life of Arthur Harding* (London: Routledge)

Harris, A. T. (2004), *Policing the City: Crime and Legal Authority in London, 1780–1840* (Columbus: Ohio State University Press)

Harris, M. (1987), *London Newspapers in the Age of Walpole: A Study of the Origins of the Modern English Press* (London: Associated University Presses)

Harris, M. (c. 1984), 'Trials and Criminal Biographies: A Case Study in Distribution', in R. Myers and M. Harris (eds.), *Sale and Distribution of Books from 1700* (Oxford: Oxford Polytechnic Press), pp. 1–36

Harrison, M. (2002), *Crowds and History: Mass Phenomena in English Towns* (Cambridge: Cambridge University Press)

Hart, E. T. (1993), *Britain's Godfather* (London: Forum)

Herring, J. (2012), *Criminal Law: Text, Cases and Materials, Fifth Edition* (Oxford: Oxford University Press)

Heller, B. (2010), 'The "Menu Peuple" and the Polite Spectator: The Individual in the Crowd at Eighteenth-Century London Fairs', *Past and Present*, 208, 1, pp. 131–57

Heller, M. (2008), 'Work, Income and Stability: The Late Victorian and Edwardian London Male Clerk Revisited', *Business History*, 50, 3, pp. 253–71

Henderson, A. (1999), *Disorderly Women in Eighteenth Century London: Prostitution and Control in the Metropolis, 1730–1830* (London: Longman)

Herbert, S. (1998), 'Policing Contested Space: On Patrol at Smiley and Hauser', in N. R. Fyfe (ed.), *Images of the Street: Planning, Identity and Control in Public Space* (London: Routledge), pp. 225–35

Hitchcock, T. (2003), '"You Bitches ... Die and Be Damned", Gender, Authority and the Mob in St. Martin's Roundhouse Disaster of 1742', in Hitchcock and Shore, *Streets of London*, pp. 69–81

Hitchcock, T. (2013), 'Confronting the Digital, Or How Academic History Writing Lost The Plot', *Cultural and Social History*, 10, 1, pp. 9–23

Hitchcock, T., and Shoemaker, R. B. (2006), 'Digitising History From Below: The Old Bailey Proceedings Online, 1674–1834', *History Compass* 4, pp. 1–10

Hitchcock, T., and Shoemaker, R. B. (2006), *Tales from the Hanging Court* (London: Hodder Arnold)

Hitchcock, T., and Shoemaker, R. B. (2015), *London Lives: Poverty, Crime and the Making of a Modern City, 1690–1800* (Cambridge: Cambridge University Press)

Hitchcock, T., and Shore, H. (eds.) (2003), *The Streets of London: From the Great Fire to the Great Stink* (London: Rivers Oram Press)

Hobbs (2013), *Lush Life: Constructing Organized Crime in the UK* (Oxford: Oxford University Press)

Hobbs, D. (1994), 'Professional and Organized Crime in Britain', in M. Maguire, R. Morgan and R. Reiner, *The Oxford Handbook of Criminology* (Oxford: Clarendon Press) pp. 441–68

Hobbs, D. (2001), 'The Firm: Organisational Logic and Criminal Culture on a Shifting Terrain', *British Journal of Criminology*, 41, pp. 549–60

Hobbs, D. (2002), 'Organized Crime Families', *Criminal Justice Matters*, 50, 1, pp. 26–7

Hobbs, D. (2006), *Bad Business: Professional Crime in Modern Britain* (Oxford: Oxford University Press)

Hopkins, E. (1994), *Childhood Transformed: Working-Class Children in Nineteenth-Century England* (Manchester: Manchester University Press), pp. 203–4

Houlbrook, M. (2013), 'Commodifying the Self Within: Ghosts, Libels, and the Crook Life Story in Interwar Britain', *Journal of Modern History*, 85, 2, pp. 321–63

Houlbrook, M. (2013), 'Fashioning an Ex-Crook Self: Citizenship and Criminality in the Work of Netley Lucas', *Twentieth Century British History*, 24, 1, pp. 1–30

Howson, G. (1970), *The Thief-Taker General: The Rise and Fall of Jonathan Wild* (London: Hutchinson)

Huggins, M. (2000), *Flat Racing and British Society, 1790–1914: A Social and Economic History* (London: Cass)

Huggins, M. (2003), *Horseracing and the British, 1919–1939* (Manchester: Manchester University Press)

Humphries, S. (1981), *Hooligans or Rebels? An Oral History of Working-Class Childhood and Youth, 1889–1939* (Oxford: Basil Blackwell)

Hurl-Eamon, J. (2004), 'Policing Male Heterosexuality: The Reformation of Manners Societies' Campaign Against the Brothels in Westminster, 1690–1720', *Journal of Social History*, 37, 4, pp. 1017–35

Hurl-Eamon, J. (2005), *Gender and Petty Violence in London, 1680–1720* (Columbus: Ohio State University Press)

Ianni, F. A. J. (1974), *Black Mafia: Ethnic Succession in Organized Crime* (New York: Simon & Schuster)

Innes, J. (2009), *Inferior Politics: Social Problems and Social Policies in Eighteenth-Century* (Oxford: Oxford University Press)

James, P. D., and Critchley, T. A. (1971), *The Maul and the Pear Tree: The Ratcliffe Highway Murders, 1811* (London: Constable)

Jenkins, P., and Potter, G. W. (1988), 'Before the Krays: Organised Crime in London, 1920–1960', *Criminal Justice History*, 9, pp. 209–30

Jones, D. V., and Bainbridge, A. (1979), 'The Conquering of China: Crime in an Industrial Community, 1842–64', *Llafur The Journal of the Society for the Study of Welsh Labour History*, 2, 4, pp. 7–37

Joyce, S. (2003), *Capital Offenses: Geographies of Class and Crime in Victorian London* (Charlottesville: University of Virginia Press)

Kift, D. (1996), *The Victorian Music Hall: Culture, Class and Conflict* (Cambridge: Cambridge University Press)

King, P. (1996), 'Punishing Assault: The Transformation of Attitudes in the English Courts', *Journal of Interdisciplinary History*, 27, pp. 43–74

King, P. (2000), *Crime, Justice and Discretion in England, 1740–1820* (Oxford: Oxford University Press)

King, P. (2003), 'Moral Panics and Violent Street Crime, 1750–2000: A Comparative Perspective', in B. Godfrey, C. Emsley and G. Dunstall (eds.), *Comparative Histories of Crime* (Cullompton: Willan Publishing), pp. 53–71

King, P. (2006), *Crime and the Law in England, 1750–1840: Remaking Justice From the Margins* (Cambridge: Cambridge University Press)

Kintrea, K., Bannister, J., and Pickering, J. (2011), '"It's just an area – everybody represents it": Exploring Young People's Territorial Behaviour in British Cities', in Goldson, *Youth in Crisis?*, pp. 55–71

Kirby, D. (2011), *The Sweeney: The First Sixty Years of Scotland Yard's Crimebusting Flying Squad, 1919–1978* (Barnsley: Pen and Sword Books)

Klingenstien, S., Hitchcock, T., and DeDeo, S. (2014), 'The Civilizing Process in London's Old Bailey', *Proceedings of the National Academy of Sciences of the United States of America*, 111, 26, pp. 9419–24

Knepper, P. (2007), 'British Jews and the Racialisation of Crime in the Age of Empire', *British Journal of Criminology*, 47, pp. 61–79

Knepper, P. (2009), *The Invention of International Crime: A Global Issue in the Making, 1881–1914* (Basingstoke: Palgrave Macmillan)

Kohn, M. (1992), *Dope Girls: The Birth of the British Drug Underground* (London: Granta)

Koven, S. (2004), *Slumming: Sexual and Social Politics in Victorian London* (Princeton, NJ: Princeton University Press)

Landau, N. (1984), *The Justices of the Peace, 1679–1760* (Berkeley: University of California Press)

Landau, N. (2002), 'The Trading Justices Trade', in N. Landau (ed.), *Law, Crime and Society, 1660–1830* (Cambridge: Cambridge University Press), pp. 46–70

Langbein, J. H. (1999), 'The Prosecutorial Origins of Defence Counsel in the Eighteenth Century: The Appearance of Solicitors', *Cambridge Law Review*, 58, pp. 314–65

Langbein, J. H. (2003), *The Origins of the Adversary Criminal Trial* (Oxford: Oxford University Press)

Laqueur, T. W. (1982), 'The Queen Caroline Affair: Politics as Art in the Reign of George IV', *Journal of Modern History*, 54, pp. 417–66

Lemmings, D. (2009), 'Introduction: Law and Order, Moral Panics, and Early Modern England', in D. Lemmings and C. Walker (eds.), *Moral Panics, the Media and the Law in Early Modern England* (Basingstoke: Palgrave Macmillan), pp. 1–21

Levi, M. (1981), *The Phantom Capitalists: The Organisation and Control of Long-Firm Fraud* (London: Heinemann)

Linebaugh, P. (1977), 'The Ordinary of Newgate and his Account', in J. S. Cockburn (ed.), *Crime in England 1550–1800* (London: Methuen), pp. 246–69

Linebaugh, P. (1991), *The London Hanged: Crime and Civil Society in the Eighteenth Century* (London: Allen Lane)

Locker, J. (2005), '"Quiet thieves, quiet punishment": Private Responses to the "Respectable" offender, c. 1850–1930', *Crime, Histoire et Sociétés*, 9, 1, pp. 9–31

Low, D. (2005), *The Regency Underworld* (Stroud: Sutton)

Macfarlane, A. (1981), *The Justice and the Mare's Ale: Law and Disorder in Seventeenth-Century England* (Oxford: Blackwell)

Macfarlane, A., with Harrison, S., and Jardine, C. (1977), *Reconstructing Historical Communities* (Cambridge: Cambridge University Press)

Macilwee, M. (2007), *The Gangs of Liverpool* (Preston: Milo Books)

Mackie, E. (2009), *Rakes, Highwaymen and Pirates: The Making of the Modern Gentleman in the Eighteenth Century* (Baltimore: John Hopkins University Press)

Marriott (2008), 'The Imaginative Geography of the Whitechapel Murders', in A. Werner (ed.), *Jack the Ripper and the East End* (London: Chatto and Windus), pp. 31–63

Marriott, J. (1999), 'Introduction', in J. Marriott and M. Matsumura (eds.), *The Metropolitan Poor: Semi-Factual Accounts, 1795–1910*, 5 vols. (London: Pickering and Chatto), pp. xi–l

Marriott, J. (2011), *Beyond the Tower: A History of East London* (London: Polity Press)

McDonald, B. (2000), *Elephant Boys: Tales of London and Los Angeles Underworlds* (Edinburgh: Mainstream)

McDonald, B. (2010), *The Gangs of London: 100 Years of Mob Warfare* (Wrea Green: Milo Books)

McGowen, R. (1990), 'Getting to Know the Criminal Class in Nineteenth-Century England', *Nineteenth Century Contexts*, 14, pp. 33–54

McGowen, R. (1999), 'From Pillory to Gallows: The Punishment of Forgery in the Age of the Financial Revolution', *Past and Present*, 165, 1, pp. 107–40

McGowen, R. (2002), 'Forgery Legislation in Eighteenth-Century England', in N. Landau (ed.), *Law, Crime and English Society, 1660–1830* (Cambridge: Cambridge University Press), pp. 117–38

McGowen, R. (2005), 'The Bank of England and the Policing of Forgery 1797–1821', *Past and Present*, 186, pp. 81–116

McGowen, R. (2007), 'Managing the Gallows: The Bank of England and the Death Penalty, 1797–1821', *Law and History Review*, 25, 2, pp. 241–82

McKenzie, A. (1998), 'Making Crime Pay: Motives, Marketing Strategies, and the Printed Literature of Crime in England, 1670–1770', in G. Smith, A. May and S. Devereaux (eds.), *Criminal Justice in the Old World and the New: Essays in Honour of J. M. Beattie* (Toronto: University of Toronto Press), pp. 235–69

McKenzie, A. (2005), 'From True Confessions to True Reporting? The Decline and Fall of the Ordinary's Account', *London Journal*, 30, 1, pp. 55–70

McKenzie, A. (2007), *Tyburn's Martyrs: Execution in England, 1675–1775* (London: Hambledon Continuum)

McMullan, J. (1984), *The Canting Crew: London's Criminal Underworld, 1550–1700* (New Brunswick: Rutgers University Press)

McWilliam, R. (1998), *Popular Politics and Protest in Nineteenth-Century England* (London: Routledge)

Meier, W. M. (2011), *Property Crime in London, 1850 to the Present* (Basingstoke: Palgrave Macmillan)

Moore, L. (1998), *The Thieves' Opera: The Remarkable Lives and Deaths of Jonathan Wild, Thief-Taker and Jack Sheppard, House-Breaker* (London: Penguin)

Morgan, G., and Rushton, P. (2007), 'Print Culture, Crime and Transportation in the Criminal Atlantic', *Continuity and Change*, 2, 1, pp. 49–72

Morgan, G., and Rushton, P. (2003), 'Running Away and Returning Home: The Fate of English Convicts in the American Colonies', *Crime, Histoire et Sociétés*, 7, 2, pp. 61–80

Morgan, G., and Rushton, P. (2003), 'The Magistrate and the Community and the Maintenance of an Orderly Society in Eighteenth Century England', *Historical Research*, 76, pp. 54–77

Morris, R. M. (2006), '"Crime Does Not Pay": Thinking Again About Detectives in the First Century of the Metropolitan Police', in C. Emsley and H. Shpayer-Makov (eds.), *Police Detectives in History, 1750–1950* (Aldershot: Ashgate), pp. 79–102

Morton (1992), *Gangland: London's Underworld* (London: Little Brown)

Morton, J. (1994), *Gangland, vol. 2: The Underworld in Britain and Ireland* (London: Little Brown)

Morton, J. (2000), *East End Gangland* (London: Little Brown)

Moss, E. (2011), 'Burglary Insurance and the Culture of Fear in Britain, 1889–1930', *The Historical Journal*, 54, 4, pp. 1039–64

Murphy, R. (1993), *Smash and Grab: Gangsters in the London Underworld, 1920–60* (London: Faber and Faber)

Nash, D., and Kilday, A. M. (2010), *Cultures of Shame: Exploring Crime and Morality in Britain, 1600–1900* (Basingstoke: Palgrave Macmillan)

Neale, M. (2011), 'Making Crime Pay in Late Eighteenth-Century Bristol: Stolen Goods, the Informal Economy and the Negotiation of Risk', *Continuity and Change*, 26, 3, pp. 439–59

Newens, S. (2007), 'The Genesis of *East End Underworld: Chapters in the Life of Arthur Harding* by Raphael Samuel', *History Workshop Journal*, 64, 1, pp. 347–53

Norton, R. (1992), *Mother Clap's Molly House: The Gay Subculture in England, 1700–1830* (London: GMP Publishers)

Paley, R. (1989), 'Thief-Takers in London in the Age of the McDaniel Gang, c. 1745–1754', in D. Hay and F. Snyder (eds.), *Policing and Prosecution in Britain, 1750–1850* (Oxford: Clarendon Press), pp. 301–41

Palk, D. (2006), *Gender, Crime and Judicial Discretion, 1780–1830* (Woodbridge: Royal Historical Society)

Palmer, S. H. (1977), 'Before the Bobbies: The Caroline Riots of 1821', *History Today*, October, 27, pp. 637–44

Partridge, E. (1950, 1989 edn.), *A Dictionary of the Underworld* (London: Wordsworth)

Paulson, R. (1991), *Hogarth: Volume 1, The 'Modern Moral Subject' 1697–1732* (New Brunswick: Rutgers University Press)

Paulson, R. (1993), *Hogarth: Volume 2, High Art and Low, 1732–1750* (Cambridge: Lutterworth Press)

Pearson, G. (1983), *Hooligan: A History of Respectable Fears* (London: Macmillan)

Pearson, G. (2011), 'Perpetual Novelty: Youth, Modernity and Historical Amnesia', in B. Goldson (ed.), *Youth in Crisis? 'Gangs', Territoriality and Violence* (London: Routledge), pp. 20–37

Pearson, J. (1973), *The Profession of Violence: The Rise and Fall of the Kray Twins* (St. Albans: Panther)

Pearson, J. (2001), *The Cult of Violence: The Untold Story of the Krays* (London: Orion)

Penfold-Mounce, R. (2009), *Celebrity Culture and Crime: The Joy of Transgression* (Basingstoke: Palgrave Macmillan)

Pepper, A. (2011), 'Early Crime Writing and the State: Jonathan Wild, Daniel Defoe and Bernard De Mandeville in 1720s London', *Textual Practice*, 25, 3, pp. 473–91

Petrow, S. (1993), 'The Rise of the Detective in London, 1869–1914', *Criminal Justice History*, 14, pp. 91–108

Petrow, S. (1994), *Policing Morals: The Metropolitan Police and the Home Office, 1870–1914* (Oxford: Clarendon Press)

Philips, D. (1977), *Crime and Authority in Victorian England: The Black Country, 1835–1860* (London: Taylor & Francis)

Philips, D. (2001), *William Augustus Miles (1796–1851): Crime, Policing and Moral Entrepreneurship in England and Australia* (Melbourne: Melbourne University Press)

Portus, G. V. (1912), *Caritas Anglicana: Or, An Historical Inquiry Into Those Religious and Philanthropic Societies That Flourished In England Between The Years 1678 And 1740* (London: Mowbray & Co)

Prothero, I. J. (1981), *Artisans and Politics in Early Nineteenth Century London: John Gast and his Times* (London: Methuen edn.)

Radzinowicz, L. (1948), *A History of the English Criminal Law and Its Administration from 1750. Vol. 1: The Movement for Reform* (London: Stevens & Sons)

Radzinowicz, L. (1956), *A History of the English Criminal Law and Its Administration from 1750. Vol. 2: The Clash Between Private Initiative and Public Interest in the Enforcement of the Law* (London: Stevens and Son)

Rawlings, P. (1992), *Drunks, Whores and Idle Apprentices: Criminal Biographies of the Eighteenth Century* (London: Routledge)

Reid, J. C. (1971), *Bucks and Bruisers: Pierce Egan and Regency London* (London: Routledge)

Reuter, P. (1983), *Disorganized Crime: Illegal Markets and the Mafia – The Economics of the Visible Hand* (Cambridge, MA: MIT Press)

Reynolds, E. (1998), *Before the Bobbies: The Night Watch and Police Reform in Metropolitan London, 1720–1830* (Basingstoke: Macmillan)

Robb, G. (1992), *White-Collar Crime in Modern England: Financial Fraud and Business Morality, 1845–1929* (Cambridge: Cambridge University Press)

Roberts, M. J. D. (1988), 'Public and Private in Early Nineteenth Century London: The Vagrancy Act of 1822 and its Enforcement', *Social History*, 13, pp. 237–94

Roberts, M. J. D. (2004), *Making English Morals: Voluntary Associations and Moral Reform in England, 1787–1886* (Cambridge: Cambridge University Press)

Rogers, P. (1980), *Hacks and Dunces: Pope, Swift and Grub Street* (London: Metheun & Co)

Rogers, P. (2005), 'Macheath and the Gaol-Breakers', *Literature and History*, 14, 2, pp. 14–36

Roodhouse, M. (2011), 'In Racket Town: Gangster Chic in Austerity Britain, 1939–1953', *Historical Journal of Film, Television and Radio*, 31, 4, pp. 523–41

Schlör, J. (1998), *Nights in the Big City: Paris, Berlin, London, 1840–1930* (London: Reaktion Books)

Sellin, T. (1994), *Pioneering in Penology: The Amsterdam Houses of Correction in the Sixteenth and Seventeenth Centuries* (Philadelphia: University of Pennsylvania Press)

Sharpe, J. À. (2004), *Dick Turpin: The Myth of the English Highwayman* (London: Profile Books)

Shoemaker, R. (2008), 'The Old Bailey Proceedings and the Representation of Crime and Criminal Justice in Eighteenth-Century London', *Journal of British Studies*, 47, pp. 559–80

Shoemaker, R. B. (1991), *Prosecution and Punishment: Petty Crime and the Law in London and Rural Middlesex, c. 1660–1725* (Cambridge: Cambridge University Press)

Shoemaker, R. B. (1992), 'Reforming the City: The Reformation of Manners Campaign in London, 1690–1738', in L. Davison et al. (eds.), *Stilling the Grumbling Hive: The Response to Social and Economic Problems in England, 1689–1750* (Basingstoke: Palgrave Macmillan), pp. 99–120

Shoemaker, R. B. (2006), 'The Street Robber and the Gentleman Highwayman: Changing Representation and Perceptions of Robbery in London, 1690–1800', *Cultural and Social History*, 3, 4, pp. 381–405

Shoemaker, R. B. (2009), 'Print Culture and the Creation of Public Knowledge about Crime in 18th-Century London', in P. Knepper, J. Doak and J. Shapland (eds.), *Urban Crime Prevention, Surveillance, and Restorative Justice: Effects of Social Technologies* (London: CRC Press), pp. 1–21

Shore, H. (1999), *Artful Dodgers: Youth and Crime in Early Nineteenth Century London* (Woodbridge: Boydell Press)

Shore, H. (2007), '"Undiscovered Country": Towards a History of the "Criminal Underworld"', *Crimes and Misdemeanours: Deviance and the Law in Historical Perspective*, 1, 1, pp. 41–68

Shore, H. (2009), '"The Reckoning": Disorderly Women, Informing Constables and the Westminster Justices, 1727–1733', *Social History*, 34, pp. 409–27

Shore, H. (2009), 'Street Children and Street Trades in the United Kingdom', in H. D. Hindman, *The World of Child Labor: An Historical and Regional Survey* (New York: M. E. Sharpe), pp. 563–66

Shore, H. (2011), 'Criminality and Englishness in the Aftermath: The Racecourse Wars of the 1920s', *Twentieth Century British History*, 22, 4, pp. 474–97

Shore, H. (2013), '"Constable Dances with Instructress": The Police and the Queen of Nightclubs in Inter-War London', *Social History*, 38, 2, pp. 193–202

Shore, H. (2014), '"Rogues of the Racecourse": Racing Men and the Press in Inter-War Britain', *Media History*, 20, 4, pp. 352–67

Shpayer Makov. (2011), *The Ascent of the Detective: Police Sleuths in Victorian and Edwardian England* (Oxford: OUP)

Sindall, R. (1983), 'Middle Class Crime in Nineteenth Century England', *Criminal Justice History*, 4, pp. 23–40

Sindall, R. (1987), 'The London Garotting Panics of 1856 and 1862', *Social History*, 12, 3, pp. 351–9

Sindall, R. (1990), *Street Violence in the Nineteenth Century: Media Panic or Real Danger?* (Leicester: Leicester University Press)

Slater, S. (2007), 'Pimps, Police and Filles De Joie: Foreign Prostitution in Interwar London', *London Journal*, 32, 1, pp. 53–74

Slater, S. (2009), 'Prostitutes and Popular History: Notes on the "Underworld", 1918–1939', *Crime, Histoire et Sociétés*, 13, 1, pp. 25–48

Slater, S. (2012), 'Street Disorder in the Metropolis, 1905–39', *Law, Crime and History*, 1, pp. 59–91

Snell, E. (2007), 'Changing Discourses of Crime: Representations of Criminality in the Eighteenth-Century Newspaper Press', *Continuity and Change*, 22, 1, pp. 13–47

Sponza, L. (1988), *Italian Immigrants in Nineteenth Century Britain: Realities and Images* (Leicester: Leicester University Press)

Spragg, G. (2003), *Outlaws and Highwaymen: The Cult of the Robber in England from the Middle Ages to the Nineteenth Century* (London: Pimlico)

Springhall, J. (1994), '"Pernicious Reading"? "The Penny Dreadful" as Scapegoat for Late-Victorian Juvenile Crime', *Victorian Periodical Review*, 27, 4, pp. 326–49

Stedman Jones, G. (1976), *Outcast London: A Study in the Relationship Between Classes in Victorian Society* (Harmondsworth: Penguin)

Stevenson, J. (1977), 'The Queen Caroline Affair', in J. Stevenson (ed.), *London in the Age of Reform* (Oxford: Blackwell), pp. 117–48

Stevenson, J. (1979), *Popular Disturbances in England, 1700–1870* (London: Longman)

Styles, J. (1980), '"Our traitorous money makers": The Yorkshire Coiners and the Law, 1760–83', in J. Brewer and J. Styles (eds.), *An Ungovernable People? The English and their Law in the Seventeenth and Eighteenth Centuries* (London: Hutchinson), pp. 172–249

Sutherland, E. (1949), *White Collar Crime* (New York: Dryden Press)

Thomas, D. (1998), *Victorian Underworld* (London: Murray)

Thomas, D. (2003), *An Underworld at War* (London: Murray)

Thomas, D. (2005), *Villains' Paradise: Britain's Underworld from the Spivs to the Krays* (London: John Murray)

Thompson, D. (2007), *The Hustlers: Gambling, Greed and the Perfect Con* (London: Sidgwick and Jackson)

Thompson, E. P. (1975), *Whigs and Hunters: The Origin of the Black Act* (London: Allen Lane)

Thrasher, F. (1927), *The Gang: A Study of 1,313 Gangs in Chicago* (Chicago: University of Chicago Press)

Tobias, J. J. (1974), *Prince of Fences: The Life and Crimes of Ikey Solomons* (London: Valentine Mitchell)

Trumbach, R. (1998), *Sex and the Gender Revolution, Volume 1: Heterosexuality and the Third Gender in Enlightenment London* (Chicago: University of Chicago Press)

Turner, J. (2013), '"Ill-Favoured sluts"? – The Disorderly Women of Rosemary Lane and Rag Fair', *London Journal*, 38, 2, pp. 95–109

Uglow, J. (1997), *Hogarth: A Life and a World* (London: Faber and Faber)

Vamplew, W. (1976), *The Turf: A Social and Economic History of Horse Racing* (London: Allen Lane)

Wales, T. (2000), 'Thief-Takers and Their Clients in Later Stuart London', in P. Griffiths and M. S. R. Jenner (eds.), *Londonopolis: Essays in the Social and Cultural History of Early Modern London* (Manchester: Manchester University Press), pp. 67–84

Walker, G. (2003), *Crime, Gender and Social Order in Early Modern England* (Cambridge: Cambridge University Press)

Walkowitz, J. (1992), *City of Dreadful Delight: Narratives of Sexual Danger in Late Victorian London* (Chicago: University of Chicago Press)

Walkowitz, J. (2012), *Nights Out: Life in Cosmopolitan London* (New Haven: Yale University Press)

Ward, R. (2012), 'Print Culture, Moral Panic and the Administration of the Law: The London Crime Wave of 1744', *Crime, Histoire et Sociétiés*, 12, 1, pp. 5–24

Warner, J., and Ivis, F. (2001), 'Informers and their Social Networks in Eighteenth-Century London: A Comparison of Two Communities', *Social Science History*, 25, 4, pp. 563–87

Warner, J., Ivis, F., and Demers, A. (2000), 'A Predatory Social Structure: Informers in Westminster, 1737–1741', *Journal of Interdisciplinary History*, 30, pp. 617–34.

Webb, S., and Webb, B. (1906), *English Local Government from the Revolution to the Municipal Corporations Act: The Parish and the County* (London: Longmans, Green and Co.)

Welshman, J. (2005), *Underclass: A History of the Excluded, 1880–2000* (London: Bloomsbury)

Wheeler, B. M. (1993), 'The Text and Plan of Oliver Twist', in C. Dickens/ F. Kaplan (ed.), *Oliver Twist, Norton Critical Edition* (London: Norton), pp. 525–37

White, J. (1980), *Rothschild Buildings: Life in an East End Tenement Block, 1887–1920* (London: Routledge and Kegan Paul)

White, J. (2012), *London in the Eighteenth Century: A Great and Monstrous Thing* (London: Bodley Head)

White, M. (2008), '"Rogues of the Meaner Sort"?: Old Bailey Executions and the London Crowd in the Early Nineteenth Century', *London Journal*, 33, 2, pp. 135–53

Wiener, M. (2004), *Men of Blood: Violence, Manliness, and Criminal Justice in Victorian England* (Cambridge: Cambridge University Press)

Wilson, G., and Wilson, S. (2007), '"Getting away with it" or "Punishment enough"?: The Problem of "Respectable" Crime from 1830', in J. Moore and J. Smith (eds.), *Corruption in Urban Politics and Society, 1780–1950* (Aldergate: Ashgate), pp. 57–78

Wilson, S. (2003), 'Moral Cancers: Fraud and Respectable Crime', in J. Rowbotham and K. Stevenson (eds.), *Behaving Badly: Social Panic and Moral Outrage – Victorian and Modern Parallels* (Aldershot: Ashgate), pp. 97–111

Wilson, S. (2010), 'Fraud and White-Collar Crime: 1850 to the Present', in A. M. Kilday and D. Nash (eds.), *Histories of Crime: Britain, 1600–2000* (Basingstoke: Palgrave Macmillan), pp. 141–59

Wiltenburg, J. (2004), 'True Crime: The Origins of Modern Sensationalism', *The American Historical Review*, 109, 5, pp. 1377–404

Wise, S. (2004), *The Italian Boy: A Tale of Murder and Body Snatching in 1830s London* (London: Metropolitan Books)

Wise, S. (2008), *The Blackest Streets: The Life and Death of a Victorian Slum* (London: Bodley Head)

Withington, P., and Shepard, A. (eds.) (2000), 'Introduction: Communities in Early Modern England', in A. Shepard and P. Withington, *Communities in Early Modern England: Networks, Place, Rhetoric* (Manchester: Manchester University Press), pp. 1–15

Wood, A. (2006), 'Subordination, Solidarity and the Limits of Popular Agency in a Yorkshire Valley, c. 1596–1615', *Past and Present*, 193, pp. 41–72

Wood, J. C. (2006), 'Criminal Violence in Modern Britain', *History Compass*, 4, 1, pp. 77–90

Wood, J. C. (2007), 'Locating Violence: The Spatial Production and Construction of Physical Aggression', in K. D. Watson (ed.), *Assaulting the Past: Violence and Civilization in Historical Context* (Newcastle: Cambridge Scholars Publishing), pp. 20–37

Wood, J. C. (2010), '"The Third Degree": Press Reporting, Crime Fiction and Police Powers in 1920s Britain', *Twentieth Century British History*, 21, 4, pp. 464–85

Wood, J. C. (2012), *The Most Remarkable Woman in England: Poison, Celebrity and the Trial of Beatrice Pace* (Manchester: Manchester University Press)

Woollard, M. (1999), 'The Classification of Occupations in the 1881 Census of England and Wales', Historical Censuses and Social Surveys Research Group, University of Essex (http://privatewww.essex.ac.uk/~matthew/Papers/Woollard_1881Classifications_no%20illustration.pdf, accessed 15 September 2014), Appendix 5, p. 42 passim

Wright, A. (2006), *Organised Crime: Concept, Cases, Control* (Cullompton: Willan)

Zedner, L. (1991), *Women, Crime and Custody in Victorian England* (Oxford: Clarendon Press)

Unpublished Dissertations

Dabhoiwala, F. (1995), 'Prostitution and Police in London, c. 1660–1760' (Oxford, D.Phil.)

Isaacs, T. B. (1979), 'Moral Crime, Moral Reform, and the State in Early Eighteenth Century England: A Study of Piety and Politics' (University of Rochester, Ph.D.)

Livie, I. M. (2010), 'Curing Hooliganism: Moral Panic, Juvenile Delinquency, and the Political Culture of Moral Reform in Britain, 1898–1908' (University of Southern California, Ph.D.)

Turner, J. (in progress) 'An Anatomy of a Disorderly Neighbourhood: Rosemary Lane and Rag Fair in the Late Seventeenth and Eighteenth Centuries' (University of Hertfordshire, Ph.D.)

Ward, R. (2011), 'Print Culture and Responses to Crime in Mid-Eighteenth-Century London' (University of Sheffield, Ph.D.)

Unpublished Papers

Church, R. (2004), 'The Rise and Changing Role of Commercial Travellers in Britain between 1870 and 1914' (http://www.econ.upf.edu/ebha2004/programme2.html, accessed 15 September 2014)

Shoemaker, R. (2013), 'Celebrating Criminality? Print Culture and the Creation of Criminal Celebrities in Eighteenth-Century London' (http://www.sipr.ac.uk/downloads/RSE_160413/Shoemaker.mp3, accessed 15 September 2014)

Index